Living Legacies of Social Injustice

Through a wide range of international and interdisciplinary case studies, this book develops the notion of legacy, and in particular, 'living legacy'—that is, it explores power relations in the context of time as a means to considering and challenging social injustice.

Legacies of social injustice are very frequently erased, denied or declared redundant. Framed by the concept of 'legacy', this book does not conceive legacy as simply referring to relics of the past, or to cultural heritage practices and artefacts. Instead, the book focuses upon 'living legacies', understood as ongoing, actively engaged in the re-constitution of power relations, and influential in the development of alternative political imaginaries. Through a variety of studies from many different contexts—including Indigenous trauma in Australia, displacement in Beirut, women travellers in Scotland, and heteronormativity in Hollywood—the book draws not only upon historiographic, sociological, legal, political, cultural and other disciplinary approaches, but also specifically makes use of feminist and postcolonial perspectives. Foregrounding the legacies of inequality and marginalisation, it contributes to a re-thinking of power and social change in ways that together suggest potential means for unsettling and reimagining such legacies.

This book will appeal to an interdisciplinary range of readers with interests and concerns in the broad area of social justice, but especially to those working in sociolegal studies, sociology, gender studies, indigenous studies and politics.

Chris Beasley is Emerita Professor in the Department of Politics and International Relations, School of Social Sciences, at the University of Adelaide, Australia, and Fellow of the Academy of the Social Sciences in Australia.

Pam Papadelos is Senior Lecturer in the Department of Sociology, Criminology and Gender Studies, School of Social Sciences, at the University of Adelaide, Australia, and Director of the Fay Gale Centre for Research on Gender.

Social Justice

Series editors
Sarah Lamble, Birkbeck College, University of London, UK
Sarah Keenan, Birkbeck College, University of London, UK
Davina Cooper, King's College University, London, UK

Feminism, Violence Against Women, and Law Reform
Decolonial Lessons from Ecuador
Silvana Tapia Tapia

Law, Judges and Visual Culture
Leslie J. Moran

Self-Declaration in the Legal Recognition of Gender
Chris Dietz

The Spaces of Mental Capacity Law
Moving Beyond Binaries
Beverley Clough

The Sexual Logics of Neoliberalism in Britain
Sexual Politics in Exceptional Times
Aura Lehtonen

The Spaces of Mental Capacity Law
Moving Beyond Binaries
Beverley Clough

Law, Registration, and the State
Making Identities through Space, Place, and Movement
Jess Smith

Living Legacies of Social Injustice
Power, Time and Social Change
Edited by Chris Beasley and Pam Padadelos

for information about the series and details of previous and forthcoming titles, see: https://www.routledge.com/Social-Justice/book-series/RCSOCJ

Living Legacies of Social Injustice

Power, Time and Social Change

Edited by
Chris Beasley and Pam Papadelos

LONDON AND NEW YORK

First published 2024
by Routledge
4 Park Square, Milton Park, Abingdon, Oxon OX14 4RN

and by Routledge
605 Third Avenue, New York, NY 10158

A GlassHouse book

Routledge is an imprint of the Taylor & Francis Group, an informa business

© 2024 selection and editorial matter, Chris Beasley and Pam Papadelos; individual chapters, the contributors

The right of Chris Beasley and Pam Papadelos to be identified as the authors of the editorial material, and of the authors for their individual chapters, has been asserted in accordance with sections 77 and 78 of the Copyright, Designs and Patents Act 1988.

All rights reserved. No part of this book may be reprinted or reproduced or utilised in any form or by any electronic, mechanical, or other means, now known or hereafter invented, including photocopying and recording, or in any information storage or retrieval system, without permission in writing from the publishers.

Trademark notice: Product or corporate names may be trademarks or registered trademarks, and are used only for identification and explanation without intent to infringe.

British Library Cataloguing-in-Publication Data
A catalogue record for this book is available from the British Library

Library of Congress Cataloging-in-Publication Data
Names: Beasley, Chris, editor. | Papadelos, Pam, 1966- editor.
Title: Living legacies of social injustice : power, time and social change / edited by Chris Beasley and Pam Papadelos.
Description: Abingdon, Oxon ; New York, NY : Routledge, 2024. | Includes bibliographical references and index.
Identifiers: LCCN 2023007622 (print) | LCCN 2023007623 (ebook) |
Subjects: LCSH: Social justice. | Power (Social sciences) | Collective memory.
Classification: LCC HM671 .L59 2024 (print) | LCC HM671 (ebook) | DDC 303.3/72--dc23/eng/20230303
LC record available at https://lccn.loc.gov/2023007622
LC ebook record available at https://lccn.loc.gov/2023007623

ISBN: 978-1-032-31890-5 (hbk)
ISBN: 978-1-032-31894-3 (pbk)
ISBN: 978-1-003-31192-8 (ebk)

DOI: 10.4324/9781003311928

Typeset in Bembo
by Taylor & Francis Books

We would like to dedicate this co-edited book to our beloved children, Perry, Alexia and Elena, who are in their way a legacy to the future to come.

Contents

List of illustrations	ix
List of contributors	x
Acknowledgements	xiii

1	Ongoing Legacies of Social Injustice: A Critical Interrogation	1
	CHRIS BEASLEY AND PAM PAPADELOS	

PART I   19

2	A Family Act: Power, Gendered Violence and the Living Legacy of Social Injustice in Papua New Guinea	21
	ALISON DUNDON	
3	A Pontian Commemoration: A Living Legacy to Remember Loss	38
	VALERIE LIDDLE	
4	'Horrors' of Honour	56
	KAMELJEET KAUR	
5	The Legacy of Stigma: American Single Mothers	73
	AMY ANDRADA	

PART II   91

6	Talking of Silence: Young Scottish Gypsy/Traveller Women in Scotland	93
	GEETHA MARCUS	
7	Young Refugees Navigating the Emotional Legacies of Displacement in Beirut Through Friendships	116
	DAVID ANDERSON AND MARY HOLMES	

viii Contents

8   The Enduring Legacies of Migration: Older Greek-born Migrants'
    Experience of Ageing in Australia   133
    PAM PAPADELOS

9   Unearthing Buried Legacies   153
    ROSEMARY WANGANEEN AND ANNA SZORENYI

PART III   171

10 The Legacy of Injustice and Resistance: Japan's Military Sexual
    Slavery   173
    MAKI KIMURA

11 Haunted by the Heteronorm: Contemporary Hollywood
    Romance   191
    CHRIS BEASLEY

12 Challenging Criminalisation in the Commonwealth: Theorising
    Legacies and Colonialities in LGBTIQ Movement Strategies   210
    MATTHEW WAITES

13 Re-imagining Legacy (Power-Time) and Social Change   231
    CHRIS BEASLEY AND PAM PAPADELOS

    Index   242

Illustrations

Figure

13.1 Masculinity – from normative to heretical   236

Tables

8.1 Demographic Characteristics   139
9.1 The Seven Phases to Integrating Loss and Grief   161

Contributors

Dr David Anderson has a PhD in Sociology from the University of Edinburgh, where his work addressed displacement, marginalisation and social space in Soacha, Colombia. He is currently a researcher on projects studying displacement and disability during COVID-19 in Ukraine (Edinburgh Napier University) and how the concept of hope might help to promote better futures for young people considered to be vulnerable and at high risk (University of Strathclyde). He co-authored *Young Refugees and Forced Displacement: Navigating Everyday Life in Beirut* (Routledge, 2021).

Amy Andrada is a PhD Sociology candidate at the University of Edinburgh. Her research focuses on deviance, family and gender studies.

Emerita Professor Chris Beasley is Emerita Professor and founder of the Fay Gale Centre for Research on Gender, at the University of Adelaide. She is a Fellow of the Academy of the Social Sciences in Australia. Her recent books include *Internet Dating: Intimacy and Social Change* (with Mary Holmes, 2021) and *The Cultural Politics of Popular Hollywood Film: Power, Culture and Society* (with Heather Brook, 2019).

Dr Alison Dundon (Senior Lecturer) is an anthropologist with long term field research in rural Papua New Guinea and is a senior lecturer at the University of Adelaide, South Australia. She has published on a wide variety of topics, including sexual and gendered health, HIV/AIDS, the anthropology of Christianity, community engagement with the state, gendered violence and on online dating interactions in PNG. Her recent book is *Shifting States: New Perspectives on Security, Infrastructure and Political Affect* (ASA Monographs), Routledge, (with Richard Vokes, 2020).

Professor Mary Holmes is Professor of Emotions and Society at the University of Edinburgh. Her research examines emotional reflexivity in a range of social spheres, particularly in relation to intimate relationships. She is one of the founding editors of the journal *Emotions and Society* and has recently published a book, with Chris Beasley, on *Internet Dating* (Routledge, 2021).

List of contributors xi

Dr Kameljeet Kaur is a teaching fellow at the University of Adelaide, situated at Wirltu Yarlu—the university's support and teaching unit for Aboriginal and Torres Strait Islanders. She is a member of the Fay Gale Centre for Research at the University of Adelaide. Her research interest are in Gender, Critical Race Studies, and Post-colonial and Decolonial Theory.

Dr Maki Kimura is Lecturer (Teaching) in Gender and Politics at University College London. She has an extensive research and teaching experience in gender and race inequality, and is particularly concerned with gender-based violence, past and present, transnational feminism, and feminist politics with intersectional and post-colonial perspectives. She is the author of *Unfolding the 'Comfort Women' Debates: Modernity, Violence and Women's Voices* (2016) (Palgrave Macmillan).

Dr Valerie Liddle completed her PhD in 2013. Her research focused on how loss is experienced by members of the Greek Pontian community in Adelaide and in Greece through certain cultural practices. She was a Visiting Research Fellow in the Discipline of Anthropology and Development Studies at the University of Adelaide between 2014 and 2021. Her most recent publication is a chapter entitled 'Pontic Dance: feeling the absence of homeland' in *Emotions, Senses, Spaces: ethnographic engagement and intersections'* (2016) edited by Susan Hemer and Alison Dundon.

Dr Geetha Marcus is a Senior Lecturer in the Division of Psychology, Sociology and Education at Queen Margaret University, Edinburgh. She is a sociologist, feminist, and teacher activist whose research and teaching interests focus on social inequalities within public education systems. Her book *Gypsy and Traveller Girls: Silence, Agency, and Power* (2019) critically explores and documents the racialised and gendered experiences of Gypsy and Traveller girls in Scotland, within public spaces of school and private spaces of home. As a South Asian and advocate of black feminist thought and methodology, her work also explores research into the multiple identities and experiences of young people and women on the margins from a postcolonial perspective.

Dr Pam Papadelos is a Director of the Fay Gale Centre for Research on Gender and a senior lecturer in the Department of Sociology, Criminology & Gender Studies. Her teaching and research focus on gender, migration, social inclusion and citizenship. She is particularly interested in cross-cultural practices for post-war migrants and the generations that follow. She is author of *From revolution to deconstruction: Exploring feminist theory and practice in Australia* (2010).

Dr Anna Szorenyi is a lecturer and researcher in Gender Studies at the University of Adelaide. Her research critiques colonial dynamics in humanitarian contexts, with particular interests in humanitarian visual culture, and in

xii List of contributors

debates around asylum seekers and human trafficking. She has also published on the ethics and responsibilities of being descended from various perpetrators of violence. All her work pursues more ethical ways of cohabiting with one another in the face of shared vulnerability.

Dr Matthew Waites is Reader in Sociology at the University of Glasgow. He is co-editor of *Human Rights, Sexual Orientation and Gender Identity in the Commonwealth: Struggles for Decriminalisation and Change* (School of Advanced Study, 2013), and author of *The Age of Consent: Young People, Sexuality and Citizenship* (Palgrave Macmillan, 2005). He has authored a range of recent chapters and articles contributing to the international political sociology of transnational LGBTI movements and global queer politics—engaged with decolonising thought—including in *Current Sociology, International Sociology, International Review of Sociology, Sociological Review* and *Journal of Genocide Research*.

Rosemary Wanganeen (MA student and health practitioner/counsellor) is a proud South Australian Aboriginal woman with ancestry and ancestral links to Kaurna of the Adelaide Plains and Wirangu from the western coast of South Australia. She is the founder, Director and CEO of the Healing Centre for Griefology, based in Semaphore, a suburb of Adelaide, South Australia.

Acknowledgements

It has taken a long while to see this book to completion. That in itself is by no means unusual. Books entailing collaboration typically do involve slow and patient work. However, in this case the book also got underway from somewhat unlikely beginnings. Indeed, it could be said to be a demonstration that, against the odds, social scientists can sometimes with very limited funding and lots of determination bring together ideas and communities across the globe to produce novel research. Chris was initially invited by the Dean of the then Faculty of Arts at the University of Adelaide, Jenny Shaw, to develop a new research network between the University of Adelaide in Australia and the University of Alberta in Canada. This research project was assisted by a small grant from the former. On this basis, Chris travelled to Edmonton and met with Susan Luhmann and Cressida Heyes. Discussions between Chris and Susan, noted down on the back of a pizza box, formed the start of an international research network including members in Australia, Britain, Sweden and Canada and resulting in three workshops in the first three of these countries. From there began the formation of the book. It almost foundered following significant care and health challenges faced by several members but, despite demanding obstacles, came to fruition through the collaboration of editors, Chris and Pam. We fortunately love working together. The strength of our friendship helps too.

Chris would like to thank Pam most of all for her astonishing persistence and intellectual generosity. Chris also wishes to acknowledge the steadfast support of her colleagues at the University of Adelaide, located in the Department of Politics and International Relations, particularly Carol Bacchi, Carol Johnson, Tiziana Torresi and Priya Chacko. And, given the starting point for this book, she is much indebted to the Fay Gale Centre for Research on Gender, especially to Megan Warin, former director. She is also deeply appreciative of the friendship and scholarly largesse of her compatriots in Canada, UK, and Sweden—that is, Susan Luhmann, Mary Holmes and Ulf Mellström. Mary and Ulf organised lively and fascinating workshops in Edinburgh and Karlstad respectively, thus providing further contexts—along with that of the inaugural

xiv Acknowledgements

workshop in Adelaide—for experiencing the work of those who eventually became contributors to the book.

Pam would like to thank Chris for her incredible enthusiasm and perceptive insights. Pam is appreciative of the support and friendship she receives from her colleagues at the University of Adelaide, particularly Megan Warin, Ros Prosser, Nathan Manning, Anna Szorenyi and Alison Dundon. She wishes to acknowledge that the book would not have been possible without the support of the Fay Gale Centre who hosted the Adelaide workshop. A special thank you goes to her sisters Dimitra and Arieta for their interest and input at various stages of this journey. Pam is most grateful for the love and support she receives from her family, including her much cherished daughters, Alexia and Elena, and her remarkable nieces Katarina, Jordan, Stavroula, Zoe and Thalia.

Matthew Waites and Taylor & Francis gratefully acknowledge permission to reproduce an extract from *Poem for the Commonwealth 2018* from: Karlo Mila (2020), *Goddess Muscle*. Wellington: Huia Publishers. Reproduced by permission of Huia Publishers.

And, finally, we both wish to thank our emotional support team for their several suggestions at various crucial moments, their capacity to offer wine and sundry other necessary condiments, and most of all for their unselfish encouragement in spite of the time this project took and the way it necessarily demanded our attention for periods. We send big grateful hugs to our partners John and Tony!

Chapter 1

Ongoing Legacies of Social Injustice

A Critical Interrogation

Chris Beasley and Pam Papadelos

This book is framed around the concept of 'legacy'. However, this approach does not conceive legacy as simply referring to acknowledged relics of the past or cultural heritage practices and artefacts, nor does it merely acknowledge that the past has some influence on the present. Instead, the approach focuses upon the notion of 'living legacy' as about power and, in particular, about an understanding of power's temporalities. *Legacy in this usage is constituted by power, is ongoing, and is actively engaged in the re-constitution of power relations along with the development of alternative political imaginaries.* Legacy is thus a core consideration in advancing social justice and consequently is central to the concerns of the Routledge *Social Justice* Series in which it is located. Indeed, we assert in this volume that it is not possible to foreground the subject of social justice without attention to legacy—that is, to power relations in the context of time. What we mean here is that for us the concept of legacy necessarily gives rise to re-thinking how power is understood and thus how prospects for social change can be investigated.

Legacy: Key focus, meaning and implications

Social Justice and Social Injustice are associated and highly evocative terminologies (Manderson, 2012) in which power relations are often not delineated in relation to time. For example, the magisterial collection edited by Michael Reisch, The Routledge *International Handbook of Social Justice* (2014), outlines historical accounts of the development of social justice as a term, yet its focus on notions of normative concepts and justice-oriented principles does not attend in its introductory overview or individual chapters to how power (and how power changes) is inextricably entwined with time. Hence, highlighting legacy as a central theme offers a novel approach which provides a substantive contribution to an emerging field of studies of injustice and social change.[1] *The conceptual framework of the theme of legacy offers a crucial means to understanding social justice questions and dilemmas in that it demands that injustice and social change cannot be understood without awareness of how power can be erased, denied or declared redundant—sometimes through normalisation—in the context of*

DOI: 10.4324/9781003311928-1

2 Chris Beasley and Pam Papadelos

time. Injustice and power relations are not self-evident, nor do they exist in isolation from their temporalities. Some scholars have attended to social justice in terms of spatial location (see for example, Grabham et al., 2009; Blomley, 2011). Here we assert the necessity of attention to power's temporal 'location'.

The specific implications of using the concept of legacy, and in particular *living* legacy, is that it points to the ways in which power relations can be insistent and long lasting, rather than just emphasising their fluidity, while nevertheless retaining a sense that they could always be otherwise. The concept brings to the fore the tension between what may be ongoing and stubbornly intransigent, the seeming permanence and natural status of relations of power established through a variety of forms of denial as well as through relentless reiteration, yet simultaneously capable of reinterpretation, re-constitution and even wholesale reworking (see for example Chapter 12). For the readers of this volume, it is intended that power can be seen as creatively ingrained in every feature of the world as it presents itself at any particular time from the most institutionally organised and explicit structures of the state to the micropolitical experience of interpersonal intimacy. Power is in this sense not to be understood as simply imposed or inserted from the outside as it were but rather as productively constitutive.

The dynamic inconsistency of power, between seeming permanence, insistent reiteration and capacity for reinvention, makes power alive, rather than the suggesting the dead hand of uncomplicated subordination, and hence our use of not merely ongoing but *living* legacy as a means to stress the ways in which power spreads and frames every day and fleshly embodied practices (see for instance Dundon, Chapter 2). 'Ongoing' and 'living' are not distinct vocabularies but linked. They are not entirely interchangeable but rather exist on a spectrum of emphasis. Hence, in many, if not all, of the chapters they are both used. In this context, what do these vocabularies bring as framing tools of analysis in the book?

Both terms are intended to draw attention to the persistence, the stickiness, of power relations and are specifically aimed at enabling and foregrounding conceptions of power as entwined with time such that power relations arising in the past continue in the present and are likely to shape the future. This focus maybe understood as in contrast to approaches which assume that social injustice is progressively and in a linear fashion overcome over time, or which relatedly assume power is enacted in distinct moments that pass, or which enunciate an over-emphasis upon power as fluid and in flux.

However, the emphasis in the terms is somewhat different. Both of the terms 'ongoing' and 'living' go beyond any notion of the past as simply influencing the present. All the same, the former term places stress upon continuities over time—even if sometimes in veiled or normalising ways which render such continuities less visible—and is rather more straightforwardly descriptive of such continuities. By comparison the latter is rather more dynamic in giving stronger emphasis to the ways in which power relations not only continue but actively shape the present and future, actuating their very constitution even as such power relations may not take exactly the same form as they interact with changes in conditions over time. The notion of continuities in power relations arises in both 'ongoing' and 'living' legacies terms but in the case of 'living' legacy appears as perhaps more strategic, more capable of some degree of shapeshifting while also more far-reaching and thoroughgoing in its impacts.

The emerging arena of analysis requires *a multidimensional orientation* in order to explore the notion of legacy in terms of that which may be obscured or deemed unimportant, yet still casts a potent long shadow in current times and in the future. For this reason, the book provides a forum for developing theoretical, empirical and experiential research dimensions across the social sciences and humanities. The range of perspectives enabled by these several methodological formats gives particular qualitative depth to the collection—a depth that we consider is less available to readers if all chapter contributions present a similar methodological stance. The majority of the chapters display a strongly theoretical or empirical focus (see for instance chapters by Beasley on cultural politics—Chapter 11—and Liddle on anthropologically inflected history—Chapter 3—respectively). Nevertheless, we see certain topics as perhaps necessarily requiring alternative approaches and displaying other strengths. For example, the chapter by Wanganeen and Szorenyi includes memoir and conversation as well as providing historical/legal background to shed light on the debilitating legacies faced by the 'stolen generations' of First Nations People of Australia. This contribution is enhanced by its experiential focus and the need to speak directly from the voice of that experience. Re-conceptualising and re-imagining social justice are advanced, we suggest, not only by what is designated as theoretical/analytical or evidential but also by other modes of analysis.

This diversity in method is accompanied by disciplinary, perspectival and qualitative range. The book draws upon historiographic, sociological, legal, political, cultural and other disciplinary approaches. It also specifically makes use of feminist and postcolonial perspectives, arising from attention to axes of gender, sexuality, ethnicity and indigeneity. These perspectives foreground inequality and marginalisation. Indeed, inequality and marginalisation are central to this collection. In this setting, the book offers a fresh and innovative wide-ranging dialogue exploring the dynamics of the four research fields (gender, sexuality, ethnicity and indigeneity), with regard to:

- re-imagining/re-conceptualising power relations—over time and in terms of 'stickiness'/sedimentation;
- interconnections between different conceptual nodes and practices of power which have implications for future research and policy development (that is, the 'intersectionality' between gender and specific other nodes including sexuality, ethnicity and indigeneity—Beasley, 2005; Koehn et al., 2013; McCall, 2005); and

4 Chris Beasley and Pam Papadelos

- interconnections between past and present which frame future possibilities regarding social injustice and inequalities (see Johnson, 2005; Marks & Worboys, 1997; Tremblay et al., 2011).

This concern with power, temporality, intersectionality and possibilities for social change signals that *attending to a singular disconnected timeframe, or a singular axis of power may result in limited understandings of social problems and even reiterate privilege. By contrast, the focus on legacy in this collection brings these elements into a cumulative conversation*—a cumulative conversation which is deepened by the diversity of contributions within the anthology.

This breadth is augmented by the variety of case studies from many different national contexts, as well as considering international settings. Such contexts include Papua New Guinea, Turkey, Greece, the UK, the USA, Scotland, Lebanon, Australia and Japan, along with the impact of global media and of colonialism in the Asia-Pacific and Britain. We consider that without a recognition and understanding of legacy, conceptualisations of social injustice and opportunities for change are seriously delimited. The reimagining of social relations associated with the term legacy requires an expansive framework that draws upon a wide variety of modes and sites of exploration.

While this book's key innovation arises in considering social justice through the novel lens of legacy—that is, through re-thinking power in terms of time, this lens demands a multidimensional approach. The book brings together a variety of methodologies and perspectives along with a strongly multi-disciplinary, international and inter-institutional framework which grew out of a wide-ranging research network, OLIRN—**O**ngoing **L**egacies of Discrimination and Violence **I**nternational **R**esearch **N**etwork. The network arose under the auspices of the Fay Gale Centre for Research on Gender at the University of Adelaide, South Australia, and encompasses researchers from four countries (Australia, Canada, United Kingdom and Sweden). It is focussed upon interrogating past, contemporary and future approaches to ongoing impacts of social injustice and driven by a concern with current theoretical debates, practical issues and political struggle.

Why is it important to attend to Legacy?

The conceptual focus, innovative features and breadth of the book should be placed in the setting of its core analysis or argument which provides its rationale. The core framing of this edited collection is around legacy, a term intended to enable a re-thinking of power and social change in ways that substantively incorporate time. We note two major ways in which legacy enables such a re-thinking—that is, analytical and practical, political considerations.

Legacy facilitates analytical reassessment of conceptualisations of power, politics, power's entanglements with time and the scope of power. In recent times feminist and postcolonial perspectives (arising in relation to both postmodernism/poststructuralism and post-humanism/new materialism) have tended to challenge understandings of power as a property owned by individuals or groups and as always involving power as domination or control by some over others. The intention has been to re-cast power as vital, fluid and dynamic rather than fixed and solid and, in emerging posthumanist versions, to move beyond the anthropocentric tendencies of postmodernism/poststructuralism (Bozalek & Pease, 2020; Braidotti, 2013; Dolphijn & van der Tuin, 2012).[2] While we support the rejection of fixity, through our use of the notion of legacy we bring to the fore quiet, slow, static, 'sticky' and long-standing normalised aggregations of power (Ahmed, 2004; Athanasiou et al., 2008; Clough & Halley, 2020) which may resist the possibility of 'lines of flight' (Deleuze & Parnet, 2007; Thornton, 2020; Deuchars, 2011). The book involves an evocative counter to recent conceptualisations of power that are inclined to emphasise ceaseless motion (Beasley, 2011). We introduce the significance of legacy to highlight some limits to contemporary feminist and postcolonial accounts of power including those influenced by Deleuze's account of vitalism as emerging connections, as process or transition (Colebrook and UK Research and Innovation, 2008; Braidotti, 2006, 2008).[3] We note the way that power relations take multiple forms and may also be articulated as sedentary (Beasley & Bacchi, 2007; Beasley, 2011). Such reconfiguring perspectives on power, necessarily involve specific attention to the political. Legacy, in our usage, prioritises the requirement to engage with 'the political' in the broadest sense of central attention to power relations (Beasley, 2017). Legacy is, above all, employed here as a political vocabulary.

Our theoretical reimagining of power in terms of legacy acknowledges the potential stickiness of power relations and hence has implications for the political, but also recognises the temporal materiality of power encompassing the past, present and the potentiality of the future—as against a conception of legacy as a feature of the past (Enright, 2018). This employment of legacy in terms of 'living legacy' exemplifies re-imagined interpretations of power and of time, and of their inter-constitutive engagements. We intend to challenge historicist and naturalised notions of time as linear, as progressive development, and as a mere container of power relations in social processes. Importantly, these conceptual concerns are associated in the empirical case studies and phenomenological approaches to particular sites of injustice within the edited collection. The focus on legacy enables readers *to reassess notions of power's temporalities as about striving, purposeful direction, speed, or exceptional moments/events* (Alexandrakis, 2016; Beynon-Jones & Grabham, 2019; Nixon, 2011; Sharma, 2014). The term is productive of analyses of power and time in the shaping of possibilities (see also Adkins, 2012; Barad, 2007; Greenhouse, 2019; Haraway, 2016).

The use of legacy, of reconfigured conceptualisation of power as entangled in time, also changes understandings of the scope of power and its forms. Legacy enables analyses of power relations which include shocking and traumatic events but also draw attention to the everyday and supposedly unremarkable. This approach refuses the separation of what is deemed 'serious' and 'important' from those of smaller and less shocking scale. It also rejects the separation of distinct and possibly striking events—which is a common feature of accounts of injustice—from steady 'normalised' continuities. One example of this point arises in Chapter 11 in which heteronormativity is insistently reiterated in contemporary Hollywood romantic comedies signifying an instance of how power relations may continue, and continue in formats that present them as normal and unremarkable. Similarly, the unusual emphasis upon axes of gender, sexuality, ethnicity and indigeneity in the anthology brings forward events and experiences which may be less visible in many approaches such as those focussed upon historical or cultural memory studies. Public memory, memorialisation and mythologising frequently favour only some representatives of cultural collectivities and render others invisible (Fredericks, 2011). Our concern to attend to several axes of power gives space to less dramatic, less obvious narratives.

We note in this setting the reconfiguring of practical, political considerations which arise alongside these theoretical concerns. One crucial starting point here is that legacies of social injustice are very frequently silenced. Indeed, a number of political processes at play here (Kimmel, 2005; Smith, 2016; Beasley, 2008), including deliberate burying entailing the production of suppressed legacies (El Kurd, 2020; Olick & Robbins, 1998; Ono et al., 2016; Poole, 2009), selective forgetting and selective memorialisation (Diprose, 2002; Van Dyke, 2016; Kundakbayeva & Kassymova, 2016), atrophication (allowing or encouraging legacies to fade into obscurity) (Bennett, 2006) and containment (partial recognition) (Thompson, 2005). It is convenient to engage in these processes, especially for those who are privileged enough to not be affected by these histories. Moreover, the compelled disappearance of histories of social injustice can be successful and, in the process, violation is enacted yet again (Frary, 2018).

There is now substantial evidence of subjective seeing and recalling, of selective attention and memory, of mental prioritising (Kiyonaga & Egner, 2013; Miller, 2021). However, we do not prioritise what is seen and remembered solely in a psychological or individualised way. Rather this selection is socio-political (Smith & Hattery, 2011; Thompson, 2007; Araújo & dos Santos, 2009; Ricoeur, 2006; Wells & Olson, 2003; Diprose, 2002; Gatens, 1996). Beasley and Brook (2019) note in this context that the socio-political and collective character of memorialising is shaped by and generates political myths of peoples and nations. Most importantly, legacies of 'the living past' (Krastev, 2019) have ongoing effects. As Stanley and Dampier (2005) point out, the 'aftermaths' of injustice remain with us (see also Orwell, 1950,

p. 204). And so, as pussy-hat singers in a January 21, 2017, Women's march in Washington, USA, point out, we '*can't* keep quiet' (Women's march anthem by MLCK, 2017).

In this context, the book is intended to draw readers' attention to a range of apposite concerns regarding the notion of living legacy. William Faulkner once famously declared '[t]he past is never dead. It's not even past' (Faulkner, 1951). He meant that the meaning and weight of the past are inexorably 'laced within the present' (Powers, 2017, p. 42; see also Sepehri, 2017). In this setting, Ric Morton has pointed out in relation to legacies of trauma that time is by no means simply a lock-step linear progression. Traumas of the past are not contained in a separate timeframe but continue and are experienced as current and ongoing (Goelitz, 2021; Morton, 2021). Acknowledging that social injustice draws inextricably on both the past and the present and is commonly intergenerational (Danieli, 1998; Luhmann, 2011) is a necessary means to enable new ways forward. As the chapters in this book remind readers, we forget or deny or discount legacies of injustice at our peril. Nevertheless, the past cannot determine our options (Santayana, 1905, p. 284; Marx, 1852). The chapters in this proposed book are intended to shed light on such an expanded range of options and encourage a more nuanced re-imagining of history, nation, public policy, sociality, embodied emotion, and resistance.

The works of Carol Johnson and Susan Luhmann provide two concrete examples of how the concept of 'living legacy' may be employed in a re-configuration of how we understand power as intrinsically temporal and as implicating past, present and future.[4] Johnson (2010), for example, in her analyses of affective citizenship points out the ways in which public apologies—though they may be appropriated to evade reparations—nevertheless provide practical instances of the ways in which recognition of memories and emotions offer authorising narratives of social legitimacy to marginalised and victimised communities. She notes that such apologies involve a refusal to place victimisation as now in the past and instead to acknowledge the ongoing connections between past and present as well as invoking claims regarding the future. They are exhortations to social re-evaluation and ongoing reform. In this setting, Johnson cites First Minister of Scotland Nicola Sturgeon's November 2017 apology to Scottish LGBTI people: "We will never again accept laws or behaviours that discriminate against you and hurt you" (Johnson 2017; Sturgeon, 2017). Apologies are not simply symbolic but are in themselves significant legitimating acts which, as Johnson points out, are not by any means an endpoint (Johnson, 2017, 2010, 2005). Recognition in this public way provides a tangible demonstration of the possibilities of the notion of 'living legacy' insofar as apologies evoke opportunities for international re-framings, as well as for nationhood, law, communities and individuals.

Luhmann's work on what she describes as 'the familial turn' in German cultural memory considers the living significance of genocidal violence in familial affective legacies. Cultural memory in this case involves the recovery,

8 Chris Beasley and Pam Papadelos

restaging and re-narration of legacies of perpetration from Germany's Nazi past through the lens of private and family life. The American documentary film *Inheritance* (directed by James Moll, 2006) shows a daughter of an acknowledged war criminal who ran a concentration camp meeting with a woman who was enslaved at the camp. Luhmann (2018) considers the film as a form of transatlantic pedagogy which obliges Germans to acknowledge complicity in relation to deeds that are often repudiated and/or rendered of restricted and past significance. She draws attention to the ways in which the present is continuously implicated in what is deemed past within collective memory and the ways in which this occurs in order to deal with the personal direct responsibility for horrific crimes undertaken by close and perhaps beloved family members (Luhmann, 2018). Here the concept of living legacy has deeply felt and compelling implications, which Luhmann takes as crucial to re-configuring social injustice over time.

As these examples suggest, this anthology engages with political melancholia, but not to offer nostalgic revivals of the past or despair about the future. Rather, delineating the haunting shadow of what we have termed 'living legacies'—revealing both the fluidity and sedentary sedimentations of power over time and in a variety of forms—is undertaken precisely in order to suggest potential means for unsettling and reimagining these legacies. We see this as moving on from what Worby and Ally (2013) describe as 'an affective politics of disappointment' to an optimistic politics of interruption enabling the cultivation of a more sanguine alterity.

Locating Legacy

This book's central concern with the notion of legacy offers an unusual contribution to theoretical, empirical and experiential accounts of power. This guiding trope is not found in a long-standing body of knowledge but rather is emergent and in development. Indeed, we consider that presently few if any volumes attend to legacy, power and time.

Scholarship attending to the significance of history, cultural memory, memorialising, and socio-political myths is usually focussed on discussions of the meaning and significance of History and historical studies (see Hunt, 2018), or on analyses of specific events/locations, typically dealing with violence and discrimination in relation to one or two axes of power relations (see Jacobs, 2010). For example, books with a more international scope most commonly maintain a singular emphasis, often around genocide or other mass violence event (see Danieli, 1998; Jinks, 2014).

While this anthology includes contributors from the discipline of History and gives attention to mass violence and state narratives, it includes many disciplinary directions, is not necessarily focused upon historical questions, and does not attend to violence and the state exclusively. The volume includes a wide range of social contexts and subjects drawing upon the work of

Ongoing Legacies of Social Injustice 9

contributors from Australia and the UK who deal with considerable range of locations. The aim is to provide a more complex composite picture of ongoing legacies of social injustice and responses to them.

In sum, the book has an intentionally inclusive ambit. This can enable attention to migration, law, film, and policy among other topics into a field of discussion alongside considerations of history and of genocidal violence. Following the Routledge *Social Justice* Series guiding imperatives, the book openly engages with power in an expansive way, and thus speaks to a wide-ranging and diverse audience. We consider this an important feature and strength of the volume. On this basis, our aim is to engage a broad readership which may include those interested in the disciplines of Sociology, Politics, Law, History, Gender Studies, Indigenous Studies, Psychology, Culture and Media Studies and Social Work.

Book plan and interconnections

While this book is divided along three complementary thematic formats to reflect the range of issues relevant to the concept living legacy, what is equally important is the crossings between, as well as within, these groupings. The first theme—state memorials, monuments, policies and law—concerns macro, public responses to what are often long-standing, sometimes normalised injustices and which may call for national and international action. Alison Dundon's chapter, 'A Family Act: Power, gendered violence and the living legacy of social injustice in Papua New Guinea' (Chapter 2) begins this section with an examination of the enduring legacy of violence against women in Papua New Guinea. Dundon asserts that justifications for violence based on 'tradition' have been challenged by grassroots, non-government, external organisations, and more recently, through new social policies and legal frameworks. Yet, the continuing legacy of violence, and Papua New Guinea's complex legal system, make it difficult for women to navigate away from forms of everyday violence.

Valerie Liddle's chapter, 'A Pontian commemoration: remembering the injustice of violence' (Chapter 3) turns our attention to Pontic Greeks who once lived in Santa, a village situated in the Pontic Alps in northern Turkey. Liddle focuses on the Pontian's annual commemoration to remember and bear witness to the massacre of their people, the destruction of their village, and those who died on enforced marches in 1921. The legacy of remembrance is augmented by two memorial sites where through their symbolic features and texts, and the commemorative rites held there, the memory of the trauma is brought into the present. These commemorations and the stories that are passed down from survivors are oriented towards political action. Pontic Greeks demand that these events constitute genocide. There is now increasing recognition of a Pontian genocide, in opposition to the stance of Turkey.

Kameljeet Kaur's chapter 'Horrors' of Honour (Chapter 4) reflects on the way that domestic violence in marginalised groups is often re-imagined and reconceptualised according to ongoing legacies of colonial narratives that stick to certain bodies. She notes that the polarising label "honour crimes", in relation to some incidents of domestic violence in the UK, not only targets marginalised communities of South Asian descent but is also a means through which (post) empire continues to describe its superiority over its (post) colonial subjects. Drawing on Sara Ahmed's (2004) model of affective economies Kaur illustrates how emotions, such as hate, when mobilised towards the foreigner/migrant, work to produce hyper affective responses of disgust and horror. These affects are fuelled by a crisis of hegemony, in which white British subjects seek to maintain dominance over migrants in this post-colonial age. Despite a seeming recognition of domestic violence, the horrors of honour rely upon the suppression and re-representation of violence against women in British South Asian communities.

The final chapter in this section, Amy Andrada's 'The legacy of stigma: American single mothers' (Chapter 5) shifts the focus from South East Asian women in the United Kingdom, to single black women in the United States. Andrada argues that conceptualisations of single mothers remain disproportionately based on race and class and continue to be actively constructed as such. This legacy of stigma has contributed to the mythologising of both the 'good mother' (married, white) and the 'bad' or othered mother (unmarried, non-white).

As discussed above, living legacies are constituted by power, temporality, intersectionality, and possibilities for social change. The contributions in Section 1 focus directly on dimensions of legacies of violence and injustice produced through cultural practice (Dundon), ethnic violence (Liddle), colonialism (Kaur), and systemic social stigma (Andrada) and the ongoing need for recognition and fundamental legal and social reform.

In Section 2—memory—the focus shifts from macro-level concerns to micro, experiential and psychological orientations. Geetha Marcus' chapter 'Talking of silence: The ongoing legacies of power and injustice in the marginalised lives of young Gypsy/Traveller women in Scotland' (Chapter 6) critically explores different forms of silence encountered in the lives of these women. They suffer from the normative absence and pathological presence of the 'Other' in policy discourse. The absence of history and identity of the Gypsy/Traveller in Scottish academic and cultural discourse renders them absent from mainstream recognition, while also ensuring they are represented as pathological victims when they do appear. Marcus employs a black British feminist framework to chart the counter-narratives and memories of Gypsy/Traveller young women in Scotland and in so doing highlights their use of silence. This use of silence can be potentially restrictive, but when used in defiance can also be empowering in shaping their oppositional gaze and enabling the possibility for alternative futures.

David Anderson and Mary Holmes' chapter 'Young refugees navigating the emotional legacies of displacement in Beirut' (Chapter 7) investigates the lives of young Syrian and Iraqi refugees living in Beirut by focusing on how their relationships with family and friends are disrupted. Anderson and Holmes' engagement with the legacies of displacement recognises a range of impacts arising from the past including distrust, exclusion, boredom and loneliness. They pay attention to how emotional legacies cause changes in friendships and also note gendered power relations that have differential effects on negotiating friendship. Anderson and Holmes argue that the young Syrians and Iraqis in their study navigate these emotional legacies to find ways of attending to friendships, while contesting some of the more corrosive influences of distrust and discrimination.

Pam Papadelos'contribution 'The enduring legacies of migration: Older Greek-born migrants' experience of ageing in Australia' (Chapter 8) draws on interviews with first generation older Greek-Australians who arrived after the Second World War and settled in three different cities in Australia (Adelaide, Perth and Darwin). She argues that while multicultural discourses have suc-ceeded culturally restrictive assimilationist policies, they have not sufficiently challenged unequal and ongoing patterns of power and privilege in Australian society. Papadelos argues that legacies of migration have a continuing impact on older Greek-Australians' perceptions of ageing positively, with past dis-crimination resulting in limited social engagement, exacerbated isolation, lone-liness, and resentment of dependency on adult children. Despite these issues, she noted that participants in her study remained actively engaged with the complex and often dissonant features of migration's legacies.

This section concludes with Rosemary Wanganeen and Anna Szorenyi's 'Unearthing buried legacies' (Chapter 9), an amalgamated text that draws on a number of sources including a memoir of Wanganeen's personal experiences as an Australian Aboriginal child subject to the laws, policies and practices descri-bed as producing 'the stolen generations'. Wanganeen tells her story to show that intergenerational suppressed and unresolved loss and grief is passed across and down the generations. She explains that as an adult she began to develop a model for personal healing that came out of her own experiences and later used this model to assist others. The chapter is informed by her insight that loss and grief experienced by past generations is a legacy that compounds and compli-cates many of the challenges that beset contemporary Aboriginal people. Wanganeen and Szorenyi describe how this perspective is not only relevant for Aboriginal people but can assist people across cultures and provide a means to reconfigure the ongoing impacts of social injustice.

These four chapters centre on experiential knowledges and raise con-siderations and questions that provide a deep understanding of the impact and political importance of the legacies of social injustice through attention to the voices of those who are marginalised. The four groups of people featured in the chapters, Gypsy/Travellers (Marcus), refugees (Anderson and Holmes), migrants (Papadelos), and First Nations People (Wanganeen and Szorenyi) are frequently silenced, marginalised, and denied recognition. The effects of past

12   Chris Beasley and Pam Papadelos

and often current traumas are not erased over time, rather these experiences continue to impact upon and shape those who experience them, requiring distinctive strategies in navigating everyday lives.

Section 3—re-imagining the future—examines ways that legacies of injustice are subverted, resisted and re-conceptualised. The final three chapters offer varied suggestions for constructing alternatives that challenge legacies of injustice and empower communities/people rather than simply recognising and condemning past actions. The third section begins with Maki Kimura's contribution 'The legacy of injustice and resistance: Japan's military sexual slavery' (Chapter 10) which examines suffering endured by victim-survivors of Japan's military sexual slavery. These women were sexually exploited by the Japanese military during World War II. Primarily from Japan, but also from its former colonies and occupied territories, they are often referred to as 'comfort women'. Supported by feminist activists, historians and other scholars, 'comfort women' have actively sought justice from the Japanese government and appealed to the international community to acknowledge sexual violence as both a serious war crime and a crime against humanity. However, Kimura notes that not only has the Japanese government evaded its legal responsibilities to these victims over the past thirty years, but also more recently has engaged in preventing memorials to 'comfort women' from being constructed. Her chapter provides a concrete instance of the politics of memorialisation, exploring how women's testimonies as well as the effects of these memorials can build resistance to this legacy of injustice.

Chris Beasley's chapter 'Haunted by the heteronorm: Hollywood romance' (Chapter 11) employs a cultural politics approach to consider the significance of popular culture in relation to power relations. This cultural politics framework offers a means to examine practices of legitimation and hegemony by noting the effect of reiterated themes in popular culture and specifically in Hollywood film—a cultural format seen by mass audiences across the globe. Beasley asserts that Hollywood movies are by no means just simple escapist entertainment but offer repeated political narratives which have substantiated effects. In this way, Hollywood movies enable social inequality to be rendered invisible and thus normalised and indeed made axiomatic. For this reason, she asks whether, and by what means, Hollywood romance films reiterate, enforce or challenge social injustice in the form of heteronormativity. The aim is to outline possibilities for innovation and social change for the future.

The final chapter in this section—'Challenging criminalisation in the Commonwealth: Theorising Legacies and Colonialities in LGBTIQ Movement Strategies—by Matthew Waites (Chapter 12) analyses the British Empire's criminalisation of sexual acts between men, and sometimes between women. He outlines this enduring legal legacy in most Commonwealth states, but also how colonial power relations influence the structure of transnational struggles for human rights by LGBTI (lesbian, gay, bisexual, trans, intersex) and queer movements. Waites' chapter offers an analysis which considers the conceptual

Ongoing Legacies of Social Injustice 13

prisms of both legacies and colonialities. Decolonial perspectives that conceptualise coloniality are engaged alongside argument that living legacy serves an additional analytical purpose. He draws on empirical research from the London Commonwealth Heads of Government Meeting's Peoples Forum (2018) in order to challenge critical dismissals of the Commonwealth by theorising the value of a multi-sited and strategic politics.

In this final thematic section, we see substantively different ways in which legacies of social injustice may also result in resistant approaches. Differential strategies outlined in these three chapters include collective action, claims directed at governments (Kimura), policy techniques aimed at altering public perceptions and encouraging government support and funding (Beasley), and tactics within government bodies and in public conventions concerned with producing legal and policy change (Waites).

The connections outlined *within* the three thematic sections do not however exhaust the links *between* the chapters. Further continuities in understanding legacies of social injustice may be recognised. These include, among others, displacement and marginalisation (Anderson and Holmes, Papadelos), gendered/sexual violence (Dundon, Wanganeen and Szorenyi, Kimura), ethnic-racial violence/colonialism (Liddle, Kaur, Wanganeen and Szorenyi, Kimura), cultural forms/artworks (Liddle, Kimura, Beasley), legal/policy discrimination in relation to sexuality (Beasley, Waites), impacts of age (Marcus, Anderson and Holmes, Papadelos), social stigma (Andrada, Marcus, Papadelos), and impacts of law/criminalisation (Dundon, Wanganeen and Szorenyi, Waites). The chapters frequently also engage directly with intersections between nodes of power. For instance, race/ethnicity/indigeneity and gender (Kaur, Andrada, Marcus, Papadelos, Wanganeen and Szorenyi), as well as sexuality and gender (Andrada, Kimura, Beasley) are but two examples here.

Whatever the subject matter, method, strategy, intersection or site that is highlighted, the contributions in this collection all employ the concept of living legacies as a means of understanding injustice as it is linked to power, and how power is necessarily interconnected with time. Our intention is that this collection will open up future discussions across a range of fields where the concept of living legacy can be utilised to generate new approaches to change (see Caswell, 2021, for related deliberations).

We now turn from this opening critical interrogation to the individual chapters with their many differing accounts of a range of actual instances of legacies. The book ends with a synthetic analysis of the implications of this initial interrogation and the individual contributions (Chapter 13) in terms of *how power and time might be re-configured to enable re-imagining and enacting social change*.

Notes

1 For related work, for example in the Routledge Social Justice Series, see Beynon-Jones & Grabham, 2019, and Valverde, 2015.

14   Chris Beasley and Pam Papadelos

2   We focus in this volume on social power relations between human beings. Though we did aim to include chapters attending to 'legacy' in terms of post-anthropocentrism, such potential contributions did not eventuate. This remains a limitation of the collection.
3   However, Bignall and others assert that influential figures like Deleuze and Foucault did not ignore power relations that remain relatively fixed over time (Bignall, 2008).
4   These two scholars are members of OLIRN and contributed to the first and third workshops in Adelaide, South Australia and Edinburgh, Scotland. Their papers were to have been included in this volume, but care and other responsibilities during the Covid pandemic prevented this. We note their works here in recognition of their several contributions.

References

Adkins, L. (2012). Out of work or out of time? Rethinking labor after the financial crisis. *South Atlantic Quarterly*, 111(4), 621–641.

Ahmed, S. (2004). Affective economies. *Social Text*, 22(2), 117–139.

Alexandrakis, O. (2016). Transformative connections: Trauma, cooperative horizons, and emerging political topographies in Athens, Greece. *History and Anthropology*, 27 (1), 32–44.

Araújo, M. P. N. & dos Santos, M. S. (2009). History, memory and forgetting: Political implications. *RCCS Annual Review. A selection from the Portuguese journal Revista Crítica de Ciências Sociais*, (1). http://rccsar.revues.org/157. Accessed June 2022.

Athanasiou, A., Hantzaroula, P. & Yannakopoulos, K. (2008). Towards a new epistemology: the "affective turn". *Historein*, 8, 5–16.

Barad, K. (2007). *Meeting the universe halfway: Quantum physics and the entanglement of matter and meaning*. Durham, NC: Duke University Press.

Beasley, C. (2005). *Gender and sexuality: Critical theories, critical thinkers*. London, Thousand Oaks: Sage.

Beasley, C. (2008). Re-thinking hegemonic masculinity in a globalizing world. *Men and Masculinities*, 11(1), 86–103.

Beasley, C. (2011). Libidinous politics: Heterosex, "transgression" and social change. *Australian Feminist Studies*, 26(67), 25–40.

Beasley, C. (2017). What matters in social change?: The uncertain significance of caring. Paper presented at the Fay Gale Annual Lecture, Academy of the Social Sciences in Australia (ASSA), University of Sydney, June 2017 and University of Adelaide, September 2017.

Beasley, C. & Bacchi, C. (2007). Envisaging a new politics for an ethical future: Beyond trust, care and generosity—towards an ethic of "social flesh". *Feminist Theory*, 8(3), 279–298.

Beasley, C. & Brook, H. (2019). *The cultural politics of contemporary Hollywood film: Power, culture, and society*. Manchester: Manchester University Press.

Bennett, J. M. (2006). The lost pasts of women's history. *Medieval Feminist Forum*, 41(1), 88–98.

Beynon-Jones, S. & Grabham, E. (Eds) (2019). *Law and time*. Boca Raton, FL: Routledge.

Bignall, S. (2008). Deleuze and Foucault on desire and power. *Angelaki: Journal of Theoretical Humanities*, 13(1), 127–114.

Blomley, N. (2011). *Rights of passage: Sidewalks and the Regulation of Public Flow*. Abingdon & New York: Routledge.

Bozalek, V. & Pease, B. (2020). *Post-anthropocentric social work: Critical Posthuman and New Materialist perspectives*. Abingdon: Routledge.

Braidotti, R. (2006). *Transpositions: On nomadic ethics*. Cambridge: Polity Press.

Braidotti, R. (2008). In spite of the times: The postsecular turn in feminism. *Theory, Culture & Society*, 25(6), 1–24.

Braidotti, R. (2013). *Post-humanism: Life beyond the self*. London: Polity Press.

Caswell, M. (2021). *Urgent archives: Enacting liberatory memory work*. Abingdon & New York: Routledge.

Clough, P. T. & Halley, J. (2020). *The affective turn: Theorizing the social*. Durham, NC & London: Duke University Press.

Colebrook, C. & UK Research and Innovation. (2008). *Vitalism and the meaning of life in the philosophy and criticism of Gilles Deleuze*. https://gtr.ukri.org/projects?ref=AH%2FE003206%2F1. Accessed September 2021.

Danieli, Y. (Ed.) (1998). *International handbook of multigenerational legacies of trauma*. New York: Springer Science & Business Media.

Deleuze, G. & Parnet, C. (2007). *Dialogues* II. New York: Columbia University Press.

Deuchars, R. (2011). Creating lines of flight and activating resistance: Deleuze and Guattari's war machine. *AntePodium*, 1–28.

Diprose, R. (2002). *Corporeal generosity: on giving with Nietzsche, Merleau-Ponty and Levinas*. Albany, NY: State University of New York Press.

Dolphijn, R. & van der Tuin, I. (2012). *New materialism: Interviews and cartographies*. Ann Arbor, MI: Open Humanities Press Imprint.

El Kurd, D. (2020). *Polarized and demobilized: Legacies of authoritarianism in Palestine*. Oxford: Oxford University Press.

Enright, M. (2018). "No. I won't go back": national time, trauma and legacies of symphysiotomy in Ireland. In S. Beynon-Jones & E. Grabham (Eds), *Law and time*. Boca Raton, FL: Routledge.

Faulkner, W. (1951). *Requiem for a nun*. New York: Random House.

Frary, M. (2018). Checking the history bubble: Historians will have to use social media as an essential tool in future research. How will they decide if its information is unreliable or wrong? *Index on Censorship*, 47(1), 70–71.

Fredericks, V. (2011). Remembering Katyn: mourning, memory, and national identity. *Memory Connection*, 1(1), 197–210.

Gatens, M. (1996). *Imaginary bodies: Ethics, power, and corporeality*. London & New York: Routledge.

Goelitz, A. (2021) *From trauma to healing: A social worker's guide to working with survivors*, 2nd edition. Abingdon & New York: Routledge.

Grabham, E., Cooper, D., Krishnadas & Herman, D. (Eds) (2009). *Intersectionality and beyond: Law, power and the politics of location*. Abingdon & New York: Routledge.

Greenhouse, C. (2019). The long sudden death of Antonin Scalia. In S. Beynon-Jones & E. Grabham (Eds), *Law and Time*. Boca Raton, FL: Routledge.

Haraway, D. J. (2016). *Staying with the trouble*. Durham, NC & New York: Duke University Press.

Hunt, L. (2018). *History: Why it matters*. Cambridge: Polity Press.

Jacobs, J. (2010). *Memorializing the holocaust*. London: IB Tauris.

Jinks, R. (2014). Thinking comparatively about genocide memorialization. *Journal of Genocide Research*, 16(4), 423–440.

Johnson, C. (2005). Narratives of identity: Denying empathy in conservative discourses on race, class, and sexuality. *Theory and Society*, 34(1), 37–61.

Johnson, C. (2010). The politics of affective citizenship: from Blair to Obama. *Citizenship Studies*, 14(5), 495–509.

Johnson, C. (2017). Affective citizenship and the politics of apology. Ongoing Legacies of Discrimination and Violence—Emotion, Memory, Representation and Policy, CrissCross conference: Inaugural OLIRN conference, University of Adelaide, December.

Kimmel, M. S. (2005). Why men should support gender equity. *Women's Studies*, 103, 102–114.

Kiyonaga, A. & Egner, T. (2013). Working memory as internal attention: Toward an integrative account of internal and external selection processes. *Psychonomic Bulletin & Review*, 20(2), 228–242.

Koehn, S., Neysmith, S., Kobayashi, K. & Khamisa, H. (2013). Revealing the shape of knowledge using an intersectionality lens: Results of a scoping review on the health and health care of ethnocultural minority older adults. *Ageing and Society*, 33(3), 437–464.

Krastev, L. (2019). The anonymous memory of the living past. 2nd International Conference on Social Science, Public Health and Education (SSPHE 2018), 196–200.

Kundakbayeva, Z. & Kassymova, D. (2016). Remembering and forgetting: the state policy of memorializing Stalin's repression in post-Soviet Kazakhstan. *Nationalities Papers*, 44(4), 611–627.

Luhmann, S. (2011). Filming familial secrets: Approaching and avoiding legacies of Nazi perpetration. *New German Critique*, 38(1), 115–134.

Luhmann, S. (2018). Nazi family matters as public pedagogy: James Moll's (2006) documentary, Inheritance. Exploring Legacies of Injustice and Inequality; Enabling Just and Equal Futures: 3rd OLIRN conference, Edinburgh, UK, December.

Manderson, D. (2012). Foreword: Social injustice. Special Issue—Thematic: Critical perspectives on social justice. *UNSW Law Journal*, 35(2), 408–416.

Marks, L. & Worboys, M. (Eds) (1997). *Migrants, minorities and health: Historical and contemporary studies*. London: Routledge.

Marx, K. (1852). *The eighteenth Brumaire of Louis Bonaparte*. New York: Die Revolution.

McCall, L. (2005). The complexity of intersectionality. *Signs: Journal of women in culture and society*, 30(3), 1771–1800.

Miller, R. R. (2021). Failures of memory and the fate of forgotten memories. *Neurobiology of Learning and Memory*, 181, https://doi.org/10.1016/j.nlm.2021.107426. Accessed June 2022.

Morton, R. (2021). *My year of living vulnerably*. Sydney: HarperCollins Australia.

Nixon, R. (2011). *Slow violence and the environmentalism of the poor*. Cambridge: Harvard University Press.

Olick, J. K. & Robbins, J. (1998). Social memory studies: From "collective memory" to the historical sociology of mnemonic practices. *Annual Review of Sociology*, 24(1), 105–140.

Ono, M., Devilly, G. J. & Shum, D. H. (2016). A meta-analytic review of overgeneral memory: The role of trauma history, mood, and the presence of posttraumatic stress disorder. *Psychological Trauma: Theory, Research, Practice, and Policy*, 8(2), 157–164.

Orwell, G. (1950). *1984*. New York: Signet Classic.

Poole, R. (2009). Two ghosts and an angel: Memory and forgetting in Hamlet, Beloved, and The Book of Laughter and Forgetting. *Constellations*, 16(1), 125–149.

Powers, T. (2017). The big thing on his mind. *The New York Review*, April 20, 42.

Reisch, M. (Ed.) (2014) *The Routledge international handbook of social justice*. Abingdon & New York: Routledge.

Ricoeur, P. (2006). *Memory, history, forgetting*, trans. Blarney, K & Pellauer, D: Chicago, IL: University of Chicago Press.

Santayana, G. (1905). *Reason in common sense: The life of reason*. New York: Charles Scribner.

Sepehri, D. (2017). 2017 Calibre Essay Prize (Second prize): "To speak of sorrow" by Darius Sepehri. *Australian Book Review*, 393(August). www.australianbookreview. com.au/abr-online/archive/2017/209-august-2017-no-393/4195-2017-calibre-essa y-prize-winner-to-speak-of-sorrow-by-darius-sepehri. Accessed June 2022.

Sharma, S. (2014). *In the meantime: Temporality and cultural politic*. London: Duke University Press.

Smith, E. & Hattery, A. J. (2011). Race, wrongful conviction & exoneration. *Journal of African American Studies*, 15(1), 74–94.

Smith, F. (2016). "Privilege is invisible to those who have it": engaging men in workplace equality'. *The Guardian*, 8 June.

Stanley, L. & Dampier, H. (2005). Aftermaths: Post/Memory, commemoration and the concentration camps of the South African War 1899–1902. *European Review of History: Revue européenne d'histoire*, 12(1), 91–119.

Sturgeon, N. (2017) Apology to those convicted for same-sex sexual activity that is now legal. Scottish National Party. www.snp.org/apology-to-those-convicted-for-sam e-sex-sexual-activity-that-is-now-legal. Accessed June 2022.

Thompson, J. (2005). Apology, justice and respect: a critical defence of political apology. Australian Association for Professional and Applied Ethics 12th Annual Conference, 28–30 September, Adelaide, South Australia.

Thompson, S. G. (2007). Beyond a reasonable doubt-reconsidering uncorroborated eyewitness identification testimony. *UC Davis L. Rev.*, 41, 1487–1546.

Thornton, E. (2020). On lines of flight: The theory of political transformation in A Thousand Plateaus . *Deleuze and Guattari Studies*, 14(3), 433–456.

Tremblay, M., Paternotte, D. & Johnson, C. (2011). *The lesbian and gay movement and the state: Comparative insights into a transformed relationship*. Ashgate Publishing.

Valverde, M. (2015). *Chronotypes of law: Jurisdiction, scale and governance*. Abingdon & New York: Routledge.

Van Dyke, R. M. (2016). Memory, place, and the memorialization of landscape. In D. Bruno & J. Thomas (Eds), Handbook of landscape archaeology (pp. 277–284). Abingdon: Routledge.

Wells, G. L. & Olson, E. A. (2003). Eyewitness testimony. *Annual Review of Psychology*, 54(1), 277–295.

Women's march anthem by MLCK: 'I can't keep quiet'. (2017). YouTube. www.you tube.com/watch?v=xgrtOO9dGsE. Accessed May 2022.

Worby, E. & Ally, S. (2013). The disappointment of nostalgia: Conceptualising cultures of memory in contemporary South Africa. *Social Dynamics*, 39(3), 457–480.

Part 1

Chapter 2

A Family Act

Power, Gendered Violence and the Living Legacy of Social Injustice in Papua New Guinea

Alison Dundon

Introduction

In Papua New Guinea (PNG), a country of 9 million people divided into approximately 800 language and ethnic groups, violence directed at women is common and its incidence widespread. While difficult to measure, given a lack of nation-wide data on prevalence, some studies indicate that gendered violence occurs across all provinces to varying levels of severity (Baines, 2012, p. 22). Spurred on by collective action generated by grassroots institutions, women's rights advocates in PNG, non-government and faith-based organisations as well as the national government and international aid donors, there has been considerable pressure to implement national legislation regarding domestic violence. Acting on the need to develop measures for the legal protection of women in the country, the Family Protection Bill (Government of Papua New Guinea, 2013) passed through the National Executive Council on the 18 September 2013 with a landslide 65–0 vote.[1] This prompted commentators at the time to suggest that this "signified strong political will" to transform very high rates of violence and was proffered as a "crucial first step to reducing violence against women" (Maladina, 2013). Despite this, recent levels of spectacular violence experienced by women has prompted the use of terms such as "epidemic", "pandemic" and "emergency" by a variety of local, national and international organisations, to highlight what Macintyre (2012) refers to an "environment of violence" for women (p. 249). Garbe and Struck-Garbe (2018) note that gender-based violence is still very much a part of everyday life and is "widely tolerated and accepted" (p. 20). As a result, Human Rights Watch (2021) argues that PNG continues to be "one of the most dangerous places to be a woman or girl, where violence against women and children is rampant" and where at least two out of three women experience domestic violence (p. 526).

It is not only episodic and spectacular violence, the "'visceral, eye-catching and page-turning power' of spectacular violence" (Nixon, 2011, p. 3), however, that women experience in PNG. They are also vulnerable to the quiet

DOI: 10.4324/9781003311928-3

unfolding of slow violence (Nixon 2011) and its interconnection with structural inequalities that profoundly harm women through the constitution of an "unjust condition" (Galtung, 1969, pp. 171, 173). For, as Christian and Dowler (2019) argue, "the binary of fast and slow violence operates as a single complex of violence" (p. 1067) in which they "thoroughly imbue each other" (p. 1072). Slow violence (Nixon, 2011), as a form of gradual and largely invisible violence that disperses across space and time and is delayed and attritional in nature (p. 2), embodies the legacy and environment of violence in which women live.

In this volume, Beasley and Papadelos (2024) argue that living legacies are (re)constituted and (re)produced through power relations, which are actively engaged not only in the creation and maintenance of these legacies but also transformed through processes of reconstituting power relations. This chapter engages the concept of 'living legacies' to critically analyse, and seek to challenge, systemic levels and forms of violence experienced by women and girls in PNG. The concept builds on the notion of legacy but moves beyond a primary focus on the past, as histories or memories. Indeed, the 'living' or, perhaps, 'liveliness' of legacies provides a meaningful framework through which the lived experience of everyday and spectacular violence, experienced by women and girls, comes to the foreground. As legacies are embedded and, both constituted and produced, in and through power relations as well as inequalities and often profound injustice, the notion of living legacies offers a way to understand the impact of legacies that stick' in the present and, even, the future. The legacy of systemic forms of violence is staunch and structural in PNG, manifest in the scars and pain women embody. Drawing on the lens of the 'liveliness' of legacies enables revelations and, potentially, acknowledgement of such inequalities and the intergenerational interplay of dynamics of slow and fast, everyday and structural violence and the harm it perpetuates across time.

In this environment of violence, state-based, legal and community power relations bolster inequalities and perpetuate harmful practices that are both rationalised and normalised. As Hukula (2012) has noted, a "common response to violence against women by Papua New Guineans is *em pasin bilong ol* (Tok Pisin: that is their way) or *em nomal ya* (TP: that's normal)" (p. 197). Such statements, she writes, suggest certain forms of violence are perceived as both traditional and the norm (Biersack 2016, p. 274). Papua New Guinean women's bodies, practices and relationships are shaped by this "living legacy" of gendered inequality and intersecting, and multiple, forms of violence. Power relations constitute gendered persons and shape perceptions of (in)appropriate behaviours, relations and expectations for both women and men. In this context, what is considered violence is highly contested, and is based on complex cultural and intergenerational perceptions of gendered capacities evident in articulations about 'tradition' and customary practices. As Jolly (2012, p. 3) notes, even "naming an act as 'violence' entails adjudications of both facts and values and these are intimately entangled". It is also recognised that perceptions of violence as abuse rather than "legitimate discipline" are culturally, historically, and individually contingent (Merry, 2009, p. 22), and the distinction between "acceptable" forms of violence and those that are understood as "abuse", are central to definitions of gendered violence (Merry, 2006, p. 25). There is an intimate relationship between gender, customary practice and violence in PNG, manifest in structural forms as well as practices based on relational premises that make women particularly vulnerable to violence across their lives. Customary practice is a highly valued temporal regime in which women and men "negotiate their temporally situated power relations with each other via discourses, histories, cultures, bodies and technologies" (Bjork & Buhre, 2021, p. 178). Nevertheless, in the case of violence against women customary temporal regimes can intersect with other temporal regimes, dialogues and structures, which render women vulnerable to discrimination and violence. Legal pathways, for example, may draw on customary practices or institutions, such as forms of compensation that rationalise and justify ongoing harm, suffering and gendered inequalities. Mawani (2014) points to the production of "discontinuities between past, present, and future" used to fortify its own "authority, sovereignty, and legitimacy" (p. 69), evident in the practice of customary law in PNG. In this context, the safety and gendered agency of women is often challenged by the "lived temporality" (Grabham & Beynon-Jones, 2019, p.5) of custom and traditional practice, which is based on politically, gendered and culturally curated notions of appropriate behaviour, mobility and capacity.

This chapter, then, foregrounds highly visible forms of violence perpetrated against women as well as the everyday, banal and slow violence that constitutes the enduring and ongoing legacy of gendered violence in PNG. In the first section, the legacy of social and legal injustice in PNG is explored through processes of normalization and widespread acceptance of violence in women's lives. This discussion also points to significant continuities between present and past forms and prevalence of violence. The following discussion of PNG's complex and pluralist legal system focusses on the experience of structural violence, which obscures the violence women encounter when engaged with legal structures and institutions. Such violence is largely invisible, often evident only in the limited access that women seeking justice to vital services, including protection under the law, legal representation, protection orders, counselling or safe spaces, experience. The negotiation of the legal system, with its focus on customary law and village courts, can prove another context in which women are both violated and disenfranchised. The final section focuses on the recent implementation of the Family Protection Act (FPA) across the country, noting the slow and structural violence that underlies its practice and progress. It traces incremental and inadequate transformations in legal, sociocultural and political processes associated with the implementation of the Act as well as the implications for women seeking justice. The chapter concludes that the

24   Alison Dundon

potential for alternate social and political futures, implied in the passing and implementation of the FPA, is certainly possible and already in progress. However, in order to transform this intergenerational legacy of violence, there needs to be a concerted challenge to existing legal, customary and gendered practices and institutions that perpetuate forms of violence and it is in this context that the framework of living legacies can aid in revealing the 'stickiness' of violence, discrimination and inequality.

'That's normal': The Living Legacy of Everyday Violence

PNG has a history of violence directed at women: Counts (1990, p. 225) noted in the 1990s that the Law Reform Commission in 1987 found that, between 1979 and 1982, 73 per cent of women murdered in the country were killed by their husbands. Conducted between 1982 and 1986, Biersack (2016, p. 274) notes that this study remains the most comprehensive survey on domestic violence in the country, which demonstrated that violence was widespread and common despite significant variation across the provinces. The research conducted for the Commission also showed that the majority of adults surveyed considered physically beating women an "acceptable, normal part of married life" (Biersack 2016, p. 274; Bradley & Kesno, 2001; Eves 2012; Macintyre 2000). Indeed, the most commonly discussed form of violence towards women in PNG is referred to (in English) as "wife beating" (Baines 2012, p. 21; Counts 1990).[2] All the same, the prevalence of wife beating is not uniform and the absence or low incidence of it in certain areas or regions has been noted in various contexts (see Counts, 1990; Human Rights Watch, 2015; Lepani, 2015; Lewis, Maruia & Walker, 2008, Mitchell, 1990; Nash, 1990; Voice for Change, 2015a).

In a report in 2008, *Violence Against Women in Melanesia and East Timor,* it was stated that violence against women was pervasive and the risk of violence a "constant presence" in the lives of women (Office of Development Effectiveness, 2008, p. 1105). The report noted that two thirds of women had experienced domestic violence and that fifty per cent of women suffered some form of sexual violence. Lewis, Maruia and Walker (2008, p. 194) cited results from a study conducted in the mid-2000s among 415 women across four provinces in PNG in which they concluded that there were considerable differences in incidence and prevalence of domestic violence. Nonetheless, 58 per cent of the sample of women reported physical and/or emotional violence in their intimate relationships, 47 per cent noted financial abuse, 44 per cent reported sexual abuse, and 38 per cent social isolation (Lewis et al., 2008, p. 194). In terms of physical and visible violence, women suffered cuts and bruises, bleeding, black eyes as well as other eye injuries, burns, and broken limbs and teeth among other injuries. Sexual violence was largely ascribed to the inability to say 'no' to sex with intimate male partners and was often accompanied by physical violence (Lewis et al., 2008, pp. 190–191). Emotional violence was experienced in terms of the use of threats to control behaviour (including physical violence), extended silence, invoking guilt and 'put-downs' (Lewis et al., 2008, p. 191). Financial abuse, including lack of access to goods and money, was also common was the isolation of women from others and having their social relations controlled or curtailed (Lewis et al., 2008. p. 193).

In a recent Human Rights Watch report, *Bashed Up: Family Violence in Papua New Guinea*, which was based on a survey conducted in June 2015 among survivors of domestic violence, police, activists, service providers and international donors and advisors, it was argued that despite "signs of progress" as a result of the passing of the FPA in 2013, there was a great deal more to do (Human Rights Watch, 2015, pp. 2–3). "He bashed me up" was a comment made often during the research, which was so common that there was "little sense of shock or outrage" (Human Rights Watch, 2015, p. 2). Similarly, in the Voice for Change Community Survey, conducted across twelve communities and involving over one thousand individuals in Jiwaka Province in 2013, wife beating was identified as the most common form of physical violence experienced by women (Voice for Change, 2015a, p. 1). In addition, communities that participated acknowledged that violence against women was widespread and that women both experienced and observed "multiple forms of violence both within their homes and in public spaces" (Voice for Change, 2015a, p. 1). In Jiwaka Province, the most common forms of violence directed at women and girls were identified as wife beating, followed by rape and sorcery-related violence. Women emphasised being overburdened with work (likening it to 'slavery'), polygamy, and their husbands taking money they had earned as the most serious forms of violence (Voice for Change, 2015b, p. 1). Other significant forms of violence reported included having market stalls destroyed, money or goods stolen, and police inaction (Voice for Change, 2015b, p. 1).[3]

It is clear, then, that women continue to experience various forms of everyday violence and encounter practices and institutions that render women vulnerable to violence, such as forms of marriage and ideals of masculinity, which are often the focus of scrutiny by global and national programs. Human Rights Watch (2015, p. 5), for example, focuses on practices such as polygamy, the payment of bride-price as the basis for marriage, financial dependence of women on their husbands and families, and attacks based on accusations of sorcery, as well as the reluctance of many police to take violence against women seriously. These intersect with chronic issues associated with law and order, as well as unfavourable economic conditions and the generation of unrealisable expectations (or desires), have also been suggested as contributing forces in the context of violence against women. Dinnen (1997) has also pointed to the complexity of issues that lie at the base of patterns of gender violence in the country, including "changing household relations, high levels of societal tolerance of violence, alcohol abuse, the breakdown of traditional restraints, and the persistence of male dominance in all fields" (p. 5).

Macintyre (2008, p. 181), however, argues that there are significant continuities between contemporary and past forms of violence. She notes that expressions of masculinity and power through violence against women, whether gang rapes, sexual assaults or domestic violence, are not solely the result of social distinctions and disjuncture wrought by modernity but have historical antecedents (Macintyre, 2008, p. 180). In a similar fashion, Kameljeet Kaur (Chapter 4) points to ways in which domestic violence is framed through the notion of 'honour crimes' in British South Asian Communities in the United Kingdom, re-imagined and co-constituted through legacies of colonial narratives that attach or stick to certain gendered bodies, and not others. In PNG, continuities of pre-colonial to post-colonial representations of women's bodies and capacities are framed through certain practices and ideals of conflict resolution, compensation and "payback" in which overt violence could be (and still is) used to punish wrongdoers for an offence or to remove individuals deemed to pose a threat to the group. In this context, certain forms of violence, such as rape, and other forms of sexual violence, have been considered justifiable (Luker & Dinnen, 2010, p. 25). Luker and Monsell-Davis (2010, p. 97) have noted that "sexual acts that state law defines as rape are 'traditionally' accepted in many cultures: such as rape for punishment, in war, as 'payback', of women who don't count, or because circumstances permit" (see also Lepani, 2008, p. 155). Biersack (2016, p. 275) notes that the shame associated with family and sexual violence, and a "culture of silence and impunity" (Amnesty International, 2011, p. 257) means that it is under-reported and data or statistics are difficult to obtain.

Macintyre (2000, p. 150) noted two decades ago that the majority of members of parliament argued against laws relating to domestic violence on the grounds that these were contrary to "traditional family life". In this context, everyday gendered violence still appears to be "culturally and socially sanctioned in PNG", and part of a widespread "acceptance of violence at the highest levels of society" (Baines, 2012, p. 22). This kind and level of violence is buttressed by activities and practices that continue to impede the reduction of violence (Baines 2012, p. 23) and potentially function to normalise and rationalise endemic levels of suffering and harm. Jolly (2012, pp. 3–4) notes the continued "widespread legitimacy of violence in general and gender violence in particular", a situation in which gender violence appears to have widespread acceptance with both women and men (Eves, 2012; Lepani, 2008; Macintyre, 2012; McPherson, 2012).

The following commentary traces women's negotiation of the complex and pluralist legal system in the context of the normalisation and acceptance of endemic and quotidian violence. In this context, a chronic lack of legal infrastructure and inadequate policing services, particularly in rural areas, means women often cannot access services they need to attain a level of judicial and, potentially, social justice.

Lifting the Lid: Women and the Violence of Law

In April 2013 PNG's Prime Minister, Peter O'Neill, argued, "[t]he lid over domestic violence is now removed and the problem exposed as a national issue needing government interventions". He went on to state that domestic violence was "contrary to the constitution and laws of PNG" (Blackwell, 2013, p. 1). The passing of the Family Protection Act five months later was initially hailed as a positive action taken on behalf of women and girls, with the aim to make legacies of everyday violence more visible in order to create more effective legal pathways for attaining justice.[4] In a report published in 2015, two years after the passing of the Act, Human Rights Watch (2015) highlighted the potential for sweeping change initiated by the FPA as "a breakthrough in public awareness about the problem" (pp. 2–3). In the meantime, however, it has become clear that the FPA is limited in its scope, primarily designed to deal only with domestic violence and put into practice "for less serious matters" (Institute of National Affairs, 2016, p. 9).

The Act operates in a complex context of legal pluralism, which is characterised as a hierarchy of laws. These are classified as the Constitution, Organic Laws, Acts of Parliament, Emergency Regulations, Provincial Laws, Laws made or adopted by or under the Constitution, and Underlying Law, including 'Customary' and 'Common' Law. In this context, written law takes precedence over underlying law, in which customary law takes precedence over common law. Customary law applies unless it is inconsistent with written law; or contravenes the National Goals and Directive Principles or the Basic Social Obligations set out under the Constitution (Government of Papua New Guinea, 2010, p. 9). Customary law, then, plays an important role in the legal system as well as in wider social institutions in the country. Customary law constitutes a broad spectrum of customary practices and institutions, and is defined in the Constitution as:

> the customs and usages of the indigenous inhabitants of the country existing in relation to the matter in question at the time when and the place in relation to which the matter arises, regardless of whether or not the custom or usage has existed from time immemorial.
>
> (PNG, 2010, p. 7)

This broad and somewhat ambiguous legal and temporal category plays an important role in PNG generally, but specifically in relation to domestic and family violence cases, which are often decided through the village court system. As the vast majority of the population live outside of the major towns and cities, village courts are most likely the primary legal institution through which women can access the judicial system. In practice, however, this complex and multifaceted legal system is characterised by an ambiguous relationship between common and customary law that makes it difficult to formulate a clear pathway for women to challenge violence or seek justice. The complex interactions between statute and customary law also play a significant role in the difficulties of pursuing domestic violence cases. In particular, domestic violence legislation is linked to the Marriage Act and whether spouses in domestic violence cases are married under statutory or customary law becomes legally significant. As most people in PNG are married under customary law, this poses a significant challenge to the uniform application of the FPA across the country. What is understood to be domestic violence, then, in this context is influenced by customary laws that are as variable as the myriad customs across this culturally diverse country.

The village court system is the largest government institution in the country. It is made of up over 1,000 courts and is the most accessible court for the majority of people. For many women, in particular, village courts represent the only accessible legal institution. Since 2004, there has been a push nationally to make more female magistrates representative in village courts (International Center for Research on Women, 2011, p. 24). Despite this, village courts often practice what McLeod (2005) has referred to as 'excessive traditionalism', which is based on a masculine model of tradition, culture and compensation. Given this context, perhaps it is not surprising that "even if opportunity avails, some forms of domestic violence and sexual assault are even less likely to be reported to or pursued by police than they are in many Western countries" (Luker & Dinnen, 2010, p. 24). Nonetheless, the majority of women remain dependent on "community-based justice" meted out in village courts, largely because they encounter problems with gaining access to the formal justice system (Stop Violence, 2013, p. 35). To complicate this process, village magistrates may lack formal training in legal processes, or have little background in law, counselling or mediation. They also charge a fee to have a case heard and fines are the usual outcome of these disputes, which many women cannot afford (Child-Fund, 2013, p. 5). Moreover, women may not wish to contact police, seeing them as the "last resort" (ChildFund, 2013, p. 7).

Village courts have been part of the formal legal system since 1973 and are characterised by informal practices like "restorative justice", community justice and policing, and conflict prevention and mediation/resolution. These play a significant role in justice systems in rural areas, but they have the capacity to undermine women's rights and needs in the process. This is particularly the case when the principle of 'restorative justice' serves to subordinate women's rights in the name of wider community needs for compensation and conflict resolution (Office of Development Effectiveness, 2008, p. 111). It has been reported that men often prefer to engage "the customary justice system of compensation and reconciliation" (Jolly, 2012, p. 9) for perhaps this very reason. Indeed, Dinnen (1997) argues that many of the mechanisms used to mediate disputes over violence against women may reinscribe and reinforce gender inequality. Women may be punished more severely for adultery than men in village courts, and understandings of marriage based on brideprice and polygamy, for example, may "accentuate a view of women as the property of men" (Dinnen, 1997, p. 5). Sometimes, women may even be offered as part of compensation payments designed to mediate disputes between groups (Dinnen, 1997, p. 5). In that context, as Senior Constable Yawa noted in 2002:

> [l]egally in Papua New Guinea the woman is often placed in the role of a jural minor. An extreme example is the case of a young woman being offered to a rival clan as a part payment of compensation during a tribal fight. In our local village courts issues of family violence are treated as minor or an offence, not against the woman herself, but against her people.
>
> (Yawa, 2002)

In addition, laws and legal interventions can be undermined when police and local court officials do not take the violence seriously or seek "reconciliation and keeping the family together over protecting the safety of the woman" (Merry, 2009, p. 51), a 'sticky' and complex legacy of colonial, political and cultural perceptions of different gendered persons Human Rights Watch (2015) reports that police do not usually see domestic violence as a serious law and order issue. In these cases, police can refuse to explore the allegations or to arrest a potential perpetrator, even if there is evidence of "extreme violence" (Human Rights Watch, 2015, p. 3). In addition, an Amnesty International Report (2011, p. 257) noted a "culture of silence and impunity" in which women were concerned about reporting violence to the authorities for fear of repercussions. Further, the "vast majority of violent acts that are illegitimate according to law" occur far from the reaches of the state, particularly those committed in rural areas (Luker & Dinnen, 2010, p. 24). As formal law and justice resources are established in cities and towns, those living in rural areas rely on village courts and, as such, it is not surprising, then that many women do not report violence that they experience.

In summary, there are common structural components of violence that women encounter when seeking to challenge domestic violence. In this case, village courts, for example, or mediations through the police, can present as harmful structures, particularly where women and others vulnerable to structural violence "may be persuaded not to perceive this at all" (Galtung, 1969, p. 137). However, Davies (2019) points to the implicit power of the "immobility and entrenchment" of these harmful structures, evident in what he refers to the "very embeddedness, fixity, and ability to appear 'natural' that gives structural violence its silent potency" (p. 5). In many cases, structural violence underlies women's engagements with legal institutions in PNG, evident in the inability to access legal institutions and other forms of legal aid and protection under the law; being unable to afford to seek justice; and the lack of appropriate, accountable and ultimately just processes and outcomes. Violence when normalised, quotidian, and largely invisible (Merry 2009, p. 5), "systematically produces or reproduces inequities that determine people's risk of being assaulted or harmed" (Wies & Haldane, 2011, p. 3). In this context, the enduring legacy of customary practices of compensation and reconciliation favour men while women can experience the laying of criminal charges or court cases as "secondary violence for the victim" (Jolly, 2012, p. 10). At that same time, legal pathways may not provide redress by police and local courts, who favour reconciliation and maintaining intact family units over the well-being of individual women. In this context, women continue to depend on community-based justice established by village courts because of the problems with "physically accessing the formal justice system and low levels of knowledge of their legal right" (Stop Violence, 2013, p. 35). The legacy of slow violence evident in the implementation of the FPA, in the next section, serves (again) to silence women's voices as time aids in detaching the experience of violence from its origins and the power relations that render such violence invisible.

Slow Violence: Implementing the Family Protection Act

The implementation of the Family Protection Act (FPA) is proving a complex and long-term process. This is partly the result of contestation and confusion over what is understood, or defined, as domestic violence and the ongoing debate about domestic violence is one of the key challenges posed by the implementation of the FPA. In October 2017 a Family & Sexual Violence Action Committee (FSVAC) secretariat in Port Moresby noted that only two convictions had come about from the 414 cases handled between 2016–17—pointing to a "very disturbing reality for victims of domestic violence" (Maribu, 2017). At that time, Ruth Kendino, a FSVAC Case Co-ordinator, called for a transformation of the law enforcement's approach to domestic violence. In one of the national newspapers in PNG, she reported that "most GBV cases are not getting prosecuted because police are not putting any urgency into the matter, treating DV/GBV as 'accepted behaviour'". This, Ruth Kendino argued, has led to a persistent lack of enforcement of the Act (Maribu, 2017). As a result, Human Rights Watch (2015) has concluded that so often women who seek aid do not see any change in terms of the prevalence or experience of violence (p. 4).

Three reports published by Médecins Sans Frontierès (2016), Voices for Change (2015), and Human Rights Watch (2015) have highlighted several issues that appear to be common to the implementation of the FPA. Included in these are concerns about law enforcement, in relation to general knowledge and use of the Act, as well as the overall understanding of the criminality of domestic violence; the problems associated with the complex ways in which customary and statutory laws intersect in the case of DV; and a chronic lack of shelters, safe houses or other kinds of essential services, including legal advice and counselling. These problems take place in a context of silence on everyday violence in extended family networks and entrenched gendered discrimination. All three reports point to:

> inadequate or inappropriate responses from the country's hybrid system of formal and traditional justice (...) patient's experiences expose a culture of impunity, and continuing reliance on traditional forms of justice to solve serious family and sexual violence cases.
>
> (Médecins Sans Frontières, 2016, p. 7)

Compensation is central to legal processes and is usually paid to the victims of crimes or their families. This means that "perpetrators often remain within their communities, exposing survivors to the threat of repeated violence" (Médecins Sans Frontières, 2016, p. 7). Mediation and compensation can, in this case, represent "a double violation of women's rights and allows perpetrators to act with impunity" (Voice for Change, 2015a, p. RS). The cost of going through the official justice system is considerable, particularly in comparison with the village courts and complainants are required to cover the cost of witnesses, court fees, summons, transport and food (Voice for Change, 2015a, p. RS). In addition, when a case goes to the formal justice system, women may experience bias in the courts or deliberations or determination (Voice for Change, 2015a, p. RS). In addition, there is still a focus on bringing the parties together to mediate or agree to an outcome, including compensation (Human Rights Watch, 2015, p. 4).

> Even after the passing of the FPA, if cases do make it to the courts, it is usually the village court system, which focuses on mediation and reconciliation rather than prosecution. Women do not usually engage the District Courts, where more serious crimes are prosecuted.
>
> (Human Rights Watch, 2015, p. 4)

In addition, there is a chronic lack of services for women facing violence, especially in rural areas, including safe houses and shelters, counselling (legal or psychosocial), and medical care. Médecins Sans Frontières (2016, p. 8) points to the need for those suffering violence to be able to leave the home and have somewhere safe to go. Yet, as Médecins Sans Frontières (2016, p. 8) reports, delays in the creation and maintenance of laws and policies on this has meant safe spaces are largely unavailable. In 2016, for example, only seven of seventeen Family Support Centres were fully functional and only six safe houses in the entire country, five of which were in the capital, Port Moresby. Many of the safe houses refuse to let children in with their mothers, which is a result of the "legal limbo" associated with the provision of accommodation for dependent children without the consent (or presence) of a legal guardian (Médecins Sans Frontières, 2016, p. 8). At this time, the other nine Family Support Centres offered varying degrees of support and services: including a limited form of medical care with a level of referrals to domestic violence services (Médecins Sans Frontières 2016, p. 8). In essence, according to Médecins Sans Frontières (2016), this means "most survivors have no hope of escape" (p. 8) from the situation they find themselves in.

Qualified counsellors are difficult to access, particularly in rural areas and where available, there is often a focus on reconciliation services (Médecins Sans Frontières, 2016, p. 7–8). Medical services are also complex and, sometimes, inaccessible (Human Rights Watch, 2015, p. 4):

> Patients face multiple obstacles for obtaining essential medical and psychological care, and they face severely limited options for accessing the legal, social, protection assistance they require. They are thus made 'double victims' – suffering first from brutal attacks, and then from failures in service provision and in the protection system.
>
> (Médecins Sans Frontières, 2016, p. 7)

In this context, the lack of social services means that women experiencing violence and who are financially dependent on partners or family, are often unable to seek shelter or safety, legal services or medical care. These circumstances create:

> obstacles to seeking safety and obtaining justice. With no way to feed themselves or their children, many simply cannot afford to leave an abusive partner. Cultural practices, such as the payment and repayment of bride price, also hinder women's ability to obtain protection, often trapping them with violent partners.
>
> (Médecins Sans Frontières, 2016, p. 8)

Médecins Sans Frontières (2016) reported that many of the patients that they treated ended up returning home to potentially further violence. In their study, they noted that one in ten women reported sexual violence, but that was only the most recent incidence in an established pattern of sexual violence (Médecins Sans Frontières, 2016, p. 7). The report indicated a need for "free, quality, confidential treatment, in addition to services beyond medical care to keep them safe" (Médecins Sans Frontières, 2016, p. 7).

In the most recent report by Human Rights Watch (2021), little seems to have changed in the last four years in relation to the Family & Sexual Violence Units established after the passing of the FPA. The report notes that these units remain limited, which exacerbates a chronic lack of services in general (p. 526). The invisibility of structural and slow violence in this case, renders women's experiences normal and largely hidden, "to the extent that it becomes exceedingly difficult to assign or demand culpability of the actors responsible" (Christian & Dowler, 2019, p. 1069). The slow violence of the implementation processes lulls rather than shocks (Christian & Dowler, 2019, pp. 1068–9), obscuring the everyday suffering of women facing violence in PNG. In the process, the political origins and causes of the violence are gradually detached from each other over time, rendering perpetrators of violence opaque and "political culpability (...) elusive" (Christian & Dowler, 2019, p. 1069).

Conclusion

The everyday and intergenerational nexus of gender, sexuality and power evident in the experiences of PNG women needs to be contexualised in terms of the complex histories of the country's 'sticky' and, often, harmful legacies, which inform and shape possible futures. This intersection is evident in other chapters in this book, such as in the experiences of Rosemary Wanganeen, an Australian Aboriginal woman and a member of 'the stolen generations'. Wanganeen points to the compounding impact of intergenerational trauma and the ongoing impacts associated with injustice (Chapter 9), an account which resonates with the experience of women in PNG.

Everyday violence is a common experience for women in PNG, whether they face gendered and sexual violence in their daily intimacies, practices and movements, or the "irrevocably linked" and largely invisible, slow violence and its attendant structural foundations (Davies, 2019, p. 5) as they operate within legal, sociocultural and political institutions. Some experience highly visible episodes of dramatic and spectacular violence, which has garnered attention from global bodies and grassroots organisations alike in recent times. The passing of the FPA, then, marks a significant moment in PNG's history regarding the perception and treatment of women, and points to an emerging impetus for sociocultural and political change. Nonetheless, as evident in the reportage of current processes to implement the FPA, women remain a potentially vulnerable group in general, and their capacities are constrained by potentially harmful institutions, agents or practices. In this context, the legacy of social (in) justice means women continue to be:

> ill-served at all levels of the male-dominated law and justice sector, ranging from the village court system to the police, where cultural assumptions about male superiority are commonly embraced, and issues that affect women, such as sexual and domestic violence, are either ignored totally or not seriously pursued.

> (Eves, 2010, p. 53)

So, as Cahill and Pain ask, "[h]ow might we come to terms with the denial and erasures of our violent legacies?" (2019, p. 1056). What are the implications of attempting to come to terms with how and why these legacies have been erased or denied in PNG and to what extent could this be a potential pathway for attaining social justice and, thus, meaningful social change for, and by, women? As Davies (2019, p. 2) suggests:

34 Alison Dundon

> [s]low violence provokes us to delve into the past to unearth the violence structures of inequality that saturate contemporary life and may well lay waste to the future (...) and take seriously the potential of bearing witness to the shifting temporalities of violence.

Bearing witness to such shifting temporalities of violence, then, may provide a pathway for the development of political alternatives (Beasley & Papadelos in this volume, 2024) in active engagement with the reconstitution of power relations in PNG. The focus on 'living legacies', then, enables an exploration of power relations and the impact on women's bodies and lives, rendering systematic inequalities and their impact, visible and audible. Living and lively legacies appear and operate in time, in bodies and, increasingly, in view.

Practices and principles that inscribe gendered inequalities and make women vulnerable to violence, such as forms of marriage practices, notions of tradition and customary practices and ideologies of masculinities, are being challenged at all levels of society. In recent times, grassroots organisations have developed a significant voice and programs are being designed to increase and enable access to support services as well as transform gendered, legal and political structures. These include programs that aim to create awareness and community mobilisation through sporting programs and organisations, for example, the Prime Ministers XIII Rugby League Match in which players promote 'Stop Violence against women' programs in a very public way (Papua New Guinea Country Report, 2008, p. 43). For this reason, as Bjork and Buhre (2021) suggest, "instead of sketching a single rhetorical temporality that might assure social justice" we might be better served to seek "a plurality of temporal frames that may make possible political emancipation" (p. 178) by "harnessing and subverting power" in the process of the "unfolding struggle for justice" (p. 179). In the process, the aim of a redistribution of power based on the principles of gender equality may bring about the possibility of a just society.

Notes

1 The Family Protection Bill (Government of Papua New Guinea, 2013) also aims to "promote safe, stable and strong families", as well as to "prevent and deter domestic violence at all levels of society" and to "ensure that there is effective legal protection for the victims of domestic violence".
2 Counts (1990, p. 2) noted that the primary victims of domestic violence were women and thus it was referred to as "wife beating".
3 A recent survey conducted by UNWomen found that, in PNG, 55% of woman and girls in marketplaces had experienced violence, including rape and gang rape, as well as verbal and visual harassment (AusAID 2013, p. 4).
4 It covered such actions as physical assault, psychological abuse, harassment or intimidation, sexual abuse, stalking, behaving in an offensive or indecent manner, causes damage to the family member's property or threatens to physically assault, sexually abuse or damage property of a family member (Government of Papua New Guinea,

2013, p. 3). In addition, the Act also provides for the possibility of ordering compensation "in accordance with custom or otherwise to the complainant" if they suffered personal injury, damage to property or financial loss (Government of Papua New Guinea, 2013, p. 8). It states that a single act can constitute domestic violence, or it can be a pattern of behaviour "even though some or all of these acts when viewed in isolation may appear to be minor or trivial" (Government of Papua New Guinea, 2013, p. 4). Part III of the Act lists the application process for a Family Protection Order (Government of Papua New Guinea, 2013, p. 4). In the same section, it establishes the conditions that relate to good behaviour, individual protection, property, and counselling and mediation in Protection Orders as well as the conditions of Interim Protection Orders (Government of Papua New Guinea, 2013, pp. 4–5).

References

Amnesty International. (2011). *Amnesty International Report 2011: The State of the World's Human Rights*. London: Amnesty International.

Baines, L. (2012). Gender-Based Violence in Papua New Guinea: Trends and Challenges. *Burgmann Journal*, 1, 21–26. Accessed 5 November 2014.

Biersack, A. (2016). Human Rights work in Papua New Guinea, Fiji and Vanuatu. In A. Biersack., M. Jolly & M. Macintyre (Eds), *Gender Violence and Human Rights: Seeking Justice in Fiji, Papua New Guinea and Vanuatu*. (pp. 271–340) Canberra, ACT: ANU Press.

Blackwell, E. (2013, April 2). PNG govt backs domestic law. *The Australian*, 1–33. www.theaustralian.com.au/news/latest-news/png-govt-backs-domestic-violence-law.

Bjork, C. & Buhre, F. (2021). Resisting Temporal Regimes; Imagining Just Temporalities. *Rhetoric Society Quarterly*, 51(3), 177–181.

Bradley, C. & Kesno. J. (2001). *Family and Sexual Violence in Papua New Guinea: An integrated long-term strategy*. Port Moresby: Institute of National Affairs.

Cahill, C. & Pain, R. (2019). Representing slow violence and resistance: on hiding and seeing. *ACME: An International Journal for Critical Geographies*, 18(5), 1054–1065.

ChildFund. (2013). Stop Violence against women and children in Papua New Guinea. www.childfund.org.au/wp-content/uploads/2017/10/Stop-Violence-Against-Women-and-Children-in-PNG-2013.pdf.

Christian, J. M. & Dowler, L. (2019). Slow and fast violence. *ACME: An International Journal for Critical Geographies*, 18(5), 1066–1075.

Counts, D. A. (1990). Beaten wife, suicidal woman: domestic violence in Kaliali, West New Britian. *Pacific Studies*, 13(3), 151–169.

Davies, T. (2019). Slow violence and toxic geographies: 'out of sight: to whom? *Politics and Space*, 40(2), 1–19.

Dinnen, S. (1997). Law, Order and the State in Papua New Guinea. *State, Society and Governance in Melanesia*. (Discussion Paper 1997/1, pp. 1–13). Canberra, ACT: SSGM.

Eves, R. (2010). Masculinity Matters: Men, Gender-based violence and the AIDS Epidemic in Papua New Guinea. In V. Luker & S. Dinnen (Eds), *Sex and Insecurity: Law, Order and HIV in Papua New Guinea*. (1st edition, pp. 47–79). Canberra, ACT: ANU E-press.

36 Alison Dundon

Eves, R. (2012). Christianity, Masculinity and Gender Violence in Papua New Guinea. *State, Society and Governance in Melanesia.* (Discussion Paper 2012/2, pp. 1–17). Canberra, ACT: SSGM.

Galtung, J. (1969). Violence, Peace and Peace research. *Journal of Peace Research,* 6(3), 167–191.

Garbe, M. & Struck-Garbe, M. (2018). Forms of violence and discrimination against women in Papua New Guinea. *Pacific Geographies,* 50, 20–25.

Government of Papua New Guinea. (2010). Responses to the list of issues and questions with regard to the consideration of the combined initial, second and third reports. Committee on the Elimination of Discrimination against Women, Forty-sixth session 12–30 July 2010. New York: Papua New Guinea Government.

Government of Papua New Guinea. (2013). Family Protection Bill 2013. https://a rchive.org/details/FamilyProtectionBillFinal19.4.13.

Grabham, E. & Beynon-Jones, S. M. (2019). Introduction. In *Law and Time* (pp. 1–28). OAPEN Open Access: Routledge.

Hukula, F. (2012). Conversations with Convicted Rapists. In M. Jolly., Steward, P. & Brewer, C. (Eds), *Engendering Violence in Papua New Guinea.* (1st edition, pp. 197–212). Canberra, ACT: Australian National University Press.

Human Rights Watch. (2015). Bashed Up: Family Violence in Papua New Guinea. www.hrw.org/publications?keyword=bashed+up&date%5Bvalue%5D%5Byear%5D=2015&=Apply.

Human Rights Watch. (2021). *World Report 2021.* https://hrw.org/world-report/2021.

Institute of National Affairs. (2016). Introduction to Human Rights Law – Papua New Guinea. www.inapng.com/pdf_files/legal-literacy–book-7.pdf.

International Center for Research on Women. (2011). Violence against Women in Melanesia and Timor-Leste. www.icrw.org/wp-content/uploads/2016/10/Vio lence-against-women-in-Melanesia-Timor-Leste-AusAID.pdf.

Jolly, M. (2012). Introduction – Engendering Violence in Papua New Guinea: Persons, Power and Perilous Transformations. In A. Biersack., M. Jolly. & M. Macintyre (Eds), *Gender Violence and Human Rights: Seeking Justice in Fiji, Papua New Guinea and Vanuatu.* (1st edition, pp. 1–46) Canberra, ACT: ANU Press.

Lepani, K. (2008). Mobility, Violence and the Gendering of HIV in Papua New Guinea. *The Australian Journal of Anthropology,* 19(2), 150–164.

Lepani, K. (2015). 'I am still a young girl if I want': relational personhood and individual autonomy in the Trobriand Islands. *Oceania,* 85(1), 51–62.

Lewis, I., Maruia, B. & Walker, S. (2008). Violence against women in Papua New Guinea. *Journal of Family Studies,* 14, 183–197.

Luker, V. & Dinnen, S. (2010). Entwined Epidemics: HIV and 'Law and Order'. In S. Dinnen (Ed.), *Civic Insecurity: Law, Order and HIV in Papua New Guinea.* (1st edition, pp. 15–44). Canberra, ACT: ANU Press.

Luker, V. & Monsell-Davis, M. (2010). Teasing out the Tangle: raskols, young men, crime and HIV. In S. Dinnen (Ed.), *Civic Insecurity: Law, Order and HIV in Papua New Guinea.* (1st edition, pp. 81–117). Canberra, ACT: ANU Press.

Macintyre, M. (2000). Hear us, women of Papua New Guinea: Melanesian women and human rights. In Hilsdon, A. M., Macintyre, M., Mackie, V. & Stivens, M. (Eds), *Human Rights and Gender Politics: Asia-Pacific perspectives.* (1st edition, pp. 147–171). London & New York: Routledge.

Macintyre, M. (2008). Police and Thieves, Gunmen and Drunks: Problems with men and problems with society in PNG. *The Australian Journal of Anthropology*, 19(2), 179–193.

Macintyre, M. (2012). Gender Violence in Melanesia and the Problem of Millennium Development Goal No.3. In M. Jolly., Steward, P., & Brewer, C. (Eds), *Engendering Violence in Papua New Guinea*. (1st edition, pp. 47–71). Canberra, ACT: Australian National University Press.

Maladina, M. (2013). Amnesty UK Blog Global Voices. 26 September 2013. www.amnesty.org.uk/blogs/global-voices/good-new-family-protection-laws-passed-papua-new-guinea.

Maribu, G. (2017, November 17). How is the Family Protection Act doing four years on. *The National*. www.thenational.com.pg/family-protection-act-four-years.

Mawani, R. (2014). Law as temporality: colonial politics and Indian settlers. *UC Irvine Law Review*, 4(1), 65.

McPherson, N. (2012). Black and Blue: Shades of violence in West New Britian, PNG. In M. Jolly., Steward, P. & Brewer, C. (Eds), *Engendering Violence in Papua New Guinea*. (1st edition, pp. 239–266). Canberra, ACT: Australian National University Press.

Médecins Sans Frontières. (2016). Return to Abuser: Gaps in services and failure to protect survivors of family and sexual violence in Papua New Guinea. March 2016. https://msf.org.au/article/project-news/return-abuser.

Merry, S. E. (2006). *Human Rights and Gender Violence: Translating international law into local justice*. Chicago, IL & London: The University of Chicago Press.

Merry, S. E. (2009). *Gender Violence: A Cultural Perspective*. Chichester: Wiley-Blackwell.

McLeod, A. (2005). Violence, women and the state in Papua New Guinea: A case note. *Development Bulletin*. 67, 115–118.

Mitchell, W. E. (1990). Why Wape men don't beat their wives: constraints toward domestic tranquillity in a New Guinea society. *Pacific Studies*, 13(3), 141–150.

Nash, J. (1990). Factors relating to infrequent domestic violence among the Nagovisi. *Pacific Studies*, 13(3), 127–140.

Nixon, R. (2011). *Slow violence and the environmentalism of the poor*. Cambridge, MA & London: Harvard University Press.

Office of Development Effectiveness. (2008). *Violence Against Women in Melanesia and East Timor*. Canberra, ACT: Australian Government.

Papua New Guinea Country Report. (2008). *Stop Violence: responding to violence against women in Melanesian and East Timor*. www.dfat.gov.au/sites/default/files/ResVAW_PNG.pdf.

Voice for Change. (2015a). *Violence against women and girls in Jiwaka Province, Papua New Guinea*. Port Moresby: Voice for Change.

Voice for Change. (2015b). *Violence against women and girls in Jiwaka Province, PNG: an analysis of the voice for change community survey*. Port Moresby: Voice for Change.

Wies, J. R. & Haldane, H. J. (2011). Ethnographic Notes from the Front Lines of Gender-Based Violence. In Wies, J. R. & H. J. Haldane (Eds), *Anthropology at the Front Lines of Gender-Based Violence*. (1st edition, pp. 1–18). Nashville, TN: Vanderbilt University Press.

Yawa, M. (2002). *Gender and Violence*. Accessed December 10, 2014. www.aic.gov.au.

Chapter 3

A Pontian Commemoration

A Living Legacy to Remember Loss

Valerie Liddle

Introduction

Every year, on the first weekend in September, a group of Greeks, known as Pontians, gather for commemorative ceremonies to remember their family forebears who came from Santa in the Pontos region of northern Turkey. Pontos began to be settled by Greek traders from the 8th century BCE and continued to have a Greek presence until the 1920s (Kokkinos, 1991, p. 313), even though it came under Muslim Ottoman rule in 1461. The area stretched along the Black Sea for almost 600 km from Sinope in the west to the border of present-day Georgia in the east. It included a flat coastal plain, rising sharply to a high mountainous region. Santa, as a collection of small villages situated just below the summer pastures in the Pontic Alps, was established in the late 17th century by Greeks who moved from the coastal regions in order to avoid the harsh demands of local feudal overlords (Bryer, 1980a, p. 122, n. 26). Living in such a remote area allowed them to be free from much of the interference of Ottoman Turks in their daily lives. Apart from being obliged to pay taxes to the sultan, they were able to develop their own village organisation and an independent lifestyle in which a central committee looked after a range of administrative and juridical affairs. In the early 1920s, as part of political unrest in Turkey, Santa came under attack from Turkish soldiers and, while their resistance fighters held out against them, eventually Santa was completely destroyed in September 1921 and many of its inhabitants were either killed or died on forced marches over the Pontic Alps into the hinterland of Turkey. Many survivors were compulsorily resettled in northern Greece.

As part of anthropological fieldwork conducted within the Pontian Brotherhood of South Australia,[1] I was staying at a memorial site called the House of Santa in the north of Greece in 2006 when the 85th commemoration of the destruction of Santa took place. My 12-month fieldwork[2] included nine weeks in Greece, when I accompanied the Pontian Brotherhood's dancers for two weeks as they performed at several venues in northern Greece. I then remained in Greece for further fieldwork. This included two weeks observing and speaking with the dancers of the Pontian Black Sea Club of Veria, two

DOI: 10.4324/9781003311928-4

weeks living with five Santa people at the memorial site, and a week with a Pontian family in the village of Nea Santa in northern Greece. I returned to the House of Santa for the 2011 commemoration. As I learnt about the history of Pontians, by listening to them, watching them dance, participating in their religious practices and attending their commemoration ceremonies, I came to understand why their intense memories of the loss of this former homeland, passed down through previous generations, trigger their grief over the tragic loss of life, their anger at the injustice over the dispossession of their land and possessions and the hardships that their forebears suffered when dispersed to another country. Even so, what is it about commemorations that gathers people to remember and in particular, what draws Santa people to a memorial site year after year to remember events that happened in a small, remote place in the Pontic Alps?

Commemorations are "elected social occasions" (Viggiani, 2014, p. 14) where members of a particular group gather at a significant physical site to remember together, engage in commemorative discourses and participate in memorialisation rites. Through commemorations the group's agreed history is reaffirmed, and their sense of a collective identity passed on to members of the younger generations. Commemorations "keep the past in mind" (Connerton, 1989, p. 72). However, what is remembered is not a "simple, unmediated reproduction of the past, but rather a selective re-creation" of it within a particular "social context, beliefs and aspirations" (Argenti & Schramm, 2010, p. 2). This production of a selective memory becomes the collective memory for the group which comes to the fore in commemorations. By holding commemorations at significant places of memory, *lieux de mémoire* (Nora, 1989) and through artefacts and memorialisation rites, commemorations "store meaning in a concentrated manner" and "assume a central role as conveyors of collective memory" (Viggiani, 2014, p. 14).

Those of the second and/or third generation who meet at the House of Santa for commemorations have a collective memory of the exile from Santa that is formed through the memories shared with them among their families and friends. From the 1980s memory studies have focused on the social component of memory. (Casey, 2004; Connerton, 1989; Fentress & Wickham, 1992; Halbwachs, 1992; Olick & Robbins, 1998). While not denying that individuals have private, personal and unique memories of their own, Halbwachs argues that these memories are acquired within a social framework. These collective memories come through or with family members, friends or others who recollect the past with us (Halbwachs, 1992, p. 22). In critique of Halbwachs (1992), Fentress and Wickham (1992, p. ix) contend that the concept of collective memory can be perceived as "disconnected from the actual thought processes of any particular person [thus making] the individual a sort of automaton, passively obeying the interiorized collective will". They, along with Olick & Robbins (1998), prefer the term "social memory" to "collective memory".

Casey (2004, pp. 21–5) clearly differentiates between individual, social and collective memory. He sees individual memory as the unique memory of the person, who recalls what or how something happened in the past. While these individual acts of remembering are "saturated with social and collective aspects, as well as with cultural and public determinants" (2004, p. 21), they remain in the domain of the individual. As distinct from individual memory, collective memory, according to Casey, taps into a memory that is "*distributed* over a given population or set of places" (2004, p. 23, italics in the original text). Those who are remembering "are remembering the same thing" (2004, pp. 23–4) such as on a national day of mourning. Casey makes a further distinction and argues that there is a social memory, which is a shared memory, because it is:

> held in common by those who are affiliated either by kinship ties, by geographical proximity in neighbourhoods, cities, and other regions, or by engagement in a common project. (…) This does not mean having the same *experience* of remembering (…) but instead [remembering] something (some event, some occasion, some physical thing, even some thought) that others in one's kin or place-group are also remembering at the time or could do so.
>
> (2004, p. 22)

The unique social memory of Santa people includes such origins, common history and shared experiences (Liddle, 2022).

Commemorations are not only instrumental in maintaining a social memory but in so doing they produce an injunction to continue to remember that becomes a living legacy for Santa people, which is transmitted to subsequent generations. Nevertheless, what is transmitted is a construction of history formed by those who have "access to power to define the parameters of the dominant historical narrative" (Kelso & Eglitis, 2014, p. 488). Commemorations, therefore, "become a powerful political tool to project and sustain narratives of legitimation and victimhood against the other faction's claims and versions of the past" (Viggiani, 2014, p. 17).

The destruction of Santa and the expulsion of its population was part of widespread political unrest in Turkey from the beginning of the 20th century, when a Turkist political group, the Committee of Union and Progress, (commonly known as the Young Turks) sought to overthrow the Ottoman sultans and establish a modern secular Muslim state under the leadership of Mustafa Kemal. Minority groups such as the Armenians, Assyrians and Orthodox Christians in Asia Minor and Pontos area came under threat. The position of Greek Orthodox people living in Turkey worsened after the so-called Asia Minor "catastrophe"[3] and the defeat of the Greek army in the Greco-Turkish war of 1920–22 resulting in organised attacks on unarmed civilians by Turkish soldiers or police (Liddle, 2022, p. 97). Entire Pontian villages were destroyed, women raped and villagers either killed or taken

A Pontian Commemoration 41

prisoners (for details of attacks in the provinces of Pontus see Ecumenical Patriarchate, 1920, pp. 4–32). Men were conscripted into labour camps, young boys were trained to be soldiers in the Turkish army and women taken into Muslim households where they were forced to adopt Islam either as wives or servants (Fotiadis, 2004, pp. 24–25; Hofmann, 2011, p. 75; Tsirkinidis, 1999, pp. 193–7). The remainder, mostly women, children and the aged, were forced to leave their homes, often in winter, by the Turkish soldiers and endure the "White Death", where they had to walk in snow over the Pontic Alps to central Turkey or even the Syrian desert. With little protection from the extreme cold and minimal provisions, a great number of people died from exposure, starvation or diseases. Others died from the brutality of their captors or at the hands of itinerant bandits. Those who were unable to walk were either shot or left to die (Hofmann, 2011, pp. 73, 77–79; Liddle, 2022, p. 97).

The violence against Pontians is described in biographies such as that of Andreadis (1993) and Halo (2000). It was reported in the newspapers of the time such as the *New York Times*, *The Times* (London) and *The Washington Post* (Hofmann, Bjørnlund, & Meichanetsidis, 2011, pp. 489–92) and in eye-witness accounts of missionaries, diplomatic staff and relief workers. One such report is from Major Forrest. D. Yowell, Director of the Near East Relief unit at Harpoot, who on 5 May 1922 wrote:

> [c]onditions of Greek minorities are even worse than those of the Armenians. Sufferings of the Greeks deported from districts behind the battlefront are terrible and still continue. These deportees began to reach Harpoot before my arrival last October. Of thirty thousand Greek refugees who left Sivas five thousand died on the way before reaching Harpoot. One American relief worker saw and counted fifteen hundred bodies on the road east of Harpoot. (...) Two thirds of the Greek deportees are women and children. All along the route where these deportees have travelled Turks are permitted to visit refugee groups and select women and girls whom they desire for any purpose (...) Their whole route today strewn with bodies of their dead, which are consumed by dogs, wolves, vultures (...) The chief causes of death are starvation, dysentery, typhus. Turkish authorities frankly state that it is their deliberate intention to exterminate the Greeks, and all their actions support this statement.
>
> (Yowell cited in Halo & Jones, 2007)

Therefore, "taking into account the flaws of Ottoman statistics, as well as difficulties with the accuracy of demographic estimates under complex conditions of war and massive flight", Hofmann considers that the overall number of Christians who died in Turkey at that time was about 3.5 million, comprising "1.5 million Armenians, 1.5 million Greeks and half a million Aramaic speaking Christians (Aramaeans, Assyrians, Chaldaeans and other denominations)" (Hofmann, 2011, p. 105). It is estimated that 353,000 Pontians, out of a population of about 700,000, lost their lives between 1915 and 1922 (Fotiadis, 2004, p. 32).

Two major conferences were convened in response to the atrocities committed at the time. The Peace Treaty of Sèvres between the Allies of World War I and the Ottoman Empire was held in 1920. Its aim was to recompense the survivors for their losses and to "try Turkish officials for war crimes committed by Ottoman Turkey against (...) the Armenians, the Greeks and the Assyrian/Aramaean Christians" (de Zayas, 2011, p. 316). Despite the fact that Turkey signed the Treaty of Sèvres, "formal ratification never followed, and the allies did not ensure its implementation" (de Zayas, 2011, pp. 316–17).

The second conference, the Conference of Lausanne in 1923, did not make reference to restitution or bringing to justice those guilty of war crimes. Instead, it negotiated a compulsory exchange of populations between Greece and Turkey (Liddle, 2022). The Convention Concerning the Exchange of Greek and Turkish Populations and Protocol was signed on 30 January 1923. The Exchange took place along religious lines. Between 1.25 and 1.4 million Greek Orthodox Christians of the Asia Minor, the Pontos and eastern Thrace regions, were deported to Greece, and approximately 356,000 Muslim Turks were forced to leave their homes in Greece and settle in Turkey (League of Nations, 1925, pp. 75–87; Liddle, 2022, p. 97).

Before I started my research, I knew nothing about Pontian Greeks. I had visited the Pontos region just six months beforehand and at that time I saw empty Greek Orthodox churches being converted into 'museums'. Even so at that time it did not occur to me that the people who had built and worshipped in them lived in the region only 80 years before my visit. Our Turkish guide told us nothing about Pontians and their history. It was only when I met a Pontian woman in Adelaide, South Australia, that I began to realise what had happened there and it gave me an impetus to find out more. Hence, my decision to direct my research to Pontians, and the Pontian Brotherhood of South Australia gave me a distinct group on which to focus. As an older Anglo-Saxon woman, I was definitely in the position of an outsider but being a wife, mother and grandmother meant that I could have rapport with older Greek women. Language, however, was a continuing limiting factor. My elementary Greek was not fluent enough for interviews and from time to time I had to rely on other informants to interpret for me. It was only when my husband started to accompany me to Pontian functions, that I began to feel a sense of acceptance. This acceptance was such that we were allowed to join the Pontian Brotherhood dancers on their tour of Greece. If that had not happened, I would not have been able to participate in the Santa commemorations.

Remembering the stories of Santa

For second or third generation Santa people, remembrance of these violent events come through the memories of those who survived the destruction of Santa. Such was the intense attachment to their villages, the sorrow at their expulsion from it and the horror of the massacre of many of its inhabitants, that the survivors felt compelled to pass on these memories to their families. They did this in such a way that my informants particularly remembered the emotional way in which these survivors spoke about Santa.[4]

Stavros[5], a 43-year-old man, told me in 2006 that in his village in Greece, which was completely composed of Santa people or their descendants, there were now only four people alive who had come from Santa, and they had come as very young children. Stavros further explained that his grandmother had come from Santa when she was 16 years of age, accompanied by her 14-year-old brother, Anastasios. Stavros told me that when his brother was born, 11 months after him, both boys were given to their grandmother to raise and then when she died, their uncle, Anastasios, who lived with them, continued to care for them. Stavros remembers that during his childhood he always heard stories about Santa from him. He said:

> [y]ou know what, we grew up with histories and fairy tales of our old people (...) Our people, Santa, don't say fairy tales, they are speaking always about Santa. Their love to their country was so, so big and they wanted to speak always about Santa, about their country, where they were born, of course.

He said that his great uncle died with "Santa on his lips"; "Santa, Santa, Santa, my country Santa" were his last words.

The memories of Santa conveyed to Stavros by his great-uncle and the way in which they were told were so vivid that as an adult Stavros felt compelled to visit the Pontos region and particularly to go to the ruins of Santa. When he came to Santa he said: "I understood I was in Santa because (...) I have in my mind the picture of Santa and when I went there, I understood, I feeled [sic] it, now I am in Santa, from inside." Stavros said that after the visit he returned to Greece with five hours of video tape and "memories and memories and memories and crying and pain and pain and pain and pain...The pain is still now, there now [indicating his heart] when I remember this place."

In developing a theory of emotions, Ahmed (2004b, pp. 8–10) posits an alternative view from both the psycho-biological one, that is, of emotions coming from the inside and showing themselves on the outside of the individual, and from the socially constructed one, that of emotions moving from a social body to affect the inner life of a person. Instead, she contends that emotions "stick" to various objects, where they work in particular ways to "make 'the collective' appear *as if* it were a body" (Ahmed, 2004a, p. 27). In

44 Valerie Liddle

yearly commemorations, when Santa people come together 'as a body', the 'stickiness' of the emotions attached to the loss of Santa is passed down to subsequent generations of Santa people. Further, as a collective they are aware of how they feel about others outside their group and in particular about Turkey, who they see as the perpetrator of their loss.

A legacy of remembrance attached to a memorial house

In 2006 approximately 400 Santa descendants attended a commemoration weekend. This took place on the grounds of the Monastery of Panagia Soumela,[6] which is situated in a mountainous area about 80 km west of Thessaloniki in northern Greece. It replicates the ancient monastery of Panagia Soumela in Pontos, now in ruins, as a religious, educational and cultural gathering place for present day Pontic Greeks. In 1963 Santa people built the House of Santa on these monastery grounds. Although the upper section of the building has overnight dormitory accommodation for a small number of people, the house is not envisaged as a hostel but rather a meeting place for the Santa community. To this end, on the ground floor there is a meeting room big enough for the large numbers of people who visit at special times during the year. In particular, the house serves as a memorial house. The many artefacts displayed in the meeting room are there to remind people of Santa. There are maps and photographs of the area; a topographical representation of the villages; photographs of those who originated from there; and artefacts such as stones and dried flora specimens collected by people who have visited the ruins of Santa in recent times. On the outside of the building, seven banners bearing the names of the Santa villages and one representing the five outer settlements are erected on the first day of the commemoration.

Commemorations are public events that have a certain "logic of composition" (Handelman, 1990, p. 17), which is linked to their structures.

> These structures have relatively high degrees of replicability. That is, whenever a particular occasion is enacted, it is put together from more-or-less similar elements; it is performed by more-or-less the same cast of characters; and it passes through more-or-less the same sequences of action.
>
> (1990, p. 12)

The programs for the 2006 and 2011 commemorative weekends I attended had the same elements. They both included a seminar session on the Saturday afternoon, a shared meal and dance in the evening, a church liturgy on Sunday morning, and memorial rituals on the Sunday afternoon. Apart from the liturgy on the Sunday morning held in the monastery church, all the other components of the commemoration weekend were conducted at the House of Santa.

A Pontian Commemoration   45

Language is central to commemorations. "In being inescapably communal, commemoration is at the same time discursive: that is to say, [it is] dependent upon language, [and takes] place *through* language" (Casey, 2000, pp. 232–3, italics in the original text). Language is embedded in the House of Santa. Not only was this so through the spoken language of a seminar session on the Saturday night of the 2006 commemoration weekend but a brief history of Santa is in a written text carved into a marble plaque and installed at the side entrance of the House of Santa.

The small top plaque ΤΗ ΣΑΝΤΑΣ Τ ΟΣΠΙΤ (THE HOUSE OF SANTA) is written in the Pontic Greek dialect.[7] The following is a part translation of the larger plaque, which is written in Modern Greek:

Santa of Pontos
   The seven villages of Santa of Pontos lay 50 km south of Trapezounda in the Pontic Alps before it was completely destroyed by the Turkish army in September 1921. It consisted of seven villages and five small settlements. Today only the ruins exist.
   The seven villages were: Pistofandon; Ischanandon; Terzandon; Zournatsandon; Pinatandon; Kozlarandon; Tsakalandon. [It then lists the names of five smaller settlements.]
   Santa was a prototype of community with a Greek and Christian ethos. It was "the Souli"[8] of Pontos and a saving ark for every Greek Christian who was persecuted by the Turks. It held and preserved the Greekness and Orthodox Christian faith of its inhabitants up to the date it was destroyed. Its inhabitants fought heroically in their struggle to protect and save it.
   But Santa did not withstand. It was destroyed and became a HOLOCAUST.
   Those of its inhabitants who were saved were forcibly displaced and dragged to exile and to the White Death. Those who survived were exchanged in the compulsory exchange of population. They took the walk of the great exodus and came as refugees to Greece in 1923.
   Every year on the first Sunday in September people who originate from Santa but live in any other place come here to this hostel and in front of the memorial for the dead make a commemoration for the victims who died during the destruction of their martyred [sic] home.[9]

As well as listing the villages of Santa and details of their destruction, the plaque reflects the key stories that form the social memory of Santa people. One of these is the heroic escape of the villagers under the leadership of Captain Efkleides[10] who, with his guerrilla fighters, waged a fierce struggle against the Turkish soldiers in an attempt to defend Santa. The following story was told to me in English by the grandson of Captain Efkleides when I was a guest at his mother's home in Nea Santa.

Santa has a terrible history. The Turks sent thousands of soldiers with heavy weapons. There were 300 women and children and 120 fighters. Captain Efkleides and other fighters told the women to go to the mountains. They all withdrew to one cave where they were attacked by the strong Turkish forces. There was only one passage out of the cave and into the forest. Everyone was in danger of being detected from the cries of the babies, so they killed them. One mother had seven children. She strangled the youngest with her own hands. She said, "I will sacrifice the one to save the others." This is a very terrible thing. That night there was a very big rain and the women and children escaped to the forest undetected by the Turks. The next day the Turkish soldiers found the children killed. The Turkish general said that it was clear that these were strong people and would not surrender (...) The story of Santa is a very big story.

I have heard similar accounts of this story from other Santa people. Although there were some variations, they always had the same elements: fighters with women and children hiding in a cave in the mountains; the Turkish army surrounding them; the Santa men, women and children escaping by night into the forest, but only by sacrificing the youngest. While it is indeed a terrible story, it is told to emphasise the heroism of the fighters and the strength and determination of Santa people in their resistance against the Turks, as part of what is remembered in the legacy of loss.

Another key event referred to on the plaque is the eviction of Santa people from their village. Known as the White Death, this event is deeply etched into the memory of Pontians. Whenever I met Pontians, in Australia or in Greece, I was always struck by the strength of their commitment to remembering what happened to their forebears. It is one of the reasons I started this research. Pavlos is a strong character and typical of many Pontians I got to know. Now in his sixties, he has lived in Australia for the past forty years but he grew up in a northern Greek village consisting only of Santa people. His parents were from Santa. Because they had already moved to adjacent Georgia at the start of the persecutions, they were not involved in the exile of its inhabitants. Pavlos recounted what he remembered hearing from his parents and from those who had survived the ordeal:

When the Turks came to the village of Santa, they gave those remaining there up to three hours to gather together their belongings. Then 720 people were forced to leave the village and to march up over the mountains. This was at the beginning of September when the weather conditions were becoming very harsh. Often it was said that if a storm came at that altitude after October no human being could survive in the open. Once they stopped overnight at a small church to protect them from the

A Pontian Commemoration   47

snow. But the church was five metres by three metres in dimension, far too small to accommodate all the people so some were forced to camp outside in the snow. Overall, of the 720 who started out, about 400 people died as a result of the cold, or by being weakened by hunger, or by diseases such as dysentery.

These two foundational stories underpin the wording engraved in granite on the plaque. Through "*what sticks*, of what connections are lived as the most intense or intimate", they become the history of Santa allowing them "to surface in memory and writing" (Ahmed, 2004a, p. 33, italics in the original text). As well as a memorial to the loss of the lives of Santa people under terrible circumstances, the house itself bears witness to the destruction of the villages of Santa. The memorabilia inside the house and banners on the outside are "marks [which] become a sign of absence, or a sign of a presence that 'is no longer'" (2004a, p. 30). The emotions attached to the loss of Santa were aroused at the memorial monument on the Sunday afternoon of the weekend.

A legacy of pain attached to a memorial monument

As a non-Pontian researcher, I could not feel the same sorrow that Santa people feel. All the same, as I watched them take part in commemorations, I could sense the pervading feeling of sadness and the close ties that hold this group of people together at these significant events. The mourning rituals for the loss of Santa, performed on the Sunday afternoon of the commemoration weekend, consisted of a number of speeches, the laying of wreaths, the singing of the two laments followed by a one minute's silence in remembrance of those who had lost their lives. These were all carried out at a monument, erected in 1968 and adjacent to the House of Santa. The positioning of the monument visually represents the geographic layout of Santa where six of the villages were on one side of the River Yambolis and one on the other. This is symbolically represented with six pine trees at the back of the monument and one in front of it. These trees by being native to the Santa region, help to bring the absent Santa into present remembrance.

In contrast to the text on the plaque on the wall of the House of Santa, the memorial monument pictorially portrays the pain and suffering of the Santa people in the form of reliefs of white marble against grey stone. (An image of 'The Holocaust of the Greeks of Santa' monument can be accessed at Imathia (http://www.greek-genocide.net/index.php/photos/40-imathia).The top one depicts the one-headed eagle, a symbol of the whole Pontian community.[11] The middle relief depicts the exile of Santa people as they leave to go on the White Death marches. It shows men and women carrying whatever they can on their shoulders or in their hands, some bent over with their burden or in grief. Two of the men are looking back. One old man with a walking stick looks back over his shoulders and in a gesture appears as if he is waving to his former home, or maybe it is a gesture of defiance. One woman is carrying a young child. Those children who are old enough are walking but two of them are clinging to their mothers as if in fear. Central to this group is an Orthodox priest positioned as if he is blessing the people as they are exiled. When I asked an informant of Santa background for his interpretation of this relief, he hesitated for a while and then said that he thought the people were saying "My God, what have we done that we suffer so much?"

The bottom section of the Santa monument has three motifs. The left-hand side depicts a Santa man with the unique Pontian headband and dressed for battle with a rifle and a bandolier and the motif on the right shows a Santa woman dressed in traditional Pontian costume. Both have their heads bowed facing the central Christian cross, again a symbol of suffering and pain. The monument has only one short directive.

> In silence, passer-by, stop and with piety meditate on the holocaust of the heroic seven villages of Santa of Pontos in 1921.[12]

In 2006 one of the laments was addressed to Captain Efkleides.

> Seven years in the resistance/in the mountains of Santa/Seven years you were torturing the Turkish souls/Captain Efkleides, where are you now?
> You who never had a fear of swords and knifes/How did it happen that you fell, into the death's hands/Captain Efkleides, where are you now?

Most people listened in hushed silence. Some sang or responded with tears; one an old man near me had tears running down his cheeks. The lament was accompanied by the lyra.[13] This instrument is one that is most associated with the Pontian community and is played in a number of different settings, each invoking different responses from joyous liveliness to sad reflection. When it is played at a commemoration ceremony for a lament, it creates a mourning mood. Because of its poignant sounds, the music of the lyra can "*reveal* the nature of feelings with a detail and truth that language cannot approach" (Langer, 1960, p. 235, italics in the original text). The emotions attached to the lyra and its sound pass down the pain and suffering that Santa people feel. It allows them to cry and grieve but also sanctions other feelings of injustice, anger and powerlessness. Why, if Captain Efkleides was so brave, was he unable to protect the village of Santa? Where is he now to address the ongoing injustices of not recognising what happened to their people? Remembering and lamenting in silence may seem to be the only option open to people when faced with overwhelming catastrophes and perceived injustices. However, silence, as Geetha Marcus points out (Chapter 6), does not necessarily mean an absence of power. The silence of a gathering of people can attest to devastations in ways that words cannot, and can also influence others to take political action.

A legacy to take political action

Santa commemorations are not overt political acts, but they are acts of "bearing witness" to the atrocities and injustices that their ancestors suffered. Oliver (2001, p. 7) argues that through the process of 'bearing witness' the powerless and oppressed are able to publicly express their pain with a view that this will be acknowledged by others. Through them Santa people hope to find a voice that will bring pressure to bear on Turkey to acknowledge that what occurred in the early part of the 20th century was in reality genocide.

The word "genocide" is not written on the plaque and or the monument even though the word was in use by the time these inscriptions were made. Instead, the word "holocaust" with its religious connotations is used. In the Old Testament a holocaust was a sacrificial offering that was completely consumed by fire. By the beginning of the 20th century, holocaust began to be used in a secular manner denoting "a wide variety of conflagrations, massacres, wars, and disaster (...) [with] no theological overtones" (Petrie, 2000, p. 55). It was deployed to refer to the Ottoman genocides of Christian minorities between 1915 and 1923.[14] During the 20th century, the word came to be closely associated with the Jewish Holocaust of World War II, which is perceived to be unique in its extent, horror, and the numbers of its victims. Although holocaust is deployed to describe the destruction of Santa, genocide has now become the term more widely used to refer to what happened to Pontians.

The word only came into the English vocabulary in 1944 (Moses, 2008, p. 8). From the Greek *genos* (race or tribe) and the Latin *caedere* (killing), the word was first coined by Raphaël Lemkin (1900–59), a Polish-Jewish lawyer, in response to the holocaust of the Jews in World War II (Hinton, 2002, p. 3). As a law student in the 1930s, Lemkin's interest had been sparked by the inability of the international courts to bring to justice those responsible for the earlier massacres in Turkey (Schabas, 2000, p. 25). From that time on, he pressed the international community to recognise these killings as a particular crime and, in the face of the atrocities committed against the Jews in World War II, he campaigned for the term genocide to be recognised as a criminal act and punishable under international law. In December 1948, the United Nations General Assembly approved the Convention on the Prevention and Punishment of the Crime of Genocide, which came into force in January 1951. Under the Convention genocide is defined as follows:

> Article II: In the present Convention, genocide means any of the following acts committed with intent to destroy, in whole or in part, a national ethnical, racial or religious group, as such:
>
> a   Killing members of the group;
> b   Causing serious bodily or mental harm to members of the group;

50 Valerie Liddle

c   Deliberately inflicting on the group conditions of life calculated to bring about its physical destruction in whole or in part;
d   Imposing measures intended to prevent births within the group;
e   Forcibly transferring children of the group to another group.(United Nations General Assembly, 1948)

The "Convention did not 'create' the crime of genocide. Rather it was intended to strengthen the pre-existing claims of victims of genocide, including the victims of the Armenian genocide and of the Holocaust" and because it is "declarative of pre-existing international law (...) it can be applied retroactively" (de Zayas, 2011, p. 312).

From the early 1970s the Armenian community through its scholars began to be particularly active in seeking recognition of the genocide of its people in Turkey and, as a result the International Association of Genocide Scholars at its international conference held in Montreal in 1997, unanimously affirmed that, "[t]he mass murder of Armenians in Turkey in 1915 is a case of genocide which conforms to the statutes of the United Nations Convention on the Prevention and Punishment of Genocide" (quoted in Dadrian, 2003, p. 80).

It was only by the late 1970s that Pontian historians, such as Fotiadis (2004) and Tsirkinidis (1999), began to access European archives to confirm that their ancestors had suffered in the same genocide as the Armenians. Their publications together with the results of the Pan-Pontian international congresses of 1985, 1988 and 1993 and lobbying by influential politicians combined to put pressure on the Greek Government to recognise the Pontian genocide. In March 1994 the Greek Government passed a motion declaring 19 May as "a day of remembrance of the genocide perpetrated against the Greek people of Pontus" (Bruneau & Papoulidis, 2011, p. 355). Over a decade later, in response to the Greek claims, the International Association of Genocide Scholars widened its earlier resolution to include other minority Christian groups, passing a resolution in 2007, which states,

> BE IT RESOLVED that it is the conviction of the International Association of Genocide Scholars that the Ottoman campaign against Christian minorities of the Empire between 1924 and 1923 constituted a genocide against Armenians, Assyrians, and Pontian and Anatolian Greeks.
> (quoted in Charny, 2011, p. 33)

Countries that have committed war crimes are often reluctant to admit responsibility for them as Maki Kimura's chapter shows in relation to "comfort women" (Chapter 10). In a similar way, the Turkish government has continued to deny that it was responsible for a genocide of its Christian minorities in the early 20th century. Turkey's position includes a number of elements: the number of deaths are exaggerated and that Turkey also suffered considerable losses; it was self-defence against the political uprisings of the Armenians and Pontians; the mass deportations away from war zones were carried out to protect civilians and their deaths were not intended; and finally, the massacres were not authorised by the Turkish officials who cannot take responsibility for the actions of irregulars or local officials who failed to understand the government's orders (Dixon, 2010, p. 471; Jones, 2006, p. 518–20; Liddle, 2022, p. 105). The claim of genocide is offensive to Turkey. It brings into question the integrity of the founder of the nation, Mustafa Kemal, and thus is perceived as an attack on the whole nation.

Turkey's stance contrasts with Germany which has acknowledged its responsibility for the genocide of the Jews in World War II. Pontians assert that Turkey should do likewise and consequentially have lobbied international governments to recognise the genocide. To do this, the legal term genocide has been adopted rather than the word holocaust, with its religious overtones. Since the 1990s the governments of Greece, Sweden, Cyprus, Armenia, the Netherlands, Austria, the Czech Republic and ten states in the United States of America, as well as two Australian states, have passed resolutions recognising the Pontian genocide.

Conclusion

This chapter shows how a legacy to remember passed down to subsequent generations of Santa descendants is encapsulated in their annual commemorations. As important events for Santa people they are a means of publicly witnessing the pain and suffering that their ancestors endured in the early part of the 20th century and that they continue to feel as a living legacy. The concept 'living legacy' provides a visceral language to characterise both the continuity and depth of emotional power the legacy of violence has for Pontians, experienced through their memories, commemorations and memorials. Terms describing memory, cultural customs and material objects do not necessarily convey this intensely alive stickiness of the past in the present and its ongoing significance in the shaping of futures.

The plaque at the House of Santa and its memorial monument set this legacy in terms of a holocaust. However, commemorations couched in terms of a holocaust are unlikely to bring pressure to bear on Turkey to acknowledge their responsibility for what happened to Santa people. To take political action, the wider Pontian community, along with the Armenian community, use the legal term genocide to describe the violent injustices suffered by Christian groups in the 20th century in Turkey. In this way, they can lobby international governments to formally recognise the genocide of their peoples. With changing power relations between Turkey and western nations over the past 30 years, and the growing number of states recognising the Pontian genocide, Pontians hope that pressure will be brought to bear on Turkey to acknowledge that what happened in the early 20th century was genocide. In

52 Valerie Liddle

the meantime, yearly commemorations serve to bear witness to what happened and foreground the legacy of loss to Santa people.

Notes

1 The Pontian Brotherhood of South Australia was established in Adelaide in 1958 for the mutual support of the fledging Pontian community.
2 In Adelaide I conducted 38 formal interviews with Pontian people ranging from 18 to 102 years of age. Ten of these informants were interviewed more than once. The length of the interviews was between a half an hour to three hours. I recorded all the interviews and later I transcribed them for my fieldnotes. Also, I had many conversations with Pontians, and as soon as possible I noted relevant comments and included them in my written fieldnotes. I also observed the Pontian Brotherhood dancers at their practice sessions and at festivals.
3 This refers to the defeat of the Greek government in its attempt to incorporate all areas of Greek settlement in the Near East into one state (Clogg, 1999, p. 6).
4 In Greece, I interviewed 17 Pontians, ten of whom were Santa descendants. In Adelaide, I interviewed one Santa descendant.
5 I have used pseudonyms for all informants in this chapter.
6 This name refers to the Virgin Mary of the Black Mountain (Miller, 1926, p. 62).
7 This is "a genuinely Greek though very peculiar and idiomatic dialect closer to Ancient Greek than is standard Modern Greek" (Kontogiorgi, 2006, p. 96).
8 Souli was a village in Epirus in Greece that was well known for its heroic fight against the Ottoman occupation in the 18th and 19th centuries. It became an example of strong resistance (Bryer, 1980b, p. 184).
9 Translated by Christos Tsoraklidis.
10 Captain Efkleides is remembered elsewhere on the monastery grounds at a monument which has an ossuary containing his bones. There was a short memorial ceremony at this monument on the Saturday afternoon of the commemoration weekend in both 2006 and 2011.
11 This was derived from the two-headed eagle, symbol of the Byzantine Empire. (Fann Bouteneff, 2002, p. 23; Hionides, 2003, pp. 113–114).
12 Translated by Christos Tsoraklidis.
13 The lyra is a three-stringed, bottle-shaped instrument about 45–60 cm in length and about 7–11 cm in width.
14 In 1929, Winston Churchill speaking of the massacre of Armenians stated that "whole districts [were] blotted out in one administrative holocaust" (Tatz, 2003, p. 18).

References

Ahmed, S. (2004a). Collective Feelings: or, the impressions left by others. *Theory, Culture and Society*, 21(25), 25–42.
Ahmed, S. (2004b). *The Cultural Politics of Emotion*. New York: Routledge.
Andreadis, G. (1993). *Tamama: The Missing Girl of Pontos*. Athens: Gordios.
Argenti, N. & Schramm, K. (Eds). (2010). *Remembering Violence: Anthropological perspectives on intergenerational transmission*. New York & Oxford: Berghahn Books.
Bruneau, M. & Papoulidis, K. (2011). Remembering the Genocide and the 'Unforgettable Homelands': The Erection of Commemorative Monuments in Greece by Refugees from Asia Minor. In T. Hofmann, M. Bjørnlund & V. Meichanetsidis

(Eds), *The Genocide of the Ottoman Greeks: Studies on the State-sponsored Campaign of Extermination of Christians of Asia Minor (1912–1922) and its Aftermath* (pp. 351–369). New York: Aristide D. Caratzas.

Bryer, A. A. M. (1980a). Greeks and Türkmens: The Pontic Exception. In *The Empire of Trebizond and the Pontos* (pp. 115–151). London: Variorum Reprints.

Bryer, A. A. M. (1980b). The Pontic Revival and the New Greece. In *The Empire of Trebizond and the Pontos* (pp. 171–190). London: Variorum Reprints.

Casey, E. S. (2000). *Remembering: A Phenomenological Study* (2nd edition). Bloomington & Indianapolis, IN: Indiana University Press.

Casey, E. S. (2004). Public Memory in Place and Time. In K. R. Phillips (Ed.), *Framing Public Memory* (pp. 17–42). Tucaloosa, AL: The University of Alabama Press.

Charny, I. W. (2011). The Integrity and Courage to Recognize all the Victims of a Genocide. In T. Hofmann, M. Bjørnlund & V. Meichanetsidis (Eds), *The Genocide of the Ottoman Greeks: Studies on the State-sponsored Campaign of Extermination of Christians of Asia Minor (1912–1922) and its Aftermath* (pp. 21–38). New York & Athens: Aristide D. Caratzas.

Clogg, R. (1999). The Greek Diaspora: The Historical Context. In R. Clogg (Ed.), *The Greek Diaspora in the Twentieth Century* (pp. 1–23). Basingstoke: Macmillan.

Connerton, P. (1989). *How Societies Remember*. Cambridge: Cambridge University Press.

Dadrian, V. N. (2003). German Responsibility in the Armenian Genocide: The Role of Protective Alliances. In C. Tatz, P. Arnold & S. Tatz (Eds), *Genocide Perspectives II: Essays on Holocaust and Genocide* (pp. 79–125). Blackheath, NSW: Bandl & Schlesinger.

de Zayas, A. (2011). The Ottoman Genocide of the Greeks and the Other Christian Minorities in Light of the Genocide Convention. In T. Hofmann, M. Bjørnlund & V. Meichanetsidis (Eds), *The Genocide of the Ottoman Greeks: Studies on the State-sponsored Campaign of Extermination of Christians of Asia Minor (1912–1922) and its Aftermath* (pp. 311–340). New York: Aristide D. Caratzas.

Dixon, J. M. (2010). Defending the Nation? Maintaining Turkey's Narrative of the Armenian Genocide. *South European Society and Politics*, 15(3), 467–485.

Ecumenical Patriarchate. (1920). *The Black Book of the Sufferings of the Greek People in Turkey from the Armistice to the End of 1920*. www.greece.org/genocide/Blackbook.htm.

Fann Bouteneff, P. (2002). *Exiles on Stage: The Modern Pontic Theater in Greece*. Athens: Επιτροπη Ποντιακων Μελετων [Committee for Pontian Studies].

Fentress, J. & Wickham, C. (1992). *Social Memory*. Oxford & Cambridge, MA: Blackwell Publishers.

Fotiadis, C. E. (2004). *The Genocide of the Pontus Greeks by the Turks* (Vol. 13). Thessaloniki: Herodotus.

Halbwachs, M. (1992). *On Collective Memory* (L. A. Coser, Trans.). Chicago, IL: The University of Chicago Press.

Halo, T. (2000). *Not Even My Name*. New York: Picador USA.

Halo, T. & Jones, A. (2007). Notes on the Genocides of Christian Populations of the Ottoman Empire: Submitted in Support of a Resolution Recognizing the Armenian, Assyrian, and Pontic and Anatolian Greek Genocides of 1914–23. Retrieved from www.genocidetext.net/iags_resolution_supporting_documentation.htm.

54 Valerie Liddle

Handelman, D. (1990). *Models and Mirrors: Towards an Anthropology of Public Events.* Cambridge: Cambridge University Press.

Hinton, A. L. (Ed.) (2002). *Genocide: An Anthropological Reader.* Malden, MA: Blackwell.

Hionides, C. (2003). *The Greek Pontians of the Black Sea* (2nd ed.). Thessaloniki: Kyriakidis Brothers.

Hofmann, T. (2011). Γενοκτονία εν Ροή – Cumulative Genocide: The Massacres and Deportations of the Greek Population of the Ottoman Empire (1912–1923). In T. Hofmann, M. Bjørnlund & V. Meichanetsidis (Eds), *The Genocide of the Ottoman Greeks: Studies on the State-Sponsored Campaign of Extermination of Christians of Asia Minor (1912–1922) and its Aftermath* (pp. 39–111). New York: Aristide D. Caratzas.

Hofmann, T., Bjørnlund, M. & Meichanetsidis, V. (Eds). (2011). *The Genocide of the Ottoman Greeks: Studies on the State-sponsored Campaign of Extermination of Christians of Asia Minor (1912–1922) and its Aftermath.* New York: Aristide D. Caratzas.

Jones, A. (2006). *Genocide: A Comprehensive Introduction* (2nd ed.). London: Routledge.

Kelso, M. & Eglitis, D. (2014). Holocaust commemoration in Romania: Roma and the contested politics of memory and memorialization. *Journal of Genocide Research*, 16(4), 487–511.

Kokkinos, D. (1991). The Greek state's overview of the Pontian issue. *Journal of Refugee Studies*, 4(4), 312–314.

Kontogiorgi, E. (2006). *Population Exchange in Greek Macedonia.* Oxford: Clarendon Press.

Langer, S. K. (1960). *Philosophy in a New Key: A Study in the Symbolism of Reason, Rite, and Art.* Cambridge, MA: Harvard University Press.

League of Nations. (1925). Convention Concerning the Exchange of Greek and Turkish Populations, and Protocol (Vol. XXXII). https://treaties.un.org/doc/Publica tion/UNTS/LON/Volume 32/v32.pdf.

Liddle, V. L. (2022). Contesting and confirming collective identity: the case of the Pontian Memorial Plaque, Migration Museum, Adelaide. *Journal of the Historical Society of South Australia*, 50, 93–108.

Miller, W. (1926). *Trebizond: The Last Greek Empire.* London: Society for Promoting Christian Knowledge.

Moses, A. D. (2008). Empire, Colony, Genocide: Keywords and the Philosphy of History. In A. D. Moses (Ed.), *Empire, Colony, Genocide: Conquest, Occupation, and Subaltern Resistance in World History* (pp. 3–54). New York: Berghahn Books.

Nora, P. (1989). Between Memory and History: Les Lieux de Mémoire. *Representations*, 26 (Special Issue: Memory and Counter-Memory), 7–24.

Olick, J. K. & Robbins, J. (1998). Social Memory Studies: From "Collective Memory" to the Historical Sociology of Mnemonic Practices. *Annual Review of Sociology*, 24, 105–140.

Oliver, K. (2001). *Witnessing: Beyond Recognition.* Minneapolis, MN: University of Minnesota Press.

Petrie, J. (2000). The Secular Word Holocaust: Scholarly Myths, History, and 20th Century Meanings. *Journal of Genocide Research*, 2(1), 31–63.

Schabas, W. A. (2000). *Genocide in International Law: The Crime of Crimes.* New York: Cambridge University Press.

Tatz, C. M. (2003). *With Intent to Destroy: Reflecting on Genocide.* New York: Verso.

Tsirkinidis, H. (1999). *At Last We Uprooted Them...The Genocide of Greeks of Pontos, Thrace and Asia Minor, Through the French Archives* (S. Mavrantonis, Trans.). Thessaloniki: Kyriakidis Brothers.

United Nations General Assembly. (1948). Convention on the Prevention and Punishment of the Crime of Genocide. www.hrweb.org/legal/genocide.html.

Viggiani, E. (2014). *Talking Stones: the politics of memorialization in post-conflict northern Ireland*. New York: Berghahn Books.

Chapter 4

'Horrors' of Honour

Kameljeet Kaur

Introduction

The following statement featured in an episode of the BBC's *Panorama* documentary series which aired in March 2012,[1] titled "Britain's Crimes of Honour":

> In multicultural Britain today, many young people from immigrant communities are well integrated. Yet in many households old traditions are still a powerful force and some cause harm. Up and down the country behind closed doors crimes are being committed, kidnap and false imprisonment, women and girls being beaten, raped and even murdered and all in the name of so-called honour. The authorities admit that they just don't know the real scale of this abuse.
>
> (Corbin, 2012)

The programme opens with a dramatic statement: "[n]o one knows how many women in Britain are being silenced by so called honour" (Corbin, 2012). The aim of the programme was to highlight a number of things: the seriousness of "honour"-related crimes, how prevalent they are, how this age-old concept continues to circulate within South Asian communities in Britain, and the silences of women living in fear of their lives because of honour (Corbin, 2012). This documentary was one of the first to provide in-depth coverage of why a so-called honour crime in the UK took place, as well as shaping public views that were then reiterated in later documentaries about honour crimes. As such it provides an important early instance of the way in which honour has continued to be employed in public discourse and captures key features of that employment which will be explored in this chapter.

The Crown Prosecution Services of the UK have defined an honour crime as:

> [a]n incident or crime involving violence, threats of violence, intimidation coercion or abuse (including psychological, physical, sexual, financial or

DOI: 10.4324/9781003311928-5

emotional abuse) which has or may have been committed to protect or defend the honour of an individual, family and /or community for alleged or perceived breaches of the family and/or community's code of behaviour.

(2019)

Honour-based crimes have been registered as a separate category of crime that is characterised by eight factors motivated by culturally based moral values, enabling them to be distinguished as distinct, striking, and particularly abhorrent (Crown Prosecution Services, 2019). Defining honour crimes as legally distinct is problematic for two reasons. First, the violence in migrant communities becomes "othered" and produces racialised representations (Gill & Brah, 2014) that are bound by colonial legacies of racism. Second, it seeks to divert attention from any commonalities between domestic violence of minority and mainstream communities in the UK.

The use of the label "honour crimes" has been contested by critics, including Gill and Brah (2014) and Razack (2008), because of the orientalist connotations the term poses when applied to British South Asian communities. Furthermore, according to the Honour-Based Violence Awareness Network,[2] honour crimes occur in specific parts of the world, including:

Egypt, Jordon, Lebanon, Pakistan, the Syrian Arb Republic, Turkey, Yemen and other Mediterranean and Persian Gulf countries, and also in western countries such as France, Germany and the United Kingdom, largely within migrant communities; India also has high levels of 'honour' based crimes, on a level with the prevalence in Pakistan.

(Honour-Based Violence Awareness Network, n.d.)

The term "honour-based violence" ascribes this form of violence to non-Western cultures, from South Asia and the Middle East to ethnic minorities in Western countries. Implicit in such articulations is a use of culture as a stand-in for racialised representations suggesting that "immigrant cultures and traditions are both backward and unchanging" (Gill & Brah, 2014, p. 73). By extension, the solution proposed resides in educating the victims, judiciary, social institutions and the general public about how honour in immigrant cultures can motivate perpetrators to commit acts of violence against women in these communities. In this context, Young's (1995) research depicts the long-standing deployment of culture in the UK to differentiate class and represent distinctions between civilised and uncivilised cultures. Here, South Asian culture is used to explain the uncivil use of honour. Hence, rejecting certain cultural values is seen as capable of reducing violence rooted in honour.

By contrast, (civilised) morality is commonly deemed to be linked to universalist humanism. For example, according to Immanuel Kant (cited in Nyholm, 2016), morality consists in a set of moral principles which guide a socially ideal society towards universally accepted social norms. Transgressing those principals is therefore a mark of the unhuman (cited in Nyholm, 2016, p. 361). In this setting, moral values such as honour, shame and guilt have been used to demarcate societies as either comprising moral civil subjects who construct a particular image of the nation or immoral subjects that become signifiers of uncivil bodies that pollute the nation. The construction of the immoral subject works not only to mark bodies out in space, but also to represent them as relics of the past in the present, reinforcing the position of the modern civil subject.

In this chapter, I argue that British Asian communities are framed as relics of the past controlled by archaic moral codes—in short, as communities which are at odds with the modern moral standards of universal humanism. In particular, colonial legacies embedded in the terminology of the "backward", and the "savage" (Pitts, 2011, p. 33) continue to codify, structure and categorise moral values of honour and "shame" in British Asian communities. These legacies are then employed to explain domestic violence within those communities. In other words, both notions of morality and deviant acts connected with these communities become racialised through the mechanics of generating moral panic—a point that will be discussed later in the chapter. The concept of 'living legacies' disrupts the normalisation of labels employed to describe domestic violence in British South Asian communities. The framework of living legacies draws attention to how colonial narratives of the Other continue to accumulate value in the present. More specifically, the theme of "backward and steeped in tradition" contextualises/sticks to present day narratives about cultural differences and moral codes.

One way to understand what constitutes the immoral use of honour, is through Donna Jeffery's paradox when she asks whether it is "ever possible for the racialised subject to be the moral liberal subject?" (Jeffery, 2002, p. 9). She argues that this is only possible when "race" is not in the equation, which is, as she points out "socially impossible" (Jeffery, 2002, p.10). Jeffery insists that the racialised subject can only be the moral subject when it is not "raced" (see also, Gilroy, 2012; Razack, 2002; Said, 1989). Thus, race becomes a crucial determining factor of a Janus-faced morality. If this is the case, then how does morality attach itself to the Western liberal subjects such that they appear inseparable, whereas immorality attaches itself to the Other?

In earlier research, I have argued that the moral liberal Western subject is only formed through the history of racialisation (Kaur, 2015). In this chapter, I will focus on disentangling the relationship between morality and the Western liberal subject by borrowing the concept of "moral economies". However, the model that I propose is different from the historical models of moral economies that were originally proposed by Thompson (1963) and later Scott (1976). These scholars describe economies that are based on ethical principles of goodness, fairness and justice to promote the survival of the small communities in contradistinction to societies that are based around maximum profit.

'Horrors' of Honour   59

The ethos of these moral economies is based on mutual obligation and not individual gain. My model differs from theirs and considers morality as a construct which gains positive value or depreciates in value as it moves through bodies. More specifically, I suggest that moral constructs gain or depreciate in emotional value as they circulate through, and stick to, particular bodies in time and space.

Moreover, as Ahmed theorises in *Affective economies* (2004), it is the circulation of moral constructs in the form of emotions that brings to the surface "individual and collective bodies" (p.117). It is not that emotions are intrinsically associated with particular moral values, let alone are innate to an object or subject, but that the circulation of emotions such as hate and love is what creates affective value—that is, emotional weight. The more such emotions circulate, the more value they have. Therefore "emotions *do things*, and they align individuals with communities, as well as bodily space with social space, through the very intensity of their attachments" (Ahmed, 2004, p. 119). In the same vein, I argue that the circulation of the moral construct, honour, is emotionally laden and, as such, its circulation creates increasing intensity. This growing intensity is expressed in moral panic. It is possible to see in the instance of honour the ways in which specific moral constructs circulate in the form of emotions within a society's moral economy and, as Ahmed outlines, thereby become attached to particular bodies in specific temporalities and locations.

In the UK, the moral construct of honour travels through the British South Asian female body, accruing colonial narratives of traditional and backward cultures, such that negative emotional value is assigned to these communities in comparison to the national mainstream. As such, this chapter demonstrates how the language of honour crimes is a political vocabulary that encompasses colonial legacies of "us" and "them" in the contemporary era, as a means to control that which is the Other. In a similar way to Chapter 2, this chapter interrogates the continual use of tradition as a marker of uncivilised moral codes, such as the use of the language of honour as a cause of domestic violence in British South Asian communities.

The moral economy model that I outline is a political construct that uses codes to mark out certain communities as unethical and immoral. The notion of economy is useful in this chapter as it highlights how moral codes such as honour appreciate or depreciate in value according to their political use as a means by which to classify minority and majority societies over time and spaces. In this context, the first section of this chapter draws upon Nietzsche's critique of nineteenth century morality to examine the hierarchical usage of morality (Nietzsche, 1887[1967]). I apply Nietzsche's analysis of morality to de-essentialise honour. I extend Nietzsche's critique by employing an account of moral economies that is influenced by Sara Ahmed's theoretical conceptualisation of "affective" economies. Here I follow Ahmed in using "affect" and "emotion" interchangeably.[3] I connect the work of Nietzsche and Ahmed

60 Kameljeet Kaur

to mount a perspective on moral economies which highlights how the language of honour may be viewed as the use of moral constructs in the form of negative emotional value to demarcate and generate criminal and colonial scripts of the Other which "stick" to migrant/diasporic bodies. I do this in three ways. First, I explain how morality functions within the moral economy to generate value. Second, I examine how honour functions to accumulate moral value, aligning some to crime and barbaric behaviours and others to universal ideals of moral liberal subjects. Having considered how the moral economy functions, I then discuss the emotions that the moral economy generates in relation to honour crimes, such as disgust, horror, fear and anger. By this means, relics of the past exist in the present, enabling historical classifications of the primitive colonised Other to surface through encoding as moral constructs which take the form of negative emotions. As Bauman argues in *Postmodern ethics*, relics like honour, may be viewed as "zombies that ought to be buried as soon as possible for their own and everyone's sake" (1993, p. 38). I suggest additionally that these emotional responses to honour can be read through psychoanalytical readings of the uncanny, in which honour from the perspective of the British white subject may be seen as the "return of the repressed". Thus, the overall impact of the moral economy results in horror attached to honour crimes.

Janus-faced honour

Nietzsche interrogates the dominant interpretations of morality because these constructs solidify what constitutes morality. He claims that morality, like science, is used to create a picture of the world—what the world and the humans in it should look like according to moral values (Nietzsche, 1887[1967]). He argues persuasively in a number of texts that morality is not value-free because of the dangers posed by the use of morals from a position of power. What we understand as morality, and therefore as supposedly unchanging universal principles, is actually only one form of morality. Nietzsche illustrates that Christian morality has been used as an obstacle to human freedom, strangling one's sense of creativity by denying the prospect of multiple moralities (Nietzsche, 1886[1966], 1887[1967]).

In this way Nietzsche unsettles the ideal of morals as essentially value-free concepts. When interrelated with power, morals become value-laden concepts through which society is structured, controlled and governed; this type of morality he terms "herd morality" (Nietzsche, 1886[1966]). Herd morality in his view is prevalent in Europe, such that it is presumed to be *the* one and only kind of morality. In other words, herd morality imposes one interpretation of morality as universal, through which values are constructed according to dichotomies of good versus bad (the Other), as means to regulate and control society (Nietzsche, 1886[1966], p. 40). Under such conditions, *a* moral perspective (here, Western) is universalised against other moral perspectives. It is at this juncture that morals can become problematic, because other moral contexts, languages or understandings may be dehumanised (Other-ed) by the West. Nietzsche's work shows how fluid moral concepts are, such that they are reconceptualised according to existing power relations (Kaufman, 2011).

In fact, honour has long been considered to have "two distinct senses, one external and one internal" (Kaufman, 2011, p. 559). This duality is construed as value-free, making it difficult to perceive that it is actually a contextual concept used as an instrument of power over particular societies. For instance, as Kaufman argues, research on shame and guilt cultures by Margaret Mead (1937) and Ruth Benedict (1946) was essentially used to mark the distinction between "honor culture and *modern* culture" (Kaufman, 2004, p. 562, emphasis added). This distinction was welcomed and adopted by various Western disciplines, such as "anthropologists, sociologists, historians and literary critics" who used such categories to identify traditional/pre-modern cultures as associated with shame and guilt (Kaufman, 2004, p. 562). Shame and guilt cultures are thus distinguished from modernity and the distinction between traditional and modern is then marked onto differentiated bodies generating binaries such as white–coloured, civilised–primitive, and coloniser–colonised. In this demarcation, the honour ideal, surfacing via shame, is turned "into the 'alien Other', on which is projected all the vices that we would like to believe our own [western] society has risen above" (Kaufman, 2011, p. 558). Colonial categories of shame and guilt cultures resurface in the postcolonial era, where honour via the language of honour crimes comes to re-make and reaffirm distinctions between white–Asian, national–diasporic and majority–minority bodies. Although the bodies are not necessarily the same and the dichotomies surrounding the notion of honour shift, what remains is the continuing legacy of binaries via the circulation of moral signs. The circulation of these moral signs through time, spaces and bodies generates emotions of fear and horror that are grounded by colonial representations of the Other as uncivilised and in need of civilising.

In *Affective economies*, Sara Ahmed shows how emotions work within the realms of the psyche and the social, by challenging the general conception that emotions are just private or that they have a positive residence within the individual that transfers outwardly towards others (Ahmed, 2004). Instead, Ahmed (2004, p. 117) argues that "emotions are not simply 'within' or 'without', but that they create the very effect of the surface or boundaries of bodies and worlds". This is not a product of one particular mechanism but a mediation between the realms of the psyche, social, individual and collective. In particular, her conception of "stickiness" and "the rippling effect of emotions" (Ahmed, 2004, p. 120) allows consideration of the relationship between morality and the Western liberal subject. The significance of Nietzsche's unsettling of notions of essential morality, along with Ahmed's development of this de-essentialising orientation through her discussion of emotions, enables moral codes to be understood as both taking the form of emotions and connected to specific power relations. In sum, morals express power relations through emotion. In this setting, moral signs "mediate the relationship between the psychic and the social, and between the individual and the collective" (Ahmed, 2004, p. 119) to bind not only the imagined white subjects to the present and future as progressive/modern, but also the imagined relic (the Other) to the backward past. The language of honour crimes demarcates bodies that are out of place, invading the civilized world of the west with their archaic morals, generating visceral emotions.

The circulation of moral signs, in this case honour, accrues emotional value through "stickiness" (Ahmed, 2004), such that the moral liberal subject becomes attached to the white Western subject, while "Asian" gets metonymically attached to the sign honour. As Ahmed (2004) argues, the purpose of metonymy is to establish links and stick words to bodies. For instance, "it can stick words like *terrorist* and *Islam*" to particular bodies (p. 132) or attach words like "animal, bad, mean, ugly" to "the Negro" (p.127). In this way, moral signs simultaneously construct the delineation of civil and uncivil bodies. The crucial point here is that the legacy, the historical context, of the sign honour is concealed.

Honour crimes rhetoric in the media draws on the living legacy of colonial narratives regarded as guilt and shame cultures, which are viewed as static, irrational cultures that kill for public recognition. The legacy of such narratives is intertwined with contemporary narratives around fundamentalism, culture clash, traditional marriage systems and the "War on Terror". The moral economy circulates feelings of disgust, horror, and anger which metonymically attach themselves to the diasporic South Asian male body.

When exploring media representations of honour crimes over a period of time, it is evident that the continual use of colonial narratives of the Other are not simply decades-old residues of racism but rather demonstrate, in a concentrated way, ongoing elements of colonialism that have continued into recent times. There are many other media stories with representations of honour crimes which, like the BBC Panorama documentary programme mentioned in the opening paragraph of this chapter, display the living legacy of colonial narratives about tradition, parenting and honour codes in South Asian communities in the UK. Some instances include, *Banaz: A love story* (Khan, 2012), *Honor diaries* (Smith, 2013), and *Murdered by my father* (Goodison, 2016). However, I have highlighted the *Panorama* programme—*Britain's Crimes of Honour* (Corbin, 2012)—because it binds 'honour crimes' to tradition, culture and backward ideals of honour and shame in British South Asian communities in a way that gives particular force to the increasing use of the term and also condensed the themes of later documentaries in a schematic fashion. While later documentaries have tended to offer a regurgitation of the Panorama themes, they tend to discuss them through an emphasis on particular incidents. Nevertheless, of all of these media representations offer much the same narratives about why such 'honour crimes' occur and as a body of representations continue to entrench the notion that migrant communities are compelled by archaic moral values which identify them as relics of the past in the present. The public circulation of such narratives encourages mainstream perceptions that "'honour killings' are a growing problem" (Talwar, 2015), and that "the scale of so-called 'honour' killings in the UK are bigger than we realise?" (Jorquera, 2019), while also generating powerful emotional responses. Such emotions have long-lasting effects in shaping legal, political and public discourses.

Ahmed's (2004) reading of the Ayran Nations website carefully maps out the role that emotions play, specifically love and hate, in marking out the bodies of the nation and the individual subject. Attachment of negative signs to others simultaneously attaches positive signs to the imagined pure subject, which is constructed through the "repetition of the signifier, 'white'" (Ahmed, 2004, p. 118). This produces a "communal" visceral response of hate that becomes justified as love—a love of whiteness, and the white nation-states to be defended from invading strangers (Ahmed, 2004, p. 119). Indeed, Ahmed argues that "[h]ate is economic" (2004, p. 120). She explains the workings of emotion as an economy, via Marx's critique of capital production, by reworking his formula "*M-C-M* (money to commodity to money) creates surplus value" accumulated via the circulation and exchange of commodities and money (Ahmed, 2004, p. 120). Analogously, Ahmed argues that the "movement between signs converts into affect" (2004, p. 120). During this process, "[s]ome signs increase in affective value as an effect of the movement between signs" (Ahmed, 2004, p. 120). Moreover, a form of repression takes place. What is repressed in relation to the process of this circulation is the concealment of multiple histories that shape the threatening character of the circulated sign. Ahmed illustrates this idea of histories alive in the present through a reading of Frantz Fanon's *Black skin, white masks* to show "how the language of racism sustains fear through displacement" (2004, p.126) which surfaces on the body of the one who is feared. In this context, morals such as honour are emotionally laden. My approach expands on that analysis and draws attention to how colonial characterisation and imagined signs of "primitive" societies continue as a living legacy, registering the temporality of power that is central to this volume and inform moral panics.

Invisible bodies *in* visible panics: Relationships between moral panics and moral economy

Hall et al. (2013) argue that moral panics do not emerge randomly. They exhibit a shape and structure and the panic follows a sequence. At times they occur according to deep-rooted fears or anxieties that can be felt at a state level. The particular crisis of honour crimes may be seen as linked to anxieties around post-World War II mass migration to Britain, which raised issues of how to regulate, incorporate, understand and integrate these new arrivals, and generated a range of analyses regarding different cultures. Some of these analyses were constructed along the lines of racial categories and emphasised distinctions between modern versus shame and guilt cultures. To put this into context, Hall et al. (2013) argue that the label "mugging", imported/borrowed from the United States to describe certain criminal activity by black youth, was imbued with racial ideologies and was not socially innocent in that it involved a policing function. This labelling was informed by analyses about crime in migrant communities as a means to control and regulate ethnic minorities.

There are clear links to be made here between the moral panic associated with mugging and those associated with honour crimes. For example, the rise of post-war immigration from Commonwealth countries, mainly an influx in Caribbean Indian and Pakistani immigrants, was regarded as the problem behind the rise of crime, such as mugging, resulting in support for restricted immigration policies. No doubt the mugging label fits into the context of Enoch Powell's statement titled "Rivers of Blood" (or "Birmingham Speech") delivered in Birmingham Town Hall in March 1968. The speech was in response to the growing black population in the UK. The speech very much reads as an expression of fear that British white identity will be lost if immigration doors are not closed to those who are not white, so much so that there was a lingering frightful notion that one day Britain may be ruled by the black man (Powell, 1968). In a similar vein, the label of honour crimes becomes a signifier of the danger that immigrant communities pose to the idea of Englishness and to Western liberal values.

A case in point is the media dissemination and judicial reporting of Shafilea Ahmed's murder. In 2003, her disappearance was reported in the print media as a consequence of arranged or forced marriage,[4] and articulated as a product of a "culture clash" (Bunyan, 2003). It was not until 2010, based on fresh evidence, that the label "honour crime" featured in the headlines—for instance, "[p]arents re-arrested over suspected 'honour' killing" (Carter, 2010). Between 2010 and 2012 the public was inundated with media coverage on the trial of Shafilea Ahmed's parents from newspaper reports to documentaries, such as the *Panorama* programme with which I opened this chapter. Interviews with women's grass roots organisations such as the South-Hall Black Sisters, and Kurdish Women's Rights Organisation, were conducted within this documentary to understand the nature of honour in South Asian cultures. The label "honour crime" and the increasingly common juxtaposition of western and traditional themes identified in the newspapers became a means to reinforce culturalist explanations. Narratives such as "culture clash", "rural village life", "rural Pakistan", "rural mentality", "abnormal", "against Western values", "traditional", "backward", "patriarchy", "arranged marriages", "forced marriage", "alien values", "Muslim parents too strict", and "more concerned about shame and honour" became the order of the day (Carter, 2010; Keaveny & Hornby, 2011; Bunyan 2003; Crilly 2012) and constituted 'the problem' as occurring amongst immigrant communities, especially Muslim communities. Race and geography became intertwined in the media coverage. The transparent association between race and crime was condensed into the rural mentality of Shafilea's parents, to which the prosecuting judge also referred in his sentencing remarks.[5] The public knowledge of honour crimes was constructed through what Stuart Hall terms "quasi-explanations" fused together to make the incomprehensible, comprehensible, by using racialised explanations of these "foreign" phenomena (Hall et al., 2013, p. 199).

The Office of National Statistics UK report of 2013 which was produced shortly after the 2012 airing of the *Panorama* programme, focused on violent and sexual crime during 2011–12 and stated that 7 per cent of women (estimated to be 1.2 million females) experience domestic violence. When these statistics are compared to actual reported incidents of honour crimes—nine per year within the UK (Honour-Based Violence Awareness Network, n.d. a) and more recently, 12 per year (Honour-Based Violence Awareness Network, n.d. b)—then, argues Ewing (2008), honour crimes feature as a moral panic. In other words, the representation of the crime in the media far outweighs its incidence. Nevertheless, this moral panic has a function that results in the attachment of a positive sign to the *white* liberal subject that carries liberal values as opposed to the negative sign that is attached to the foreigner who has been tolerated even though they carry counter values to that of the white British majority. White British values accumulate positivity, while horror concerning the values of the foreigner are heightened. This intensifying horror arises as more and more (often concealed) signs attach to honour. Ahmed (2004) names this a "rippling effect" that moves sideways in the present but also backwards as it connects moral signs, emotions and bodies. Thus, what sticks to subjects is also bound up with the "absence present" of historicity (Ahmed, 2004, p. 120).

This fear of the Other is deep-rooted and born out of what Gilroy (2005) states is a "crisis of hegemony" (p. 102). He argues that moral panics are symptomatic of post-imperial or postcolonial melancholia, in which Britain's collective memory loss in the face of imperial decline manifests itself as an identity crisis, expressed through racist violence, which distinguishes the Other from the national majority. This violence serves to recreate, re-homogenise and purify the notion of a national identity of the state (Gilroy, 2005), thus creating folk devils (Hall et al., 2013). Gilroy's (2005) *Postcolonial melancholia* provides a historical context for the honour crime moral panic that has emerged in the contemporary era. Honour crimes provide a platform from which the nation-state can re-assert its lost power over the immigrant, resurrecting the empire through dualistic categories of domestic violence that are played out on the diasporic female British Asian body. Contextualised thus, the language of honour crimes brings life to the discourse of the "brown woman being saved from the brown man" (Spivak, 1994, p. 52). The immigrant becomes a colonial subject again, allowing Britain to play out its colonial

66 Kameljeet Kaur

fantasises of rescue, education, protection and salvation (Bhattacharyya, 2008; Lewis, 1996; Mohanty, 1988).

While Gilroy (2005) identifies this crisis emerging out of postcolonial melancholia, I am interested in how ethnically marked female bodies are central to the ways in which this melancholia is played out. In an attempt to reinsert a sense of British identity, the female body becomes a site upon which colonial fantasies are once again recalled and dramatised. By constructing a new label to describe and criminalise domestic violence, murder or child abuse in British South Asian communities, the west once again in the name of civilisation performs the act of the liberator.

Sticky honour: Uncanny effects of the moral economy

The moral economy generates feelings of disgust, horror and loathing as signs of historical narratives circulate through time, space and bodies. For instance, returning back to the BBC *Panorama* programme, *Britain's Crimes of Honour* (Corbin, 2012), it is evident how these feelings of disgust, horror and loathing are expressed outwardly towards the Other. From the start, the reporter of the documentary conjures up a scene in which "traditional" (read: non-modern, non-Western) crime, is "lurking in the heart of Britain" (Corbin, 2012). This is supported by an interview with Nazir Afzal, who explains how ancient and traditional values and attitudes of honour did not simply die out with the older generation. Additionally, the programme carried out an opinion poll of 500 people to show that there was a significant proportion of young Asian people (both women and men) who believed that women should live according to honour (Corbin, 2012). The poll does not demonstrate that this is an Asian-specific issue. Yet the responses to the programme that were uploaded to YouTube presented it as a matter crucially associated with Asian communities. Various remarks expressed concern and exhibited a range of strongly negative emotions. Some angrily called for the return of the death penalty: "sick, sadistic murder (…) Fucking crazy bastards! I would introduce the death penalty, eye for an eye". Others evoked disgust through associating Muslims with animals: "Muslims think that divorce is shameful and dishonourable but domestic violence and killing young innocent women brings honour? F*ckin animals (no offence to animals)". Others expressed contempt through marking Muslims as primitive and even calling for them to be gassed: "you guys are so fawking primitive (…) stupid ignorant third world savages. Gas chambers for everyone!" (Corbin, 2012).

These emotions are exacerbated because the South Asian female body is already historically bound-up by narratives of oppression and repression, stuck in traditional and pre-modern cultures. As a result, the attachment of honour crime to the endangered Asian female body is significant. This circulation of the sign honour thus re-marks/re-makes boundaries between the immigrant populations of Britain and the British majority. This boundary construction can also be read through Ahmed's analysis of psychoanalysis in reference to emotionality (Ahmed, 2004, p. 120). While Ahmed (2004, pp. 119–120) does not limit affective economies to just the psychic realm, she does nevertheless draw on Freud's notion of:

> unconscious emotions, where an affective impulse is perceived but mis-construed, and which becomes attached to another idea. What is repressed from consciousness is not the feeling as such, but the idea to which the feeling may have been first (but provisionally) connected.

Affirmation of binary cultural difference in the aftermath of colonialism, I would argue, is also best understood as being emotionally felt as the uncanny return of the repressed. In Sigmund Freud's influential 1919 essay, *The uncanny*, he elaborates the concept by way of two German terms: *hemlich* which trans-lates into "home", a familiar, cosy accessible place, and *unheimlich* which is unfamiliar, strange, inaccessible and unhomely (Freud, 1919, p. 348). At first, both terms seem totally opposed. In actuality, Freud argues that they circulate through each other. It is not only the unfamiliar that generates the anxiety of the uncanny feeling, but the combination of the familiar and the unfamiliar. Thus, the uncanny "is something that is secretly familiar", which stems from our repressed feelings that are concealed to ourselves (Freud, 1919, p. 349). In other words, the uncanny feeling arises when unconsciously we are reminded of own forbidden thoughts, our feelings which were repressed become pro-jected onto the Other, who becomes a threat. In this sense, it is not that the word 'honour' is repressed and then returned but rather the discomforting history of British colonialism which is buried and then resurrected through a particular usage of the term, especially in conjunction with aberrant crime. The return of the repressed thus enables historical violence to be displaced onto the outsider—onto that which is outside the self, outside mainstream national identity.

Discourses concerning honour crimes from those who conceive themselves as insiders, as intimately and self-evidently belonging to the national home, as British, may be viewed as the return of colonial conceptions of the traditional or barbarism, as some of the responses suggest. The language of honour crimes enters Western discourses because it is the uncanny return of colonial perspec-tives that have been estranged via the process of repression. The outrage of honour crimes results from the thought that this conceptualisation of honour is still present in modern society. This leads to an exacerbated sense of danger, disgust, horror and contempt that is aimed towards the migrant communities as pollutants of national space (Ahmed, 2004; Puwar, 2004). British subjects who deem themselves to be self-evident national citizens are struck by fear because they feel that they, the national majority, may be overrun by barbarians endangering *their* way of life.

Further, as honour circulates and sticks to relics of the past, we see how heinous crimes committed during colonialism reveal the very act of colonisation to be embodied by the boomerang effect in which even the "most civilized man" is dehumanised through the very savagery of the colonial enterprise (Cesaire, 1972, p. 41). The boomerang effect is prevalent in the language of honour crimes, in which we witness the postcolonial return of the repressed colonialism. As Homi Bhabha argues, the stereotypes that attempt to fix the Other as unfamiliar are actually more familiar than one is made to believe, because they are created by the repressor (Bhabha, 1994). Thus, the responses to the *Panorama* documentary series evoke a traumatic and pathological response, a visceral reaction to the Other who has crossed the line and is literally too close for comfort. As Žižek (2008) argues, today's liberal tolerance toward Others is carried out by ensuring that they keep their distance. Therefore, the word "tolerance" is intolerable when the Other crosses a "zone of habitability" (Žižek, 2008, p. 35). One way to create and maintain that distance is to stick the horrors of honour, associated with the past, onto bodies that have been subjected to colonial narratives of uncivil, traditional, backward societies that are not quite human.[6] The horror expressed at these crimes is represented not only through sympathy and horror, but also through the use of symbolic violence toward the Other in "our" society through the orientalist tropes and stereotypes that distance the self from the Other (Said, 1979). Domestic violence in British Asian communities then is no longer simply a crime, but a *barbaric* crime that unnerves *our* civilised sensibilities.

It is through this symbolic status of honour crimes that they become an internal spectacle disseminated across the internet, television and newspapers. The viewers participate in the theatre of primitive horror, and the pornographic spectacle of diasporic brutality. The dramatic emotional responses to the *Panorama* programme perpetually perform a disavowal of the violence through their proclamations of disbelief that such a crime could exist in the twenty-first century. This disbelief is a product of the fact that while honour violence is not unknown within Anglo European societies, violence against women has been conveniently disassociated from the modern British mainstream (Frevert, 1998). This simultaneously functions to displace the violence onto its societal Others—Others who become fetishised, disavowed and abjected from humanity disavowal (Ewing, 2008). Only the barbaric, or in Gilroy's more specific terminology, the "infra-human", are capable of such brutality (Gilroy, 2005, p. 102). Importantly though, it is the Asian female body which becomes the site upon which demarcations of us and them are made. In this sense, the horrors of honour rely upon the suppression, representation and labelling of violence in British Asian communities as that which cannot be understood through the existing discourse of domestic violence. This violence is conveniently displaced into essentialised social binaries distinguishing the Western liberal subject from the Other—binaries that allow the colonial legacy to live on when presented through a culturalist paradigm (Brah &

Minhas, 1985; Puar, 1996). The re-contextualisation of so-called honour crimes in the UK in relation to masculine domination offers a way forward beyond the enduring legacies of the rhetoric of honour and of colonial racism.

Conclusion

This chapter re-examines the honour crime discourse through conceptualising moral economies. In the moral economy, the sign honour becomes attached to some bodies as a means of creating and sustaining a national identity that is supposedly built upon ideals of (modern) liberalism rather than (primitive) honour codes. The notion of moral economy helps uncover the ways in which crime in ethnic minorities becomes racialised and, at the same time, ethnic honour is rendered primitive and shame is imputed in relation to the ethnic body. Emphasising hierarchically constituted cultural difference and shaming ethnic bodies is one way to regulate minority communities. My use of moral economy not only points out that moral signs, here honour, are employed politically such that morality marks the boundaries between the civil and uncivil but also how the female body is vital when marking these distinctions. The moral constructs associated with honour are emotionally created, generated and mobilised at specific points in time through moral panics. The label "honour crime" is not just moved from one place to another but is a product of the circulation of the sign honour through bodies, time and space. Throughout it all, women's bodies remain the primary sites upon which morality is regulated and monitored.

In the online response to honour crimes in the *Panorama* documentary— employed as an exemplary instance of the way in which such crimes are conceived in public—it is possible to see how the emotional responses of anger, disgust and horror are generated as an uncanny effect of the moral economy. The common remark that the crime is barbaric suggests the return of the repressed—the uncanny's leitmotif. Yet, this return is a result of specific historical narratives that conceal the history of colonialism through use of the language of honour. The concept of 'living legacies' challenges the resurrection of colonial constructions regarding migrant communities as homogeneous, backward, steeped in tradition and relatedly uncivilised. Thereby, it is conceptual framing which enables refusal of the employment of honour as a means to describe domestic violence in British South Asian communities. Instead, it draws attention to the ways in which power relations evident in the past are by no means extinguished but rather continues to accumulate value in the present. Arguably the west has constructed its own monsters, who have come back to haunt them. It is perhaps pertinent to recall Kristeva's, argument that the west's relationship with foreigners "depends on how familiar they are with their ghosts" (Kristeva, 1991, p. 89).

Notes

1 This documentary was released at the height of the debate and aired two months before the well-publicised murder case of Shafilea Ahmed.
2 The Honour-Based Violence Awareness Network, comprising both white and non-white professionals and scholars, is an international digital resource centre providing an understanding and awareness of Honour Killings, Honour Based Violence and Forced Marriages. It undertakes researching, collating and documenting what, how, where and why these forms of violence occur. It also offers training for professionals who may come across victims of this form of violence.
3 The interchangeable use of affect and emotion is debated, but I do not have scope in this chapter to deal with this further.
4 Anitha and Gill (2015) argue that the overrepresentation of forced marriages created a moral panic about South Asian cultures.
5 For further detail, see the transcript of the court proceedings titled as: Regina V Iftikhar Ahmed and Farzana Ahmed (2012) T20117279 at 1.
6 By contrast, there are many instances of whiteness that are honoured in Britain, instances from its imperial past and in recent times (see Baird, 2021; Clarke, 2021; Mizatani, 2011).

References

Ahmed, S. (2004). Affective economies. *Social Text*, 22(2), 117–139.
Anitha, S. & Gill, A. K. (2015). A moral panic? The problematization of forced marriage in British newspapers. *Violence against women*, 21(9), 1123–1144.
Baird, R. P. (2021, April 20). The invention of whiteness: The long history of a dangerous idea. *The Guardian*. www.theguardian.com/news/2021/apr/20/the-invention-of-whiteness-long-history-dangerous-idea Accessed December 12 2022.
Bauman, Z. (1993). *Postmodern ethics*. Oxford: Blackwell.
Benedict, R. (1946). *The chrysanthemum and the sword*. Boston: Houghton Mifflin.
Bhabha, H. K. (1994). *The location of culture*. London: Routledge.
Bhattacharyya, G. (2008). *Dangerous brown men: Exploiting sex, violence and feminism in the war on terror*. London: Zed Books.
Brah, A. & Minhas, R. (1985). Structural racism or cultural difference: Schooling for Asian girls. In Gaby Weiner (Ed.), *Just a bunch of girls*. Milton Keynes: Open University Press.
Bunyan, N. (2003, December 19). Parents of missing "culture clash" teenager are arrested. *The Telegraph*. www.telegraph.co.uk/news/uknews/1449831/Parents-of-missing-culture-clash-teenager-are-arrested.html. Accessed February 2013.
Carter, H. (2010, September 2). Parents re-arrested over suspected "honour" killing. *The Guardian*. www.theguardian.com/uk/2010/sep/02/parents-arrested-suspected-honour-killing. Accessed February 2013.
Cesaire, A. (1972). *Discourse on colonialism*. New York: Monthly Review Press.
Corbin, J. (Reporter) (2012). Britain's Crimes of Honour (Television series episode). In F. Lloyd-Davies (Producer), Panorama. London, British Broadcasting Company.
Clarke, A. (2021). Recognising British bodies: The significance of race and whiteness in 'post-racial' Britain. *Sociological Research Online*. doi:10.1177/13607804211032232. Accessed December 15 2022.

Crilly, R. (Reporter) (2012). 'The culture of rural Pakistan helped kill Shafilea'. *The Telegraph.* http://blogs.telegraph.co.uk/news/robcrilly/100174697/the-culture-of-rural-pakistan-helped-kill-shafilea. Accessed February 2013.

Crown Prosecution Services. (2019). So-called honour-based abuse and forced marriage: Guidance on identifying and flagging cases. www.cps.gov.uk/legal-guidance/so-called-honour-based-abuse-and-forced-marriage-guidance-identifying-and-flagging. Accessed December 12 2022.

Ewing, K. P. (2008). *Stolen honor: Stigmatizing Muslim men in Berlin.* Stanford, CA: Stanford University Press.

Freud, S. (1919). The Uncanny. In J. Strachey (Ed., Trans.), *The Standard Edition of the Complete Psychological Works of Sigmund Freud.* London: Hogarth Press and The Institute of Psycho-Analysis.

Gill, A. K. & Brah, A. (2014). Interrogating cultural narratives about "honour"-based violence. *European Journal of Women's Studies,* 21(1), 72–86.

Gilroy, P. (2005). *Postcolonial melancholia.* New York: Columbia University Press.

Gilroy, P. (2012). "My Britain is fuck all" zombie multiculturalism and the race politics of citizenship. *Identities,* 19(4), 380–397.

Goodison, B. (Director) (2016, March). Murdered by my father (television series). BBC Three.

Hall, S., Critcher, C., Jefferson, T., Clarke, J. & Roberts, B. (2013). *Policing the crisis: Mugging, the state and law and order.* London: Macmillan Education UK.

Honour-Based Violence Awareness Network. (n.d. a.). http://hbv-awareness.com/honour-based-violence. Accessed December 10, 2012.

Honour-Based Violence Awareness Network. (n.d. b.). http://hbv-awareness.com/honour-based-violence. Accessed January 20 2022.

Jeffery, D. I. (2002). A terrain of struggle: Reading race in social work education (Doctoral Dissertation). University of Toronto.

Jorquera, N. (Reporter) (2019, 12 July). Is the scale of so-called 'honour' killings in the UK bigger than we realise? *ITV News.* www.itv.com/news/2019-07-14/honour-killings-day-of-memory-shafilea-ahmed-qandeel-baloch. Accessed December 12 2022.

Kaufman, W. (2004). Is there a "right" to self-defense? *Criminal Justice Ethics,* 23(1), 20–32.

Kaufman, W. (2011). Understanding honor: Beyond the shame/guilt dichotomy. *Social Theory and Practice,* 37(4), 557–573.

Kaur, K. (2015). Diasporic Honour: The politics of honour crimes in British South Asian Communities (Doctoral Thesis). Retrieved from PhD Thesis (International studies), University of South Australia. Accessed January 2022.

Keaveny, P. & Hornby, M. (2011, September 7). Parents charged with "honour" killing. *The Independent.* www.independent.co.uk/news/uk/crime/parents-charged-with-honour-killing-2350674.html. Accessed March 2013.

Khan, D. (Director) (2012). Banaz: A love story (documentary film). Fuuse Films.

Kristeva, K. (1991). *Strangers to ourselves.* New York: Columbia University Press.

Lewis, R. (1996). *Gendering orientalism: Race, femininity, and representation.* New York: Routledge.

Mead, M. (1937). *Cooperation and competition among primitive peoples.* New York:

Mizutani, S. (2011). *The meaning of White: Race, class and the 'domiciled' community in British India, 1858–1930.* Oxford University Press: Oxford.

Mohanty, C. T. (1988). Under Western eyes: Feminist scholarship and colonial discourses. *Feminist Review*, 30(1), 61–88.

Nietzsche, F. W. (1886[1966]). *Beyond good and evil: Prelude to a philosophy of the future.* New York: Vintage Books.

Nietzsche, F. W. (1887[1967]). *On the genealogy of morals.* New York: Vintage Books.

Nyholm, S. (2016). On Kant's idea of humanity as an end in itself. *European Journal of Philosophy*, 24(2), 358–374.

Office of National Statistics. (2013). Part of crime statistics, focus on: Violent crime and sexual offices, 2011/12. www.basw.co.uk/resources/focus-violent-crime-and-sexual-offences-201112. Accessed March 2013.

Pitts, J. (2011). Empire, Progress, and the Savage Mind. In Levy, J. T. (Ed.). *Colonialism and its legacies.* London: Lexington Books.

Powell, E. (1968). Speech at Birmingham 20 April. www.enochpowell.net/fr-79.html Accessed March 2013.

Puar, J. (1996). Resituating discourses of "Whiteness" and "Asianness" in Northern England: Second-generation Sikh women and constructions of identity. In M. Maynard and J. Purvis (Eds), New Frontiers in Women's Studies: Knowledge, identity and nationalism. London & Bristol, PA: Taylor & Francis (pp. 127−149).

Puwar, N. (2004). *Space invaders: Race, gender and bodies out of place.* Oxford: Berg Publishers.

Regina v. Iftikhar Ahmed and Farzana Ahmed. (2012). T20117279 1.

Razack, S. (Ed.) (2002). *Race, space, and the law: Unmapping a white settler society.* Toronto, ON: Between the Lines.

Razack, S. (2008). *Casting out: The eviction of Muslims from Western law and politics.* Toronto, ON: University of Toronto Press.

Said, E. (1979). *Orientalism.* New York: Vintage Books.

Said, E. W. (1989). Representing the colonized: Anthropology's interlocutors. *Critical Inquiry*, 15(2), 205–225.

Scott, J. C. (1976). *The Moral economy of the peasant: Rebellion and subsistence in Southeast Asia.* New Haven, CT: Yale University Press.

Smith, M. (Director) (2013). Honor diaries (documentary film). Clarion Project.

Spivak, G. (1994). Can the subaltern speak? In P. Williams & L. Chrisman (Eds), *Colonial discourse and post-colonial theory: A reader* (pp. 46–93). Hertfordshire: Harvester Wheatsheaf.

Talwar, D. (Reporter) (2015, 9 July). "Honour killings" are a growing problem, say campaigners. *BBC News.* www.bbc.com/news/av/uk-33456745. Accessed December 12 2022.

Thompson, E. P. (1963). *The making of the English working class.* London: Gollancz.

Young, R. (1995). *Colonial Desire: Hybridity in Theory, Culture and Race.* London: Routledge.

Žižek, S. (2008). *Violence: Six sideways reflections.* London: Profile.

Chapter 5

The Legacy of Stigma
American Single Mothers

Amy Andrada

Legacies are inherited histories that shape our notions in the present day. However, some legacies are built on myth, and not all legacies are just. Such is the case for the traditional (or nuclear) American family and its antithesis, single mothers. In this paper, I argue that the mythologisation of the 'traditional' American family is responsible for the stigmatisation of single mothers. By examining these families through a critical socio-historical lens, the work traces, challenges, interrogates and unburies modern 'social facts' of American motherhood. Over time, this lens reveals a legacy of ongoing social injustice evident in the origin of the 'American family' myth maintained throughout the 20th and 21st centuries. As a result, today's American families are conceptually framed by bifurcated (and/or hierarchal) motherhood that has produced a legacy of stigmatising single mothers, which informs modern notions and/or experiences about these women and their families.

In this respect, the persistence of nostalgic arguments of a past white-nuclear-suburban-family—often juxtaposed against the present decline in traditional "family values" (that is, non-nuclear families) in a rapidly modernised world—has resulted in a mythologised dream that once held the fabric of America together (Cootnz, 1992[2016]). However, this forgotten dream is a product of "post/memory" (Stanley, 2008), or memory made after the fact, responsible for constructing present-day American motherhood. According to Coontz (Cootnz, 1992[2016], pp. 1–7), this myth is a "collective nostalgia" that denies family diversity, as well as its social injustices, has resulted in a "nostalgia trap" that simplifies and idealises a past reality. Thus, the mythologisation of the 'traditional' American family has created an ongoing legacy that is incomplete and inaccurate, resulting in the marginalisation of families outside the 'traditional' family as un-American and thus are essentially *othered*. Moreover, as family and parenthood are central to femininity (Andrada, 2019; Kessler & McKenna, 1985), the preoccupation with "family values" effectively produces two extremes among American women: the *ideal* or 'good mother' identity (that is, white, married/coupled, non-poor) (May, 2008, 2004; Gross, 2005) and the 'bad' or *othered* mother (that is non-white, unmarried, [perceived as] lower class) (Bartky, 2012). In short, the latter are single mothers

DOI: 10.4324/9781003311928-6

(Andrada, 2019) or mothers without a (romantic) male partner in parenthood and family life—for example, never-married, separated, divorced, or widowed.

Evidence of these extremes is apparent when examining current trends on the topic. However, this argument is produced in two interconnected ways: explicit criticism of single mothers on the one hand, which indicates implicit support of married ones on the other. For instance, in the U.S., a quick google search of the term "single mother" will net narrowing results, often encapsulating stereotypes and misinterpreted statistics (see Best, 2001). Unsurprisingly, news articles embody these themes and approaches as ethos when examining the group. Articles range from headlines proclaiming, *Blacks struggle with 72 percent unwed mothers rate* (Washington, 2010) to highlighting societal concerns (and hysteria) over the historical precedence of *The unbelievable rise of single motherhood in America over the last 50 years* (Badger, 2014), with an albeit off-beat head nod to *How poor single moms survive* (Semuels, 2015).

Although these headlines represent only a few articles about single mothers—and most accounts are often inaccurate and ill-defined—even reputable sources sometimes lack comprehensive assessments when publishing (and framing) information about the group. For instance, Pew Research Center published a review that stressed a global dilemma in how the *U.S. has world's highest rate of children living in single-parent households* (Kramer, 2019), with even the U.S. Census emphasising the *Percentage and number of children living with two parents has dropped since 1968* (Hemez & Washington, 2021). And although these sources collectively highlight persistent concerns regarding single mothers (such as, poverty, being unpartnered/unwed, lone parenting, and [presumably] racial minority status), their preoccupation with family type often negates poverty as a significant predictor of these outcomes.

For instance, when examining American family households, the U.S. Census Bureau (2014, 2016) cites that about 23 per cent of children in the U.S. live with a single parent. However, single-mother families comprise of *less than* 9 per cent of U.S. households (Brady et al., 2017). Also, the term "single-parent family" is misleading regarding household living arrangements, as these mothers (21 per cent) live in an assortment of housing environments (including with other adults) (Livingston, 2018; London, 2000). Furthermore, academics tend to centre their preoccupation on the 'poor' segment (about one third) of single mothers (often owing to their vulnerable status) (see Walker et al., 2008)— rather than the group as a whole.

Moreover, though single mothers' total income and poverty status are lower than the average U.S. household (Lu et al., 2020), recent research identifies that *most* single-mother families are not impoverished (U.S. Census Bureau 2017, 2019a, 2019b[1]; U.S. Department of Health and Human Services, 2019)[2] and do not contribute significantly to poverty rates in the United States (Brady, et al., 2017). Furthermore, more often than not, women of 'poor' single mother families are more likely to be impoverished *before* becoming parents, with parenthood often exacerbating existing wealth inequalities (McLanahan et al., 2019)—factors reflected even among 'poor' divorced and/ or separated mothers who entered poverty as a result of partner-family separation (Hogendoorn et al., 2020).[3] And finally, being maritally 'single' does not mean unpartnered, for even research among poor(er) unmarried mothers found about one-half were cohabiting with fathers at the time of birth of their child, emphasising both parents desired parental (and partnered) involvement (McLanahan et al., 2019) in their families.

Collectively, the undertone of these articles implies that 'single' mothers are implicated in the demise of the two-parent 'traditional' family—concerns that are generally founded on poor child outcomes (McLanahan et al., 2019). However, as McLanahan et al. (2019) indicate, these consequences are similarly evident even among poor cohabiting partnered parents and poor married families in the United States. Thus, concerns about single parenthood may not be (only) poverty-based. As such, when examining single-mother families, the use of transparent and accurately contextualised data aid in highlighting mis-representations regarding unpartnership (or being without a partner) as a causal factor of non-traditional (or non-nuclear) and/or problematic families (for example, broken families). Arguably, poverty is the underlining factor of numerous family concerns, *regardless* of family type. However, the preoccupa-tion with single mothers is more likely magnified because mothers are unpart-nered (Andrada, 2022) *and* the historical legacy attached to the group rather than because a portion is impoverished.

Effectively, the "culture narrative", or the stigma discourse surrounding single mothers (Lubiano, 1992), is a byproduct of the country's fixation with the 'traditional' family—centred on a preoccupation of coupledom and partnering. This mythologisation has produced a spectrum of femininity around motherhood founded on partnership, resulting in the construction of the American mother as *ideal* and any *othered* as un-American. Though research on single mothers has been exhaustive, the following analysis advances this argument by examining how motherhood acts as a patriarchal norm in maintaining an idealised version of femininity—one that often undermines *othered* mothers (via stigma) and constrains idealised mothers into fixed notions of femininity, particularly one dependent on maleness (or the presence of men) to define 'good mothers' and/or proper (nuclear) families (see Andrada, 2019).[4]

Using a feminist lens (D'Ignazio & Klein, 2018), evidence of this phenom-enon is captured by reexamining the socio-historical biography of the single mother. Doing so reveals an unfiltered—and thus, a more 'complete'—histor-ical account (Worby & Ally, 2013, p. 461) of the following. The postwar era, punctuated by white backlash towards the Civil Rights movement, was centred on family arguments on 'concerns' of (il)legitimacy (or unwed mothers) throughout the 1950s until the 1970s. These 'concerns' evolved into class (and race) disparities of (non)access to reproductive rights during the 1970s–90s. After this the (reinvigorated) "welfare queen" and the rise of "single by choice" mothers (among white women) set a precedent in which current unpartnered mothers are situated.

Although single mothers exist in every facet of ethnicity and race in American families (Raley et al., 2015), the analysis in this chapter situates its argument between black and white American motherhood(s). This focus is foundational to American motherhood as it frames the experience of motherhood for most women in the United States. Specifically, historical black motherhood has embodied stigmatised motherhood, while white motherhood has inherited the ideal. Thus, this spectrum of motherhood reveals the contingent realities most American women navigate in negotiating their motherhood(s) with respect to their own racial and ethnic backgrounds (see Andrada, 2022).

In this light, the re-examination offered here enables a (de)construction of the single mother to uncover "legacies denied and repressed histories" that have produced intergenerational social injustice with bifurcated results among American mothers (Luhmann, 2011, p. 120). In short, in the present-day, *ideal* mothers have inherited a legacy of privilege *owing to* the legacy of injustice *othered* (single) mothers have inherited. Thus, *decon*structing historical motherhood opens up the possibilities for pursuing other "lines of flight" (or trajectories for personal becoming) (Winslade, 2009, p. 337) in which American mothers can create a spectrum of possibilities rather than reproduce predetermined outcomes (Diprose, 2006). Furthermore, new light shone on socio-historical accounts offers current (and future) women (and society) an opportunity to critique and challenge the ongoing legacies of social injustice that present-day single mothers inherit while simultaneously dismantling social prestige maintained by *ideal* mothers (and their descendants) (Luhmann, 2011). Thus, understanding the stigma of single mothers reveals these construction(s), their legacies and (hopefully) an avenue towards their dismantlement.

1950s–70s: *Leave it to Beaver* and the Myth of June Cleaver— Constructed (Il)legitimacy

Following the post-war era, images of the American family as nuclear were crystallised in popular television shows such as *Leave it to Beaver* (1957), the *Donna Reed Show* (1958) and *Father Knows Best* (1954)—even though only a tiny fraction of Americans actually lived like those in such shows (Cootnz, 1992[2016]). While these shows presented a romanticised myth, the American family became culturally known as "two parents and at least that many offspring", which defined a modern version of "womanhood" (and femininity) as intrinsically tied to motherhood (Solinger, 1991, p. 19). Furthermore, Solinger (1991, p. 19) argues that these statuses "could not be achieved without a husband, outside a properly constructed family".[5] In short, American "womanhood" required a man.

In turn, these definitions transformed marriage from a marker of conformity to an indicator of prestige (Cherlin, 2004), making the nuclear family the American norm (Cootnz, 1992[2016]) with both (marriage and family) desired as forms of social status (Goffman, 1951; Haller, 1981). This evolution of marriage and family illustrates a historical turn in the division between (non) married women/mothers that incurs a moral cost—evident in the cultural and institutional (dis)advantages of marriage. However, even before the 1950s, the success of U.S. marriages and the 'American family' had been distinctly founded on economics (Bennett et al., 1989). Thus, marriage not only signified a 'complete' woman but a successful one.

As this new version of "womanhood" defined modern femininity, the demand for women to uphold and maintain these statuses became conditional to the point that severe social sanctions were imposed upon women that contravened them—evidenced in the treatment of unwed mothers. Framed by moral anxieties over (il)legitimacy, fearing unwed mothers would compromise traditional "family values", the tactics of racist adoption policies, coerced "shotgun weddings" (or a rushed marriage owing to an unplanned pregnancy) and discriminatory welfare practices ensured women that breached social conventions during this era endured severe penalties. Race (and intrinsically class) were the defining factors of these outcomes (Akerlof & Yellen, 1996; Solinger, 1991).

During this period, explicit racist practices were embedded into policy and community initiatives. (Il)legitimacy debates spiked during the 1960s—though not as a result of any significant rise in total unwed births (Akerlof et al., 1996), but as a white backlash to the advancing civil rights movement. For instance, Solinger (1991, p. 21) argues that race-specific distinctions were one strategy to uphold "race hierarchy" when it was most threatened. This was evident in tactics that framed sexual mores through the high rate of black unwed mothers—serving as a "convenient counterpoint" (D'Emilio & Freedman, 1988) against similar white sexual behavior—to further support for biological determinism amongst the races (Solinger, 1991, p. 21). Furthermore, these arguments conveniently ignored the "public attitudes, policies, and practices" (Solinger, 1991, p. 31) that black women experienced, which *were* largely defined by race. Thus, the response to illegitimate (or unwed) births differed because of the political climate around race *not* owing to changes in the cohort of lone mothers.

These responses extend into the political climate in which states' reactions to unwed mothers differed dramatically based on race. In this instance, social work and/or adoption programmes were upheld for whites, while welfare services were generally directed towards blacks (Solinger, 1991, p. 21). Regarding the former, unwed white mothers could remain *unseen* via the availability of maternity homes and/or convents and/or be "rehabilitated" by

78 Amy Andrada

becoming "not-mothers" by giving up their babies for adoption.[6] However, as Solinger (1991) contends, unwed black women were excluded via racist policies and practices. In addition, and contrary to social (mis)perception, birthrates of married black women were actually *higher* than whites; while the practice of coerced "shotgun weddings" was more commonplace amongst whites (Akerlof et al., 1996).[7] Therefore, these patterns demonstrate that white women exhibited similar sexual behavior to black women, except that the state and community made concerted efforts to conceal white impropriety. As a result, these practices were superimposed to ensure the *invisibility* (or active forgetting) of (almost) unwed white mothers in these debates. As such, these revelations alter and/or "complete" the "hidden histories" of white women, otherwise rendered (intentionally) *invisible* (Worby & Ally, 2013, p. 461).

Furthermore, welfare recipients were generally poor white families, despite concerns that welfare services were directed towards an 'overrepresented' black populace. Though some black families may have needed these services, most blacks could not receive government and/or welfare assistance (Solinger, 1991). The concerted efforts of politicians (Hymowitz, 2005), social commentators and attitudes among (white) taxpayers, led to a "resistance against tax-supported welfare programmes for blacks [and opposition] against civil rights for blacks" led to these programmes being black-*identified* (Solinger, 1991, p. 21). As a result, such programmes consequences were construed as costing white taxpayers. This was then effectively used to 'justify' (white) political outrage (see also Crandall & Eshleman, 2003). As Ahmed (2014) argues, the "stickiness" (or legacy of disgust) attached to welfare, being identified as "black" begins. The association, between welfare and black, marks out the origin of stigmatisation. Collectively, these connections led to the (constructed) *visibility* of the single mother as, essentially, black women. In the process, black women were perceived as contravening modern 'womanhood', resulting in black women becoming a scapegoat for failing to maintain a 'traditional' family and thus compromising "family values" (Coontz, 1992[2016]).

A (re)examination of nostalgia arguments founded in this era (Cootnz, 1992 [2016]) reveals histories that were actively buried or suppressed (Worby & Ally, 2013), served to revere and preserve white women while denigrating black ones—conditions still evident today. Athanasiou et al. (2008, pp. 13–18) argue that questioning history alerts us to "problems that are still alive or invested with emotion and value". As this history embodies trauma and traumatic events, such problems become embedded into the "construction of identity" through the "historical transmission[s] of the past", which generate meaning for the present. Highlighting divergent (black/white) motherhood(s) as tied to "womanhood" aids in disentangling stigma and privilege—and with it enables the dismantling of "social facts" and their traumas (Athanasiou et al., 2008; Durkheim, 1894) tied present-day mothers. As the postwar era closes amid the sexual revolution, a propagandised divide between white (female) propriety and black illegitimacy is substantiated—one that continues onward

The Legacy of Stigma 79

through alternative means of lacking access to reproductive rights, furthering the class (and racial) divide into the 1970s on throughout the 1990s.

The 1970s–90s: The Sexual Revolution and the Woman's Movement—The Fight for Reproductive Rights... But *Whose?*

The era began with the landmark decision by the Supreme Court in *Roe v. Wade* (1973), which granted abortion rights to women. The decision had a significant ripple effect on society, especially concerning women and families. These effects could be seen in declining marriage rates, shotgun weddings and adoptions (Akerlof et al., 1996). Thus, with the decline in patterns that dominated the previous era, a shift in this era was reflected in an increase in contraceptive use, abortion services and a rise in birthrates among unmarried white women[8]—albeit, comparatively, with a marked decrease among black women (Akerlof et al., 1996).[9] However, the rise in reproductive services also deepened the divide among women based on (non)access to those services—opportunities largely based on class (and, relatedly, race). Hence, the debate regarding (un)motherhood (or mothers and non-mothers) and single motherhood also become entrenched in the class divide.

Though *Roe v. Wade* granted abortion rights to women, the state was not required to fund these services—leaving poor women with limited options to pursue these opportunities (Raider, 2005). Thus, barriers to access help explain inconsistencies between increased reproductive rights and rising birth rates among unmarried women. As a result, Akerlof et al. (1996) argue social scientists of the time focused on black unwed birthrates (despite higher rates among unwed whites) when arguing that generous federal welfare benefits and the decline of the marriageability of black men (often as a result of job shortages linked to de-unionisation)[10] were responsible for high black birthrates. Furthermore, their data shows that welfare benefits fell throughout the 1970s–80s—when unwed births rose—explaining only a small fraction of the increase in unwed births. Therefore, according to Akerlof et al. (1996, p. 279), reproductive rights and unwed birth rates increased owing to the "erosion of the custom of shotgun marriages", producing a "reproductive technology shock". In short, cultural shifts in attitudes towards sexual behavior via access to reproductive rights *and* services were responsible for the decline in marriage rates, the rise in unwed motherhood and (arguably) lower stigma towards single mothers. Nevertheless, this stigma decreased largely in relation to white women, but not necessarily black women.

The preoccupation with unwed black mothers becomes evident when examining the relationship between (non)access and class. For although women gained reproductive rights during this era, the framing of the (un) motherhood debate evolved to centre on concerns of (un)desired pregnancy/ motherhood among white middle-class women—one that usually abandoned the plight of poor (and racial minority) women. As Rowley (2015, p. 16) argues, the class divide was evident in that:

> those with access to private physicians were more likely to obtain a[n] [abortion] procedure than poorer patients who relied on municipal or religious-based hospitals. [Specifically], Catholic hospitals almost never officially allowed abortions, even when women's lives were at stake.
>
> (2015, p. 16)

However, (non)access to medical services proves to be a more significant issue for poor women in other ways. For example, lacking access to reproductive services *and* penalisation practices within those services were more severe for poor women of colour (Schoen, 2005). For instance, although the women's movement aligned with support for welfare services for poor women, concerns regarding 'welfare abuse' (or use by the black populace) did not necessarily dissipate during the era but evolved into forced and/or coerced sterilisation. These was rationalised as "eugenic and [for] welfare cost purposes", but were, in fact, (racial) population control measures (Rowley, 2015, p. 63). Because these issues centred on black and minority statuses (as opposed to only 'poor women'), these issues were largely ignored by white middle-class women (and the state) (Allen, 1977). Therefore, it is within the practices of (non)access and reproductive penalisation that class (and race) are more readily seen or *visible* (Worby & Ally, 2013). This relationship aids in understanding how the trauma produced by these practices is felt in the present day (Athanasiou et al., 2008).

Thus, the combination of the courts' ruling in denying state financial support to fund reproductive services (see Hyde Amendment)[11], the white-middle class framing of the (un)motherhood debate, along with the states' hysteria (or 'concerns') regarding 'welfare abuse,' are responsible for the penalised efforts and/or outcomes (such as population control measures) and medical non-access experienced by mothers of colour (specifically, unwed black mothers). These influences and interventions show that access to reproductive services relied heavily on economic and state infrastructure (Rowley, 2015). The availability of these services produced dual results: the lack of access to reproductive services suppressed (and thus oppressed) poor women and women of colour, while simultaneously ensuring continued access to reproductive rights and services to white (middle-class) women.

As such, the outcome perpetuates a "collective nostalgia" (Cootnz, 1992 [2016]) founded on social injustice in the prior era, which evolved further into an intergenerational injustice during this time (Luhmann, 2011). White women become connected with access to (un)motherhood while unwed and/ or single motherhood becomes inextricably tied to black women (albeit with a more *visible* layer of class dimensions). And yet, both groups of women (white, black) inherit more than privilege and/or oppression. They inherit a legacy. White women are linked with a perpetuation of the past stamped onto the

The Legacy of Stigma   81

virtues of the (present) self/group such that past and present representations cannot be "neatly cleaved from one another" (Luhmann, 2011, p. 132), while black women are further constrained by a constructed identity founded on imposed traumatic events (Athanasiou et al., 2008).

As the era morphs into the 21st century (the 1990s–2010s), a democratic and (seemingly) more liberal state appears to enshrine the country. In this respect, the single mother debate also becomes framed by more liberal ideologies, specifically "choice" parenthood. In this respect, the spectrum of motherhood is increasingly pulled in different directions: a portion of white women abandon marriages to pursue "single by choice" motherhood, and a reinvigorated focus on black women typecasts them as "welfare queens" who (not ironically) practice the same ideologies.

The privileged/oppressed binary among women as single mothers, separated (and imbued) by a historical legacy of race and class disparities which further substantiate the legacy of stigma among single mothers.

1990s–2010s: "Choice" Motherhood: (White) Single Mothers and the (Black) "Welfare Queen"

As the country endorsed a new democratic president in the 1990s, an explicit (re)focus on the middle-class American family dominated the political and social landscape (Weaver, 2000). The sentimentality of (neo)liberal ideologies is evident in social policy, specifically among tax cuts for the middle- and working- classes, with concerted efforts to limit welfare benefits for the poor (Carcasson, 2006). Informed by historical archetypes in welfare policy, spending cuts directed towards the poor were rationalised to prevent (imagined) further 'welfare abuse' by "welfare queen[s]" or women seen as the "dominant mother responsible for the moral degeneracy of America" (Hancock, 2004, p. 98).[12] Collins (1991, pp. 67–78) argues the "welfare queen" represents a "controlling image" in which "cultural narratives" (Lubiano, 1992) embody dominant discourse, values and beliefs. As a result, the "welfare queen" was (re)used by President Clinton as an impetus to rationalise the "War on Poverty" to garner public support for spending cuts among the poor (Carcasson, 2006; Hancock, 2004; Weaver, 2000).

Despite the cultural preoccupation with single mothers as "welfare queens" and recent welfare cuts, single motherhood rates had risen among *both* white and black women (Akerlof et al., 1996)—except with a newly added caveat of "single mothers by choice" (or SMCs) prominent among white middle-class women (Bock, 2000). This new trend revealed several things. Without the previous social pressures to have a "shotgun marriage" combined with conservative anti-abortion rhetoric (Carbone & Cahn, 2014) and women's lack of interest in "marrying down" (or marrying someone of a lower social class) (Schwartz et al., 2016), a portion of women abandoned marriage and entered parenthood as single mothers. However, as a result of the historical legacy or trauma (Athanasiou et al., 2008) attached to the single mother trope, these women entered motherhood "inherit[ing] the stigma of their poorer sisters" (Bock, 2000, p. 63). As Coontz (1992[2016]) argued, it is the presence of middle-class white women in the single motherhood debate that challenged discourse regarding 'legitimate' families—not the presence of black women (despite variations in social class).

The language of "single by choice" is distancing and disingenuous. As Bock (2000, p. 64) states, it exemplifies "entitlement to make this [single mother] decision", yet also implies a "single-parent hierarchy" in which other mothers "do not enter single motherhood by choice, or at least, not by a choice as responsible as their own". The effect is to separate SMCs from "allegedly [mothers] who are the 'real' problem" or, in other words, "welfare queens". Thus, even the construction of these white mothers contributes to the *invisibility* of *othered* single mothers while simultaneously making their single-mother debate *visible* within the social and political landscape. As a result, the *(in)visibility* of single mothers becomes further ensconced in the notion of 'legitimate' families, with white mothers' 'choosing' their lone motherhood and black mothers experiencing it by consequence. This affective language, derived from a nostalgic past, evidences how notions of (il)legitimacy transmuted into the present debate.[13]

Although SMCs represent a "transgression" (Beasley, 2011) against their historical backdrop, this is at the cost of distancing themselves from notions assigned to blacks—an approach that ultimately undermines the former group's liberal pursuits. As Diprose (2006, p. 440) argues, unless privileged groups transform their heritage, the future will be a "reproduction of one's [existing] heritage, and hence no future at all". Therefore, any redirection of "lines of flight" (Winslade, 2009) requires "transgressions" that remove one's privilege (Beasley, 2011), entailing questioning and being responsive to their legacies and their contributions to others (Diprose, 2006). Historically, middle-class white women have been framed as maintaining American "family values" (Cootnz, 1992[2016]). However, as they entered single motherhood (as SMC, or *othered*), they encountered the legacy of stigma attached to single mothers—one which they actively avoided and to which they had (inadvertently) previously contributed. As a result, the participation of SMCs provided an additional dimension to the motherhood debate. The previous bifurcated spectrum of motherhood which encompassed two opposing positions—(non-poor) white married mothers and (poor) black unwed mothers—now included a hierarchal element complementary to the SMC constituents. Thus, motherhood was reframed yet again and, consequently, so was American "womanhood".

As women attempt to navigate the (re)framing of the (single) motherhood debate, resulting in culture shifts from the 1990s–2010s, these trends continue onward into the present day—one in which mothers (single or otherwise) must contend with a concocted legacy in which race, class and gender disparities are intertwined. The intersection of these historical underpinnings, which perpetuated intergenerational social injustice in this era (Luhmann, 2011), is carried forward and further defines the context of the next era.

2010s–Present: The Construction of the 'Single Mother'— Outcomes of a Legacy of Injustice

The history outlined, specifically the legacy of injustice tied to the single mother, also details a legacy of stigma, represented by the historical (re) construction of black illegitimacy throughout the 20th and 21st centuries. This is a history founded on the backdrop of slavery and substantiated by social and political (il)legitimacy, economic (non)access and social intolerance—factors presently evident in social stigma towards single mothers and the institutional discrimination still endured (Smith, 2019).[14] More importantly, these events illustrate that the construction of the single mother is founded on a traumatic past, which marks her identity as traumatic by default (Athanasiou et al., 2008).

Not surprisingly, this legacy also coincides with its constructed antithesis, *ideal* women/mothers—in other words, middle-class (coupled) white women/parents. In this respect, unearthing the legacy of idealised mothers ensures her *visibility*, revealing an idealised version of femininity (Connell, 1987) or "emphasized feminine". As Connell (1987) argues, this figure is not real but imagined—evident in its reinforced construction. And though she is a construction, the idealised mother or "middle-class female identity" (Gross, 2005) defines the 'good mother', despite any actualities. In doing so, she inherits social prestige while perpetuating the construction of the idealised American mother as herself (see Andrada, 2019). SMCs fail to maintain this construction and are not successful in distancing themselves from the stigma of *othered* single mothers (such as black women) as unpartnered mothers. This occurs despite the recent rise of unwed parenthood among SMCs and a noted decline among archetypal single mothers (that is, non-white single mothers).[15]

This is noteworthy because the term intersectionality suggests that positionality informs current experiences, in which identities are a product of "status characteristics" (Collins, 1991; Cottom, 2018). And although intersectionality aids in explaining an aspect of the continued stigma towards non-white single mothers, on its own, it is insufficient in accounting for the experiences of white (middle-class) single mothers. For instance, research on American middle-class single mothers discovered prejudice, discrimination and stigma, because of of mothers' being unpartnered (Andrada, 2022). This finding highlights 'conflicting' intersectional identities of prestige and stigma. Stigma was maintained *despite* intersectional privilege (such as being middle-class, non-black and non-minority), while simultaneously reinforced by oppressed intersectional identities (or being a black woman). And yet, all these

84 Amy Andrada

single mothers were *othered*, owing to their 'single-mother' status, regardless of intersectional privilege(s) (Andrada, 2019). In short, the legacy of stigma of being a 'single mother' was the source of their discrimination.

Like other scholars, Ahmed (2014) argues that the "politics of disgust" are responsible for the lingering historical subjective reality with which under-privileged and/or minority groups continually contend. Thus explaining—as with intersectionality—how the "stickiness" of "disgust' perpetuates past their origin and/or factual realities. However, such approaches underscore the power of stigma (Link & Phelan, 2001) as a social artefact. The social construction of the single mother (or unwed black mother) produces a legacy of stigma frames the single mother group and their experiences as a whole—despite any hierarchal placements in the present.

Thus, contrary to any intersectional privileges (white, middle-class and so on), all members inherit a legacy of injustice that outperforms and/or overshadows any 'privileges' derived from other intersecting identities. In theory, this explains the unsuccessful distancing of SMCs in the single motherhood debate. Magee and Galinsky (2008) argue 'steepness' exists within parallel hierarchal placements, which may explain reduced stigmatis-ing experiences among non-black single mothers and substantiate a main-tained stigma for all group members.[16] In this respect, the legacy of stigma among present-day single mothers is founded on the legacy of injustice based on the historical construction of the single mother, set against a nostalgia myth of the American family (or *ideal* coupled mothers) (Cootnz, 1992 [2016]). As a result, this construction demonstrates *both* mothers as fabrications, with the former embodying a legacy of oppression and the latter a legacy of prestige.

Unearthing the historical injustice of single mothers in this chapter or gypsy/traveleer women in the following one (see Chapter 6), requires a feminist lens (D'Ignazio & Klein, 2018) and (re)examination of historical accounts. Such a process unearths "hidden histories" (Worby & Ally, 2013, p. 461) by making the invisible visible. With regard to American mother-hood, exposing its constructed production renders visible both a legacy of stigma attached to single mothers and a legacy of privilege tied to the *ideal* mother—thus explaining the latter's preferential status in U.S. society (Cherlin, 2004). Through this analysis, both legacies can be known as tied to each other over time. Thus, remembering a more "complete" history may dismantle our "collective nostalgia" (Cootnz, 1992[2016]) enabling us to generate new meanings for ourselves, each other and future women (Athanasiou et al., 2008; Johnson, 2005).

Notes

1 It is important to note coupled lesbians mothers in this argument. As coupledom is framed through a heteronormative lens, lesbian mothers are still subjected to this

The Legacy of Stigma   85

lens, particularly in maintaining a coupled-nuclear family unit (Matapanyane, 2016). Stigma experienced by gay and lesbian families owing to sexuality and/or homophobia is arguably a testament to the heteronormative conceptual foundations of partnering and family (Hopkins et al., 2013).

2 'Impoverished' is based on a nuclear family standard of two adults and two children at <$25,750 in 2019.

3 U.S. Census Bureau (2019a, 2019b) identifies the income distributions of female householders with children under age 18 (and no other adult). Collectively, these data indicate the group is largely situated between working-class and lower-middle-class incomes for the 2019 year.

4 Estimates ranged between one-quarter and one-third of divorced and/or separated women enter poverty.

5 Prior to World War II, unwed mothers were generally considered to be "proper mothers" to their "bastard children", despite the lack of husbands/partners (Solinger, 1991).

6 Specifically, "not-mothers" were unwed mothers encouraged to give up their illegitimate babies for adoption. In exchange, these women were 'rehabilitated' back into their communities.

7 Bear in mind that economic (non)access for women may have significantly contributed to shotgun marriage trends during this period (for example, see arguments regarding the Equal Pay Act of 1963 via the Supreme Court Historical Society, 1971).

8 These trends align with the Equal Pay Act of 1963, the Supreme Court legalising birth control for unmarried people in 1972 and abortion rights in 1973.

9 Akerlof et al. (1996) argue that from the 1960s–80s, births for unmarried women roughly doubled for whites but fell by 5–10 per cent for blacks.

10 Arguably, rises in unemployment only accounted for a fraction of the shrinking black marriage pool (Akerlof et al., 1996).

11 The Hyde Amendment (1976) barred the use of federal funds to pay for abortion in most cases. As a result, women could only obtain an abortion based on funds and/or (limited) services available; a landmark decision that overwhelmingly affected poor women and women of colour (Rowley, 2015).

12 For example, see Hays (2004) regarding the "welfare queen" popularised by President Ronald Regan—a perspective which folds into President Bill Clinton's era.

13 As the historical language of 'unpartnered mothers' has changed over time (for example, see changing terms like unwed, single, lone, SMC and so on.), the stigma directed towards them has lessened but has been maintained. This is evident in the re-labeling of the group and the group's tendency to distance itself from the stigma associated with being a 'single mother' (see Bock, 2000). The central issue maintained in each of these terminologies is their disassociation from a male partner within the family. This reveals that stigmatised and idealised versions of American motherhood are not strictly founded on mothering but centred on the male presence within families (see Andrada, 2019). A male presence is a notion honoured as central to the nuclear family within the American consciousness, evident in social attitudes and family policy in the United States.

14 Understanding stigma and its functions are at the heart of this analysis. In this respect, stigma persists regardless of choice and/or consequence of limited options. Stigma results from deviation from normative ideals (Link & Phelan, 2013). Regardless of the social position of women (including black women) raising children outside of romantic partnerships, these women tend to endure stigma as unpartnered mothers because they operate as mothers outside the idealised partnered-mother norm, whatever their personal views. This reinforcement maintains

idealised mother[hood] as partnered, purposely discounting women's autonomy in support of this social norm.

15 See for example, Livingston and Brown's (2014) arguments regarding declines in unwed birthrates among poor/women of colour.

16 Magee and Galinsky (2008) argue within rungs of a hierarchy are levels of "steepness" in which the "intensity" of privilege and/or oppression may be identified within inter- and/or intra- related groups and/or groups within similar "levels".

References

Ahmed, S. (2014). *Cultural politics of emotion.* Edinburgh: Edinburgh University Press.

Akerlof, G. A., Yellen, J. L. & Katz, M. L. (1996). An analysis of out-of-wedlock childbearing in the United States. *The Quarterly Journal of Economics,* 111(2), 277–317.

Allen, J. E. (1977). An appearance of genocide: a review of governmental family-planning program policies. *Perspectives in Biology and Medicine, 20*(2), 300–306.

Andrada, A. (2019). 'Woman' and (Un)Partnered Mother: An Intersectional Perspective, In Buchanan, F. & Zufferey, C. (Ed.), *Intersections of Mothering: Feminist Accounts.* Abingdon: Routledge.

Andrada, A. (2022). The Scarlett Letter Effect: Evidence of a Single Mother Narrative (unpublished doctoral dissertation). University of Edinburgh, United Kingdom.

Athanasiou, H. & Yannakopoulos, K. (2008). Towards a New Epistemology: The "Affective Turn." *Historein,* 8, 5–16.

Badger, E. (2014, December 18). The unbelievable rise of single motherhood in America over the last 50 years. *The Washington Post.* Retrieved October 22, 2021 from www.washingtonpost.com/news/wonk/wp/2014/12/18/the-unbelievable-rise-of-single-motherhood-in-america-over-the-last-50-years.

Bartky, S. L. (2012). *Femininity and Domination: Studies in the Phenomenology of Oppression.* New York: Routledge.

Beasley, C. (2011). Libidinous politics: Heterosex, 'transgression' and social change. *Australian Feminist Studies,* 26(67), 25–40.

Best, J. (2001). *Damned Lies and Statistics: Untangling Numbers from the Media, Politicians, and Activists.* Berkeley, CA: University of California Press.

Bennett, N. G., Bloom, D. E. & Craig, P. H. (1989). The divergence of black and white marriage patterns. *American Journal of Sociology,* 95(3), 692–722.

Bock, J. D. (2000). Doing the Right Thing? Single Mothers by Choice and the Struggle for Legitimacy. *Gender & Society,* 14(1), 62–86.

Brady, D., Finnigan, R. M. & Hübgen, S. (2017). Rethinking the Risks of Poverty: A framework for analyzing prevalences and penalties. *American Journal of Sociology,* 123 (3), 740–786.

Carbone, J. & Cahn, N. (2014). *Marriage Markets: How Inequality is Remaking the American Family.* Oxford: Oxford University Press.

Carcasson, M. (2006). Ending Welfare as We know It: President Clinton and the Rhetorical Trans formation of the Anti-welfare Culture. *Rhetoric & Public Affairs,* 9(4), 655–692.

Cherlin, A. J. (2004). The Deinstitutionalization of American Marriage. *Journal of Marriage and Family,* 66(4), 848–861.

Collins, P. H. (1991). *Black Feminist Thought: Knowledge, Consciousness, and the Politics of Empowerment.* New York: Routledge.

Connell, R. (1987). *Gender and Power: Society, the Person and Sexual Politics*. Cambridge: John Wiley & Sons.

Coontz, S. (1992[2016]). *The Way We Never Were: American Families and the Nostalgia Trap*. New York: Basic Books/Hachette.

Cottom, T. M. (2018). *Thick: And Other Essays*. New York: The New Press.

Crandall, C. S. & Eshleman, A. (2003). A Justification-Suppression Model of the Expression and Experience of Prejudice. *Psychological Bulletin*, 129(3), 414–446.

D'Emilio, J. & E. Freedman. (1988). *Intimacy Matters: A History of Sexuality in America*. New York: Harper & Row.

D'Ignazio, C. & Klein, L. (2018). Chapter One: Bring Back the Bodies. *Data feminism*. Retrieved October 14, 2021 from https://mitpressonpubpub.mitpress.mit.edu/pub/zrlj0jqb.

Diprose, R. (2006). Derrida and the Extraordinary Responsibility of Inheriting the Future-to-Come. *Social Semiotics*, 16(3), 435–447.

Durkheim, É. (1894) Les Règles de la Méthode Sociologique. *Revue Philosophique de la France et de l'Étranger*, 37, 465–498.

Goffman, E. (1951). Symbols of class status. *The British Journal of Sociology*, 2(4), 294–304.

Gross, N. (2005). The Detraditionalization of Intimacy Reconsidered. *Sociological Theory*, 23(3), 286–311.

Haller, M. (1981). Marriage, women, and social stratification: A theoretical critique. *American Journal of Sociology*, 86(4), 766–795.

Hancock, A. M. (2004). *The Politics of Disgust: The Public Identity of the Welfare Queen*. New York: NYU Press.

Hays, Sharon (2004). *Flat Broke with Children: Women in the Age of Welfare Reform*. New York: Oxford University Press.

Hemez, P. & Washington, C. (2021, April). Percentage and Number of Children Living With Two Parents Has Dropped Since 1968. Washington, DC: United States Census Bureau. Retrieved October 24, 2022 from www.census.gov/library/stories/2021/04/number-of-children-living-only-with-their-mothers-has-doubled-in-past-50-years.html.

Hogendoorn, B., Leopold, T. & Bol, T. (2020). Divorce and Diverging Poverty Rates: A Risk-and-Vulnerability Approach. *Journal of Marriage and Family*, 82(3), 1089–1109.

Hopkins, J. J., Sorensen, A. & Taylor, V. (2013). Same-Sex Couples, Families, and Marriage: Embracing and Resisting Heteronormativity 1. *Sociology Compass*, 7(2), 97–110.

Hymowitz, K. S. (2005, Summer). The Black Family: 40 Years of Lies. *City Journal*, 15 (3). Manhattan Institution for Policy Research. Retrieved October 28, 2021 from www.city-journal.org/html/black-family-40-years-lies-12872.html.

Johnson, A. G. (2005). *The Gender Knot: Unraveling Our Patriarchal Legacy*. Philadelphia, PA: Temple University Press.

Kessler, S. J. & McKenna, W. (1985). *Gender: An Ethnomethodological Approach*. Chicago, IL: University of Chicago Press.

Kramer, S. (2019, December 12). US Has World's Highest Rate of Children Living in Single Parent Households. Washington, DC: Pew Research Center. Retrieved October 4, 2021 from www.pewresearch.org/fact-tank/2019/12/12/u-s-children-more-likely-than-children-in-other-countries-to-live-with-just-one-parent.

Link, B.G. and Phelan, J.C. (2013). Labeling and Stigma. In Aneshensel, C. S., Phelan, J. C. & Bierman, A. (Eds) *Handbook of the Sociology of Mental Health. Handbooks of Sociology and Social Research.* Dordrecht, NE: Springer.

Link, B. G. & Phelan, J. C. (2001). Conceptualizing stigma. *Annual Review of Sociology,* 27(1), 363–385.

London, R. A. (2000). The Dynamics of Single Mothers' Living Arrangements. *Population Research and Policy Review,* 19(1), 73–96.

Livingston, G. (2018, April 25). The Changing profile of Unmarried Parents. Washington, DC: Pew Research Center. Retrieved November 11, 2021 from www.pewresearch.org/social-trends/2018/04/25/the-changing-profile-of-unmarried-parents.

Livingston, G. & Brown, A. (2014). Birth Rate for Unmarried Women Declining for First Time in Decades. Washington, DC: Pew Research Center. Retrieved November 13, 2021 www.pewresearch.org/fact-tank/2014/08/13/birth-rate-for-unmarried-women-declining-for-first-time-in-decades.

Lu, Y. C., Walker, R., Richard, P. & Younis, M. (2020). Inequalities in Poverty and Income Between Single Mothers and Fathers. *International Journal of Environmental Research and Public Health,* 17(1), 135–148.

Lubiano, W. (1992). Black ladies, welfare queens and state minstrels: ideological war by narrative means." In T. Morrison (Ed.), *Race-ing justice , en-gendering power: Essays on Anita Hill, Clarence Thomas and the construction of social identity.* New York: Pantheon, pp. 323–363.

Luhmann, S. (2011). Filming Familial Secrets: Approaching and Avoiding Legacies of Nazi Perpetration. *New German Critique,* 38(1), 115–134.

Magee, J. C. & Galinsky, A. D. (2008). 8 Social Hierarchy: The Self-Reinforcing Nature of Power and Status. *Academy of Management Annals,* 2(1), 351–398.

Matapanyane, M. (2016). *Motherhood and Single-Lone Parenting: A 21st Century Perspective.* Bradford, ON: Demeter Press.

May, V. (2004). Narrative Identity and the Re-Conceptualization of Lone Motherhood. *Narrative Inquiry,* 14(1), 169–189.

May, V. (2008). On Being a 'Good' Mother: The Moral Presentation of Self in Written Life Stories. *Sociology,* 42(3), 470–486.

McLanahan, S., Garfinkel, I., Waldfogel, J. & Edin, K. (2019). Fragile Families and Child Wellbeing Study, 1998–2017. *Inter-university Consortium for Political and Social Research.*

Raider, D. L. (2005). Abortion restrictions: "Undue burden" to women and society. (Doctoral dissertation). Retrieved October 8, 2021 from ProQuest Dissertations & Theses Global (Order No. 3166967).

Raley, R. K., Sweeney, M. M. & Wondra, D. (2015). The growing racial and ethnic divide in US marriage patterns. *The Future of Children/Center for the Future of Children, the David and Lucile Packard Foundation,* 25(2), 89.

Rowley, S. B. (2015). "No Middle Ground": The Rise of Abortion Politics, 1960s-1980s. (Doctoral dissertation). Retrieved October 6, 2021 from ProQuest Dissertations & Theses Global (Order No. 3716258).

Schoen, J. (2005). *Choice & Coercion: Birth Control, Sterilization, and Abortion in Public Health and Welfare.* Chapel Hill, NC: University of North Carolina Press.

Schwartz, C. R., Zeng, Z. & Xie, Y. (2016). Marrying up by Marrying Down: Status Exchange Between Social Origin and Education in the United States. *Sociological Science*, 3, 1003–1027.

Semuels, A. (2015, December 1). How Poor Single Moms Survive. *The Atlantic*. Retrieved October 9, 2021 from www.theatlantic.com/business/archive/2015/12/how-poor-single-moms-survive/418158.

Smith, M. H. (2019). Reproduction in the Welfare State: Public Spending for Family Planning and Abortion Services in the United States. (Doctoral dissertation). Retrieved October 30, 2021 from ProQuest Dissertations & Theses Global (Order No. 13886757).

Solinger, R. A. (1991). "Wake up Little Susie": Single Pregnancy and Race in the Pre-Roe v. Wade Era, 1945–1965. (Doctoral dissertation). Retrieved October 26, 2021 from ProQuest Dissertations & Theses Global (Order No. 9130374).

Stanley, L. (2008). *Mourning Become…: Post/Memory and Commemoration of the Concentration Camps of the South African War 1899–1902*. New York: Manchester University Press.

Supreme Court Of The United States. (1971) U.S. Reports: *Reed v. Reed*, 404 U.S. 71.

U.S. Department of Health and Human Services. (2019). HSS Poverty Guidelines. Washington, DC Retrieved October 29, 2021 from https://aspe.hhs.gov/topics/poverty-economic-mobility/poverty-guidelines.

U.S. Census Bureau. (2014). Historical Living Arrangement of Children: Children Under 18 Years Living With Mother Only, by Marital Status of Mother, 1960–2014. Retrieved October 23, 2022 from www.census.gov/data/tables/time-series/demo/families/children.html.

U.S. Census Bureau. (2016, November 17). The Majority of Children Live with Two Parents (CB16–192). Retrieved October 21, 2022 from www.census.gov/newsroom/press-releases/2016/cb16–192.html.

U.S. Census Bureau. (2017). America's Families and Living Arrangements: One-parent Unmarried Family Groups With Own Children Under 18, By Marital Status Of The Reference Person (Table FG6). Retrieved October 11, 2021 from www.census.gov/data/tables/2017/demo/families/cps-2017.html.

U.S. Census Bureau. (2019a). Presence of Children Under 18 Years Old by Total Money Income in 2019, Type of Household, Race and Hispanic Origin of Householder (HINC-04). Retrieved October 22, 2022 from www.census.gov/data/tables/time-series/demo/income-poverty/cps-hinc/hinc-04.2019.html.

U.S. Census Bureau. (2019b). Income Limits for Each Fifth and Top 5 Percent of All Households: 1967 to 2019 (Table H-1). Retrieved October 21, 2021 from www.census.gov/data/tables/time-series/demo/income-poverty/historical-income-households.html.

Walker, J., Crawford, K. & Taylor, F. (2008). Listening to Children: Gaining a Perspective of the Experiences of Poverty and Social Exclusion from Children and Young People of Single-Parent Families. *Health and Social Care in the Community*, 16 (4), 429–436.

Washington, J. (2010, November 7). Blacks struggle with 72 percent unwed mothers rate: Debate is Growing in and Outside the Black Community on How to Address the Rising Issue. *NBCNews*. Retrieved October 13, 2021 from www.nbcnews.com/id/wbna39993685.

Weaver, R. K. (2000). *Ending Welfare As We Know It*. Washington, DC: Brookings Institution Press.

Winslade, J. (2009). Tracing Lines of Flight: Implications of the Work of Gilles Deleuze for Narrative Practice. *Family Process*, 48(3), 332–346.

Worby, E. & Ally, S. (2013). The Disappointment of Nostalgia: Conceptualising Cultures of Memory in Contemporary South Africa. *Social Dynamics*, 39(3), 457–480.

Part II

Chapter 6

Talking of Silence
Young Scottish Gypsy/Traveller Women in Scotland

Geetha Marcus

Introduction

Building on the analysis of other ongoing manifestations of the living legacies of power and injustice in this book, this chapter foregrounds the oppression—seen and unseen, overt and disguised—which shapes the lives of Gypsy/Travellers in Scotland,[1] and in the lives of young Gypsy/Traveller women in particular.[2] It begins by initially situating the study which produced the data for this work and providing some background and context on Gypsy/Travellers in Scotland.

Little is known about Gypsy/Travellers (Dawson, 2007). Traditionally known as the 'pilgrims of the mist' (Stewart, 2008), this chapter seeks to reveal the unrelenting legacies of silencing linked to erasure, misrepresentation, denial and, of course, violent suppression from the dominant society, which has parallels with Kaur's approach (in Chapter 4) on honour-based crimes in South Asian communities. However, Gypsy/Travellers experience the legacies of silencing and also operationalise silence as a means of strategic resistance, self-exclusion and protection from the majority culture and population in Scotland. Perceived as 'folk devils' in the collective public imagination, they exercise their 'weak power', as Belton (2013) argues, to exclude the included. Silence becomes a way of communicating.

The tapestry of their narratives is then placed within a black feminist and postcolonial frame, in order to show that much of what they experience are part of ongoing colonising processes (Beasley and Papadelos, 2024; Waites, Chapter 12 of this volume). A discussion outlining why and how a postcolonial, intersectional perspective is employed is offered and linked to the theme of "living legacy as power" (Beasley and Papadelos, 2024). Additionally, the chapter points out similarities between the experience of Gypsy/Travellers and other racialised experiences. The remainder of the chapter then turns to the different forms of silence that arise in relation to Gypsy/Travellers, against the backdrop of historical oppressions and the shapeshifting processes of dominance that continue to endure.

DOI: 10.4324/9781003311928-8

The chapter is in keeping with the central theme of this book—that as social analysts we must try to understand the complex ghosts of the past in order to make sense of how they intricately haunt the present (Beasley and Papadelos, 2024; Gordon, 2008). Virdee (2019, p. 1) contends that "viewed from the marginalised vantage point, the history of the modern world has been a catastrophe marked by land dispossession, genocide, enslavement, forced migration, structural discrimination, everyday racism and grieving for lives made unlivable". As racialised outsiders in Scotland, the lives of Gypsy/Travellers have been marked by such oppression, but as Heuss (2000, p. 52) explains, their cultures also "expose and provoke the pathologies of European culture".

Situating the Study

The chapter draws upon an original study of the educational experiences of Scottish Gypsy/Traveller girls and seeks to centre the girls' voices and perspectives, initially considered through a series of papers and publications produced during the course of my research (Marcus, 2013a, 2013b, 2014a, 2014b, 2015a, 2015b, 2016). These works arose in the context of a continuing lack of significant data and scholarly works on the lived experiences of Scottish Gypsy/ Travellers and of young Gypsy/Traveller women in particular. The writings that exist are mostly anthropological and historical (Murray, 1875; Wilson and Leighton, 1885; Mackenzie, 1883; MacRitchie, 1894; McCormick, 1907; Rehfisch and Rehfisch, 1975; Williamson, 1994; Neat, 1996; Kenrick, 1993; Reid 1997) or about the communities as a whole (Clark, 2001, 2006, 2008, 2013; Clark and Taylor, 2014; Shubin, 2010).

The research outlined here draws primarily on the lives of 17 young Gypsy/ Traveller women aged 12 to 21 and was at first focused upon their educational experiences in Scottish schools (Marcus, 2019). The young women had different family, living circumstances, attendance and achievements in school and came from a wide variety of areas in Scotland. This qualitative, inductive study gave space for multiple voices gathered via in-depth semi-structured interviews. The interviews included those with the young women and over 30 stakeholders in education, healthcare, third sector and government agencies and were generated alongside a review of legislation, policy documents and guidelines.

The overarching aim of the study was to improve the Scottish mainstream understanding of Gypsy/Travellers in Scotland. However, their previously unheard stories exposed the need to examine their lives within Scottish schools, families and communities. The study revealed that there were ongoing and distinct legacies of oppression, injustice and misuse of power within colonising processes that continue to this day. In keeping with black feminist interrogation of such oppression and power relations, the study also raised and questioned possibilities for transformational and meaningful change (Crenshaw, 1991; Collins, 2000; Yuval-Davis, 2011; Bilge, 2014).

Postcolonial and Black Feminism Tools for Understanding and Action

Colonising Processes as Living Legacies

In keeping with postcolonial thinking, I assert that colonial exploitation and processes are political decisions and have several common features from the past that have not only impacted on the present but continue to exist. Following Hall (2021, p. 3) "[t]he political| is understood here in terms of the different modalities of power (cultural, moral and intellectual, as well as economic and political); the play of power within and between different sites [or communities]". In previous work (Marcus, 2021) I describe power relations as a sort of "shapeshifting beast" that can be obvious, overt, violent, but also silent, passive, hidden (see also Trepagnier, 2010). This view of power can be employed to reveal the complexities of colonialism as well as patterns, conflicts, contradictions and tensions in the intersecting experiences of colonisers and colonised which play out to this day", in the UK and beyond (Marcus, 2021). Colonial histories are not contained to a particular period or particular cultures. Indeed, certain features of colonial regimes such as racialised othering can be seen in a variety of times and locations and as such provide an exemplary means to consider the language of 'living legacies'.

Relations of power in colonialism are crucially concerned to 'divide and rule', to designate those who belong and are humanised and those that do not and consequently are de-humanised (Marcus, 2021). Indeed, racialised differentiation is a key element of the continuing existence of colonialism. Lopez's book *White by Law* (2006) offers an account of the impact of racialisation enshrined in law which captures the deeply rooted character of the project of 'othering'. A postcolonial frame thus problematises power dynamics in the systems and structures that influence our lives and, as the term is consciously political, enables interrogation of both macro and micro levels of power. However, postcolonialism is a framework that also goes beyond the racialisation of others. Issues of race intersect with other modes of social oppression.

Here post colonial thinking connects with black feminist approaches and the terminology of intersectionality in ways that are useful for understanding and analysis of the experiences of Gypsy/Traveller women. Indeed, a combined methodological approach in my study was productive of rich, nuanced and multi-layered data about their lived experiences. Intersectionality is key to this combined approach as it "allows us to see women in their particular context, without minimising the effects of differences between different forms of subjugations or concealing one form in another" (Marcus, 2019, p. 113). Mirza (2015, p. 4) asserts that intersectionality "valorises [localised], situated experience which is at the heart of black feminist epistemology".

Black Feminism, intersectionality and Living Legacies

Race is a crucial element of black feminism, but black feminists argue that in order to understand race, the intersecting vectors of gender, class, sexuality and other social locations, need to be explored. Hence, the term *intersectionality* becomes crucial (Crenshaw, 1989). Though intersectionality is inextricably linked to understandings of race, it brings into focus an expanded range of heterogeneous modes of power. In this context, African American feminist Audre Lorde argues "there is no such thing as a single-issue struggle because we do not live single-issue lives" (2007, p. 138). She explains that we "cannot afford the luxury of fighting one form of oppression only" (Lorde, 1983 p.9). In the same vein, I note that black feminism is a multi-dimensional, inclusive framing which aims to consciously disrupt existing relations of power and in the process allows for a 'reframing' of historicity, narratives and perspectives (Marcus, 2021). Furthermore, Mirza (2015) and Bilge (2014) argue that black feminism is "a political challenge to white supremacy in feminist politics and feminist social science" (cited in Marcus, 2019, p. 108).

In this setting, Carbado et al. (2013, p. 303) maintain that intersectionality is today viewed as "a method and a disposition, a heuristic and analytic tool". I suggest that it has enabled representation of black women's struggles but has also journeyed beyond to involve other local, national and international efforts for change (Marcus, 2019, p. 112). Carbado et al. similarly affirm that "actors of different genders, ethnicities and sexual orientation have moved inter-sectionality to engage an ever-widening range of experiences and structures of power" (2013, p. 305). Analysing the narratives and lived experiences of young Gypsy/Traveller women in my study involved using a multidimensional fem-inist approach which considered colonialising processes as well as black femin-ism and the term intersectionality. Such an approach reveals the impact of living legacies of continuing and unrelenting racialised and gendered violence on them. However, as this chapter will show, such legacies do not inevitably generate ongoing subordination. In other words, Gypsy/Traveller women are not just 'victims'.

Gypsy/Travellers in Scotland: connections and persecution

Scottish Gypsy/Travellers have lived in Scotland since the 12th century making them one of Britain's oldest nomadic communities. Divisive narra-tives peddled by mainstream media focus on unfounded myths and stereo-types and ignore positive connections between the history of Scotland and that of Gypsy/Travellers (Amnesty International, 2012b). As mentioned earlier, Gypsy/Travellers continue to be under-represented, misunderstood, or erased. However, some scholars in the field agree that "it would also be incorrect to imply that all Gypsy/Travellers suffered relentless persecution across centuries in Britain, as they have from time to time lived and worked harmoniously alongside settled populations" (Kenrick & Clark 1999, p. 51; Marcus 2019). There were, in fact periods of conversation, community and unity (Cannadine, 2013). Green (cited in Marcus, 2019, p. 43) states that "the oral traditions of Scottish Gypsy/Travellers have contributed to Scotland's national identity and its legacy; and that the history of Gypsy/Travellers is part of Scottish heritage, tradition, culture, and language". Hence, Gypsy/Travellers "are a Scotland in miniature" (Dawson, 2007, p.10). Along with Kenrick & Clark (1999) and Neat (1996), I have noted that 'there are similarities and differences between the history of Gypsy/Travellers and mainstream Scottish heritage, and the two have been necessarily and inextricably linked for centuries, as have their social relations of power. While there have close and sometimes harmonious connections between them, deep divisions are also a feature of their interactions.

Centuries of Persecution

Marked divisions propagated by unrelenting legacies of power have caused disturbing conflict, hatred and fear over centuries. Gypsy/Travellers, in common with the European Roma, have experienced multiple forms of persecution and marginality spanning centuries. These include the death penalty in the mid-16th century, deportation to the colonies, ethnic cleansing, removal of children from their parents to be sent to Australia and Canada and forced assimilation via school and healthcare programmes. Like their Roma counterparts, they have faced a demonising and dehumanising public perception as 'other' (see Marcus, 2019, p. 46). Indeed, Gupta et al. (2007, p.114) state that "indigenous peoples are among the most disadvantaged on earth, given that they are the most diverse grouping of humanity and constitute a large percentage of the global population". Like many indigenous peoples, this Celtic minority has also been colonised.

A sustained "matrix of domination" (Collins, 2000, p.18) has led to perceived cultural clashes and adversarial identities (Marcus, 2019). Clark (2001, p.24) emphasises that "the overall picture which emerges from the research is that Gypsy/Travellers are misunderstood, unheard and subject to a type of discrimination and prejudice that could be termed, specifically, 'anti-Gypsyism'". Amnesty International (2012a; 2012b; 2013, p.1) has accused the media and Scotland's 32 Local Authorities of perpetuating discrimination against Gypsy/Travellers, declaring at the time that "despite four inquiries by the Scottish Equal Opportunities Committee over the past 12 years, little or no progress has been made". There have since been more reports, inquiries, guidance on how to support and care for Gypsy/Travellers, but progress is glacial, exacerbated by the global pandemic of 2020.

Gypsy/Travellers were officially recognised as having a separate ethnic status in Scotland only as recently as 2008,[3] and granted protection under the *Race Relations Act* (1976) (Scottish Government, 2014). However, recognition of their status in law has done little to give the communities space and power

(Razack, 2002) to live as they wish. Neither have there been meaningful forms of compensation or acknowledgement for the ongoing harms associated with racialised and gendered inequalities. The impact on physical and mental welfare persists and is intergenerational.

The Impact of an Abusive Legacy in the 21st Century

A survey completed by the Minority Ethnic Carers of People Project in 2012, (see Marcus, 2019, p. 50) lists various ongoing manifestations of discrimination. For example, doctors' surgeries are still able to refuse to accept Gypsy/Travellers onto their patients' list despite there being vacancies and over 50% of Gypsy/Travellers in Scotland will have spent at least part of their lives without access to running water. According to the Equality and Human Rights Commission (2017), "the life expectancy for Gypsy/ Traveller men and women is 10 years lower than the national average. Gypsy/Traveller mothers are 20 times more likely than the rest of the population to have experienced the death of a child". Moreover, Gypsy/Traveller men appear to be particularly likely to suffer mental health issues (Minority Ethnic Carers of People Project, 2022). Annual surveys of Scottish public opinion, the *Social Attitudes Survey* (Scottish Centre for Social Research 2010, 2015) confirm that there are negative and racist views held towards Gypsy/Travellers. According to the charity, Save The Children Scotland (2005), 92 per cent of young Gypsy/Travellers in Scotland say that they have been bullied because of their racialised identity. Most of the young women I interviewed spoke of racist bullying in the primary schools they attended and as a result "excluded" themselves from mainstream secondary education as a form of protection. The life experiences of some Gypsy/Travellers in key areas—social inclusion, healthcare, accommodation, employment and education—reflect an unacceptable level of gross mistreatment and marginalisation (see also Marcus, 2019, p. 52).

Limited attempts, via laws, policies and reports, have been made to recognise the hardships Gypsy/Travellers face, aimed at re-distributing resources and challenging exclusion. However, the action stops there. Ahmed (2004) calls this "non-performativity" where the act of policy making is an end in itself. Nevertheless, participants in this study suggest that through continuing self-exclusion and electing to stay hidden and silent, they exert a measure of control leading to a form of protective self–segregation, and as Rochat (2020, p. 63) argues, strategic "self-essentialism".

Self-Exclusion for Self-Protection

Gypsy/Travellers employ a range of self-segregating strategies. They continue, for example, to live with extended family groups on local authority managed traveller sites. Women and girls are often accompanied when they leave the site. Inter-marriage of Gypsy/Traveller women with 'gadjos' (non-Travellers;

outsiders) is still considered taboo. Girls are often not enrolled in school or leave education early for their protection from "contamination" by gadjo boys and girls (Okely, 1983, 1994; Douglas, 2003). Moreover, girls still tend to be carers and home makers as having a career is discouraged. It remains the masculine role to provide for and protect family. Gypsy/Travellers tend not to share their ethnicity, address and data in surveys, to the frustration of policy makers who are viewed with suspicion. Gypsy/Travellers number approximately 4,500, according to the last Scottish national census in 2011,[4] but a more accurate figure is not known as many refuse to self-identify out of fear. The data reveals many similarities with the racialising of South Asian women and British Muslim women (Archer, 2002; Basit, 1996, 1997, Talbani and Hasanali, 2000; Emejulu, 2013). This also occurs in relation to black African communities. They, like Gypsy/Travellers, are disparaged as they live together in areas viewed by many as ghettos and continue to face significant barriers (Black Equity Organisation, 2022). Indeed, racialised assumptions generally continue to shape public perceptions and policy for various groups in the UK as is evident in the so-called 'Trojan Horse Affair '(New York Times, 2022). This telling moment arose when an anonymous letter sent to Birmingham city council in 2013 (revealed later to be a hoax) alleged a plot to take over and run local state schools according to strict Islamist principles and was then taken up by government as demonstrating that violent extremism was blossoming and used as justification to drive controversial reforms in counter-terrorism policy. While the difficulties faced by Gypsy/Travellers are by no means exclusive to them, their experience of and response to racialised marginalisation is nevertheless specific.

The Ongoing Legacy of Silence

My focus now shifts to attempting to define and illustrate the functions of silence and what is considered relevant silence as a means of outlining the particular ways in which Gypsy/Travellers have responded to their persecution (Dijk, 2008; Sbisà, 2002; Schröter, 2013). Drawing on the work of several key theorists (Ferguson, 2003; Ladson-Billings, 2009; Mirza, 2015; Schröter, 2013; Trepagnier 2010), I highlight the different forms of silence encountered throughout my research. Silence, I argue, is intricately linked with power; but silence does not necessarily imply an absence of power (Hall, 1991; Gordon, 2008; Belton, 2013; Johnson, 2011). Evidence from my research suggests that silence is nuanced and multifarious.

Schröter (2013, p. 1) argues that:

> present political and communicative culture cherishes verbal communication. The last decades have seen (…) a huge increase in the provision of mediated political [and social] communication up to the tipping point of over-saturation.

Whilst talking and verbal exchanges are perceived as positive and desirable, verbal silence in Western democracies tends to be perceived as negative, unproductive and unhelpful, leading to normative pre-occupations on how to discourage or eliminate it (Dingli, 2015). Conflict situations in particular require that the private becomes public for the general good. Foucault (1979, p. 27), however, argues "there is not one but many silences, and they are an integral part of the strategies that underlie and permeate discourses".

Silence is not just about the absence of speech, whether "self-imposed or imposed by others" (Donnan & Simpson, 2007, p. 6). Silence and its subsequent interpretation are bound by the context in which it occurs. Silences hold multiple meanings which are tentative and "open to (re)interpretation" (Poland & Pederson, 1998, p. 308). Ferguson (2003, p. 49) contends the complexity of silence "operates in diverse ways". As a noun, silence infers the absence of speech, but it can also imply lack of communication, concealment and secrecy. As a verb, silence can be a powerful tool of control, as in the act of silencing—used to muffle, suppress and degrade. Equally it can be a tool of resistance and "community formation" (Ferguson, 2003, p. 49), as in the act of defiance or non-cooperation. Glenn (2004, p. xi) argues, "silence can deploy power [or] it can defer to power. It all depends".

This chapter maintains that silence and silencing are part of colonisation processes that exist to this day. The silencing of narratives, experiences, voices, histories, alternative modes of thinking and doing, are ongoing legacies of structural, cultural and moral violence. Silence thus will be discussed as political discourse, as phenomena and as process. Silence can be a tool of marginalisation, violence, fear, defence, protection, agreement, disagreement, but its impact and consequence depend on the motives of the individual, community or organisation putting it to use. Johnson (2011, p. 57), writing about how silence is operationalised in asylum cases in the UK, warns that "the equivocal nature of silence imparts a vulnerability to interpretation, rendering it subject to the imposition of unsolicited meaning. Silence's indeterminacy, it is suggested, should give pause". Thus, in developing a political understanding of silence, it is crucial analytically to differentiate between *silencing* as being prevented from speaking through centuries of ongoing exclusion and oppression (Ephratt, 2008) and *silence* as a deliberate choice. I will now clarify the ambiguous character of silence.

Silence as Erasure and Denial by the Dominant Power

The political discourse of silence and power around Gypsy/Travellers in Scotland occurs in multiple ways. Through erasure of their histories and voices in public discourse and consciousness, 'the Gypsy/Traveller' as a racialised minority is as Mirza (2015, p. 3) notes, normatively absent yet pathologically present" in the Scottish imagination. They appear "as a group of people collectively assigned as 'other'. In other words, they are essentialised as a

Talking of Silence: Young Scottish Gypsy/Traveller Women in Scotland 101

homogenous group reflecting the Scottish public's 'moral panic' over these 'folk devils' (Cohen, 1972; Morris, 1994). They are feared and are absent and excluded from daily mainstream socio-political activity and discourse. In their exclusion, they are nevertheless negatively included as a means to reiterate the dominance of the mainstream (Du Bois, 1935; Fanon, 1968). In settled populations there are misperceptions, fears, prejudices and racist attitudes revealed in a general reluctance to associate with, befriend and intermarry those in Gypsy/Traveller communities.

Gypsy/Travellers are ignored, erased, or demonised as a well-known disparaged 'Other' in both the European and Scottish imagination. The manipulation of their history and identity within Scottish culture, within some academic texts, policy documents and administrative data, silences other historical accounts. This imposed silence streamlines, cleanses and sidelines other perspectives. It is silence by erasure. 'Master narratives' (Lyotard, 1979[1984]) demand that certain histories are hidden, thereby constricting both collective and individual historical memory, commemoration and memorialisation. Silencing creates single perspectives and obstructs understanding of 'othered' histories.

Richardson's (2006) work, *The Gypsy Debate: Can Discourse Control* provides a contemporary and incisive account of the social shaping of Gypsy/Travellers, outlining what is said about the community and the effect this has on their daily, lived experiences via theories on power, control and discourse (Bauman, 1989; Cohen, 1972; Foucault, 1980). Richardson (2006, p. 35) argues negative, degrading and controlling language against Gypsy/Travellers, often racist and bigoted, is perpetuated and reinforced through legislation, government policy and the media. Moreover, as Richardson points out, the "Gypsy debate" is not a balanced one, as Gypsy/Travellers do not possess equal political representation and a right to reply. The imbalance silences and is silence as process.

The legacy of this lack of parity is particularly reflected in the history, discourse and effects of legislation in the UK (O'Nions, 1995). In the past 50 years, Gypsy/Traveller communities have experienced draconian legislation, particularly regarding accommodation and camping sites, which have undermined the communities' traditionally semi-nomadic way of life, affecting their physical, emotional and mental wellbeing (Minority Ethnic Carers of People Project, 2012). The *Housing (Scotland) Act 2001* places a duty on Local Authorities to regularly review and update their Local Housing Strategy to meet the accommodation needs of Gypsy/Traveller communities in Scotland, but Scottish local authorities currently do not have a legal duty to *provide* suitable caravan site accommodation for Gypsy/Travellers. However, *The Children Act (Scotland)* 1995 states that public authorities and services have a duty to safeguard and promote a child's welfare and "any intervention by a public authority in the life of a child must be properly justified" (Scottish Government, 2006).

The paucity of stopping sites for Gypsy/Traveller families, the denial of space and time to rest, hiding from the police, together with the consequences of being evicted, has negative impacts on children and their education. Stopping and camping sites, authorised or unauthorised, do not fit into traditional concepts of 'home' held by settled populations and policy-makers and are viewed instead as squatting, invasions upon space as real estate. The majority settled community sees itself as host and Gypsy/Travellers as unwanted guests. The conflicts and controls over space can have direct links with race and power. In her work on *Race Space and the Law,* Razack (2002, p. 1) maintains, "spaces [can be] organised to sustain unequal social relations and (…) these relations [in turn] shape spaces". Space can be used to empower some and disempower others, and in the process a child's educational experiences may be adversely affected, as I have discovered from some of the young women I met.

Their concept of home and method of travelling has been criminalised for centuries. In 1541 the first wave of anti-Gypsy laws was introduced in Scotland, and in the 1570s Scottish Gypsy/Travellers were also ordered to stop travelling, leave Scotland or face the death penalty (Marcus, 2019). A few decades later in 1609, a further law in Scotland declared that since all Gypsies were thieves by habit or repute, they should be put to death or transported to the Americas (Marcus, 2019). Staying hidden and invisible kept Gypsy/Travellers safe, but their visible absence further corrupted their image in popular discourse and marginalised them (Marcus, 2019). The continuing impact that stems from this criminalisation has not ceased. but is only marginally relieved when Gypsy/Traveller families are forced to settle under brick and mortar, with implications for their sense of identity and mental wellbeing (MECOPP, 2012).

The stereotype of the Gypsy/Traveller is a powerful negative image that has been, consciously or subconsciously, structurally embedded in the minds of the settled community for hundreds of years and this process shows little sign of relenting. Prospects for positive social change and social justice for Gypsy/Traveller communities in Scotland appear slim.

The Silent Legacy of Absence and Presence

Gypsy/Travellers are "pathologically present," but also made "normatively absent" (Mirza, 2015, p. 3) through structural, institutional and discursive hegemonic systems. Absence and presence can co-exist: dialogue occurs, and information is disseminated about the subject, but both take place with the subject itself excluded from the conversation. The subjects are silent and silenced. In keeping with the *1895 Scottish Traveller Report* (Dawson, 2005), many government and non-governmental reports do not include direct evidence from Gypsy/Travellers themselves, with a few exceptions. If they are included, often the same few are given space to speak. Their voices are then used, interpreted and re-interpreted. "Thus caution is needed in assuming that power relations can be changed through the elicitation of (…) talk" (Arnot & Reay, 2007, p. 311). Gypsy/Travellers are still generally discussed and written about by 'non-Travellers', albeit by those who work closely with Gypsy/Traveller communities. In a recent consultation exercise by the Scottish Government on *Improving Educational Outcomes for Children and Young People from Travelling Cultures* (Scottish Government, 2017, p. 5), declared that "a Traveller teacher" was part of their working group and the rest were non-Travellers or "representatives who support Traveller families (…) and third sector representatives".

Silencing Gypsy/Traveller Women

The gap in the existing literature on Gypsy/Traveller women exacerbates the complexity of silence, censorship and absence. Within the limited studies that are available, it is significant that Gypsy/Traveller women are perceived as being a problem, having problems, being polluted and unclean or having the potential to pollute and dishonour their communities (Clavell-Bate, 2012; Dawson, 2005; Lloyd, 2005; Okely, 1983). Underlying the constructed image and discourse used about Gypsy/Traveller women is the language of sex and sensuality, pollution, shame and risk, and more recently their hypersexualisation through television programmes like *My Big Fat Gypsy Wedding* (Channel 4, 2010).

The lack of contemporary research about Gypsy/Traveller women follows a long tradition of women either being erased from the Gypsy/Traveller experience or being discussed in sexist and racist ways. Women are either ignored or constructed in problematic terms in existing literature. For instance, the *1895 Scottish Traveller Report* (Dawson, 2005) hardly mentions the experiences of women. The little that is written in this report is negative. Gypsy/Traveller women are described as "drunken wives (…) a very difficult problem in connection with the School Board (…) [because] fathers frequently ascribe their incapacity to send their children to school owing to having drunken wives" (Dawson, 2005, p. 19). The Chairman of this Victorian inquiry gives support to this account in his testimony at the hearing, saying of women, married or pregnant that, "[m]y experience is that directly they get money they go to drink, and when drunk they give way to disorder and brawling (…) [leaving] their children untended on the roadside during the night" (Dawson, 2005, p. 39). A further witness, Reverend Mackenzie reveals that "the mothers get drunk and fall over their children" (Dawson 2005, p. 46). Such a moralising discourse about motherhood is also commonly used against working class women in poverty, alongside suggestions of child neglect and excessive reproduction of 'feral' children (Allen & Osgood, 2009; Romagnoli & Wall, 2012). Additionally, a manager of a girls' industrial school in Perth reported to the committee, "[a]s these Tinker girls grow older, they deteriorate in intelligence

104   Geetha Marcus

very much" (Dawson, 2005, p. 45). The manager also believes that Tinker girls do well when separated from their parents and sent abroad. Women are labelled "immoral" because "girls of 15, 16 and 17, and lads of the same age, and their parents all lodge and sleep" together (Dawson, 2005, p. 15).

Gypsy/Travellers were not called upon to testify and their voices were missing. In Scotland, the erasure or negative representation in this 1890 report exemplifies the ongoing symbolic cultural and political violence directed towards women from Gypsy/Traveller communities to this day. The marked impact and persistence of this violence is evident in my research.

Being silenced and using silence: young Gypsy/Traveller women

One of the most striking findings is the liminality of their positioning betwixt and between complex intersections of space, race, gender, class, culture and intergenerational tensions. Preliminary interviews in my research (Marcus, 2015, p. 72) revealed that some young women seemed doubly oppressed by systemic institutional inequities and fixed gender expectations from within their culture and families; whilst others express strong views and aspirations about their future roles as women, which may challenge stereotypical perceptions. Their families and communities are crucial here. Skye (16) and Rona (19) stated emphatically that, from their view, most Gypsy/Traveller girls are not allowed to go to school because their families and communities do not see any need for them to do so.

SKYE: They have like no choice in anything and that really sucks!
RONA: I'm going to make sure my kids are in school.
SKYE: You're surrounded by other Travellers [at the mobile school] and maybe if you pick the wrong thing to do (…) maybe if like the boy picked something that wasn't (…) manly enough.
RONA: I've kind of noticed that as well.
SKYE: He'd be sort of picked on by the rest of the Travellers as well (…)
RONA: Or like a girl becoming a mechanic!
SKYE: Travellers are quite sexist. There's like no gender equality among Travellers, they're just like the women and men *have* to (…) they have like no choice in anything and that really sucks because like I won't (…) when I grow up, I want to have my own job and everything and I don't want to have to live off (…) like (…) a man (…). Yeah, it's ridiculous! The man will bring in all the money all the time.

The young women's accounts reveal that they are "governed by their family and their locality, by the physical, social, and emotional spaces they inhabit" (Marcus, 2015, p. 73). Their varied experiences illustrate Lorde's argument (Lorde 2007, p. 53) that "there are many kinds of power, used and unused, acknowledged or otherwise". They experience multiple constraints reflecting their captivity within long-standing institutional, structural, political and cultural agendas.

Gypsy/Traveller women are subject to *being* silenced both in racialised and gendered ways, but also *use* silence as a form of limited power to manipulate, to withhold. Power relations take multiple forms—through discourse, policies, legislation and, as the editors of this collection acknowledge, quiet, slow, static and "sticky" aggregations of power (Ahmed, 2004; Athanasiou et al., 2021; Beasley & Papadelos, 2024) may be just as provocative.

Acknowledging how external and internal structural inequalities affect some Gypsy/Travellers in Scotland, particularly young women, is key to improving understanding and taking committed action to tackle these power imbalances, restore trust and heal centuries of conflict. However, there remains not only a range of levels of recognition with regard to such imbalances, but also a lack of concerted effort amongst various groups, institutions, government departments and Gypsy/Traveller communities themselves to alter them. All parties concerned lack the bridging capital to connect with one another, recognise commonalities and value differences. In his seminal work *The Art of Listening*, Backs (2007, p.5) argues "the capacity to hear has been damaged and is in need of repair". The powerful often cannot visualise or hear the lived experience of those they marginalise. Those that are marginalised often do not have the opportunity nor feel the invitation to enable connection.

Silence as Resistance

Gypsy/Travellers are demonised, marginalised and controlled through discourse and silence, but arguably there are signs of agentic action through self-exclusion, remaining silent and hidden, given that they have opposed centuries of persecution and survived. Ladson-Billings (2009, p. 85) contends that "silence can be used as a weapon (…) silence can be used as a means of resistance that shuts down [unwanted] dialogic processes". One participant, Sandray (aged 22) pointed out that Gypsy/Travellers not only see themselves as being separate and different, but better than 'non-Travellers': "[y]ou feel like you're superior to everybody around you because you've got your own language, you've got your own ways, you dress your own way, it's just (…) It's just a good feeling". May (aged 12) was particularly adamant that her community should live separately from other communities:

> I'd rather stay with my own kind (…) because like I'm with my own kind and I'm not like mixing because they don't understand me and I don't understand them, like not being disrespectful or anything (…) if we are not mixing, then there's no trouble.

Of the 17 young women I interviewed, most strongly asserted their right and need to live apart from the rest of society because, as they insisted, "we are different". May claims she is happy at the youth centre she attends twice a week for basic literacy and numeracy lessons because "it's like all my kind [of people] here". However, Sandray did reveal that this is not straightforward for her and added, "I'm not going to lie (...) to me it's not [real] because there's a real world out there, you cannae just stay in your bubble". However, many of the young women acknowledged that it is not safe for them to be out in the real world unless they 'pass' as simply White Scottish, rather than openly self-identify as Scottish Gypsy/Traveller. Of course, the danger stems from centuries of ongoing persecution, leading to living legacies and processes of exclusion, marginalisation and intergenerational trauma (Herman, 2015). Furthermore, the young women highlighted the ingrained sexism within their families and communities that places undue pressure on their honour and propriety and limits their aspirations. As Rushdie (1983, p. 173) notes, "[r]epression is a seamless garment; a society which is authoritarian in its social and sexual codes, which crushes women beneath the intolerable burdens of honour and propriety, breeds repressions of other kinds as well". The young women are doubly oppressed, facing the trauma of centuries of racialised and gendered patriarchy. Their resistance has to be maintained on several fronts—community, family and school.

My study revealed that nearly all the young women interviewed noted racist bullying in the primary schools they attended and in consequence 'excluded' themselves from mainstream secondary education as a form of protection. A very small number reported the bullying to their teachers because they felt that if they did staff would not listen or care. The enduring legacy they face is one of collective perceptions of educational spaces as unsafe and risky. The young women's accounts also indicate that through self-exclusion from mainstream education and electing to stay hidden and silent, they and their families exert a measure of control leading to a form of protective segregation (see Marcus, 2019, pp. 164–165). Unsurprisingly, those who indicated success in attainment and enjoyment of school, affirmed that positive school experiences with non-Traveller peers and school staff, proved germane to their optimistic outlook for their future as women. Only four out of the 17 young women remained in further education after primary school.

As they are located within a specific cultural and geographical space within which they experience racialised discrimination, the young women self-exclude as a form of protective segregation. Ahmed (2012, p. 36) reminds us "how tiring and debilitating it can be as a racialised woman to co-exist in spaces of whiteness (...) and the emotional labour that it takes to have spaces of relief". These "spaces of relief" represent a form of self-exclusion and retreat into spaces of much needed silence as sanctuary.

Gypsy/Traveller family structures tend to involve extended families that live in tight, closed communities. Fathers are heads of families who work for income, and mothers are homemakers who care for children and elderly relatives. Boys are trained to help their fathers to earn, and daughters are schooled to help their mothers at home. Restrictions and obligations within the private world of family had either to be accepted or delicately negotiated in the public spaces of education and the workplace (Emejulu, 2013, p. 59). Silence was part of that strategy of negotiation and manipulation of well-established cultural norms and taboos.

None of the young women I interviewed, or their families discussed matters to do with class, poverty (which was clearly visible at times) and sexuality. Sex is a taboo topic of conversation for Gypsy/Travellers, and sex education is recognised as a major reason why Gypsy/Traveller parents do not permit their daughters to attend secondary school. Most of the young women stated they aspired for a career, but also believed that their dream career could not be fulfilled. Most those interviewed expect to follow tradition and get married soon after reaching 16 years of age. Some of the women I met seemed content to accept that this condition is just part of who they are as Gypsy/Travellers Eight young women acknowledged that despite their aspirations to have a career, they knew it was expected that they would marry and have children, unless they had their family's approval to do otherwise. Their silent acceptance of the status quo reflected their respect for their parents, but also propagates the community's traditions and existence. To challenge that status quo would mean being ostracised which threatens the community, as I discovered through my conversations with two older Gypsy/Traveller women.

Rhona (70) heard about my project and made contact (personal communication, August 6, 2015). She said that she wanted to talk to me about her life as a Gyspy/Traveller woman because she wanted "others to know what it is like to be a Traveller and understand". Over a series of telephone calls Rhona shared her experiences. She explained that she used silence to remain quiet about her identity for over 50 years. She was ostracised, but also excluded herself from her family, choosing instead to 'pass' as a 'non-Traveller'. She explained that she remained hidden and silent out of fear, but also to "learn to read and write", pursue her love of learning, "be independent", and to be free from persecution. Gypsy/Traveller writer, storyteller and singer, Jess Smith (67), also talked about being ostracised by her family, because she chose to write about her community, to break the silence (personal communication, May 14, 2014). Discussion around their aspirations and notions of success reinforced findings that some of the women are beginning to challenge the binding spaces of long held values and traditions, imagining circumstances in which they have greater agency. However, an ongoing and very live legacy of silence, fear, conflict, and tension is intertwined in their narratives.

This was evident in the views of Gypsy/Travellers who refused to take part in my research. They were understandably suspicious and afraid they might get into trouble with the authorities because their children were not in school.

They often reported that they did not see the point of talking, as nothing was going to change for them. They refused to give information to government authorities who could exact control. In a digital age where many of us inadvertently or willingly share data about every aspect of our lives to the State and corporations, it is instructive perhaps that Gypsy/Travellers tenaciously hold on to theirs. This deep suspicion of public and government formats was confirmed by all the participants and their families, reflecting their inclination towards invisibility as a form of meaningful absence. The inability to gather accurate data on Gypsy/Travellers in twice-yearly counts introduced in 1998 and various other statistical data collection methods, including the most recent national census, remains frustrating for government. Scottish Government (2010) data suggest that the exact population figure of Scottish Gypsy/Travellers is unknown (Marcus, 2019, p. 122). Neither are they visibly identifiable, because their phenotypical features are not dissimilar to the White Scottish majority. Unlike people of colour, and Muslims, Sikhs, or Jews in religious paraphernalia, Gypsy/Travellers in Scotland "hold a pigmentary passport of privilege that allows [some] sanctity within the racial polity of whiteness" (Johal, 2005, p. 273).

Their invisibility protects their identity and privacy and is a silent obstacle to the researcher or those in positions of authority keen to capture accurate data. Staying hidden or invisible has kept them safe over centuries, but their visible absence arguably has further corrupted their public image and contributed to their marginalisation. Silence in this case is strategic. Their withholding of information, their silence, accords them protection and a measure of power. Living outside certain norms and strictures, their refusal to be visible, to participate and cooperate, disempowers the State and its outreach and frustrates the possibilities for policymaking.

Gypsy/Travellers use silence to their advantage, and in this way, silence is as Ferguson (2003, p. 50) suggests not "merely an impediment to community". The idea that power and control only exist in the hands of governing institutions denies the power of both communal and individual human agency. Citing Stuart Hall's (1991) notion of 'weak power', Belton (2013), who identifies as a Gypsy, theorises that it might also be in the interest of the marginalised to maintain and take advantage of that marginality (Marcus, 2019, p. 55). In this context, Belton (2013, p. 287) suggests that "oppression can be a means to gain resources, [privileges and protection]".

Conclusion

Using a postcolonial black feminist framework, the chapter supports the ideas and arguments shared in the various contributions within this book. Understanding and interrogating living legacies of power in the lives of the marginalised and othered is a core consideration in advancing social justice. Without it, the editors and chapter authors argue that it is not possible to re-imagine prospects for positive social transformation. However, the road to renewal is hard (Hall, 2021).

In interrogating the past and contemporary impact of ongoing social injustice associated with the racialised and gendered patriarchy experienced by young Gypsy/Traveller women, silence is used as erasure and denial by the dominant power, and simultaneously, it is employed as a means of resistance by Gypsy/Travellers who prefer to remain in the shadows, separate and distinct. Silence is a form of political discourse, process and phenomenon in itself.

Current approaches to stem these injustices look bleak as these tend to remain fixed in the power dynamics associated with an ongoing colonisation process. Young Gypsy/Traveller women, along with those in their own communities and those of many other racialised communities, continue to struggle to navigate socio-economic and institutional systems in Scotland. Despite their resilience, these young women remain underrepresented, particularly in the political sphere. They continue to dodge the relentless overt and covert oppression when forced to assimilate, or 'pass' as White Scottish, or remain hidden. As is highlighted in this chapter, ongoing and decidedly living legacies of discrimination are reflected when silence is operationalised via erasure and denial and simultaneously, through resistance by the colonised. However, in terms of their future, this legacy of suppression and fear imposed through various means is only disrupted when Gypsy/Travellers, including young Gypsy/Traveller women, silence their own heritage, community and identity. It would seem that the project of othering, demonising, and exclusion continues and arguably has succeeded in criminalising and fragmenting one of the oldest nomadic communities in Britain. However, Gypsy/Travellers in Scotland continue to exist, resist and unite as communities on the periphery; and in understanding this periphery, the living legacies of power at the centre also come into view.

Notes

1 The term "Gypsy/Traveller", as is used in this chapter, is the Scottish Government's (2014) most recent official terminology and is used in some academic literature as the preferred term, although not all Gypsy/Travellers agree with the labelling. Like many forms of external ascription, it is "ambiguous and fluctuating" (Liégeois, 1998, p. 33).
2 Young Gypsy/Traveller women are often considered by their families and communities to be young women when they reach puberty. By 12 years, they tend to leave formal education and are not enrolled in secondary school, learning instead to care for their homes, elderly relatives, and siblings.
3 Gypsy/Travellers were officially recognised as having a separate ethnic status in Scotland in 2008, K.MacLennan vs Gypsy/Traveller Education and Information Project (Scottish Parliament, 2010).
4 The Scottish National Census takes place in 2022, unlike the National Census in the rest of the UK, which took place in 2021.

References

Ahmed, S. (2004). Declarations of whiteness: The non-performativity of anti-racism. *Borderlands EJournal*, 3(2). www.borderlands.net.au/vol3no2_2004/ahmed_declarations.htm.

Ahmed, S. (2012). *On Being Included: Racism and Diversity in Institutional Life*. Durham, NC: Duke University Press.

Allen, K. & Osgood, J. (2009). Young women negotiating maternal subjectivities: The significance of social class. *Studies in the Maternal*, 1(2), 1–17.

Athanasiou, A., McIvor, D. W., Hooker, J., Atkins, A. & Shulman, G. (2021). Mourning work: Death and democracy during a pandemic. *Contemporary Political Theory*, 20(1), 165–199.

Amnesty International. (2012a). On the Margins. www.amnesty.org.uk/sites/default/files/amnesty_international_on_the_margins_2012.pdf.

Amnesty International. (2012b). *Caught in The Headlines*. www.amnesty.org.uk/sites/default/files/amnesty_international_caught_in_the_headlines_2012.pdf.

Amnesty International. (2013). Scottish Gypsy Travellers. www.amnesty.org.uk/content.asp?CategoryID=12418.

Arnot, M. & Reay, D. (2007). A sociology of pedagogic voice: Power, inequality, and pupil consultation. *Discourse: Studies in the Cultural Politics of Education*, 28(3), 311–325.

Archer, L. (2002). Change, culture and tradition: British Muslim pupils talk about Muslim girls' post-16 'choices'. *Race, Ethnicity and Education*, 5 (4), 359–376.

Backs, L. (2007). *The Art of Listening*. New York: Berg Publishers.

Back, L. & Solomos, J. (2013). *Theories of race and racism: A reader*. London: Routledge.

Basit, T. N. (1996). 'I'd hate to be just a housewife': Career aspirations of British Muslim girls. *British Journal of Guidance and Counselling*, 24(2), 227–242.

Basit, T. N. (1997). 'I want more freedom, but not too much': British Muslim girls and the dynamism of family values. *Gender and Education*, 9(4), 425–440.

Bauman, Z. (1989). *Modernity and the Holocaust*. Ithaca, NY: Cornell University Press.

Beasley, C. & Papadelos, P. (2022) *Living Legacies of Social Injustice: Power and Social Change*. London: Routledge.

Belton, B. (2013). 'Weak power': community and identity. *Ethnic and Racial Studies*, 36 (2), 282–297.

Bilge, S. (2014). Whitening Intersectionality. *Racism and Sociology*, 5, 175.

Black Equity Organisation. (2022). News: State of Black Britain Report, September 26. https://blackequityorg.com/state-of-black-britain-report.

Cannadine, D. (2013). *The undivided past: Humanity beyond our differences*. London: Penguin.

Carbado, D. W., Crenshaw, K. W., Mays, V. M. & Tomlinson, B. (2013). Intersectionality. *Du Bois review: Social Science Research on Race*, 10(2), 303–312.

Channel 4. (2010). My Big Fat Gypsy Wedding. Jes Wilkins.

Clark, C. R. (2001). 'Invisible lives': the Gypsies and Travellers of Britain (Doctoral dissertation, University of Edinburgh).

Clark, C. (2006). Defining ethnicity in a cultural and socio-legal context: the case of Scottish Gypsy-Travellers. *Scottish Affairs*, 54(1), 39–67.

Clark, C. (2008). Introduction themed section care or control? Gypsies, Travellers, and the state. *Social Policy and Society*, 7(1), 65–71.

Clark, C. & Taylor, B. (2014). Is nomadism the 'problem'? The social construction of Gypsies and Travellers as perpetrators of 'anti-social' behaviour In Britain. In Pickard, S. (Ed.), *Anti-social behaviour in Britain: Victorian and contemporary perspectives*. Basingstoke: Palgrave Macmillan, pp. 166–178.

Clavell-Bate, R. (2012). Elective home education: Supporting access to education for children and young people within the Gypsy, Roma, and Traveller community. In J. Visser, H. Daniels, and T. Cole (Eds), *Transforming troubled lives: Strategies and interventions for children with social, emotional, and behavioural difficulties*. (pp. 175–191). Bradford: Emerald Group Publishing.

Cohen, S. (1972). *Folk Devils and Moral Panics*, Oxford: Blackwell.

Collins. P. H. (2000). *Black feminist thought. Knowledge, consciousness and the politics of empowerment*. London: Routledge.

Crenshaw, K. (1989) Demarginalizing the intersection of race and sex: A black feminist critique of antidiscrimination doctrine, feminist theory and antiracist politics. *University of Chicago Legal Forum*, 1, 139–167.

Crenshaw, K. (1991). Mapping the margins: Intersectionality, identity politics, and violence against women of color. *Stanford Law Review*, 43(6), 1241–1299.

Dawson, R. (2005). *The 1895 Scottish Traveller Report*. Derbyshire: Dawson & Rackley.

Dawson, R. (2007). *Empty Lands: Aspects of Scottish Traveller Survival*. Derbyshire: Dawson Publishing.

van Dijk, Teun A. (2008). *Discourse and Context. [Electronic Resource]: A Sociocognitive Approach*. Cambridge: Cambridge University Press.

Dingli, S. (2015). We need to talk about silence: Re-examining silence in International Relations theory. *European Journal of International Relations*, 21(4), 721–742.

Donnan, H. & Simpson, K. (2007). Silence and violence among Northern Ireland border Protestants. *Ethnos* 72(1), 5–28.

Douglas, M. (2003). *Purity and danger: An analysis of concepts of pollution and taboo*. London: Routledge.

Du Bois, W. E. B. (1935). *Black reconstruction*. San Diego, CA: Harcourt, Brace and Howe.

Emejulu, A. & Bassel, L. (2015). Minority women, austerity and activism. *Race & Class*, 57(2), 86–95.

Emejulu, A. (2013). Being and Belonging in Scotland: Exploring the Intersection of Ethnicity, Gender and National Identity among Scottish Pakistani Groups. *Scottish Affairs* 84(1), 41–64.

Ephratt, M. (2008). The Functions of Silence. *Journal of Pragmatics* 40(11), 1909–1938.

Equality and Human Rights Commission. (2017). *Gypsies and Travellers: Simple solutions for living together*. Retrieved from Gypsies and Travellers: simple solutions for living together | Equality and Human Rights Commission (equalityhumanrights.com).

Fanon, F. (1968). The Fact of Blackness in Black Skins. *White Masks*, (trans.) Charles Lam Markmann. London: MacGibbon & Kee.

Fraser, A. (1995). *The Gypsies*, 2nd edition. Oxford: Blackwell.

Ferguson, K. (2003). Silence: A politics. *Contemporary Political Theory*, 2(1), 49–65.

Foucault, M. (1979). *The History of Sexuality*, Vol. 1. London: Allen Lane.

Foucault, M. (1980). *Power/Knowledge: Selected Interviews and Other Writings, 1972–1977*. New York: Pantheon.

Glenn, C. (2004). *Unspoken: A Rhetoric of Silence*. Carbondale, IL: Southern Illinois University Press.

Gordon, A. F. (2008). *Ghostly matters: Haunting and the sociological imagination*. Minneapolis, MN: University of Minnesota Press.

Groome, F. H. (1890–91). Transportation of Gypsies from Scotland to America. *Journal of the Gypsy Lore Society* 2(1), 60–62.

Gupta, D. T., James, C. E., Maaka, R. C. A., Galabuzi, G. E. & Anderson, C. (2007). *Race and racialisation. Essential readings*. Toronto, ON: Canadian Scholars' Press.

Hall, S. (1991). Ethnicity: Identity and difference. *Radical America* 23(4), 9–20.

Hall, S. (2021). *The hard road to renewal: Thatcherism and the crisis of the left*. London: Verso Books.

Herman, J. L. (2015). *Trauma and recovery: The aftermath of violence—from domestic abuse to political terror*. London: Hachette UK.

Heuss, H. (2000). Anti-Gypsyism research: the creation of a new field of study. In: Acton, T. (Ed.) *Scholarship and the Gypsy struggle: commitment in Romani Studies*. Hatfield, University of Hertfordshire Press, pp. 52–67.

Johal, G. S. (2005) Order in KOS on race, rage, and method. In *Counterpoints*, pp. 269–290.

Johnson, T. A. (2011). On silence, sexuality and skeletons: Reconceptualizing narrative in asylum hearings. *Social & Legal Studies*, 20(1), 57–78.

Kenrick, D. (1993). *From India to the Mediterranean: the migration of the Gypsies* (Vol. 3). Hatfield: University of Hertfordshire Press.

Kenrick, D. & Clark, C. (1999). *Moving On: The Gypsies and Travellers of Britain*. Hatfield: University of Hertfordshire Press.

Ladson-Billings, G. (2009). Silences as Weapons: Challenges of a Black Professor Teaching White Students. *Theory into Practice* 35(2), 79–85.

Liégeois, J. P. (1998). *School provision for ethnic minorities: The gypsy paradigm* (Vol. 11). Gypsy Research Centre : University of Hertfordshire Press.

Lloyd, G. (2005). *Problem Girls: Understanding and Supporting Troubled and Troublesome Girls and Young Women*. London:Psychology Press.

Lopez, I. H. (2006). *White by law: The legal construction of race*. New York: New York University Press.

Lorde, A. (2011). *I Am Your Sister: Collected and Unpublished Writings of Audre Lorde (Transgressing Boundaries: Studies in Black Politics and Black Communities)*. New York: Oxford University Press.

Lorde, A. (1983). There is no hierarchy of oppressions. *Bulletin: Homophobia and Education*, 14(3–4), 9.

Lorde, A. (2007). *Sister Outsider: Essays and Speeches*. 1984. Berkeley, CA: Crossing Press.

Lyotard, J.-F. (1979[1984]) *The Postmodern Condition*. Manchester: Manchester University Press.

Mackenzie, A. (1883[2012]) *The History of the Highland Clearances*. Lenox, MA: Hard Press Publishing.

MacRitchie, D. (1894). *Scottish Gypsies Under the Stewarts*. Edinburgh: D. Douglas.

Marcus, G. (2013a). The Educational Experiences of Gypsy and Traveller Girls in Scottish Schools. Paper presented at the Interweaving: Connecting Educational Research Within, Across and Between Perspectives conference (August 21), Moray House School of Education, University of Edinburgh.

Marcus, G. (2013b). From the Margins to the Centre: The Educational Experiences of Gypsy and Traveller Girls in Scottish Schools. Paper presented at the British

Educational Research Association (BERA) Postgraduate Symposium (October 11), School of Education, University of Glasgow.

Marcus, G. (2014a). From the Margins to the Centre: The Educational Experiences of Gypsy/Traveller Girls in Scotland. Paper presented at the Kaleidoscope Conference: Opening Up the Ivory Tower (May 29–30), Faculty of Education, University of Cambridge.

Marcus, G. (2014b) From the Margins to the Centre: The Educational Experiences of Gypsy/Traveller Girls in Scotland. Paper presented at the British Educational Research Association Annual Conference (September 23–25), Institute of Education, London.

Marcus, G. (2015a). Marginalisation and the Voices of Gypsy/Traveller Girls. *Cambridge Open-Review Educational Research e-Journal*, 1(2), 55–77.

Marcus, G. (2015b). The Intersecting Invisible Experiences of Gypsy/Traveller Girls in Scotland. Paper presented at the Childhood and Youth Studies Network Seminar conference (November 25), School of Social and Political Science, University of Edinburgh.

Marcus, G. (2019). *Gypsy and Traveller girls: Silence, agency, and power.* Cham & New York: Springer.

Marcus, G. (2021, April 21). Decolonising the curriculum: Silence is not an option. [Blog post] Retrieved from: QMU Blog | Queen Margaret University | Decolonising the Curriculum: Silence is not an Option.

Mayall, D. (1995). *English Gypsies and State Policy.* Hatfield: University of Hertfordshire Press.

McCormick, A. (1907). *The Tinkler-Gypsies.* Dumfries: J. Maxwell & Son.

Mies, M. (1983). Towards a methodology for feminist research. In G. Bowles & R. Klein (Eds), *Theories of women's studies* (pp. 117–139). London: Routledge & Kegan Paul.

Minority Ethnic Carers of People Project. (2012). Hidden carers, unheard voices: Informal caring within the Gypsy/Traveller community in Scotland. www.mecopp. org.uk/files/documents/gypsy%20traveller/HiddenCarers-Unheard%20Voices% 20Report.pdf.

Minority Ethnic Carers of People Project. (2022). *Men aloud: Engaging with Gypsy/Traveller men in Scotland Report*, March 2022.

Mirza, H. S. (2015). "Harvesting our collective intelligence": Black British feminism in post-race times. *Women's Studies International Forum*, 51, 1–9.

Morris, L. (1994). *Dangerous classes. The underclass and social citizenship.* London: Routledge.

Murray, R. (1875[1983]). *The Gypsies of the Border.* Galashiels: RC Hodges.

Neat, T. (1996). *The Summer Walkers: Travelling People and Pearl-Fishers in the Highlands of Scotland.* Edinburgh: Canongate.

New York Times. (2022). The Inside Story of How a 'Bogus' Letter Roiled Britain. 7 Takeaways From 'The Trojan Horse Affair' Podcast (nytimes.com).

O'Nions, H. (1995). The marginalisation of Gypsies. *Web Journal of Current Legal Issues, 3.* www.bailii.org/uk/other/journals/WebJCLI/1995/issue3/index.html.

Okely, J. (1983). *The Traveller-Gypsies.* Cambridge: Cambridge University Press.

Okely, J. (1994). Constructing difference: Gypsies as "other". *Anthropological Journal on European Cultures*, 3(2), 55–73.

Poland, B. & Pederson, A. (1998). Reading Between the Lines: Interpreting Silences in Qualitative Research. *Qualitative Inquiry* 4(2), 293–312.

Razack, S. (Ed.). (2002). *Race, space, and the law: Unmapping a white settler society.* Toronto, ON: Between the Lines.

Rehfisch, A. and Rehfisch, F. (1975). Scottish Travellers or Tinkers. In Rehfisch, F. (Ed.) *Gypsies, Tinkers and other Travellers.* London: Academic Press, 271–283.

Reid, W. (1997). Scottish Gypsies/Travellers and the folklorists. *Romani culture and Gypsy identity.* Hatfield: University of Hertfordshire, 29–37.

Richardson, J. (2006). *The Gypsy Debate: Can Discourse Control?*Exeter: Imprint Academic.

Rochat, P. (2020). *Moral acrobatics: How we avoid ethical ambiguity by thinking in Black and White.* Oxford: Oxford University Press.

Romagnoli, A. & Wall, G. (2012). 'I know I'm a good mom': Young, low-income mothers' experiences with risk perception, intensive parenting ideology and parenting education programmes. *Health, Risk & Society,* 14(3), 273–289.

Rushdie, S. (1983). *Shame.* Toronto: Vintage Canada.

Save the Children Scotland. (2005). Having our Say. www.gypsy-traveller.org/your-family/young-people/educational-reports-and-resources.

Sbisà, M. (2002). Speech Acts in Context. *Language & Communication* 22(4), 421.

Schröter, M. (2013). *Silence and Concealment in Political Discourse* (Vol. 48). Amsterdam: John Benjamins Publishing.

Scottish Centre for Social Research. (2010). Scottish Social Attitudes Survey 2010. www.scotland.gov.uk/Resource/Doc/355763/0120175.pdf.

Scottish Centre for Social Research. (2015). Scottish Social Attitudes 2015: Attitudes to discrimination and positive action. www.scotland.gov.uk.

Scottish Government. (2006). Scotland's children: The Children (Scotland) Act 1995: Regulations and guidance, Volume 1: Support and protection for children and their families. www.scotland.gov.uk/Publications/2004/10/20066/44708.

Scottish Government. (2010). Review of the Twice-Yearly Count of Gypsies/Travellers in Scotland. www.scotland.gov.uk/Publications/2010/03/05103811/0.

Scottish Government. (2014). Gypsy/Travellers. www.scotland.gov.uk/Topics/People/Equality/gypsiestravellers.

Scottish Government. (2017). Improving Educational Outcomes for Children and Young People from Travelling Cultures. https://consult.scotland.gov.uk/support-and-wellbeing/improving-educational-outcomes-for-children/.

Scottish Parliament. (2010). PE1363: Apology from Scottish Government to Scottish Gypsy/Traveller Community. https://archive.parliament.scot/business/petitions/pdfs/PE1363.pdf.

Shubin, S. (2010). "Where can a Gypsy stop?" Rethinking mobility in Scotland, *Antipode,* 43 (2), 494–524.

Stewart, S. (2008) *Pilgrims of the mist: The stories of Scotland's Travelling people.* Edinburgh: Birlinn Publishers.

Talbani, A. & Hasanali, P. (2000). Adolescent females between tradition and modernity: Gender role socialization in South Asian immigrant culture. *Journal of Adolescence,* 23 (5), 615–627.

Trepagnier, B. (2010). *Silent Racism: How Well-Meaning White People Perpetuate the Racial Divide.* Boulder, CO: Paradigm Publishing.

Thompson, T. W. (1928). Gleanings from Constables' Accounts and Other Sources. *Romani Studies*, 7(1), 30–48.

Virdee, S. (2019). The Racialized Outsider as the Conscience of Modernity. British Sociological Association Conference Keynote Lecture. Glasgow.

Williamson, D. (1994). *The Horsieman: Memories of a Traveller 1928–1958*. Edinburgh: Canongate Press.

Wilson, J. M. & Leighton, A. (1885). *Wilson's Tales of the Borders and of Scotland: Historical, Traditionary, and Imaginative, with a Glossary* (Vol. 2). Glasgow: William MacKenzie.

Yuval-Davis, N. (2011). *The politics of belonging: Intersectional contestations*. London: Sage.

Chapter 7

Young Refugees Navigating the Emotional Legacies of Displacement in Beirut Through Friendships

David Anderson and Mary Holmes

Years after the outbreak of the Syrian civil war and the rise and fall of the Islamic State in Syria and neighbouring Iraq, Lebanon remains one of the primary host nations for refugees from these conflicts and the country with the highest number of refugees per capita in the world (United Nations High Commissioner for Refugees, 2021). The vast majority of these refugees are from Syria, numbering almost 900,000—taking into account unregistered refugees, this may be closer to 1.5 million (United Nations High Commissioner for Refugees, 2021, p. 1).[1] In Beirut, the capital, Iraqi refugees settled within the sectarian geographies of the city, divided according to religion and ethnicity while Syrians found shelter in the city's long-established Palestinian camps and more recent informal settlements (Chatty & Mansour, 2011; United Nations High Commissioner for Refugees/United Nations International Children's Emergency Fund/World Food Programme, 2017). Over time, most Syrian refugees in Beirut have transitioned to permanent shelter, with more than 90% now living in residential housing (United Nations High Commissioner for Refugees/United Nations International Children's Emergency Fund/World Food Programme, 2022, p. 46). Yet, while these families have found themselves increasingly integrated into the physical space of the city, the legacy of displacement continues to be felt in their everyday lives through exclusion and vulnerability. Syrian refugees are entangled within the complex history and geopolitics between Lebanon and Syria and are frequently stereotyped as inferior and immoral others by Lebanese locals, leading to social exclusion (Chatty, 2017, pp. 28–29; Riga, Holmes, Dakessian, Langer & Anderson, 2021, pp. 87–112). They experience extremely high levels of poverty and instability through food and livelihood insecurity, with only a little over half of children in education (United Nations High Commissioner for Refugees/United Nations International Children's Emergency Fund/World Food Programme, 2022, p. 11). Half of Syrian refugee children report experiencing physical or psychological violence and there are specific gendered vulnerabilities, with young boys more likely to be at risk of child labour, and young girls more likely to be married at a young age (United Nations High

DOI: 10.4324/9781003311928-9

Commissioner for Refugees/United Nations International Children's Emergency Fund/World Food Programme, 2022, pp. 11, 162).

In this chapter, we offer an account of young refugees as actively navigating the geopolitical and intimate shifts in power that forced displacement has caused within their lives. While many refugees live in precarious circumstances and have crucial humanitarian needs, it is important to place these within the social context of refugees' lives (Chatty, Crivello & Lewando Hundt, 2005, p. 397; Wernesjö, 2012). Refugees must navigate new political realities as they settle into host nations and interact with humanitarian bureaucracies (Askins, 2015; Feldman, 2019; Marshall, 2013, 2014), and many experience profound changes to their intimate lives through the loss or re-shaping of their relationships with family and friends (Culcasi, 2019; Kallio, 2019). Despite this, scholarship examining *how* friendships are made and performed for young refugees is relatively rare (but see Bergnehr, Aronson & Enell, 2020; Butler, 2021; Nathan et al., 2013; Spaaij, 2015).

Here, we extend our previous work with young Iraqis and Syrians in Beirut (Riga et al., 2021, pp. 27–50) to ask, 'what are the emotional legacies of forced displacement for these young refugees and how are friendships important in how they navigate these legacies?' Drawing on Beasley and Papadelos (in this volume), we conceptualise these legacies as 'living' for young refugees. A legacy is not just about the past or inherited practices of power but involves the re-shaping of power relations in the present, and this close connection with political acts and imaginaries intimately links living legacies with social change. By looking at displacement, we can see that emotions play an important part in how the legacies of the past live on and yet shift and are resisted. Emotions relating to past power relations within and between the homeland and their host nation shape the present. Legacies *live* partly because they continue to be felt. Past occupations, oppressions, injustices and flights from danger are remembered with feeling, and the feelings are passed on to younger generations, but as they are passed on they are also altered. In the lives of the young refugees in our study, displacement is not a fixed, past event but one that continues to unfold and change, not only in their lives but through the social and political landscapes of Beirut. We understand this as an outcome of the exercise of power through geopolitics, resulting in the loss of homes and livelihoods for displaced families. Power, in some instances, has also accumulated, become sticky or solidified in the environs of Beirut and the places where these young refugees now live. In becoming refugees these young boys and girls—and their families—have to understand, reflect on and navigate the new political realities of their lives, both on an intimate and public scale. The legacies of displacement that they experience include injustices not only related to their status as recipients of humanitarian aid and new racialisations encountered through refugeedom (Riga et al., 2021), but the ways in which family dynamics and close relationships with friends change. Displacement, like other forms of injustice and violence, causes harm—harm that can travel from past to present, having material and emotional effects on families (see, for example, Cernea & Maldonado, 2018; Gilmartin, 2021). As explored by others in this volume, the ways in which power reshapes intimate relationships can produce powerful feelings of loneliness and isolation (Papadelos, Chapter 8), and experiences of grief and loss are transmissible across time and generations (Wanganeen & Szorenyi, Chapter 9). Emotional reflexivity is an important concept for understanding how young refugees navigate these effects in the immediate present, and how these navigations indicate the reshaping of friendships. We use the term 'navigation' here in a similar sense to William Reddy (2001) to refer to how people weave their way between, around and with feelings, as they encounter power as a dynamic, temporal force. Emotional reflexivity describes how feelings are reflected and acted upon as we relate to others (Holmes, 2010, p. 140).

Through examining the different ways in which these young refugees respond to their displacement—viewing this as a living legacy that continues to affect their lives and broader social and political realities—we see their use of emotional reflexivity to gauge, understand and act on the emotional changes they experience in their friendships and families. The young refugees spoke of what appear to be emotional legacies of displacement: of distrust, of their anger or disgust at injustice and exclusion, and of boredom and loneliness. What the displaced inherit is often opaque and cause and effect are unclear (cf. Lupu & Peisakhin, 2017, pp. 836–7). However, we argue that these young people reflect on this ambiguity themselves. The Syrians discussed to what extent a climate of distrust arising from displacement infected their friendships, while the Iraqis reflected on their collective struggles to stay connected. We also found that intersections of gender and racialised power meant that the boys and the girls varied in how they formed, maintained and used friendships to reflexively navigate the changes in their lives. For the boys, football was vital for social connections; for girls, it was difficult to keep friendships beyond their family active. Nevertheless, we argue that the young Syrians and Iraqis exercised emotional reflexivity to understand and act on these changes to their friendships, allowing them to navigate the emotional legacies of displacement.

Study Background

We learned about the feelings and experiences of 51 young Syrian and Iraqi refugees in Beirut as part of a British Academy funded study between 2016 and 2017 (Riga et al., 2021). We partnered with three local humanitarian organisations, who helped us recruit refugees aged eight to 17: half boys and half girls. All the young refugees we worked with had been in Lebanon for some years at the time of our four fieldwork trips. They were living in Beirut with their families (often extended families), either in the Palestinian 'camps' of

Dbayeh, Shatila, Burj el-Barajneh and Mar Elias or the poorer outskirts of the city in the neighbourhoods of Mouseitbeh, Mazraa and Sed el-Bouchrieh. This chapter draws mostly from several focus groups on trip three, in which both authors participated. The groups took place at the premises of our partner organisations or on a local university campus. Our partner organisations arranged those groups according to our request that we see an even mix of refugee girls and boys, a range of ages, and as many of the young people from our earlier trips as possible (some having moved on). In the groups we discussed who and what was important to these young people, asking questions such as 'who do you trust?' and 'what makes you happy?' We asked them to tell us stories about the last time they had felt happy or lonely or angry. From what they told us we built a picture of the ways in which their emotions inform and guide their understandings of family and their family practices (Morgan, 2011) as they navigated the disruptions of displacement.

Ethical concerns were central to this study. Family life was not always a place of safety and we met some of the young people through a child protection organisation. Ethical agreements prevented us discussing the family violence and the potentially distressing details of the wars that had displaced them and how they had come to Beirut. The particularly precarious and difficult situation of displaced Syrians in Beirut and the smallness of the humanitarian care circles also required a high level of anonymisation.

Friendships require and aid emotionally reflexive navigations of distrust

Distrust appeared to be one emotional legacy of displacement related to the history of power in the sectors of the city where the young people lived, and to other histories of displacement. The young Syrians typically lived in or around the 'camps' originally formed for Palestinians fleeing the formation of the state of Israel in 1948. The camps of Beirut are a legacy of conflict and distrust in Lebanon and the wider region; they are places that pass on an "embodied relation with the world" (Cresswell, 2014, p. 69), and arguably an emotional legacy endures through the heritage of disempowerment present in their history and politics. While it has been argued that the camps in Beirut bequeath low levels of trust and result in "not very strong or loyal" (Afifi et al., 2016, p. 352) relationships between residents, others have suggested they can foster connection and solidarity (Joseph, 1993; Martin, 2015). However, camp inhabitants are largely excluded from Lebanese society, residents lack education and employment rights and many factions and political tensions exist within them, exacerbated by the more recent arrivals of Syrians and displaced Palestinians from Syria (Riga et al., 2021, pp. 6–7; see also, Afifi, Afifi, Merrill & Nimah, 2016; Chatty, 2017; Kelley, 2017; Martin, 2015; Sayigh, 1994). Over time the camps have become more permanent and have been absorbed as everyday features of the city, blurring into the surrounding suburbs and low-income, informal settlements (Martin, 2015). Yet, the camps leave their mark on how young people learn to feel.

All of the young refugees in our study spoke (sometimes when asked whom they trusted, sometimes spontaneously) of how betrayal and distrust impacted their friendships, but these issues seemed particularly present for the young Syrians living in or near the camps. Most arrived in those neighbourhoods before they were ten but found that making and maintaining friendships could be challenging. The young people witnessed much adult anger, frustration and despair in response to social exclusion (Ramadan & Fregonese, 2017, pp. 953–954). Distrust was not necessarily the outcome but almost all the Syrians spoke of finding trust difficult to maintain and often broken, and our conversations with them suggested that legacies of distrust could impact on friendship. They exercised considerable reflexivity around whether to trust friends. Ala, a 12-year-old Syrian girl attending school in one of the suburbs surrounding a Palestinian camp, revealed how she had a good school friend, saying: "we talk to each other about all our problems, but I don't go into depth about everything because you can't trust just anyone." No matter how close the friend, Ala limited sharing her problems, especially family problems. In a focus group on our fourth trip, she reflexively considered how she related to different kinds of friends. Trust appeared vital in how she distinguished authentic from instrumental or fun friendships (Spencer & Pahl, 2006). She outlined three categories: "genuine friends," others who "support you if it suits their own interests" and others who "if you don't make them laugh, they are not your friends." For Ala, what made a genuine friend was emotionally "being there" (Brownlie, 2011) to "support you no matter what." Additionally, Ala's categorisation showed awareness of how wider prejudices and power relations might limit friendship; she said that some people would "always dislike you, you will always be a thing to them." These were highly reflexive, politicised considerations of whether different kinds of friends helped her navigate the problems with trust that her specific displacement situation in the camps brought.

However, the Iraqi refugees in the study could reflexively navigate legacies of distrust more collectively with their friends because of their particular displacement history. These Iraqis had fled their homeland along with most of their Christian community, and together they attended daily the same organisation where we met them. Friendships often stretched back to before their time in Beirut, and these friendships gained sustenance from the sharing of past experiences (Policarpo, 2016, pp. 29–30). Sixteen-year-old Sarah was just one of the many who spoke fondly of how these bonds were strengthened by being together at the organisation: "now our village is in Lebanon. We knew each other in Iraq, [but] now our family is right here (...) We are like a family here." These family-like relationships had advantages for the young Iraqis, keeping them in close contact, and

Young Refugees Navigating the Emotional Legacies of Displacement 121

allowing them opportunities to try and untangle the changes displacement had brought to their friendships. The young Iraqis discussed some of these issues.[2]

YOUNG REFUGEE 1: In our group (...) let's imagine that there are two very close friends in this group, when there's a problem, they both blame each other and spill each other's secrets.

YOUNG REFUGEE 2: In Iraq we didn't live in the village, we lived in Baghdad. I didn't have a lot of Christian friends, just the ones from the church. But no matter how much time we'd all spent together there were never any issues [between Muslims and Christians]. They have their faults, but we were all friends and we lived a good childhood together. Since we came here, though, we have been having a lot more problems.

INTERVIEWER: Why do you think that's the case? That you have more fights here than you did there?

YOUNG REFUGEE 3: Because we don't confront each other and everybody speaks behind each other's back.

YOUNG REFUGEE 2: These things happened in Iraq, depending on where one lived.

YOUNG REFUGEE 1: Because now we are a bigger group now, like eight or nine [people], so that creates more room for problems. If someone says something to another person then that other person will tell their secrets to the rest of the group, and that's why we have problems.

YOUNG REFUGEE 4: No, I think differently. I think there are people who have different mentalities, and that's why we have more problems.

YOUNG REFUGEE 2: Everyone has a different interpretation of things. Each village has its own mentality. For example, if Karima doesn't like Yara then she will try to get her friends not to talk to Yara. It wasn't like that in Iraq.

YOUNG REFUGEE 1: There's something else I have to say: in Iraq we were kids. We were young, we were innocent, we didn't know how to hate people and make problems. Now we're older we see things differently and think about things differently, so that has something to do with it as well.

The group showed considerable collective emotional reflexivity about how and why their relationships changed. While they acknowledged the changes—particularly in a lack of trust and talking behind each other's backs—it remained unclear to them what the exact causes were. The problems that they felt they now encountered were blamed on a variety of reasons: religious differences (between Christians and Muslims); the expanded size of their friendship group; individual differences or greater group diversity (different mentalities); a sense of ageing and change (loss of innocence); and learning to place themselves in political conflicts (how to hate people). Some of the group thought these problems were part of growing up, others related them to their situation living as refugees within Beirut, while some thought such problems also happened back in Iraq.

The humanitarian organisations in Beirut offered the young refugees many emotional resources, but their carers struggled to address the disempowering legacies related to being othered as a refugee (Riga et al., 2021, p. 52), and its impacts on friendships—for example, the difficulty of maintaining relationships with friends outside Beirut. Being together at the organisation provided both space and resources to try and enable more trusting friendships, and the young Iraqis were aware of this. They explained that they learned about emotions from the psychologist at the organisation, who taught them about "emotions, and (…) good behaviour" and "how to treat [their] friends"; to reflect on what and how they felt and to use this in acting; "not to hit anyone, to talk to people instead." However, they appeared to get little guidance on dealing with the loss of friendships, with cousins often being close friends (Riga et al., 2021, p. 32). Elena said: "I miss my cousins. They're all in Australia. My grandmother, both my aunts (from father's side). They're all there, but we are here." In the same workshop Danyal and Rachel, for example, told us about friends from Iraq who had left or who they hadn't spoken to for a while. Sarah, one of the older teenagers, described trying to maintain her relationship with a friend from Iraq.

SARAH: In Iraq, I had a friend who was very close to me, I met her at school (…) She moved close to us and we became neighbours. We were best friends. (…) She was very nice, she understood me, and she used to come over, we used to eat together, do each other's nails and hair, we used to study together. I miss her a lot.

INTERVIEWER: Do you still speak to her?

SARAH: Yes, I do, but not recently because she's doing her official exams. But we're still friends, and we still talk a lot on [social media].

INTERVIEWER: And if she were to come, would she come here?

SARAH: Well, I wouldn't know, but she doesn't need to leave. She's not a Christian, she's a Muslim. But we were very good together.

Reflections upon the past inevitably led to comparisons with the present, and an awareness of differences between the two could lead to memories evoking "a sense of past belonging that brings pleasure (and pain) in the present" (May, 2017, p. 411). For Sarah, online contact maintained the friendship but it was inferior in comparison to its more embodied aspects (cf. Policarpo, 2016, p. 34). The previous physical closeness of sharing food, grooming and studying are in the past and although the girls were "still friends" and talked a lot, Sarah missed her friend. She believed that her friend's different religion meant it was unlikely she would leave Iraq, and so she showed awareness of the politics of displacement and how this had different impacts on her and her friend. The use of the past tense in "we were very good together" alluded to a felt sense of loss regarding their friendship; it had survived but was diminished.

What these young people could do in the face of friendships made precarious by displacement and geopolitical and interethnic distrust was heavily framed by what access they had to resources such as social media, travel, opportunities for other friendships and places or people who would listen to how they had been hurt. The difficulty of forming new friendships can arguably put existing friendships under strain. Of course, not only refugees experience ups and downs in their friendships when they are young (Jamieson & Highet, 2014), but the need to evaluate and address things that go wrong may be greater when friends are hard to find. Here we see how displacement can offer a window into the operation of living legacies, illustrating how outcomes have changed for these young refugees in their family and friendships—in loss, both of friends themselves, and also the trust necessary to maintain friendships. However, displacement for these young refugees was also felt in the specific limitations their new lives imposed on who they could interact with, and where. This was evident not only in the camps or organisations, but even football pitches.

Navigating exclusion through football

It became clear from them constantly speaking of it that, for the boys, football was of major importance in navigating some of the exclusionary legacies of displacement and finding space for friendships, if not feelings of belonging. One Iraqi boy stated that without it they "don't do anything" and just "stay at home." For the young Syrians and Iraqis that we spoke with, playing football could provide limited help in navigating their experiences of discrimination and exclusion. Some spoke of using designated football grounds as places where they could befriend adult supervisors or 'gatekeepers' such as local police to gain some protection from racialised bullying and harassment by Lebanese youth. Yet, while sport can foster feelings of belonging and integration for refugee and immigrant youth, this is by no means guaranteed and can lead to the opposite, with closed social and cultural groupings furthering exclusion and reinforcing hierarchical relationships (Bradbury, 2011; Dukic, McDonald & Spaaij 2017; Nathan et al., 2013; Spaaij, 2015). Places for playing football were neither available to all the young boys we spoke to, nor free from the same dynamics that resulted from the political and cultural landscape of Beirut.

Both the Iraqi and Syrian boys recounted being treated badly by Lebanese youth and excluded from their games. For Syrian refugees, living by a Palestinian camp, this exclusion was accompanied by a reflexive awareness of politicised relationships and their emotional impacts.

OMAR: On our team—for example, I'm Syrian, yeah? There's this guy in the camp, he has money, he plays before us. He [the coach] always starts him and always puts us out of the game.

MAJID: That guy is Palestinian. So, interest comes before football.

(...)

OMAR: There's this guy, for example (...) he's Syrian. He never gets to play. Never. Every match he comes, he sits, doesn't play, cries, and then goes home.

MAJID: And then there are people who play because they're the sons of the coaches, or the sons of older players [from more senior teams], and they don't even know how to control the ball.

OMAR: There's this other coach, for example, his son doesn't play well at all, but he plays every single game.

MAJID: And this Syrian guy who comes is a much better player than him, but the coach prefers to always play the other guy.

Such statements made it clear that these Syrian boys were acutely aware of the inheritance of political and racial hierarchies that influenced their everyday lives within the Palestinian camps (see Riga et al., 2021, pp. 4–8), and how these extended even to their games of football. The power relationships inherent within the camps placed them at the bottom of a hierarchy predicated on ethnicity, influence, money or connections; all things that, as recently arrived Syrian refugees, these boys lacked. This exclusion was perceived even in the spaces that they were able to play football, where "you wouldn't know that it's a football pitch (...) there's garbage, dirt. It's disgusting" (Majid).

Although football spaces were often far from ideal these boys persevered in playing; it was so crucial to how they emotionally navigated their sense of powerlessness and connected their present to the past. Being familiar with a sport and with the actions, rules and bodily movement of it can create positive feelings of control and connection (Evers, 2010; Wacquant, 2004), key parts of fostering a sense of home, even in displacement (Back, 2007, pp. 51–70; Boccagni, 2017). Football helped these boys to find friends and spaces to navigate some of the difficulties they faced in Beirut; it could also provide a positive way to engage with the past. When asked, several of the young refugees specifically mentioned playing football in their country of origin as some of the best memories that they have.

INTERVIEWER: What are some of your best memories with your friends?

YOUNG REFUGEE: The last time we played football in Iraq.

INTERVIEWER: How did that make you happy?

YOUNG REFUGEE: We were playing against a different town, and my friend was in the same team with me.

Another boy, asked to tell us any story about himself, told us of winning a local football tournament with his friends in Iraq. The association with friendships, success and happiness meant that football was a connection, a positive legacy, reminding them of life and places before displacement that could help maintain intimate relationships in Beirut, even if in a limited or less than perfect form.

Football, for these young refugees in Beirut, emerged as a significant form of navigating ongoing legacies of exclusion and discrimination resulting from their displacement—and more specifically their displacement to Beirut and the intersecting political and racial hierarchies there. As a lynchpin in their efforts to maintain and forge new friendships football presented a means of contesting exclusion from other avenues of sociality and belonging within the city and allowed these young Syrians and Iraqis to stake a claim to at least some public space. It also demonstrated some of the ways in which these young boys were using placed, embodied and relational forms of emotional reflexivity in how they navigated interactions with others, their peers, and the places where they now lived. Considering displacement as a living legacy—where power relations change over time, become sticky and adhere to people and places—is particularly evident in the social and physical limitations that these young boys felt within their day-to-day attempts at enacting friendship through play. However, in its ability to recall happier times, football also allowed these young refugees to contest the relegation of their previous homes and relationships to the past, allowing reflexive comparisons with the present (cf. May, 2017; Miller, 2003) that could maintain a sense of agency. Girls, on the other hand, were excluded from these spaces and inherited some different challenges in making their way through displacement.

Navigating boredom, loneliness and marriage

The young women in our study worked hard to draw on friendships in navigating legacies of displacement that could reinforce limitations arising from gendered power relations. Previous studies have suggested that intimacies among Arab refugee families in Beirut are framed by a "patriarchal connectivity" in which family members identify themselves and others in relation to the father and/or oldest brother (Joseph, 1993). Senior men have considerable control or influence over women and younger men and extended kin are important in young people's lives, especially their cousins. The homogeneity of their neighbourhoods in displacement may reinforce what one of the young Syrian women we met called an "Arab mentality" among their parents regarding who they could be close to and how. Non-kin friendships may be difficult to maintain in the face of this "mentality" (Riga et al., 2021, pp. 27–50) and because friendships have to be navigated around the central importance of families. Kin networks are overlapping and often intricate, which can bring problems such as surveillance by kin and neighbours, as well as benefits

(Forster, 2021). Malika, who was around twelve years old, lived in a Syrian neighbourhood on the edge of the city. She told us a story about her friend Cala, who joined us for that focus group, and how she fell out with her because of Cala's friends (some of whom were her relatives).

> One day I went over to hers and they started to make fun of me a bit (…) so, I got upset and I told her that, "look, it's done, I don't want to speak to them, we can stay friends but I don't want to have anything to do with these others." And then I went home. [But later] they came and made amends.

In order for Malika to continue to be friends with Cala she also had to be friends with these other friends and relatives, even though she didn't like them. Forming intimate friendships beyond their extended families did seem difficult for the young women in our study as there were only so many children who would be acceptable as friends, given the gendered constraints of family politics on one side and discrimination against them as Syrians on the other.

Girls' often hard-won friendships also played a somewhat ambiguous role in helping them navigate fears of early marriage that are a gendered emotional legacy of displacement. Parents have responded to the very real racialised violence experienced by Syrian girls in Beirut through arranging early marriage (Bartels, Michael & Bunting, 2020; Charles & Denman, 2013). Syrian girls in Beirut are almost three times as likely to be married off at a young age (under 18) than they would have been in pre-crisis Syria (Abdulrahim, DeJong, Mourtada & Zurayk, 2017; Bartels et al., 2020). These displaced girls had to steer around their parents' fears, discrimination and violence against them, 'honour' codes, the possibility of early marriage, the above-mentioned structures of distrust, their domestic responsibilities (Suárez-Orozco & Qin, 2006) and their own feelings.

It appeared to be difficult for the young Syrians to draw on friendships to avoid early marriage and loneliness and boredom could result. Malika, mentioned earlier, and Rukan, both Syrian, came to Lebanon when they were young. They told us they enjoy meeting people of other nationalities and backgrounds, but they described their parents as being wary of the girls' relationships, particularly with boys. Going out was limited. Rukan, who was 15, reported that she stayed at home a lot. In one focus group, she described when she had last felt lonely—an emotion word, picked out at random from a hat during an activity: "Lonely. I am the oldest girl, so I always wash dishes or help my mother, since my sister, she goes out sometimes with Mum and Dad and I stay home to do some housework." On our fourth trip she said that since we last saw her, she had been "bored" and wanted "to go back to Syria so I don't have to be in the house anymore". She was not completely without freedom; we know that she and another girl walked quite a long way to be with us at the first workshop. However, the restrictions of being the eldest girl kept her home, and fears of early marriage restricted Rukan's freedom and her friendships.

> We are five friends who are very close. Now we're all very close, nobody likes one person more than they like the other, but my friend Hibah got married about a year ago (...) now she lives far away, at least three hours away. So, I see her maybe once a month, or sometimes not at all, so I don't see her maybe for three months (...) she's like a very good friend and I love her. She's going to be a mum now.

Rukan loves her friend Hibah, but at 15 Hibah was married, lived far away and was expecting her first child. They are seldom able to meet or even speak on the phone. Parents and their young daughters navigated these legacies of displacement with difficulty (Bartels et al., 2020; Cherri, Gil Cuesta, Rodriguez-Llanes & Guha-Sapir, 2017; Merry, Pelaez & Edwards, 2017). Rukan remained unmarried but as a young Syrian woman in displacement in Beirut she recognised the limited options for overcoming her loneliness and boredom. She remembered, or imagined, that in Syria she would be free from the violent legacies of displacement that, in addition to cultural ideas about gender and honour, kept her stuck at home. Yet loneliness, boredom and early marriage were not inevitable outcomes of displacement for the girls we met and in following up with our partner organisations later we were told that Rukan (still unmarried) and her family had relocated to another country where early marriage, and hopefully also boredom, might be more easily avoided.

The Iraqi Christian girls in the study, who were mostly a little younger (from 11 to 16), talked less of loneliness and boredom, but displacement apparently restricted friendships to within their communities. We have already noted their talk of Muslim friends left behind. In Beirut they lived with their families and near other Iraqis in the poorer outskirts of the city. Their daily contact at our partner organisation helped girls make and cement friendships, mostly as Ala and Mina told us, "spend[ing] the day at home together with our families." They often went to each other's houses on a Sunday, to watch a movie "and eat of course" (Randa), although that meant the girls helping their mothers to prepare food while "the boys just play[ed] piano and football" (Sarah). The girls also spoke of occasional outings with their family or the organisation, or going to buy ice creams. However, one legacy of displacement appeared to be a politicisation of these young refugees (Riga, Langer & Dakessian, 2020), which prompted some of the young women to seek social change outside their communities. Outside of the recorded parts of our workshops and focus groups, two of the girls, including Syrian refugee Ala mentioned above, showed us some of the inspirational videos and documentaries that they made to share on social media beyond Beirut. Often about love, inclusivity and hope, we heard less about these videos than

128   David Anderson and Mary Holmes

about football, but they were clearly important to the girls and showed their creativity in finding connections. These ethical and political instances of sociality would benefit from further research. What we did learn was that these young Syrians and Iraqis were emotionally reflexive and showed political acumen in navigating the legacies of displacement.

Conclusion

Experiences of friendship in displacement highlight how legacies of power live on through emotions, but not unaltered. The friendships of these young refugees both required and aided their reflexive navigations of the emotional legacies of displacement. These legacies lived within their and Beirut's present as ongoing feelings about place, community, family, friends and self that were made sense of and acted on in relation to each other, and to ethnic and sectarian power struggles. We argue that these young refugees developed a politically astute emotional reflexivity through which they reflected on the past and present and hoped and acted for change. Importantly, the distinctive characteristics of their displacement had shaped their emotional experiences in the city. The young Syrians seemed more individualised in learning to categorise and discriminate, to help them find friends to provide some emotional support amid sticky forms of disempowerment and distrust within the Palestinian camps of Beirut. The Iraqis, resourced and enabled by their daily contact within a humanitarian organisation, seemed more able to navigate away from distrust and hate together and they reflexively debated what had been the influences of their shared past. However, the organisations these young refugees attended could not always compensate for discrimination or disconnection from the past, especially the loss of friends from other communities who were outside Beirut. The ways in which friendships were used to navigate the emotional legacies of displacement were also gendered. For the boys, football was not an escape from the politicised relationships and exclusion all around them but was vital to using their friendships to feel and claim somewhere and someone to be. Most of the girls were also politicised by the injustices of displacement, but some were left feeling lonely and bored as gendered restrictions limited friendships in the face of the wider discrimination against their displaced communities. Looking at forced displacement through the lens of living legacies allows us to see how shifting power relations have 'stuck' to these young refugees' emotional lives, impacting their friendships and families. It may be that this results in an intergenerational transfer of loss and grief, or that this cycle could be broken (Wanganeen and Szorenyi, Chapter 9). For example, more research would be welcome on how some of these young refugees make political choices to pass on lessons of tolerance and love, instead of perpetuating distrust or hate. Legacies can be ended. Using emotional reflexivity these young refugees learnt from and reacted to the changes that forced displacement and refugeedom had brought, finding new ways of continuing relationships and connecting through politicised reflections on the past, present and future, infused with hopes for change.

Notes

1 At the time of our original study, 2016–17, Lebanon was host to 1,468,431 refugees. However, this may not take account of unregistered refugees. See https://data.worldbank.org/indicator/SM.POP.REFG?locations=LB.
2 Although detailed notes were taken of who was in each focus group, it was not always possible to identify who was speaking when we transcribed the recordings.

References

Abdulrahim, S., DeJong, J., Mourtada, R. & Zurayk, H. (2017). Estimates of early marriage among Syrian refugees in Lebanon in 2016 compared to Syria pre-2011. *European Journal of Public Health*, 27, Issue suppl_3, November 2017, ckx189. 049. doi:10.1093/eurpub/ckx189.049.

Afifi, T., Afifi, W., Merrill, A. & Nimah, N. (2016). "Fractured communities": Uncertainty, stress, and (a lack of) communal coping in Palestinian refugee camps. *Journal of Applied Communication Research* 44(4), 343–361. doi:10.1080/00909882.2016.1225166.

Askins, K. (2015). Being together: Everyday geographies and the quiet politics of belonging. *ACME: An International Journal for Critical Geographies*, 14(2), 470–478. www.acme-journal.org/index.php/acme/article/view/1175. Accessed April 2 2022.

Back, L. (2007). *The art of listening*. Oxford: Berg.

Bartels, S. A., Michael, S. & Bunting, A. (2020). Child marriage among Syrian refugees in Lebanon: At the gendered intersection of poverty, immigration, and safety. *Journal of Immigrant & Refugee Studies*, 19(4), 472–487. Routledge. doi:10.1080/15562948.2020.1839619.

Bergnehr, D., Aronson, O. & Enell, S. (2020). Friends through school and family: Refugee girls' talk about friendship formation. *Childhood*, 27(4), 530–544. doi:10.1177/0907568220923718.

Boccagni, P. (2017). *Migration and the search for home: Mapping domestic space in migrants' everyday lives*. New York: Palgrave Macmillan.

Bradbury, S. (2011). From racial exclusions to new inclusions: Black and minority ethnic participation in football clubs in the East Midlands of England. *International Review for the Sociology of Sport* 46(1), 23–44. doi:10.1177/1012690210371562.

Brownlie, J. (2011). "Being there": Multidimensionality, reflexivity and the study of emotional lives. *The British Journal of Sociology* 62(3), 462–481. doi:10.1111/j.1468-4446.2011.01374.x.

Butler, R. (2021). Moral childhoods: The role of morality in friendship-making among children from refugee backgrounds in rural, multicultural settler Australia. *Children's Geographies*, 1–15. doi:10.1080/14733285.2021.1988513.

Cernea, M. M. & Maldonado, J. K. (Eds). (2018). *Challenging the prevailing paradigm of displacement and resettlement: Risks, impoverishment, legacies, solutions*. Routledge.

Charles, L. & Denman, K. (2013). Syrian and Palestinian Syrian refugees in Lebanon: The plight of women and children. *Journal of International Women's Studies; Bridgewater* 14(5), 96–111.

Chatty, D. (2017). The Syrian humanitarian disaster: Understanding perceptions and aspirations in Jordan, Lebanon and Turkey. *Global Policy* 8(S1), 25–32. doi:10.1111/1758-5899.12390.

Chatty, D., Crivello, G. & Lewando Hundt, G. (2005). Theoretical and methodological challenges of studying refugee children in the Middle East and North Africa: Young Palestinian, Afghan and Sahrawi refugees. *Journal of Refugee Studies*, 18(4), 387–409. doi:10.1093/refuge/fei037.

Chatty, D. & Mansour, N. (2011). Unlocking protracted displacement: An Iraqi case study. *Refugee Survey Quarterly*, 30(4), 50–83. doi:10.1093/rsq/hdr012.

Cherri, Z., Gil Cuesta, J., Rodriguez-Llanes, J. M. & Guha-Sapir, D. (2017). Early marriage and barriers to contraception among Syrian refugee women in Lebanon: A qualitative study. *International journal of environmental research and public health* 14(8), 836. doi:10.3390/ijerph14080836.

Cresswell, T. (2014). *Place: An introduction*. Chichester: Wiley Blackwell.

Culcasi, K. (2019). "We are women and men now": Intimate spaces and coping labour for Syrian women refugees in Jordan. *Transactions of the Institute of British Geographers*, 44(3), 463–478. doi:10.1111/tran.12292.

Dukic, D., McDonald, B. & Spaaij, R. (2017). Being able to play: Experiences of social inclusion and exclusion within a football team of people seeking asylum. *Social Inclusion* 5(2), 101–110. doi:10.17645/si.v5i2.892.

Evers, C. (2010). Intimacy, sport and young refugee men. *Emotion, Space and Society*, 3 (1), 56–61. doi:10.1016/j.emospa.2010.01.011.

Feldman, I. (2019). *Life lived in relief: Humanitarian predicaments and Palestinian refugee politics* [ebook edition]. Oakland, CA: University of California Press. doi:10.1525/california/9780520299627.001.0001.

Forster, R. (2021). No city is the same: Livelihood opportunities among self-settled Syrian refugees in Beirut, Tripoli and Tyre. *CMI Insight, Chr. Michelsen Institute*, March. www.cmi.no/publications/7709-no-city-is-the-same-livelihood-opportunities-among-self-settled-syrian-refugees-in-beirut. Accessed April 2 2022.

Gilmartin, N. (2021). 'Ending the silence': Addressing the legacy of displacement in Northern Ireland's 'Troubles'. *International Journal of Transitional Justice*, 15(1), 108–112. doi:10.1093/ijtj/ijaa027.

Holmes, M. (2010) The emotionalization of reflexivity. *Sociology* 44(1), 139–154. doi:10.1177/0038038509351616.

Jamieson, L. & Highet, G. (2014). Troubling loss? Children's experiences of major disruptions in family life. In J. Ribbens, McCarthy, C. A.Hooper & V. Gillies (Eds), *Family troubles? Exploring changes and challenges in the family lives of children and young people* (pp. 135–150). Bristol: Policy Press.

Joseph, S. (1993). Gender and relationality among Arab families in Lebanon. *Feminist Studies* 19(3), 465–486. doi:10.2307/3178097.

Kallio, K. P. (2019). Leading refugee lives together: Familial agency as a political capacity. *Emotion, Space and Society*, 32, 100541. doi:10.1016/j.emospa.2018.08.002.

Kelley, N. (2017). Responding to a refugee influx: Lessons from Lebanon. *Journal on Migration & Human Security* 5(1), 82–104. doi:10.1177/233150241700500105.

Lupu, N. & Peisakhin, L. (2017) The legacy of political violence across generations. *American Journal of Political Science* 61 (4): 836–851. doi:10.1111/ajps.12327.

Marshall, D. J. (2013). 'All the beautiful things': Trauma, aesthetics and the politics of Palestinian childhood. *Space and Polity*, 17(1), 53–73. doi:10.1080/13562576.2013.780713.

Marshall, D. J. (2014). Save (us from) the children: trauma, Palestinian childhood, and the production of governable subjects. *Children's Geographies*, 12(3), 281–296. doi:10.1080/14733285.2014.922678.

Martin, D. (2015). From spaces of exception to 'campscapes': Palestinian refugee camps and informal settlements in Beirut. *Political Geography* 44, 9–18. doi:10.1016/j.polgeo.2014.08.001.

May, V. (2017). Belonging from afar: Nostalgia, time and memory. *The Sociological Review* 65(2), 401–415. doi:10.1111/1467-954X.12402.

Merry, L., Pelaez, S. & Edwards, N. C. (2017). Refugees, asylum-seekers and undocumented migrants and the experience of parenthood: A synthesis of the qualitative literature. *Globalization and Health* 13(1), 75. doi:10.1186/s12992-017-0299-4.

Miller, L. (2003). Belonging to country—A philosophical anthropology. *Journal of Australian Studies* 27(76), 215–223. doi:10.1080/14443050309387839.

Morgan, D. (2011). *Rethinking family practices.* Basingstoke: Palgrave Macmillan. www.palgrave.com/us/book/9780230527232. Accessed April 2 2022.

Nathan, S., Kemp, L., Bunde-Birouste, A., MacKenzie, J., Evers, C. & Shwe, A. T. (2013). "We wouldn't of made friends if we didn't come to Football United": The impacts of a football program on young people's peer, prosocial and cross-cultural relationships. *BMC public health* 13(1), 1–16. doi:10.1186/1471-2458-13-399.

Pahl, R. & Spencer, L. (2004). Personal communities: Not simply families of 'fate' or 'choice'. *Current Sociology* 52(2), 199–221. doi:10.1177/0011392104041808.

Policarpo, V. (2016). "The real deal": Managing intimacy within friendship at a distance. *Qualitative Sociology Review* 12(2), 22–42. doi:10.18778/1733-8077.12.2.02.

Ramadan, A. & Fregonese, S. (2017). Hybrid sovereignty and the state of exception in the Palestinian refugee camps in Lebanon. *Annals of the American Association of Geographers* 107(4), 949–963. doi:10.1080/24694452.2016.1270189.

Reddy, W. M. (2001). *The navigation of feeling: A framework for the history of emotions.* Cambridge: Cambridge University Press.

Riga, L., Holmes, M., Dakessian, A., Langer, J. & Anderson, D. (2021). *Young refugees and forced displacement: Navigating everyday life in Beirut.* London: Routledge.

Riga, L., Langer, J. & Dakessian, A. (2020) Theorizing refugeedom: Becoming young political subjects in Beirut. *Theory and Society* 49(4), 709–744. doi:10.1007/s11186-020-09393-2.

Sayigh, R. (1994). *Too many enemies.* London: Zed Books.

Spaaij, R. (2015). Refugee youth, belonging and community sport. *Leisure Studies* 34(3), 303–318. doi:10.1080/02614367.2014.893006.

Spencer, L. & Pahl, R. (2006). *Rethinking friendship: Hidden solidarities today.* Princeton, NJ: Princeton University Press.

Suárez-Orozco, C. & Qin, D. B. (2006). Gendered perspectives in psychology: Immigrant origin youth. *International Migration Review* 40(1), 165–198. doi:10.1111/j.1747-7379.2006.00007.x.

United Nations High Commissioner for Refugees. (2021). Lebanon factsheet—November 2021. https://reporting.unhcr.org/document/1262. Accessed April 2 2022.

United Nations High Commissioner for Refugees/United Nations International Children's Emergency Fund/World Food Programme. (2017). VASYR 2017—Vulnerability assessment of Syrian refugees in Lebanon. https://data2.unhcr.org/en/documents/details/61312. Accessed April 2 2022.

United Nations High Commissioner for Refugees/United Nations International Children's Emergency Fund/World Food Programme. (2022). VASYR 2021—Vulnerability assessment of Syrian refugees in Lebanon. https://reliefweb.int/sites/reliefweb.int/files/resources/VASyR%202021.pdf. Accessed April 2 2022.

Wacquant, L. (2004). *Body & soul: Notebooks of an apprentice boxer.* Oxford: Oxford University Press.

Wernesjö, U. (2012). Unaccompanied asylum-seeking children: Whose perspective? *Childhood*, 19(4), 495–507. doi:10.1177/0907568211429625.

Chapter 8

The Enduring Legacies of Migration
Older Greek-born Migrants' Experience of Ageing in Australia

Pam Papadelos

Introduction

Australia, like many other developed countries, has an increasing ageing population with a rise in the proportion of people aged 65 and over (15.9 per cent in 2019), which is largely attributed to low fertility rates and an increased life expectancy (Australian Bureau of Statistics, 2019). Of those born overseas there are approximately 20 per cent who were born in non-English-speaking countries (Australian Institute of Health and Welfare, 2018). This relatively high number reflects Australia's history of post-war migration, which peaked between 1950 and 1970 (Jupp, 2002). For this reason, Brandhorst, Baldassar and Wilding (2021, p. 250) suggest a 'migration turn' in the aged care sector to deal with "the ongoing impact of past migration and of long-term migrant settlement". Post-war Greek migrants are of particular interest as they are the largest cohort (88.4 per cent) of ageing citizens from non-English speaking countries in Australia, closely followed by post-war Italian migrants (87.9 per cent).[1]

This chapter utilizes the concept 'living legacies' to explore post-war Greek migrants' experiences of ageing in Australia. Legacy here refers to the "quiet, slow, static, 'sticky' and long-standing normalised aggregations of power" as an ongoing process and therefore 'living', rather than an event fixed in the past (Chapter 1 of this volume). In this context, legacies of migration in this chapter relate to the impact of past injustices and traumas experienced as a result of migration and their ongoing and often unforeseen relationship to perceptions of ageing positively. In this setting, it is useful to draw attention to both ongoing and living legacies of migration. As stated in Chapter 1 (Beasley & Papadelos) in this collection, 'ongoing' and 'living' are not interchangeable terms but they are also not altogether different. Ongoing notes what 'sticks' or continues over time, whereas the term living refers to relations of power which are ongoing but show signs of alteration in keeping with political, cultural and environmental changes or factors in the present such that continuities in power are undercut or even effectively disguised. Thus, while ongoing suggests that some aspects of power relations from the past may push through

DOI: 10.4324/9781003311928-10

time, in a relatively static and unchanged way, the language of living legacy attends to the way that power relations not only continue but actively shape the present and future thereby impacting on lives in unexpected, unpredictable or even inadvertent ways.

Legacies of migration are not officially recognised by the state and are either forgotten, repressed, or remembered at the individual/community level. Ongoing and living aspects of the impact of migration are to be found at this non-official level. According to Loriggio (1996, p. 117):

> [t]here are strong and weak globalities (colonialism has produced a strong variety, in so far as its legacies are officially and publicly inscribed in the social or political fabric of the ex-colonies; migrations a weak variety, in so far as its legacies are non-official, do not commit the state to anything, are left to private individuals to acknowledge or not).

Thus, it is important that researchers address these often neglected historical legacies of migration and the socio-structural injustices (low levels of cultural and social capital)[2] that resonate for ethnic minorities in the present. For many participants emotional and other psychological problems stemming from legacies of migration have negatively impacted on ageing (see also Damousi 2013). These issues are not easily overcome. However, by recognising or identifying the harmful effects of migration legacies, opportunities arise to enact change in the present.

An analysis of 37 in-depth interviews with older Greek-born Australians residing in Adelaide, Brisbane and Darwin who immigrated to Australia between 1947 and 1975 are used to inform the discussion about the impact of legacies of migration on ageing. This paper begins with an overview of post-war Greek migration to Australia, followed by a brief history of multi-culturalism in Australia. These sections provide the necessary context for understanding the experiences of ageing for older Greek-Australians..

Post-war Greek migration to Australia: An Overview

Although there were small Greek communities dotted throughout Australia prior to World War II, the majority of Greeks arrived between 1952 and 1970. This increase in Greek migration was a direct result of the Menzies Coalition Government's decision to actively pursue immigrants beyond recuperating losses sustained during the Depression (1930s) and World War II (Kunz, 1971). European migrants including Southern Europeans, such as Greeks and Italians who could pass as "a darker shade of white", were explicitly sought between 1950 and 1970, principally because they were viewed as a lesser evil than Asian migrants or the "yellow peril" (Hage, 2002, p. 424). Efforts to attract migrants from Greece by Australia's first Minister of Immigration, Arthur Calwell, were welcomed by the Greek Government which

The Enduring Legacies of Migration 135

was caught up in the aftermath of a brutal Civil War (1946–49) that devastated a country yet to recover from World War II.

Post-war Greek migration to Australia started in small numbers after World War II and escalated after 1952 with the signing of the Intergovernmental Committee for European Migration agreement between Greece and Australia (Glenn et al., 2017). The majority of early arrivals were young, able-bodied, single men, followed by families. This created a significant gender imbalance (ratio of 1:5) prompting the government to specifically target female migrants in order to address the issue of "unhappy, disillusioned, lonely and frustrated [migrant men who] would sooner go home to uneasy Europe than stay" in Australia (*The Australasian Post* 1953 cited in Simic, 2014, p. 159). Thus, from 1957 to at least 1963 single women arrivals outnumbered single men—many arriving on what were referred to as 'bride ships' (Janiszewski & Alexakis, 2015). Between 1952 and 1972 a total of 71,221 Greeks travelled to Australia by ship with assisted passage, although the total number (assisted and self-funded) exceeded 180,000 arrivals (Palaktsoglou, 2013, p. 294). There was also an influx of Greek Cypriots from 1963 to 1974 as a result of displacement caused by the forced division of Cypress into the Turkish north and Greek south (Georgiades, 2015, p. 1538). Despite the disparate geographic differences most migrants were unskilled, had low levels of education, and did not speak English. The majority of post-war Greek migrants settled in Victoria and New South Wales with fewer migrants settling in South Australia and other parts of Australia (Glenn et al., 2017).

While migration to Australia was voluntary, over 214,000 Greeks were compelled to migrate between 1947 and 1972 as a result of poverty, trauma and violence (Damousi, 2013, p. 13). Migrants who did not have relatives or friends to support them on arrival were "conscripted to designated jobs" in remote areas of Australia or interned in former army camps, such as Bonegilla (operational from 1947 until 1971) in rural Victoria (Teicher, Shah & Griffin, 2002, p. 212).

Despite the urgent pleas from the Arthur Calwell, the first Minister for Immigration in the late 1940s, for 'white Australians' to welcome the newcomers as 'new Australians', they were quickly labelled the "'Dago Menace', the 'Olive Peril', the 'Greasy Wog' and the 'Olive Trash'" (Andreoni, 2003, p. 81). In addition, southern European migrants were initially considered "aliens" and did not have access to "public welfare services" available to British migrants on arrival (Birrell & Jupp, 2000, p. 2). Post-war Greek migrants were successful in maintaining their cultural traditions, including language and religion, in many cases to the detriment of English language acquisition and general community engagement outside of their own cultural circles (Avgoulas & Fanany, 2016, p. 107).

It is estimated that more than 300,000 Australians with Greek heritage permanently reside in Australia. However, the number of Greek-born Australians is decreasing as a result of limited infrequent arrivals since 1970 and an increase in mortality rate with age. The 2016 Census reported that Victoria has the largest population of Greek-born migrants (47,240), followed by New South Wales (29,481) and then South Australia (8,682) (Australian Bureau of Statistics, 2017). Post-war Greek migrants resisted the pressure to assimilate by forming community groups/associations and a strong connection to the Greek Ortho- dox Church, which also invested in Greek language classes for future genera- tions. However, the inadequacy and even failure of assimilationist policies at a national level—evidenced by resistance to assimilation (in varying degrees) even by the third generation (Papadelos, 2021)— contributes to the construction of the Greek migrant as the 'perpetual-foreigner-within' (Nicolacopoulos and Vassilacopoulos, 2005, p. 275) or 'the stranger at home' (Vasta, 2017, p. 36). In this context, following Sara Ahmed's (2004) observation, 'sticky words' or 'sticky signs', such as migrant in this case, become associated with particular bodies.

Multiculturalism in Australia: An overview

There are a number of key phases of Australian Migration Policy according to Jupp (2007): the White Australia Policy (1880–1973); assimilation policies (1946– 1960s); integration policies (1960s–early 1970s); multicultural policies (since the late 1980s); and more recently a backlash against multiculturalism (since the late 1990s). It is worth noting that these phases and the sentiments attached to their logic are not strictly linear. Nevertheless, recent studies show that feelings of reverse discrimination fuelled by high profile far-right politicians, like Pauline Hanson, maintain and reinforce perceptions that a multicultural approach to migration will threaten Australian identity and disadvantage 'white' Australians (Sharples & Blair, 2021). It is not within the scope of this paper to provide a detailed account of each of the phases identified by Jupp (2007). However, while the discussion will focus on multiculturalism and the way that it incorporates policies offering protections around cultural, religious and linguistic differences, comment on the other phases will be incorporated where relevant. I argue that the legacy of past policies continue to impact on the shaping of multiculturalism and its potential to enact change. Moreover, simply repealing or rescinding racist policies will not erase the negative consequences of these legacies because they have already hindered migrants' ability to accumulate essential skills, or what Bourdieu (1986) refers to as social and cultural capital, that will enhance their experience of old age. A living legacies framework holds the past accountable for present and future injustices.

Immigration was a priority for the newly Federated Commonwealth gov- ernment of Australia, formed in 1901. For the first two hundred years of colonisation there was a strong British influence in Australia in line with a vision for "a new Britannia" (Jupp, 2002, p. 5).[3] This vision was embedded in the first Act passed by Prime Minister, Edmund Barton's government, the *Immigration Restriction Act* 1901 (Commonwealth), later known as 'The White Australia Policy'. The Act, through various strategies, the most insidious being "a dictation test [administered] in any European language", freed the Government of the day to be selective about who could enter the country while circumnavigating accusations of racism (Bashford, 2014, p. 32). The White Australia Policy was strictly adhered to for the first part of the twentieth century and reinforced "a racial causal logic linking White racial identity and high civilized standards of living" (Hage, 2002, p. 423). Thus, the policy was based on maintaining a "homogeneous [British] culture", underpinned by an ideology of white supremacy, which justified the exclusion of undesirable immigrants until the end of World War II (Stratton, 1998, p. 15).

Despite these problematic government policies following on from Australia's colonial beginnings, in recent times Australia has a diverse population with 30 per cent of Australia's population born overseas (Australian Bureau of Statistics, 2021).[4] Australian multiculturalism is based on an ideology that recognises and celebrates this cultural diversity (Gow, 2005). In this setting, government sanctioned policies were put into place to protect the rights of minority groups and promote everyday "intercultural encounters" (Wise, 2005). Yet, as Stratton (1998, p. 10) notes, these multicultural policies have a "very conservative understanding of culture", which fail to address or acknowledge the "different moralities" of cultures other than Anglo-Celtic in origin. Instead, multicultural policies adhere to "a metaphorical spatial structure in which migrant, 'ethnic' cultures are peripheral to a core culture" that primarily comprises of white British and Irish settlers (Stratton, 1998, p. 10).

Australia's first Minister of Immigration, Calwell, was tasked with increasing Australia's population through active immigration initiatives, or "planned immigration" at the end of World War II (Tavan, 2012, p. 209). The rationale behind the population increase was twofold: first, to address the potential threat of Asian invasion, fuelled by a Cold War mentality, captured in the phrase "populate or perish" (Meaney, 1995, p. 177) and, second, to source unskilled labourers to build much needed infrastructure (Markus, 1984). The hope was that most of the new migrants would come from Britain or Ireland, but for the first time in Australia's history its government actively encouraged non-British immigrants from southern European countries, like Greece and Italy, heralding a new direction in Australia's immigration policy.

Calwell's passion for immigration, intensified by a growing "invasion complex" (Papastergiadis, 2004, p. 9), was tempered by his ongoing commitment to a white Australia demonstrated through additional financial support for British immigrants (described as 'Ten pound Poms'),[5] and his 1949 publication "I stand by White Australia". This commitment was further evidenced through policies of assimilation where new immigrants were required to cast aside their 'cultural baggage' and blend into their new environment.

However, after the mass influx of post-war migrants the ideology of assimilation became difficult to sustain (Vasta, 2006). Many non-British post war migrants maintained linguistic and cultural practices of their home countries, owing in part to language barriers and in part to the racism of assimilation agendas (Nicolacopoulos & Vassilacopoulos, 2014, p. 24). In other words, despite measures by governments, "institutional and informal racism" encouraged a resistance to assimilation, with post war migrant groups forming enclaves that maintained cultural distinctions (Vasta, 1993, p. 210). For instance, first-generation Greek migrants maintained language, religion and cultural traditions by closely aligning with other Greek migrants and resisting, or at the very least mitigating, the effects of racism by forming institutions that served their needs (that is, churches, schools and social clubs). Moreover, the plethora of regional clubs (Cyprian, Macedonian and Spartan, among others) fought the erasure of "the collective historical experience of specified groups" (Carangio, Farquharson, Bertone & Rajendran, 2020, p. 5) and the homogenisation of source cultures (Stratton 1998, 34). According to Damousi:

> [t]he assimilation policy which framed migration objectives after World War II did not allow for recognition of an immigrant's history. The discourse of the nation-state was premised on a denial of past connections to home and indeed a repression of these memories.
>
> (2013, p. 15)

By the late 1970s, Australian policies had moved away from a politics of assimilation towards a strategy of multiculturalism in line with Canada's multicultural policies (Stratton & Ang, 2001, p. 154). Multicultural policies were developed to account for a growing public awareness of the diverse ethnic makeup of society, to address conspicuous socioeconomic disparities and celebrate diversity. Since adopting the new policy there has been a push to forget the racism implicit in Australia's colonial past and celebrate diversity whereby the migrant's ethnic identity "coexists with the national" (Ang, 2014, p. 1184). In the words of Sara Ahmed (2007, p. 131), this approach to multiculturalism was intended to produce "a happy smiling multiculturalism". Ahmed, among others, is critical of this version of multiculturalism as it is predicated on integrating into the dominant culture, where the onus is on the migrant "to let go of the pain of racism by letting go of racism" not only to secure their happiness but also for "the generation-to-come" (Ahmed, 2007, p. 133). While the shift from assimilation to multiculturalism was welcomed by many, it leaves "unquestioned the construct of the 'nation', nationalism and continued inequalities in Australian society" (Ashton, 2009, p. 385). Instead the focus is diverted to a tokonistic "celebration of costumes, customs and cooking" (Gunew, 1994, p. 22).

Australia's commitment to the White Australia Policy, while the cause of much discomfort in recent history, has left a legacy that persists in varying degrees (Carangio et al., 2020). The outcome of many legacies can only be discernible as positive or negative retrospectively, yet negative consequences (intentional or unintentional, evident or disguised) are rarely addressed or mitigated in a meaningful way. The shift to multiculturalism benefited the dominant culture in the

The Enduring Legacies of Migration 139

form of economic growth and cultural diversity and provided protections for minority cultures and communities, while failing to adequately address past injustices that continue to disadvantage migrants into old age. This background provides a basis for understanding the complicated relationship between past injustices and current issues faced by ageing Greek-Australians.

Method

Participants were recruited through community groups, church groups and service providers. Primary data was collected through in-depth interviews. A total of 37 in-depth interviews were carried out with participants in Adelaide (n=17), Brisbane (n=10) and Darwin (n=10). Participants were interviewed in their homes with the average interview lasting approximately ninety minutes in duration. Ethical approval was received before data collection began and consent was obtained from the participants prior to the interview. Interviews were mostly conducted in Greek (89 per cent) and a number of questions, both qualitative and quantitative, were asked and audio-recorded. The interview included some demographic questions on age, education levels, living

Table 8.1 Demographic Characteristics

Variables		*(n=37)*
Gender	Female	56.8% (21)
	Male	43.2% (16)
Age	Youngest 67 and oldest 92	77 mean
Age arrived in Aust.	Youngest 4 and oldest 49	21 mean
Marital Status	Married	67.6% (25)
	Widowed	29.7% (11)
	Divorced	2.7% (1)
Education	Some primary school	37.8% (14)
	Completed primary school	37.8% (14)
	Some Secondary School	16.2% (6)
	Completed Secondary school	0% (0)
	Trade Qualification, Apprenticeship, Diploma	2.7% (1)
	University Degree	5.4% (2)
Preferred Language	Greek	89.2% (33)
	English	10.8% (4)
Spoken English proficiency (self-assessed)	Very good	10.8% (4)
	Average	27% (10)
	Very Poor/not at all	62.2% (23)
What was the main reason for your move to Australia?	For a better future	56.8% (21)
	To meet family	24.3% (9)
	To get married	8.1% (3)
	To find work	10.8% (4)

140   Pam Papadelos

arrangements, housing, mobility, English language proficiency, social activities and perceptions of participants' general health. Open-ended questions explored life course information about migration experiences, perceptions and histories since arriving in Australia and personal beliefs about ageing and what participants consider makes them happy.

In accordance with characteristics of the older Greek-born population most participants had low levels of formal education with the majority not completing secondary school (92 per cent). High rates of home ownership (92 per cent owned outright) and residential stability was evident among this population with a mean period of 34 years spent living at the same address, which indicates that participants are well established in their current neighbourhoods and are familiar with their local environment.

Trauma, loss and isolation: an analysis of the interview data

Early assimilation policies necessitated a 'forgetting' of the past predicated on a will to succeed that often required long hours at work and relying on children to act as cultural and language interpreters (Vasta, 1993). Retired, ageing migrants in this study dwelt on these aspects of their migration experience often weaving together past and present experiences, especially traumatic experiences, into a non-linear narrative where memories of the past were constantly present. The legacies of early assimilationist policies, such as the White Australia Policy, resonate and linger in their accounts of trauma, loss and isolation demonstrating their ongoing effects. Trauma, Máiréad Enright (2019, p. 72) explains, "does not make its mark at the time", but rather the effects of trauma continue into the present shaping everyday life. For many participants the events that lead to migration and subsequent treatment on arrival were experienced and remembered as traumatic events. The concept of living legacy is important in providing insights into the current issues faced by these post-war migrants as they are ageing. While some features of the traumas of migration are evidently ongoing, others are less easily recognised. Such features shape who they are now, how they came to be in Australia and what support is required as they age. This chapter explores three dominant themes that emerged from the data: a sense of loss and isolation; a strong expectation that their children should look after them based on memories of life in Greece prior to migration; and the ongoing impact of the World War II and the Civil War. These themes were often interconnected.

Sense of loss, social isolation and longing for 'home'

> My memories of Greece are beautiful. I left my village with tears in my eyes.
> (80 year-old-woman, migrated aged 26)

Longing for 'home' or what Avtar Brah (2005, p. 189), called "homing desire" was strongly expressed by some participants. However, the desire for home was not straightforward as it became clear "that 'home' is a mythic place of desire in the diasporic imagination, (...) it is a place of no return, even if it is possible to visit the geographical territory that is seen as the place of origin" (Brah, 2005, p. 188). Participants spoke of wanting to go 'home' or missing their homes, while also recognising that their 'home' no longer exists or is not a realistic option for them and that Australia is now home. Thus, as Ahmed states "it is not simply that the subject does not belong anywhere" but that they belong in "more than one place" (Ahmed, 1999, p. 330). The loss of one's preferred 'home' caused by displacement is expressed in the following comments.

> I have one thing that I would like to be different. I would like to be in my village, even if my life is a little worse off than here. I would be happier in my own village rather than in this strange land. But there were no opportunities to go back, and by the time we could afford it the children did not want to go. So, the moment passed and now I can't go back.
>
> (74 year-old-man, migrated aged 20)

> I wish we did not have to leave Greece, but that wasn't a choice. I wish we didn't have to come here. That I could have stayed with my parents, my siblings, not to be in a strange land with no relatives, it was very bad. This is something that we all had in common when we came to Australia; everyone missed their family. We wished to be back in Greece but now this is lost to us for ever. Now we can never go back for good, we have too much to lose—we have our house, our children our grandchildren, so we can't leave. Also we have our doctors and know how the system works here. Greece is our mother and Australia is our stepmother, not a bad stepmother, but not the same.
>
> (81-year-old woman, migrated aged 25)

Their desire for home was more than a longing for Greece; homeland represented family and belonging. In spite of the care and companionship offered by their adult children, some participants spoke of regrets about migrating to Australia, particularly in relation to loneliness. These emotions govern their everyday experiences and are rooted in decisions made in the past, which they claimed were not through choice but 'forced' on them. In particular, participants spoke of the impact of war on their decision to leave Greece and later marginalisation from mainstream society, which occurred in an effort to resist racism (Vasta, 1993). Loneliness and isolation was a common theme, particularly among widowed participants.

The social isolation is what will kill us. This is the worst thing about coming to Australia. Sitting here all alone day after day, waiting for our children. I think this is why so many Greeks have dementia. There were no cases of dementia in our village. It was unheard of. Here we are alone and we ponder on the past. I came to Australia in 1962. I don't want to remember those years as things were so difficult. The racism was awful. We were called names. In those days people seemed very ignorant and nasty. People would spit at us in the street. I was especially sad for my children because the schools did nothing about it. Australia is my home but it is not really my home. I sometimes think that I would rather have fallen in the sea and have been eaten by the fish than come here. It is too late now, but I wish I never came. Years later I still cry. My children tell me not to be silly that things are good here, but I don't feel that way. It worries me this bitterness I feel. For me the worse thing about ageing is having bad memories because they get worse as you age.

(75-year-old woman, migrated aged 21)

The thing that upsets me the most is my loneliness. Who can help with that? From 5pm to the morning I am on my own, my mouth is closed and my throat constricts. Not like in Greece where there are many people to talk to, people who speak your language. That's why older people have a better life there than here; they are not as isolated.

(85-year-old man, migrated aged 38)

In other words, the difficulties they endured, and for some continue to endure, are presented as unavoidable and direct consequences of past and ongoing processes of migration. The isolation and loneliness felt by many participants was mitigated somewhat by the care and companionship of their children and to a lesser extent their grandchildren. Thus, deep sadness and regret (associated with never seeing their parents, siblings, aunts and uncles again) and nostalgia (for the life they imagined they might have lived), was often interrupted with an acknowledgement that they are grateful for the opportunities available in Australia, especially economic and academic opportunities available to their children. Their feelings of disconnectedness, even after 40 or more years of living in Australia, points to a legacy of refusing/resisting assimilationist policies. The participants' sense of disconnection is typically associated with being unable and/or unwilling to socialise with other communities in Australia, most notably as a result of language barriers. However, their experience of ongoing isolation from the general community has not been officially recognised or addressed under the more recent policy of multiculturalism. In other words, the legacies of previous policies that have built up over time that have built residues that shape current experiences. The notion of living legacies allows us to acknowledge and interrogate these

The Enduring Legacies of Migration   143

sediments thereby enabling identification of areas where change can be enacted, and where these legacies can be overcome or at the very least mitigated. Moreover, because these legacies remain 'live', they can be recognised and dealt with in ways that are appropriate for individuals and communities.

Expectation that family members would look after them: 'Happiness comes from family'

Most participants expressed a strong reliance on their children to act as interpreters and "cultural brokers" (Bauer, 2016). Earlier studies reflect findings that children, predominately daughters, are more likely to provide care, reassurance and companionship as parents age (Connidis & Davies, 1992; Papadelos, 2019). The majority of participants stated that their daughters undertook most of the domestic and care responsibilities, while their sons mostly dropped by to share food, have a Greek coffee and occasionally translate letters and explain unknown bills. The following provides an illustrative account of the work done by participant's daughters.

> My daughter comes every Saturday because she works every day. My other daughter comes to wash and hang my clothes and do some ironing. They also help with bills, go to the pharmacy and doctors with me. We are still very independent and we don't expect anything from our children as we know that they are busy.
>
> (80-year-old woman, migrated aged 26)

> My daughter lives close-by. She was 10 when we came to Australia and speaks Greek well, but sometimes she does not know all the words. My son was born here and doesn't speak Greek very well, but we understand each other. I see my daughter every day and we call a hundred times a day. She cooks and brings me food here and I go to her house 3–4 times a week to eat.
>
> (85-year-old man, migrated aged 40)

The expectation that family members should look after the elderly was clearly articulated by all bar one participant who migrated to Australia aged four. For the majority of participants the belief that family members should care for their elders stems from their memories of village life and the non-nuclear family unit that included extended family. Greek traditions, or way of life in the villages, was mostly remembered as communal and loving. Many participants expressed feelings of nostalgia, loss and yearning, in relation to the value and significance of the extended family in caring for the elderly.

> From a young age we were taught to respect the elderly—uncles, aunts and relatives. There was a lot of hardship and hard work, but plenty of love and

happy times too. No matter what problems/issues arose, there was support and strength from the whole family, young and old, to overcome them.

(75-year-old woman, migrated aged 22)

The old people in our village lived very well. They sat outside their homes and talked to everyone who passed. I respected old people a lot. The most important thing for a person when they age is that their family looks after them. I have three children and seven grandchildren and don't think they should abandon me in my old age.

(76-year-old woman, migrated aged 17).

We had grandmother (γιαγιά) and grandfather (παππού) living with us. Everyone did their bit, so they were not a burden. There was nowhere for old people to go. There were no pensions, nursing homes or anything. They lived well because they were looked after by everyone and had their family around them.

(76-year-old man, migrated aged 28)

The old people there were old but not unhealthy, whereas in Australia there are a lot of illnesses. The elderly saw their children every day and they were happy. The evenings were particularly lovely with everyone keeping each other entertained. Sometimes there were festivals (πανηγύρια) where the whole village and neighbouring villages came together to celebrate.

(76-year-old woman, migrated aged 19)

While family, and to some extent community, was noted as important it did not mask the hardship faced by all, especially the old. Some accounts were not as positive as the ones above. Indeed, some participants recounted memories of the difficulties older people faced in the village because there was limited access to health services and all able-bodied family members would be out in the fields during the day:

I remember seeing the elderly [in Greece] and thinking, 'Let's not grow old (…) better that we die young before we grow old'; see, now we are elderly and we haven't died. Ageing then was not a happy/enjoyable time.

(78-year-old woman, migrated aged 33)

I loved all the old people in our village. I felt for them and always tried to be helpful. The old people back then had some hardship because there were no doctors or medical facilities.

(85-year-old man, migrated aged 38)

They were very hard times. The elderly didn't have access to proper conveniences, or a proper diet. Their diet usually consisted of rice,

The Enduring Legacies of Migration   145

pasta, and whatever was made in the home. Bathing was limited to washing your feet, arms and head as there were no showers like there is today. There were no nursing homes in those days, so the elderly would be left in the house by themselves as the children/family had to work in the fields during the day. People in those days died young.

(79-year-old man, migrated aged 30)

In an effort to work against the racist assumptions of assimilation into the Anglo-Celtic mainstream, while ameliorating the related threat of social isolation, post-war Greek migrants countered by developing their own social supports. They created social (clubs and halls), religious, and educational spaces (ethnic schools) that maintained their separate identity (Vasta, 1993, p. 210). The role or function of the Greek Orthodox church for Greek-Australians continues to be significant in maintaining culture, but for older migrants it is also vital for social and psychological well-being (Damousi, 2013). For these reasons, religious and ethnic identities are inseparable for many Greeks, as Orthodoxy is considered "an integral indispensable element of Greek identity" (Roudometof, 2008, p. 71). However, this element of culture is most strongly associated with older migrants. My earlier research on third-generation Australians of Greek heritage found that most young people attended church for special occasions only and looked elsewhere for social and psychological support (Papadelos, 2021). By contrast, the majority of these first-generation participants said that they attended church regularly with approximately 80 per cent attending at least once a week. Difficulty with transport or mobility issues were significant factors for those who attended less frequently.

We go to church every Sunday because we are Christians. But you also get the chance to talk to someone. It is important to meet with people.

(79-year-old man, migrated aged 30)

I think it is important that I attend church regularly. I want my children to be healthy and praise God (Δόξα τω Θεώ), so that he doesn't forget them.

(78 year old woman, migrated age 33)

We used to go to church every Sunday but we don't go anymore because we have no one to take us. I can't leave my husband alone as he is not mobile.

(83-year-old woman, migrated aged 19)

I want to die knowing that my children and grandchildren are healthy, safe and happy, praise God (Δόξα τω Θεώ).

(71-year-old woman, migrated aged 19)

146 Pam Papadelos

During the interviews many of the participants crossed themselves and praised God (Δόξα τω Θεώ) for their good fortune and the blessings bestowed upon their children. While participants were very grateful for the level of care provided by their children, they resented or lamented their dependence, which they claimed was a consequence of migration. The legacy of racist policies has not dissipated with time. Instead their influence is ongoing in that participants are unable to overcome barriers to participation in mainstream society. Despite the creation of supportive structures within their own communities including the support of the Greek Orthodox church, limited culturally appropriate services in their adopted home leads elderly Greek-Australian migrants to rely upon old traditions and look to family members, particularly daughters, for help and care (including transport, domestic duties and translation) and companionship. While the additional work taken on by their children is largely presumed to be axiomatic, nevertheless this demand placed upon their families add to their sense of disconnection and loss associated with migration from an originating 'home' community as participants acknowledge that their adult children often struggle with juggling paid work and childcare. In this instance, migration not only resulted in ongoing legacies associated with past reliance on family, but these legacies proved increasingly problematic in the changed circumstances of Australian family life.

The Wars

In the previous paragraphs the ongoing legacies of migration were linked to aged post-war migrants' feelings of loneliness and isolation along with reliance on their children. Research on post-war migrants rarely focuses on their experiences prior to migration. Thus, Damousi's (2013, 2015) work on the psychological consequences of, not only the Second World War, but also the ensuing Civil War on older Greek migrants and their children is an important contribution. Damousi (2013, p. 12) claims that assimilationist policies necessitated the "suppression of individual and collective memory" of trauma, which lead to unresolved grief. For many participants memories of the wars continue to haunt them.

> They were 'black years' I try not to think of them; the Germans, the war—best not to think of them as I get upset. My doctor tells me not to dwell on the past as it is not good for me especially as I am on my own [widowed], but sometimes it is hard not to. During the day it is not so bad but at night it is not so good.
>
> (85-year-old man, migrated aged 38)

> I have a lot of pain in my heart. The brutality I witnessed during the war and the death of my brother are particularly painful memories. I take

The Enduring Legacies of Migration 147

comfort in my religion and my family, they help me forget the pain of the past.

> (82-year-old woman, migrated aged 27)

I came to Australia out of desperation. We were poor and the Germans stole our wealth and we couldn't do anything about it. Then we had the civil war and the situation got worse as Greeks fought with Greeks.

> (81-year-old woman, migrated aged 25)

There was the war and then we had the guerrillas—I saw people been killed at a very young age. And later, after the war, my family would talk about these events. It is impossible to forget this time.

> (75-year-old woman, migrated aged 21)

There is some evidence that Greek-born migrants are more likely to suffer from anxiety and depression compared to Anglo-Australians (Kiropoulos et al., 2012). Higher rates of depression are attributed to a combination of stressors, including missing family in Greece, nostalgia for homeland, isolation/loneliness, mobility or health issues (Georgiades, 2015), and, less recognised, unresolved trauma experienced pre-migration (Damousi, 2013).

Restrictive assimilation policies failed to recognise migrants' "past connections to home" especially grief related to traumatic memories of war (Damousi, 2013, p. 15). Their unresolved trauma has produced an enduring legacy for many of these migrants. However, trauma is not necessarily experienced as having a fixed effect. This legacy may also be reshaped by older migrants for future generations because they "can find a way of living (…) that feels better through the process of speaking about the past, and through exposing the wounds that get concealed by the 'truths' of a certain history" (Ahmed, 2004, p. 201). Participants talking about their stories prior to migration, as well as stories of home-sickness and building new families after migration, and lastly stories of isolation and restriction in older age, potentially enable ways of coming to grips with the complex legacies of migration.

Conclusion

> I look forward and not back, otherwise it gets depressing; we have to move forward. I went back to Greece and didn't recognise many people. Many left and others are dead. I miss my sisters, but not like my children and grandchildren, so I always come back. I don't belong anywhere [laughs].
>
> (76-year-old man, migrated aged 28)

This paper attempts to provide insight into post-war Greek migrants' experiences of ageing in Australia and utilises the concept 'living legacies' to understand past injustice and the ongoing challenges produced as a result of migration and discriminatory government policies. The concept of 'living legacies' is useful here as it provides a framework for understanding the ways in which past injustice and disadvantage both shape and interact with conditions in the present. These legacies also live through the stories that are told by one generation to another and have an ongoing impact on belonging for generations to come (see Papadelos 2021). Interviews with 37 first-generation migrants reveal that unresolved pre-migration trauma and post-migration stress and discrimination produce legacies which not only hinder ageing positively but continue to have generational flow-on effects. Issues such as poor language acquisition and isolation were not significant issues in the first few decades after migration and thus governments did little to provide services that addressed them. However, failing to provide adequate language classes, for instance, is now a significant barrier to ageing positively. While these migrants did not think it possible to learn English at this stage in their lives, there were and are other ways to support migrants to feel less isolated and part of their communities. In the present day it would be advantageous for example to fund cultural events for seniors that include transport to and from events.

Participants, as is described in the quotation above, frequently claimed that "they didn't belong anywhere" or that they were Greeks living in Australia, rather than Australians or Greek-Australians, even after living in Australia for over 40 years. While migrants' spoke of hardship on arrival, they did not have time to dwell on these issues as they were busy working, building a strong Greek community and raising their young families. Their family, church and community sustained them in their youth and made English language acquisition optional. Unfortunately, as they aged it became more difficult to sustain community life, owing to limited social connections and their energies became more narrowly focused on the church and their family. This limited social engagement exacerbated isolation, loneliness and resentment of dependency in old age. Older migrants in this study remained actively engaged with the complex and often dissonant features of migration's legacies.

The task ahead is to understand the legacies of migration and use this knowledge to provide support for current and new migrants to achieve full participation in society and a strong sense of belonging sustaining them as they grow older in their adopted home. Recognition of such legacies can enable re-imaginings of their lives in the present and in the future. In everything from innovations in aged care facilities, to transport and community development, incorporation of the impact of legacy offers a means to re-invent the future of ageing migrants.

Notes

1 In addition, I am fluent in Greek language and culture and was able to transcribe the interviews in full to facilitate familiarisation through immersion in the data.
2 See Bourdieu (1986) for more details on the different forms of capital.
3 Aboriginal Australians inhabited Australia for over 40,000 years prior to colonisation in 1778 (Bourke et al. 2006). After colonisation, Indigenous people were denied claim to the land and social and cultural practices that existed for thousands of years were decimated in favour of British values. For information on Indigenous sovereignty, see Moreton-Robinson (2007).
4 For the purpose of comparison, the foreign-born figure in the United States is 13.4 per cent of its population (US Census Bureau, 2019).
5 'Ten pound Poms' is a colloquial expression for English migrants who paid £10 for passage to Australia.

References

Ahmed, S. (1999). Home and away: Narratives of migration and estrangement. *International Journal of Cultural Studies*, 2(3), 329–347.
Ahmed, S. (2004). Affective economies. *Social Text, 22(2)*, 117–139.
Ahmed, S. (2007). Multiculturalism and the promise of happiness. *New formations*, 63(1), 121.
Andreoni, H. (2003). Olive or white? The colour of Italians in Australia. *Journal of Australian Studies*, 27(77), 81–92.
Ang, I. (2014). Beyond Chinese groupism: Chinese Australians between assimilation, multiculturalism and diaspora. *Ethnic and Racial Studies*, 37(7), 1184–1196.
Ashton, P. (2009). 'The Birthplace of Australian Multiculturalism?'Retrospective Commemoration, Participatory Memoralisation and Official Heritage. *International journal of heritage studies*, 15(5), 381–398.
Australian Bureau of Statistics. (2017). 3412.0 – Migration, Australia, 2015–2016. www. abs.gov.au.
Australian Bureau of Statistics. (2019). 3101.0 – Australian Demographic Statistics, June 2019. www.abs.gov.au.
Australian Institute of Health and Welfare. (2018). Older Australia at a glance (Cat. no. AGE 87). www.aihw.gov.au/reports/older-people/older-australia-at-a-glance.
Australian Bureau of Statistics. ABS Media Release 23 April 2021. www.abs.gov.au/m edia-centre/media-releases/30-australias-population-born-overseas.
Avgoulas, M.-I. & Fanany, R. (2016). Greek as a marker of identity in Melbourne, Australia. *Ζητήματα Δι/Πολυγλωσσίας, Διαγλωσσικότητας και Γλωσσικών Πολιτικών στην Εκπαίδευση* (3rd Crossroads of languages & cultures: Issues of Bi/Multilingualism, Translanguaging and Language Policies in Education), May 30–31, 2014, Aristotle University of Thessaloniki & Polydromo, p. 4.
Bashford, A. (2014). Immigration restriction: rethinking period and place from settler colonies to postcolonial nations. *Journal of Global History*, 9(1), 26.
Bauer, E. (2016). Practising kinship care: Children as language brokers in migrant families. *Childhood*, 23(1), 22–36.
Birrell, R. & Jupp, J. (2000). *Welfare recipient patterns among migrants*. Canberra: Department of Immigration and Multicultural Affairs.

Bourdieu, P. (1986). The Forms of Capital. In J. G. Richardson (Ed.), *Handbook of Theory and Research for the Sociology of Education* (pp. 241–259). New York: Greenwordpress.

Bourke, C., Edwards, B., Bourke, E. & Edwards, W. H. (Eds). (2006). *Aboriginal Australia: An introductory reader in Aboriginal studies*. St Lucia, QLD: Queensland University Press.

Brah, A. (2005). *Cartographies of diaspora: Contesting identities*: Routledge.

Brandhorst, R., Baldassar, L. & Wilding, R. (2021). The need for a 'migration turn'in aged care policy: a comparative study of Australian and German migration policies and their impact on migrant aged care. *Journal of Ethnic and Migration Studies*, 47(1), 249–266.

Carangio, V., Farquharson, K., Bertone, S. & Rajendran, D. (2020). Racism and White privilege: highly skilled immigrant women workers in Australia. *Ethnic and Racial Studies*, pp. 1–20.

Colic-Peisker, V. & Farquharson, K. (2011). Introduction: A New Era in Australian Multiculturalism? The Need for Critical Interrogation. *Journal of Intercultural Studies*, 32(6), 579–586.

Connidis, I. A. & Davies, L. (1992). Confidants and companions: Choices in later life. *Journal of Gerontology*, 47(3), S115–S122.

Damousi, J. (2013). Silence and noise: Legacies of war and migration for second generation Greek-Australians. *Agora*, 48(2), 11–18.

Damousi, J. (2015). *Memory and Migration in the Shadow of War: Australia's Greek Immigrants after World War II and the Greek Civil War*. Cambridge: Cambridge University Press.

Enright, M. (2019). "No. I won't go back": national time, trauma and legacies of symphysiotomy in Ireland. In S. Beynon-Jones & E. Grabham (Eds), *Law and Time* (1st edition, pp. 46–74). Boca Raton, FL: Routledge.

Georgiades, S. (2015). Greek Immigrants in Australia: Implications for Culturally Sensitive Practice. *Journal of immigrant and minority health*, (5), 1537–1547.

Glenn, D., Cosmini, D., Palaktsoglou, M. & Bouvet, E. (2017). Icons and Rosaries in my Suitcase: A Study of Religious Objects and Practices of Ageing Italian and Greek Migrants in South Australia. *Flinders University Languages Group Online Review*, 5(2).

Gow, G. (2005). Rubbing shoulders in the global city: Refugees, citizenship and multicultural alliances in Fairfield, Sydney. *Ethnicities*, 5(3), 386–405.

Gunew, S. M. (1994). *Framing marginality: Multicultural literary studies*: Carlton, Vic.: Melbourne University Press.

Hage, G. (2002). Multiculturalism and white paranoia in Australia. *Journal of International Migration and Integration/Revue de l'integration et de la migration internationale*, 3(3–4), 417–437.

Janiszewski, L. & Alexakis, E. (2015). Greek currents in Australian waters: Greek-Australians and the sea, 1810s–2013. *Reading, Interpreting, Experiencing: An inter-Cultural Journey Into Letters*, pp. 73–96.

Jupp, J. (2002). *From white Australia to Woomera the story of Australian immigration*. New York: Cambridge University Press.

Jupp, J. (2007). Australia's immigration policy. In A. Hassam & A. Sarwar (Eds), *Australian Studies Now* (pp. 267–274). New Delhi: Indialog Publications.

Kiropoulos, L. A., Meredith, I., Tonkin, A., Clarke, D., Antonis, P. & Plunkett, J. (2012). Increased psychosocial stress in Greek-born immigrants compared to Anglo-

Australians with coronary heart disease: the healthy heart, healthy mind study. *Heart, Lung and Circulation*, 21(12), 794–802.

Kunz, E. F. (1971). European migrant absorption in Australia. *International Migration*, 9, 68–79.

Loriggio, F. (1996). Going South. In F. Loriggio (Ed.), *Social Pluralism and Literary History. The Literature of the Italian Emigration* (pp. 91–121). Toronto, ON: Guernica Editions.

Markus, A. (1984). Labor and immigration: Policy formation 1943–5. *Labour History*, 46, 21–33.

Markus, A. (2014). Attitudes to immigration and cultural diversity in Australia. *Journal of Sociology*, 50(1), 10–22.

Meaney, N. (1995). The end of 'white Australia'and Australia's changing perceptions of Asia, 1945–1990. *Australian Journal of International Affairs*, 49(2), 171–189.

Moreton-Robinson, A. (Ed.). (2007). *Sovereign subjects: Indigenous sovereignty matters*. Allen & Unwin.

Nicolacopoulos, T. & Vassilacopoulos, G. (2005). *On the Methodology of Greek-Australian Historiography*. Paper presented at the Biennial International Conference of Greek Studies, Adelaide: Flinders University Department of Languages(Modern Greek).

Nicolacopoulos, T. & Vassilacopoulos, G. (2014). Migrants' struggles to transform the political landscape of post-war Australia. *Agora*, (2), 24–32.

Palaktsoglou, M. (2013). The 'invisible'immigrants: Greek immigrant women in Australia (1952–1972). *Journal of Modern Greek Studies Special Issue*, 290–304.

Papadelos, P. (2019). Living between two cultures: reflecting on Greek orthodox mourning practices. *Social Identities*, 25(2), 254–268.

Papadelos, P. (2021). "Greeks are different to Australians": understanding identity formation among third-generation Australians of Greek heritage. *Ethnic and Racial Studies*, 44(11), 1975–1994.

Papastergiadis, N. (2004). The invasion complex in Australian political culture. *Thesis eleven*, 78(1), 8–27.

Roudometof, V. (2008). Greek Orthodoxy, territoriality, and globality: religious responses and institutional disputes. *Sociology of Religion*, 69(1), 67–91.

Sharples, R. & Blair, K. (2021). Claiming 'anti-white racism' in Australia: Victimhood, identity, and privilege. *Journal of Sociology*, 57(3), 559–576.

Simic, Z. (2014). Bachelors of misery and proxy brides: Marriage, migration and assimilation, 1947–1973. *History Australia*, 11(1), 149–174.

Stratton, J. (1998). *Race daze: Australia in identity crisis*. Sydney: Pluto Press.

Stratton, J. & Ang, I. (2001). Multicultural imagined communities: cultural difference and national identity in the USA and Australia. In D. Bennett (Ed.), *Multicultural States: Rethinking Difference and Identity* (pp. 135–162). New York & London: Routledge.

Tamis, A. (2005). *The Greeks in Australia*. Cambridge: Cambridge University Press.

Tavan, G. (2012). Leadership: Arthur Calwell and the Post-War Immigration Program. *Australian Journal of Politics & History*, 58(2), 203–220.

Teicher, J., Shah, C. & Griffin, G. (2002). Australian immigration: the triumph of economics over prejudice? *International Journal of Manpower*, 23(3), 209–236.

US Census Bureau. (n.d.). Foreign Born. Accessed December 16, 2019. www.census.gov/topics/population/foreign-born/about.html.

Vasta, E. (1993). Multiculturalism and ethnic identity: The relationship between racism and resistance. *The Australian and New Zealand Journal of Sociology*, 29(2), 209–225.

Vasta, E. (2006). Migration and migration research in Australia. In E. Vasta & V. Vuddamalay (Eds), *International migration and the social sciences: Confronting national experiences in Australia, France and Germany* (pp. 13–78). Hampshire: Palgrave Macmillan.

Vasta, E. (2017). The migrant 'stranger'at home:'Australian'shared values and the national imaginary. In J. Lloyd & E. Vasta (Eds), *Reimagining home in the 21st century* (pp. 36–54). Cheltenham & Northampton: Edward Elgar Publishing.

Wise, A. (2005). Hope and belonging in a multicultural suburb. *Journal of Intercultural Studies*, 26(1–2),171–186.

Chapter 9

Unearthing Buried Legacies

Rosemary Wanganeen and Anna Szorenyi

Rosemary Wanganeen is a proud South Australian Aboriginal woman with ancestry and ancestral links to Kaurna of the Adelaide Plains and Wirangu from the western coast of South Australia. She is the founder, Director and CEO of the Healing Centre for Griefology. She has worked in health, welfare and social justice for Aboriginal people for more than 30 years, including campaigning for and subsequently working as a researcher for the Royal Commission into Aboriginal Deaths in Custody. Her clinical work is based on the study of (Aboriginal) ancestral unresolved grief that has compounded and complicated contemporary (Aboriginal) descendants' losses, guaranteeing (Aboriginal) disadvantage, inter-generationally. Wanganeen considers that this approach provides a foundation for grieving processes that will heal and restore prosperity, as well as assisting people across cultures in addressing the ongoing impacts of historical and contemporary forms of colonial warfare and welfare. Rosemary Wanganeen is currently completing a Master of Philosophy at the University of Adelaide, where she is writing a memoir about the personal experiences that led to the development of her model, 'the Seven Phases to Integrating Loss and Grief©*, which resulted in an innovative field of work she terms 'Griefology'.*

The amalgamated text below includes edited material from a previously published paper (Wanganeen, 2010), work from her MPhil dissertation in progress, extracts from a recorded conversation with her principal supervisor, Anna Szorenyi, on 11 October 2021,[1] and some collaboratively written sections.[2] This structure kept Wanganeen's voice and language in the forefront, while also drawing out the implications of her work for the concept of 'living legacy'.

Background: The Stolen Generations

To set the context, it is helpful to know about Australia's history of 'The Stolen Generations'. From the early stages of invasion of the continent by Europeans, Aboriginal children were taken from their communities for the purposes of labour exploitation (Human Rights and Equal Opportunity Commission, 1997, p. 22). Initial policies of segregation turned into policies of control (euphemistically termed 'protection'), as Aboriginal people were confined to reservations and missions. At the same time, the white invaders/

DOI: 10.4324/9781003311928-11

settlers relentlessly pursued Aboriginal women, producing anxieties among the authorities about 'miscegenation'. In the first half of the 20th century, increasingly formalised policies of 'assimilation' argued that Aboriginality could be progressively 'bred out' "of mixed 'blood'"[3] descendants, while "full blood" descendants were expected to 'naturally' die out in the face of the evolutionary superiority of the European (Read, 2014). The invaders/settlers were not above hastening this process through deliberate spreading of disease and massacres of local groups (Foster, 2012; Colonial Frontier Massacres, 1788 to 1930, 2021). These combined racist and paternalistic attitudes justified the widespread removal of children from the 'influence' of their parents, in the name of improving their prospects so that they would disappear into white society. These policies are often characterised as enabling a form of 'genocide'. Whether this terminology is used or not, there is no doubt that they sought to erase Aboriginality as a culture and identity (Human Rights and Equal Opportunity Commission, 1997, p. 190; Moses, 2004; Read, 2014; van Krieken, 1999).

The intergenerational legacies of these policies for the families and communities affected cannot be underestimated. Aboriginal and Islander adults who were taken, contrary to the intent of the policy, are no more likely to be educated or employed than those who grew up in their Aboriginal communities (Human Rights and Equal Opportunity Commission, 1997, pp. 12–14). They are, moreover, more likely to suffer from addictions, homelessness and isolation, and to be imprisoned (Human Rights and Equal Opportunity Commission, 1997, pp. 12–14). In addition, families and communities suffered from the loss of their next generation. The *Bringing Them Home Report* states,

> [m]ost significantly the actions of the past resonate in the present and will continue to do so in the future. The laws, policies and practices which separated Indigenous children from their families have contributed directly to the alienation of Indigenous societies today.
>
> For individuals, their removal as children and the abuse they experienced at the hands of the authorities, or their delegates, have permanently scarred their lives. The harm continues in later generations, affecting their children and grandchildren.
>
> (Human Rights and Equal Opportunity Commission, 1997, p. 4)

After much public debate, Prime Minister Kevin Rudd made a formal Apology to the Stolen Generations, delivered in Parliament House in 2008 (2008: National Apology to the Stolen Generations, 2022). While met with great formal seriousness by Aboriginal communities, that apology now rings hollow, given that children then continued to be removed from their families at higher rates than ever before (Douglas & Walsh, 2013; Funston & Herring, 2016; Behrendt, 2017).

The impact of intergenerational injuries in childhood, adolescence and beyond (Wanganeen)

Under the 1911 Aborigines Act (SA) the Chief Protector[4] could "cause" every:

> aboriginal[5] or half-caste[6] to be kept within the boundaries of any reserve or aboriginal institution, or to be removed to and kept within the boundaries of any reserve or aboriginal institution, or to be removed from one reserve or aboriginal institution to another" (*Aborigines Act 1911* (SA) s. 17(1)).

As an Aboriginal child of the 1950s, I was born into the above policy!

After my birth in 1955 in a white mainstream country town, my parents were forced by law to return me and their first four babies to our Mission, called Point Pearce in South Australia.[7] I need to describe what I believe are the psychological impacts not just upon my family but the Aboriginal community in relation to the 1911 Aborigines Act, as it was not just meant to contain, and control us, physically. It was an era where Aboriginal people had no legal rights to leave the mission and were forced to depend on 'welfare'. I have strong memories of the women lining up for supplies, including my mother and grandmothers.

Along with the 1911 policy, I was also born into the existing 1940 Exemption Certificate (SA).[8] This policy was designed to increase divisions within Aboriginal society. To gain this Certificate and hence to escape the legal and other restrictions of Mission life, we as a family had to reject our Aboriginality. This also meant that, once exempted, we were not allowed to "consort" with our family members who remained on Point Pearce Mission.

The South Australian 1911 and 1940 policies were designed to relate to each other and just as cruel was a third one I was born into, called the 1951 Assimilation Policy. It was described at the 1961 Native Welfare Conference of Federal and State Ministers, as requiring that all Aborigines were eventually expected to "attain the same manner of living as other Australians and to live as members of a single Australian community enjoying the same rights and privileges, accepting the same customs and influenced by the same beliefs, as other Australians" (cited in Reynolds, 1972, p. 175).

In 1960 I was 5 years of age and, under the umbrella of the three policies I've described, my family moved into Clare—a white mainstream country town in South Australia. We were given a three-bedroom home with a massive backyard. Several years ago, I learnt we were the first and only Aboriginal family in Clare for at least five years. This is also a part of the cultural genocide because Aboriginal families like ours couldn't continue practicing our 'Nunga English' (Nunga is a South Australian word for Aboriginal people) or any traditional or contemporary cultural ways.

Aboriginal families had a multitude of significant reasons to want to leave 'Mission-life': better education for their children; marriage for their children to white people for status and greater opportunities; greater opportunities in the workforce in the hope racism would not be a barrier to equal opportunities. On reflection it stands to reason that mum and dad moved off Point Pearce Mission to enable their children to have a better chance of being educated and having more job opportunities. However, mum and dad wouldn't have known the consequences of their decision. For us as a family, as with every other Aboriginal family who applied for and received them, the passports were designed to trigger unwritten policies of 'grooming' Aboriginal families for 'white privilege'. The execution of these policies came with the threat of being revoked if the Aboriginal families didn't assimilate. They would then be unceremoniously "driven" back to their Mission! To avoid this, mum, dad and us kids were expected to abandon our Nunga English and speak Anglo-Saxon English which was to reflect the mannerisms of white people, and this became more pronounced when we left the family home.

It must be acknowledged, I grew up on Mission, never hearing anyone talking traditional languages because, several generations before my generation, Aboriginal people were already forbidden to partake in cultural practices including speaking any traditional languages. I consider the three outlined policies a combined legacy of intergenerational cultural genocide. My family is an example of cultural genocide, as we were and still are today, fluent in the English language only.

In the early days of my family moving off the Mission, the Exemption Certificate's intention was to keep us, and particularly mum and dad, apart from our extended family. I'm confident such restrictions on access to his male relatives back on the Mission were designed to funnel dad into using alcohol and eventually family violence towards mum and his children. Similarly, mum was restricted from access to her female relatives for practical support and guidance about her husband's alcohol consumption and violence. This funnelled her to turn to white people in Clare: a further continuation of cultural genocide. By this time, almost none of our cultural heritage remained. The flow-on meant us kids had minimal to no contact with our cousins, aunties and uncles, or grandparents back on Point Peace. In real practical terms, it meant we couldn't run and laugh freely with them on or off the Mission.

Over the next four years, I became one of eight children and as a kid, I don't have any memories of white people coming to our home either as other children to play or as adults coming for any reason. It seemed we were family and friends to each other as if we didn't need anyone outside of my family to befriend us. Mind you, mum and dad might have been too afraid to have white people into our homes out of fear of being shamed, blamed or judged over something!

Dad returning home from work every evening would be greeted by his screaming brood. Even though I remember the violence in my family, I remember the love my mum and dad had for each other – they were teenage sweethearts. I remember how they would help me with my homework which I think helped me find my love for learning and school. I loved learning about new things. I remember being a good student. When I brought my homework back to my class teacher, she would put a gold star on it, or she would write 'well done, Rosemary' and I have strong memories of standing in my pride and intelligence with a big smile on my face! I'd take it home and the praise continued at home from my mum and dad! But one day at school the love I had for it turned into fear.

Let me introduce you to my seven-year-old self who remembers experiencing raw and overt racism in front of her whole class and at a most vulnerable and tender age. I don't remember what made my seven-year-old self late for school. The teacher stopped the lesson and said, we should put cardboard carton on this side of your desk, in front of your desk and on the other side of your desk so you can't see the children and the children can't see you and just write 'dunce' all around it! I didn't flinch; I was too afraid to cry! Something 'snapped' inside of me that day. Until I was in my 30s I believed I was nothing more than a "dummy" for being late for class. My seven-year-old remained trapped inside of me, warning me not to over-extend myself into the education space because, as she would always remind me, "they might see we're just dummies"! This experience stayed a barrier to further education until well into my adult life.

Alongside this, I was exposed to several experiences of childhood family violence and alcohol for the first time. Some years ago, I applied for my mums' records from our South Australian State Government (Centre for Youth and Family Solutions Adoption & Family Information Service, n.d.) and I found a page that supports my childhood memories when mum was trying to get help from the police and welfare. The state government department writes it up in mum's file that the "house was becoming more frequently visited by undesirable persons who usually arrived with alcohol."

I have the memory of dad being drunk and yelling and screaming at mum and seconds later, his dinner plate and the kitchen wall collide with each other yet again. Scenarios like this would intensify the fear among us children on several occasions, and if mum couldn't manage dad and the situation escalated, we had to flee our family home and head for a 'safe house' somewhere in Clare among white people. As much as I was afraid of dad when he was like this, I have strong memories of being afraid for him left alone in the house. What if something happened to him and no one was there to help him? What if he died?

Another memory etched into my eight-year-old childhood memory was the day us kids were playing outside when I heard screams—dad screaming at mum and mum screaming with what sounded like fear, again! I snuck around the back of the house and snuck into our tiny laundry. Mum's screams seemed to be different that day and I didn't know why. I thought, I gotta see what's going on today, because it was my job to put a stop to their domestic violence situation. Trouble is I was seconds too late.

Just as I stood on our laundry step looking into the kitchen, I witnessed my dad hit my mum in the stomach! Frozen on the step, I stopped breathing. I still stayed there long enough to realise that mum could see one of her "little ones" frozen in fear.[9] She nudged dad and using eye contact she's telling him I was watching everything. Now I was the subject of his uncontrollable rage whereupon he screamed at me 'top note', to 'get outside and play'. I'm so terrified but where do I run to hide! I find myself running into our big back yard, so my tears can flow and freely sob. The tears and sobbing were not just because my dad screamed at me—one of his "little ones"—but also because now I'm afraid for my mum. Leaving her behind like that, I'm now afraid she might die without her "little one" to get her out of that situation.

It was just a matter of time before 1964 rolled around and I became my nine-year-old self but my already fractured young life shattered into even smaller pieces. Mum was off to have her ninth baby, but our mother—dad's young and very much-loved wife—died suddenly on 20 May 1964. This is described in mum's state government records as "heart failure" after an operation but was "not noticed by the surgeon"! The very next day, the 21 May was my ninth birthday and it's safe to assume it was the first of many life-less birthday parties that followed.

Mum's state records confirm how the 1940 Exemption Certificate (South Australia) forced restrictions upon some Aboriginal families. After mum's death, this certificate applied to my family's life in real terms. Six out of eight kids became a part of the Stolen Generation or as affectionately known in the Aboriginal communities, 'welfare'. I'm nine-and-a-half years old when it happens to me. I don't remember dad, nana or grandfather sitting me down to tell me we are going to be taken away by "our" white welfare officer, Mr. Rice, to go live in the big city with all white people and not come back home! They would have told me, surely; it's just that I don't have the memory.

On the day I was taken away, I was being removed under the 1911 Aborigines Act that made the Chief Protector of Aborigines "the legal guardian of all Aboriginal and half-caste children under 18 years of age" (The Aborigines Act, 1911). But how would I know this; I'm just a kid and everything looks normal. The family wakes up with breakfast looking and sounding just like any other breakfast. But why is nana so unusually quiet and looking a bit sad? Then the knock comes to the front door and nana goes and answers it. There stands Mr. Rice with a sad and sorry half-smile etched onto his face.

We arrive in Adelaide and the Department of Aboriginal Affairs place us in what I call a "holding pen" which is an Aboriginal hostel called Sussex Street in North Adelaide. We're held up there until our first white foster family are ready for us, but I was never ready for them! They are a mother, a father and their six-year-old daughter! I'm so young, and of course I don't have any say or choice, so we (my sister and I) move in with them.

Like most white foster families of Aboriginal children, it was just a matter of time before this family shattered my trust. The father became a perpetrator of physical abuse with sexual tendencies. I only have the one distinct memory of being violated in this family! Being only a child, I can't remember what I did to deserve such a beating, but he told me to go into their bedroom, pull my underwear down, lay face down across their bed and wait until he comes in. When he finally arrives, he's carrying a 'copper stick' and like all copper sticks it had to be made from very strong wood. I know what it was because nana had to use a copper stick to drag out the boiling hot linen from the copper and plunge them into a nearby, laundry sink of cold water. He then proceeds to beat my bare backside, making it so painful I can't even scream out or cry in pain; the pain sent me into a state of shock, I lost control of my little body and I slid onto the floor that was cold with floor tiles. I shut down! The abuse became so unbearable that my sister kept running away out of fear and I stayed out of fear, but I have a memory of finding a notepad, a biro and a stamp and somehow, I found my childlike courage to write a note to nana to "dob in" this man.

Before too long Mr. Rice arrived to "remove" us. My sister and I were separated, and I was "re-fostered". I then met with another white couple who were so old they were grandparents. I went from bad to worse with this family. It was about three months before the "old man" began grooming me and about six months into my time with them, he began sexually molesting me.

In between the day I arrive and his grooming I had another racially motivated comment that shattered my now wafer-thin Nunga identity, proving that assimilation is still in progress and is doing what it is designed to do. We were being taught Australian Studies and the topic of this subject was the "arrival of 1788"—that is, the arrival of white people. The teacher was so emotionally caught up in the topic that he spat out with such venom "and Aboriginal people were savages". I was the only Nunga kid in the classroom and my twelve-year-old self internalised this statement by saying to myself, "shame job, how can my mob do that to those poor white people". The psychological legacies of the policies just kept on coming and the impact had me sympathising with the 'poor white people', ashamed of my Aboriginality and blaming my ancestors for being 'the savages'.

I left this second foster home after the day the "old man" and I were in the lounge and coincidently, just as his wife walked past the kitchen/lounge room door, he inappropriately touched me yet again. She must have witnessed this, because seconds later, she quietly closed the sliding door. My immediate memory after she slides the door, is screaming out to the old man 'I can smell gas' and I'm a child witness to something no 12-year-old child should ever experience. His wife was committing suicide by gassing herself using their gas oven.

After a time, Mr. Rice came knocking on my door. He looked so sad and I got the feeling he was really concerned for my wellbeing. He asked me to pack only what I needed. Even though I had known Mr. Rice all these years, he was still someone I couldn't trust enough to tell him what happened in this house of horrors.

You can imagine my shock and happiness when the next move meant I arrive at Wiltja Girl's Hostel to be greeted by my two older loving sisters. This is where I was now allowed to reconnect to family through my two sisters. Some years later I caught up with nana, who by then had moved into the Adelaide suburbs. Even though this is finally a time in my young life I can reconnect to my family, I must acknowledge I'm still a "welfare kid". All the girls in this hostel are "welfare kids".

It's now 1967 and I'm just twelve-years-old and in South Australia there are two significant things that shaped my life. Since 1788, according to white man's law, I *was not* a citizen of Australia. I grew up as a non-citizen. Secondly, I'm one of many Aboriginal kids still being managed under the 1923 Aborigines Act (Training of Children) that enabled the Chief Protector of Aborigines to:

> "commit any aboriginal child to any institution within the meaning of the State Children Act, 1895, under the control of the said Council, to be there detained or otherwise dealt with under the said Act until such child attains the age of eighteen years."
>
> (*Aborigines (Training of Children)* Act 1923 (SA) s. 6(1))

Going Forward: Responding to intergenerational injuries—integrating loss and grief into personal healing and assisting others

The legacies of racist laws, formal policies and informal practices did not just disappear. I found the ongoing impact of intergenerational violations of cultural genocide and community/family abuse and violence enacted in childhood and adolescence were reiterated in adulthood. This became evident in my own life.

In 1987 I was in Sydney in a women's shelter. I was disfigured, bruised and battered yet again. I had no idea how I got there, how I came to be a part of three violent relationships and other mentally and emotionally abusive relationships. How is it that I have been a victim but also on the spectrum of a perpetrator of family violence? I needed to find out where I came from to be so angry, so full of rage, that sometimes escalated to violence. There were times when I was mentally, emotionally and physically abusive to my children. Sometimes alcohol only served to fuel my anger, rage and violence in love relationships. Yes, I'm a wife, a mother, a woman, a colleague and yet on leaving the women's shelter I was so traumatised as I wondered, 'who the hell is Rosemary Wanganeen?' At this time, I feel only half a person. I'm still living in depression and having suicidal thoughts. While I know intellectually that I am an Aboriginal person, emotionally and spiritually I do not feel a Nunga—what the hell is that about?

I felt inept inside, then I realised that the lack of my Nunga identity had me experiencing my life with a lot of deep-seated shame. I had lost pride, faith and trust in myself being Aboriginal. In order to figure out how I ended up in this emotional whirlpool a 'voice' told me to go back into my past. This terrified the hell out of me. All my adult life I had been conditioned to stay away from the past: "what's happened has happened, you can't change it so just move on". Yet I know that it is time to feel the fear of my past.

In the latter part of 1992, while in the Pitjantjatjara[10] lands reconnecting with my ancestors, I began putting pen to paper to design my 'Seven Phases' approach to loss and grief based on the past five years of self-healing. Then, in 1994, I completed a loss and grief course[11] that enabled me to finally put a name to all the loss and suppressed unresolved grief I had experienced. Although the course opened up my consciousness to approaches concerned with loss and grief in relation to death and dying,[12] there's so much more to loss and grief than death and dying. It was several months before I began conceptualising my approach to include loss of one's culture and much more. This enabled me to reconcile with my childhood and break the cycle in my future. By 1994 I developed my own version of an evidence-based model outlining the Seven Phases. These include, for example:

Table 9.1 The Seven Phases to Integrating Loss and Grief

Phases	Description
Phase 1	Contemporary major grief reaction to Aboriginal disadvantage
Phase 2	Childhood & adolescent losses & suppressed unresolved grief
Phase 3	Ancestral losses and intergenerational suppressed unresolved grief
Phase 4	Physical practices of ancient ancestral traditional cultures
Phase 5	Spiritual practices of ancient ancestral traditional cultures
Phase 6	Reclaiming Griefology in a contemporary setting
Phase 7	Reformation of disadvantage to prosperity

The basis of the Seven Phases approach, developed for both personal healing and helping others as a health practitioner/counsellor, lies in actively reflecting upon my own personal experiences. In this chapter I have concentrated upon those of my experiences relevant to Phase One and Two and made brief mention of experiences linked with Phases Three, Six and Seven.[13]

As I have described previously, major loss experiences took place in my childhood and adolescence. In my Seven Phases model these experiences do not constitute an inner child in the singular. By experiencing these multiple experiences at these ages, they become collectively what I call unhealed and violated inner children in the plural. As I grew into my adult self with all these unhealed and violated inner children trapped inside my now adult body, they developed multiple personalities in their own right. And they would experience immature, childlike, grief reactive triggers when they sensed they could be exposed to what happened to them in childhood. They would make sure that I, the adult Rosemary would experience covert or overt tantrums as they went into a panic when faced with adult intimate relationships, tantrums which prevented me from being able to stay in loving, happy relationships or be at ease with pleasure and happiness. For example, when my 9-year-old 'little one's' mum suddenly died, she interpreted this as, 'I must have loved my mum too much and I killed her!' My nine-year-old developed patterns of sabotage to save anyone she loved from 'imminent death'. My adult-self had no control over her! My little one was thinking to herself: Why would I risk experiencing love and happiness again? It's like putting my hand into a fire knowing, *I'm risking getting severely burnt, blistered, and scarred, again*! To transform those interpretations, my adult-self had to help my 9-year-old grieve to reclaim her ability to feel safe and to love again.

It is important to understand the legacies of psychological effects that are experienced by many Aboriginal children and teenagers as they grow up in a society dominated by non-Aboriginal systems and people, particularly the 'welfare'. I lived in grief-fear of mainstream services for decades because it was mostly non-Aboriginal people who delivered the services and system. Throughout my childhood and adolescence, I was often afraid I would experience racially motivated comments or behaviours within the services because I'd already 'accumulated' a number of those experiences. Today, I believe racism is 'man-made' and designed to make many Aboriginal people feel so afraid of accessing mainstream services, many will stay away from many services and consequently stay trapped in Aboriginal disadvantage. I have lived in grief-fear for most of my teenage and early adult life as a legacy of this system.

Working with Griefology (extract from a conversation between Anna Szorenyi and Rosemary Wanganeen, October 2021)

AS: *What do you do now?*
RW: It was only in the last few years that I coined the label 'Griefology', because I realised there is more to loss and grief than death and dying.

Post my training with Bereavement Educational Services, I had an epiphany that loss of culture wasn't on the radar in the training. No-one was talking about the loss of Aboriginal culture. I then knew I had a responsibility to 'use' my experiences to help the Aboriginal community. Griefology is a decolonising methodology as it understands and seeks to resolve the relationship between (Aboriginal) ancestral losses and the suppressed unresolved grief that has compounded and complicated contemporary (Aboriginal) descendants' own losses and suppressed unresolved grief.

AS: *Do you want to tell us a bit about what you do in your work?*

RW: I work with Aboriginal and non-Aboriginal people. It doesn't matter what gender one identifies as, or what cultural background they come from or what age, because loss and grief is a human experience that doesn't discriminate.

AS: I understand that you help people in working with loss and grief? Do you want to tell us a bit about how you go about doing that?

RW: I do an introduction and background to myself and my work, then I invite them to share with me their story. Then as I'm listening to their story, I'm listening for their major losses and what grief emotion/s they seemed to be trapped in and where it's unresolved. I'm also listening for their unhealed inner children or adolescents who were violated or harmed in some way. I share my model of finding their "little ones" as opposed to what they are experiencing at their chronological age sitting in the room.I will give them feedback, summarise their story, and put it into my loss and grief framework. I then invite them to share their thoughts on whether the summary of their losses and unresolved grief of the younger versions of themselves is making sense to them based on what they've just shared with me and more often than not, it does. (It is important to acknowledge that some people can take more than a few sessions to really get a good grasp of their "little ones", so as to apply them in their everyday life.)

AS: With regard to the Seven Phases model, do you think it contributes something to working with loss and grief as historical injustices, that other approaches don't do?

RW: Many popular approaches to loss and grief, such as Elizabeth Kubler-Ross' 'Five Stages of Loss' (see Kubler-Ross & Kessler, 2005), don't take into account historical injustices. When I did the training with Harold Jones at the Bereavement Education Centre, I thought afterwards, 'he didn't address historical, intergenerational losses' and I made that part of my approach, as have other Aboriginal scholars working with trauma and grief such as Judy Atkinson (2000; see also McKendrik et al., 2017). As Aboriginal people I think we have a responsibility to incorporate ancestral losses. Look, my intuitive research question didn't ask only 'what happened when 1788 arrived so inhumanely?', but also 'why did it happen so inhumanely?' Why did this patriarchal society commit such cruelty upon another human being and why couldn't they see, feel and hear the cries of pain and sheer terror of my ancestors?' So, both loss and grief, and historical violence, were now on my radar. Then a random series of events led me to discover a description of Plato's attitude to grieving, summarised as 'Grief is not only illogical, but a weakness' (Walters 1997, p. 56).[14] I'm not an academic and haven't researched this at length, but to me this statement encapsulated something; it deeply resonated with me and at the time I didn't know why. I started to ponder whether the suppression of healthy grief-anger among Europeans could have escalated to unhealthy grief-anger, rage, violence, inhumane atrocities, psychopathic behaviours, making them insensitive to what they were doing to other human beings. This became my 'aha moment' which enabled me to bring Australia's violent past into the 20th and 21st century, without any shaming, blaming or demonising of those who arrived in 1788, to enable future generations to break the cycle not just of Aboriginal disadvantage, but Australia's (human) disadvantage. After all, loss and grief are human experiences!

Let me emphasise that the model is named The Seven Phases to Integrating Loss and Grief because it gently guides the individual to integrate their ancestral losses and unresolved grief that have compounded and complicated their contemporary losses and suppressed unresolved grief. Based on my own journey through this process, I know its healing abilities—because that's what happened for me. I intuitively integrated all that happened to me into my life, as a human being. I intuitively knew not to look for closure, even though that was in my face, you know, hearing it all the time, particularly through media. For me there was something abnormal about looking for closure. It's about integrating all that's happened to us as human beings. For me to sustain a client from the beginning of their session and bring them out the other side of their grief journey, it was critical for me grieve and heal my inner children so as not to have their grief triggers 'flying all over the place' in the sessions. As a clinical Griefologist of 28 years, I've also been able to sustain my health and wellbeing.

AS: *You've worked extensively with prisoners. Do you want to discuss how that work goes?*

RW: Yeah, I've recently done a program delivered over twelve half-days with eight Aboriginal men, aged 19 to 42. I knew the Seven Phases was going to be culturally appropriate, but I went in with an abundance of caution. However, they kept returning to each session because they've never heard of loss and grief from their perspective and to have an Aboriginal educator teach this perspective they stayed engaged. They were shocked but inspired. To have me take them into this deep place of what happened to our ancestors (phase three), then gently, gently weave in their childhood and specifically their unhealed multiple inner children, was so emotionally moving. We then discussed what their parents would have endured growing up and what their grandparents would have had to endure and the experiences of those who were a part of Stolen Generation, through the lens of their losses and unresolved grief.

In phase six of the programme, I shared with them my story of my "little ones", as a segue into acknowledging their own "little ones". I encouraged them to think about violations of their little ones which could have led them into becoming a part of the welfare and into juvenile justice system. All of these young men had experiences with the welfare in their families and all experienced the juvenile justice system in their teenage years and then they went into the adult prison system. We then began discussing recidivism. I introduced it to them by asking them "you know how we've been talking about my little ones and your little ones, what do you think little ones need, what do you think little kids need, to be able to feel safe, growing up?" So, they started to say things like, 'well, they need a home', yeah, they chimed in then they started bouncing off each other, "yeah they need a bed, they need clean sheets, they need food, they need showers, they need to feel safe". Then I said, "I think it's one of your little ones, that needs to keep coming back into prison, because he is getting all of his needs met in prison, that he knows he can't get from in his family". And we just all stopped to absorb what we just "unravelled". I reminded them, this is why it's not about you who's in this room at your chronological ages of 19 or 42. It's about you at your chronological age acknowledging and healing your little ones, so they don't have you wanting to go back into jail to have their needs met, again. Childhood and adolescent experiences of unresolved loss and grief are a practical factor in understanding recidivism that I think is misunderstood. You can put into place many practical support structures but if attention to loss and grief in counselling and programs is missing, recidivism could continue, intergenerationally.

In Adelaide on January 26 2022, I attended the Survival Day march and a young Aboriginal man re-introduced himself to me and I knew him immediately as one of the lads who attended the prison program. He went onto to share with me that he has a full-time job and doesn't touch alcohol and drugs. The outcome for this lad seems to confirm that in his family, intergenerational suppressed, unresolved grief did get passed across and down the generations. To resolve future injustices upon humanity, we as human beings all have a right, a role and a responsibility to respectfully find our way back to culturally appropriate grieving processes. This includes supporting and respecting those who have been victims of all forms of violations without shaming, blaming or demonising perpetrators, because all human beings once upon a time were children, therefore all their unhealed inner children have their own story to tell.

Concluding comments: Unresolved grief as a living legacy of social injustice

Maybe the question here should be, who keeps the flame of 'living legacies' burning? The first generations who were in the front lines of an inhumane invasion began living in harmful and violent grief behaviours. These misunderstood violent grief behaviours become learnt behaviours particularly throughout childhood and adolescent years, clearing a pathway for the next generation to learn them. According to Griefology, the emotion of unresolved grief is itself the legacy—a response to loss and damage, inflicted under highly unequal power relations. When this legacy is forgotten, denied or suppressed, its effects can perpetuate the injustice so that it keeps surfacing with impunity, haunting people's lives in many different forms. The central contribution of this theory of loss and grief is that processing and integrating grief in appropriate ways must be crucial in any effort to integrate the legacies of past injustices and violence.

An integrating loss and grief model can also help to shift power relations, by putting on the record who is actually responsible for what, so that what might have appeared as personal fault can be understood as a legacy of historical injustice. Asking such questions can reverse 'the colonial gaze' that has long positioned Aboriginal people and culture as 'the problem' and the object of study (Rigney, 1999). Instead, we can ask, what happened to the Europeans to make them so cruel? This is a way of refusing to take violence and racism for granted. The question itself comes from a founding assumption that humans are not naturally prone to treating one another with callous violence: it must have been, in some way, learnt behaviour. Culturally appropriate grieving processes, on the other hand, can help to heal in the present and the future. Aboriginal people are often told to 'get over' the past, to 'forget' and 'move on' (Haebich, 2011). Here instead we see how breaking the silence of grief will break the cycle of it being passed on to future generations.

Liddle's chapter in this volume also shows the importance of grief in remembering what has been lost to genocide. Importantly, Liddle's contribution shows how grief is not just about the past, but about constructing visions of justice for the future. Grief, then, can emerge as a crucial form of 'living legacy', according to the definition proposed by Beasley and Papadelos in Chapter One of this volume. In this approach, grief is not just an ongoing effect of the past, but a site where power relations can continue to emerge and shift in the present. Sometimes this emerges as the intractable patterns of repetition that we call 'unresolved grief', but sometimes it can become an opportunity for healing and change. We could even say that culturally appropriate grieving processes are a method for transforming the first kind of legacy into the second.

RW: Griefology can be such a process. I don't know if it's going to be in my lifetime but, before I leave this earth, I'd love to see humans developing and honouring loss and grief, so that we can find our way back to living in harmony with ourselves, human to human, and with mother earth—with mother nature, thriving intergenerationally!

Notes

1 Rosemary Wanganeen's MPhil in progress is co-supervised by Dr Kam Kaur.
2 We wish to acknowledge Chris Beasley's efforts in providing framing and detailed editorial assistance in developing this chapter.
3 The terms "mixed 'blood' " and 'half-caste' were used by colonial authorities to designate those of mixed Aboriginal and white parentage, and 'full blood' to designate those without white parentage. After a long history of being used to justify policies of control, child-stealing, and assimilation, these terms are now considered offensive by most Aboriginal people in Australia (Human Rights and Equal Opportunity Commission, 1997, p. 22). The terms are used only in historical context to explain the cruel and inhumane policies of the era.
4 The colony of South Australia established an Aboriginal 'Protector' in 1839. In 1844 the Protector was officially declared legal guardian of 'unprotected' children (that is, orphans and those whose parents were 'unknown') (Human Rights and Equal Opportunity Commission, 1997). The 1911 Aborigines Act (SA) granted increased powers to detain and control the movements of all Aboriginal people (Aborigines Act 1911 (SA). s.17), and legal guardianship of all people of Aboriginal descent under the age of 21 (Aborigines Act 1911 (SA) s. 10(1)).
5 The descriptor 'aboriginal' used in colonial and other historical accounts is now almost invariably capitalised as 'Aboriginal'. More recently, other descriptors such as Indigenous or First Nations peoples have also come into use. However, this chapter is Wanganeen's story and as an Aboriginal person she uses 'Aboriginal' rather than 'Indigenous'. Wanganeen finds the latter offensive because of its use in relation to flora and fauna. She asserts in this context that 'words truly matter. They can be on the spectrum of deeply offensive or inspirational.'
6 The term 'half-caste' is another term that is no longer used and is deeply hurtful to Aboriginal people, because of its embeddedness in racist theories of eugenics and its use by the authorities to justify child stealing.
7 Point Pearce was established as a mission in 1868 on Narungga land on the Yorke Peninsula, and taken over by the South Australian Government on the recommendation of the 1913 Royal Commission 'to inquire into and report upon the control, organisation and management of institutions (…) set aside for the benefit of Aborigines' (Human Rights and Equal Opportunity Commission, 1997).
8 The 'Exemption Certificate' allowed particular Aboriginal people assessed as possible candidates for assimilation to leave reserves and missions and live in the non-Aboriginal community, where unlike their relatives on the mission, they could access social security, and purchase land and alcohol.
9 Wanganeen uses the phrase "little ones" within her therapeutic practice, where it refers to the ongoing legacy of injuries arising in a person's childhood past which continue to cause pain and shape their lives unless the perspectives of these "little ones" are paid due attention.
10 Pitjantjatjara is a language of 'Western Desert' Indigenous people whose Country is located at the intersection of the remote north-west of South Australia, Western Australia and the Northern Territory (Russell, 2022). Many Pitjantjatjara people live

on the APY, APY Lands or just the Lands, a local government area brought into being by the Anangu Pitjantjatjara Yankunytjatjara Land Rights Act 1981 ("About Us," 2020).

11 This training comprised several workshops held in Adelaide over 1994–5 (Jones, 1994; Wessels, 1994; Jones, 1996).

12 Such approaches derived from a combination of the training at Bereavement Educational Services and Wanganeen's personal lived experiences, through grieving. The Bereavement training possibly referred to the popular work of Elisabeth Kubler-Ross (see Kubler-Ross & Kessler, 2005), but Wanganeeen does not directly use this source.

13 For more details on this framework, see Wanganeen 2008, 2010, 2011 and 2014.

14 Walters bases his summary of Plato's attitude on Plato's *Phaedo* (trans. 1969) and *Republic* (trans. 1945), arguing that Plato's attitude to grief is logically consistent with his doctrine of the immortal soul—that is, it is illogical to grieve for a temporary and weak body when the soul lives on, and that grief is an expression of that bodily weakness (Walters, 1997, pp. 55–56). Walters argues that this attitude became widespread in Christian Europe through a Platonic revival during the early years of the Church, and then through the influence of the work of Augustine (see p. 56). This chapter is not the place for any extended discussion of this interpretation, but for further accounts of Plato's concerns about the dangers of grief, see Spelman (1997).

References

2008: National Apology to the Stolen Generations. (2022). National Museum of Australia. www.nma.gov.au/defining-moments/resources/national-apology.

About Us. (2020). Anangu Pitjantjatjara Yankunytjatjara. www.anangu.com.au/en/about-us.

Atkinson, J. (2000). *Trauma Trails, Recreating Song Line: The transgenerational effects of trauma in Indigenous Australia*. North Melbourne, Vic.: Spinifex Press.

Behrendt, L. (2017). After the Apology: Director's Statement. Ronin Films. www.roninfilms.com.au/feature/16485/after-apology.html.

Centre for Youth and Family Solutions Adoption & Family Information Service: GRG 29/172 Case File No: 6817 (South Australian Government).

Colonial Frontier Massacres, Australia, 1788 to 1930. (2021). https://c21ch.newcastle.edu.au/colonialmassacres/map.php.

Douglas, H. & Walsh, T. (2013). Continuing the Stolen Generations: Child protection interventions and Indigenous people. *International Journal of Children's Rights*, 21(1), 59–87.

Foster, R. (2012). *Out of the silence: The history and memory of South Australia's frontier wars*. Kent Town, SA: Wakefield Press.

Fowler, M., Roberts, A. & Rigney, L.-I. (2016). The 'very stillness of things': Object biographies of sailcloth and fishing net from the Point Pearce Aboriginal Mission (Burgiyana) colonial archive, South Australia. *World Archaeology*, 48(2), 210–225. doi:10.1080/00438243.2016.1195770.

Funston, L. & Herring, S. (2016). When will the stolen generations end?: A qualitative critical exploration of contemporary "child protection" practices in Aboriginal and Torres Strait Islander communities. *Sexual Abuse in Australia and New Zealand*, 7(1), 51–58. doi:10.3316/informit.201569927296804.

Haebich, A. (2011). Forgetting Indigenous histories: cases from the history of Australia's Stolen Generations. *Journal of Social History*, 44(4), 1033–1046.

Human Rights and Equal Opportunity Commission. (1997). *Bringing Them Home: Report of the National Inquiry into the Separation of Aboriginal and Torres Strait Islander Children from Their Families.* https://humanrights.gov.au/sites/default/files/content/pdf/social_justice/bringing_them_home_report.pdf.

Jones, H. (1994, November). Managing loss and grief. Training held at Bereavement Educational Services, South Plympton, South Australia.

Jones, H. (1996, March). Assisting People in the Community in Grief Recovery. Training held at Grief Management Services, Christie Downs, South Australia.

Jones, T., Corowa, M., Rudd, K., ABC-TV & Australian Broadcasting Corporation. (2008). *The Apology to the Stolen Generations of Australia.* ABC Commercial.

Kubler-Ross, E. & Kessler, D. (2005). *On Grief and Grieving.* New York: Scribner.

McKendrick, J., Brooks, R., Hudson, J., Thorpe, M. & Bennett, P. (2017) Aboriginal and Torres Strait Islander Healing Programs: A Literature Review. Healing Foundation. https://healingfoundation.org.au//app/uploads/2017/02/Aboriginal-and-Torres-Strait-Islander-Healing-Programs-A-Literature-Review.pdf.

Moses, A. D. (2004). *Genocide and settler society: Frontier violence and stolen Indigenous children in Australian history.* New York: Berghahn Books.

Plato. (trans. 1945). *The Republic of Plato.* (F. M. Cornford, Ed. & Trans.). Oxford: Oxford University Press.

Plato. (trans. 1969). *The Last Days of Socrates* (H. Tredennick, Trans.) London: Penguin.

Read, P. (2014). Reflecting on the Stolen Generations. *Indigenous Law Bulletin* 8(13), 3–6. www8.austlii.edu.au/cgi-bin/viewdoc/au/journals/ILB/2014/24.html.

Reynolds, H. (1972). *Aborigines and settlers: The Australian experience, 1788–1939.* North Melbourne, Vic.: Cassell Australia.

Rigney, L.-I. (1999). Internationalization of an Indigenous anticolonial cultural critique of research methodologies: A guide to Indigenist research methodology and its principles. *Wicazo Sa Review*, 14(2), 109–121. doi:10.2307/1409555.

Russell, S. (2022). Aboriginal people of South Australia: Pitjantjatjara. State Library of South Australia. https://guides.slsa.sa.gov.au/Aboriginal_peopleSA/Pitjantjatjara.

Spelman, Elizabeth V. (1997). *Fruits of Sorrow: Framing our attention to suffering.* Boston, MA: Beacon Press.

van Krieken, R. (1999). The barbarism of civilization: Cultural genocide and the 'stolen generations'. *The British Journal of Sociology*, 50(2), 297–315. doi:10.1111/j.1468-4446.1999.00297.x.

Walters, G. (1997). *Why Do Christians Find it Hard to Grieve?*Carlisle: Paternoster Press.

Wanganeen, R. (2008). A loss and grief model in practice. In A. Day, M. N. Nakata & K. Howells (Eds), *Anger and Indigenous Men: Understanding and Responding to Violent Behaviour* (pp. 73–85). Annandale, NSW: Federation Press.

Wanganeen, R. (2010). Dealing with Loss, Grief and Trauma: Seven Phases to Healing. In N. Purdie, P. Dudgeon & R. Walker (Eds), *Working Together: Aboriginal and Torres Strait Islander Mental Health and Wellbeing Principles and Practice* (1st Ed., pp. 267–284). Barton, ACT: Australian Government Department of Health and Ageing.

Wanganeen, R. (2011). Integrating personal and professional experiences: Seven Phases to integrating loss and grief. *Grief Matters* 14(3), 78–88.

Wanganeen, R. (2014). *Seven Phases to Integrating Loss and Grief. In P. Dudgeon, H. Milroy & R. Walker (Eds.) Working Together: Aboriginal and Torres Strait Islander Mental*

Health and Wellbeing Principles and Practice (2nd Ed., pp. 475–492), Barton, ACT: Australian Government Department of the Prime Minister and Cabinet.

Wessels, C. (1994, December). Managing Loss and Grief #1. Training held at Grief Management Services, Christie Downs, South Australia.

Legislation

Aborigines Act 1911 (South Australia): An Act to Make Provision for the Better Protection and Control of the Aboriginal and Half-Caste Inhabitants of the State of South Australia. Australian Institute of Aboriginal and Torres Strait Islander Studies. https://aiatsis.gov.au/sites/default/files/docs/digitised_collections/remove/54205.pdf.

Aborigines (Training of Children) Act 1923: An Act to make Better Provision for the Care, Control, and Training of Aboriginal Children, for placing Aboriginal Children under the Control of the State Children's Council, to amend the Aborigines Act, 1911, and for other purposes. Australian Institute of Aboriginal and Torres Strait Islander Studies. https://aiatsis.gov.au/sites/default/files/docs/digitised_collections/remove/54206.pdf.

Part III

Chapter 10

The Legacy of Injustice and Resistance
Japan's Military Sexual Slavery

Maki Kimura

Introduction

Since the start of Japan's invasion of Manchuria during the 1930s and its subsequent participation in the Asia-Pacific War, hundreds of thousands of women from Japan, its colonies and occupied territories, fell victim to a systematic form of sexual slavery by the Japanese military. Contrary to the popular belief that the existence of these women, often referred to as 'comfort women', had only come to light in the 1990s, their experiences had been recorded in the Allied forces investigations at the end of the war and regularly featured in diaries and memoirs of soldiers published after the war. However, the injuries and injustice these women suffered only gained a delayed recognition in the 1990s, some 50 years after the end of the war. The ordeal they endured, recounted by Kim Hak-sun from South Korea (the first officially recognised victim-survivor of the system), and many other women who followed her, shook not only feminists, but also a wider public in Japan, other Asian countries and beyond. Supported by transnational feminist activists, historians and other scholars, the victim-survivors have actively sought justice from the Japanese government. They helped the international community recognise sexual violence as a serious war crime and a crime against humanity, and problematised ongoing gendered violence in conflict today.

Nevertheless, over the past 30 years, their cry for justice has met with a strong rebuttal from the Japanese government which has repeatedly refused its legal responsibility towards these victims. More recently, the Japanese government has made numerous attempts to prevent memorials to 'comfort women' from being erected in victim-survivors' countries of origin, as well as in Europe and in the USA, perpetuating further injustice to the women. This political confrontation has led to this issue becoming a crucial site of the politics of memorialisation. Looking at transnational feminist activism surrounding the building of memorials for these women and their new reading of women's testimonies, this chapter aims to explore how the material and spatial effects of these memorials and people's engagement with them, as well as the women's testimonies, create an emotionally engaged 'affective' community and build

DOI: 10.4324/9781003311928-13

resistance, which could potentially challenge this legacy of injustice. Legacy here indicates complex power relations that materialise the connection between past, present and future. In the context of the debates over 'comfort women', legacy concerns political processes of the memorialisation of the past, that is, determining what is to be remembered and how. Here we recognise the power dynamics at play in understanding and acknowledging these women's experiences of violence and trauma past and present. Legacy in this setting makes us consider how we can advance social justice today, but also strongly influences how we identify and redress social injustice in the future, in particular around issues of sexual exploitation and violence.

Many victim-survivors of this form of sexual slavery have repeatedly objected to being labelled 'comfort women' ('ianfu'), as their experience is far from (providing) 'comfort' and the term has also historically been associated with prostitution. The victim-survivors have instead maintained that the term 'sexual slaves' would be more appropriate to describe their experience of suffering. As the term 'comfort women' is widely used in the discussion of this issue and the movement for redress, in this chapter I will continue to use the term, but only to refer to this specific system of Japan's military sexual slavery. In addition, in order to acknowledge the controversy around how the term 'comfort women' is understood and how it represents the victim-survivors, it will be employed with inverted commas. The battle over the naming of Japan's system of military sexual slavery itself in part represents its living legacy but other struggles such as those over recognition and redress reveal the ongoing and multi-directional impact of this legacy of violence and trauma.

Political controversy surrounding Japan's military sexual slavery

In August 1991 Kim Hak-sun (1924–97), from South Korea, publicly testified to the physical and psychological damage and injustice she had suffered from her experience of sexual slavery. Subsequently, she became the first formally recognised victim of Japan's military sexual slavery during World War II (commonly referred to as the 'comfort women' system), as many other victim-survivors of the system also began to share their experience encouraged by Kim's brave testimony. Until these women came forward and illuminated the state involvement in their abuse, they were long identified as military prostitutes who provided 'sexual service' to Japanese military personnel and civilian employees, and simply considered as 'unfortunate' victims of poverty who had been sold into prostitution and war when sexual violence was prevalent.

While most women kept their painful pasts to themselves, their testimonies have also demonstrated that some of them had revealed their experience of sexual slavery long before they came forward in the 1990s, in an attempt to have their hardship and trauma acknowledged (Kimura, 2021, pp. 292–93). However, their voices were only listened to in the 1990s, when systematic sexual violence in conflict and other forms of violence against women began to widely attract the attention of (transnational) feminist communities. These victim-survivors' injuries were at long last acknowledged as a case of structural exploitation of and violence against women perpetrated by the state through gender, class, race, ethnicity and militarism. This well illustrates how these women's experience of past violence and trauma represents a living legacy as power dynamics today operate to determine what happened in the past, as well as to inform what we understand as social injustice in the future.

The exact number of women who fell victim of Japan's military sexual slavery is still debated and the true extent of victimisation will likely never be known. However, it is often suggested that at least 200,000 women suffered from this system of sexual violence and exploitation. These women came from diverse national and ethnic backgrounds including Korean, Taiwanese, indigenous Taiwanese, Chinese, Filipina, Indonesian, Timorese, Dutch, Malay, Vietnamese, Thai, Burmese, Indian, Chamorro, and Eurasian backgrounds, along with Japanese women, though the majority were not ethnic Japanese (Fight for Justice, 2022a). The women became subjected to sexual slavery through deception, sex trafficking, kidnapping and forcible enlistment and recruitment by Japanese officials, including the military and local collaborators. They were raped and exposed to other forms of violence and abuse in 'comfort stations' which spread over Japan, its colonies, occupied territories and conflict areas in East, Southeast and Pacific Asia during the 15 years of war in China and the Asia–Pacific accompanying Japan's ambitions to expand its military and colonial power. Some researchers argue that the Japanese government introduced the system to implement more rigorous measures to control the spread of venereal diseases and to prevent rape of local women, though evidence suggests that the development of the system did not help reduce the occurrence of rape but actually justified systematic violence against women (Kimura, 2016a, pp. 41, 100, 106).

A significant number of 'comfort stations' may be identified, but there were substantial differences in the ways that they were operated. Some were managed by the military or run as private businesses, modelled on the licensed prostitution system operating in Japan and its colonies at the time. Others were less structured in temporary and makeshift places, but the women were still kept in captivity and were continuously subjected to sexual and other forms of violence. For these women, life after 'comfort stations' was equally challenging and traumatic. Many could not go back to their family, knowing they would be rejected or indeed disowned by their relatives, and also had lives of economic difficulty. Opportunities to get married were limited, and even if they did marry, they were often abused by their husbands and in-laws because of their infertility and other residual physical injuries. Life accounts narrated by victim-survivors instigated intense, often emotive, debates in Japan (as well as in South Korea, other Asian countries and beyond). Japanese society became divided over the degree of responsibility to be attributed to the Japanese government and how the suffering of these women could be acknowledged and represented in history and remembered today. In particular, critical tensions arose between on the one hand, survivor-activists and other transnational feminists and activists who sought justice for victims from the Japanese government, and, on the other, Japanese right-wing politicians and critics[1] who underplay the responsibility of the Japanese government for the atrocity of the 'comfort women' system and the violation of fundamental human rights it involved.

Debate on the criminality of this system of sexual exploitation originally centred around the role of the Japanese military and other officials in organising 'comfort stations', and the level of coercion in 'recruiting' women. Right-right politicians and other critics have claimed that the involvement of Japanese authorities was only minimal and restricted to regulating private brokers who ran 'comfort stations' and protecting those civilians who 'worked' in 'comfort stations' in conflict-affected areas. They understate the responsibility of the Japanese authority in the operation of the 'comfort women' system arguing 'comfort stations' were organised on a commercial basis, and the women were sold into prostitution and not forcibly taken by the Japanese authority. By contrast, survivors and other activists maintain that even though the level of involvement of the Japanese military and other authorities in managing 'comfort stations' varied, they were overall responsible for the introduction and implementation of 'comfort stations'. Activists have also emphasised that the coercion process does not simply cover whether the women were taken forcibly or not but includes recognition of whether these women were taken unaware of what lay ahead of them and kept enslaved and captive against their will.

The redress movement of victim-survivors seeking justice from the Japanese government that has continued over 30 years has revolved around developing a transnational network involving a range of communities including survivors, scholars, artists, and various citizen groups and challenging right-wing discourses such as those noted above. With the support of feminist groups that address other examples of sexual violence during war, such as in former Yugoslavia and Rwanda, victim-survivors have successfully brought the attention of the international community to this legacy of violence and trauma. They subsequently managed to gain recognition of sexual violence during conflict as not simply a war crime, but also as a crime against humanity. Working closely with local support groups, transnational feminist activists and citizen groups that organised public hearings and meetings, the survivor-activists travelled within Asia and beyond to share their testimonies and experience of social injustice. Feminist scholars and artists recorded these women's testimonies, translated and published them, and made films and other artworks about their lives (Women Active Museum, 2013, p. 67; Nakano et al., 2017, pp. 13–19; and Fight for Justice, 2022a). Ten lawsuits were filed against the Japanese government in Japan between 1991 and 2001 by victim-survivors, supported by these feminist and citizen networks. However, all except one

The Legacy of Injustice and Resistance 177

case were rejected or not accepted by the District Courts and Appeal Courts of Japan, and all cases and their appeals were finally turned down by the Japanese Supreme Court by March 2010 (Women Active Museum, 2013, pp. 38–39).

Redress movements have been strengthened by bringing activists from Asia together, holding regular Asian Solidarity Conferences on the Issue of Military Sexual Slavery. The first one of these was held in Seoul in August 1992 and attended by activists from Hong Kong, Japan, the Philippines, South Korea, Taiwan and Thailand (Yang, 2020, p. 23). The Conference has been held regularly since then, with the most recent 15th Conference in Seoul in March 2018 (The Korean Council, 2022). Another successful transnational collaboration has involved developing and organising the Women's International War Crimes Tribunal for the Trial of Japanese Military Sexual Slavery that took place on December 8–12, 2000. Civil society groups in Japan and Asian countries where victim-survivors came from, as well as groups in other countries working on violence against women (in conflict), planned and managed the event (VAWW-NET, 2002; pp. 9–15, Women Active Museum, 2006, pp. 62–3).

The Tribunal was attended by survivor-activists and citizen groups from North and South Korea, China, Taiwan, Malaysia, the Philippines, Indonesia, East Timor, the Netherlands, drew an audience of over 1,000 people every day and involved a number of nationally and internationally renowned lawyers as legal advisors, Country Prosecutors, Chief Prosecutors and Judges (Women Active Museum, 2006, p. 59). The Summary of Findings on December 12, 2000, and the Final Judgement on December 4, 2001, delivered by four judges, concluded that Japan had acted in violation of international law and found Emperor Hirohito and Japanese military officials guilty (The Women's International War Crimes Tribunal for the Trial of Japan's Military Sexual Slavery, 2001). The Public Hearing on Crimes Against Women in Recent Wars and Conflicts was also held after the Tribunal. Testimonies of women from 17 countries, including Asia, Middle East, Africa, Europe, North America and Latin America, who had recently suffered sexual violence were shared (The Women's International War Crimes Tribunal for the Trial of Japan's Military Sexual Slavery, 2001). It illuminated how the impunity afforded by the perpetrators of the crimes of the 'comfort women' system would bring impunity for current and future violence against women in conflict, linking the 'comfort women' issue with the violation of present and future. Thus, the legacy of violence and trauma suffered by victims of the 'comfort women' system was by no means simply a matter of past distress and injustice but vigorously enabled strengthening of feminist transnational networks today which fight against (various forms of) gendered violence (Women Active Museum, 2006, p. 68–75).

Feminist groups have also been actively utilising the UN system sending delegates and submitting reports in the process of, for example, the Universal Period Review of the UN Human Council, and the State Periodic Review of the Convention of Elimination of All Forms of Discrimination against Women. These actions contribute to raising international awareness of the issue and put international pressure on the Japanese government to take responsibility. Furthermore, at the 11th Asian Solidary Conference in Taipei in 2012, it was decided that August 14, the day that Kim Hak-soon publicly testified about her ordeal, should be marked as the International Memorial Day for 'Comfort Women'. The first International Solidarity Demonstration was organised in Seoul on August 14, 2013 and many citizen groups organised demonstrations across the globe on the day (The Japan Nationwide Action, 2020).

While victim-survivors and other feminist activists were successful in developing transnational feminist networks to fight for justice, they are required to constantly challenge right-wing discourses which deny women's suffering. Over the past 30 years the Japanese government has made some, albeit limited, acknowledgement of the direct involvement of the Japanese military and authorities in organising the 'comfort women' system. Also, a certain level of coercion in its operation has been acknowledged, as exemplified by the 1993 Kono Statement issued by Kono Yohei, then Chief Cabinet Secretary. The Japanese government has, however, maintained its default position that since all the issues of reparation, restitution and compensation had already been settled by the San Francisco Peace Treaty, bilateral treaties and other agreements, in particular, by the 1965 Treaty on Basic Relations between Japan and the Republic of Korea, no individual compensation would be necessary (Kimura, 2016a, pp. 5–6, p. 220).

Nevertheless, in recognising its moral responsibility for victim-survivors, in 1995 the Japanese government established the Asian Peace and Friendship Fund for Women (the Asian Women's Fund) in partnership with civil society as an expression of atonement. This Fund offered 'atonement money' of 2,000,000 yen (US\$18,500) to victim-survivors from a pool donated by the public. Secondly, under the auspices of the Fund, victim-survivors were issued a letter from the Prime Minister expressing sincere remorse and apology to the former 'comfort women'. Thirdly, the Fund provided medical and welfare support for victim-survivors through government funding. These developments went ahead despite the refusal of many women to accept the atonement money. The offer of such money was criticised as an 'alternative measure' to formal compensation that effectively blurred the legal responsibility of the Japanese government (Kimura, 2016a, pp. 4–5).

The continuation of the Japanese government's denial of its responsibility has largely been shaped by right-wing views held by many politicians of the ruling Liberal Democratic Party as well as wider sections of society in Japan. The influence of right-wing ideas has become noticeable since the 1990s but has intensified over the past 15 years. The visible presence of right-wing discourses in the international scene can be demonstrated by a paid advertisement entitled 'The Facts (about "comfort women")' which appeared in *The Washington Post* on 14 June, 2007. The advertisement claimed that these women were prostitutes (Onozawa, 2013, p. 47). In addition, under the second Abe Shinzo government (2012–20) the withdrawal of the 1993 'Kōno

Statement' (mentioned previously) was seriously considered, though the then Prime Minister Abe and Chief Cabinet Secretary, Suga Yoshihide, eventually confirmed that the government would retain the position of the 'Kōno Statement' (House of Councillors of Japan, 2014, pp. 2–3).

Denying government responsibility for the organisation of the 'comfort women' system, and instead claiming this system functioned as a form of military prostitution, right-wing critics maintain that this topic is unsuitable to teach schoolchildren and intervened in the development of the school curriculum, attempting to remove teaching about Japan's military sexual slavery at primary and secondary schools (Kimura, 2016a, pp. 16–17; 126–7; Nagai, 2017, pp. 113–115, Tawara, 2013). In Japan, schools (particularly state primary and secondary schools) are required to use ministry approved textbooks in their teaching which meet the requirement of national Curriculum Guidelines. Private publishers organise teams of experts to produce textbooks in the subjects such as Japanese, English, mathematics, science and social studies (including history and citizenship studies) and submit their draft textbooks to the Ministry of Education, Culture, Sports, Science and Technology for examination and approval. Since the women who are survivors of sexual slavery came forward to testify about their experience, whether to include or exclude the reference to the system of 'comfort women' and the experience of these women in and from history textbooks have become the subject of heated national debates.

A short commentary on 'comfort women' in textbooks first appeared in 1997. In order to challenge this inclusion, some right-wing critics set up a group called Japanese Society for Textbook Reform to create history and citizenship studies textbooks to reflect their version of history aiming to sustain a Japanese imperial-centred historical view. In the face of such organisations and the related general political drift to the ideological right wing, the number of textbooks which make reference to the system of 'comfort women' has declined throughout the first decade of 2000, and by 2010 the commentary on 'comfort women' system had disappeared from all government approved textbooks.[2] Meanwhile, the first history and citizenship studies textbooks that the Japanese Society for Textbook Reform produced were approved by the Ministry of Education in 2001, followed by further approvals in following rounds of examination. These textbooks have officially been used in schools where local education councils (including that in Tokyo) adopted these textbooks as part of their teaching materials.

In addition to textbook debates, feminists have been fighting over the media and cultural as well as academic representation of the issue and victim-survivors. One of the most recent incidents was the publication of an article by Professor J. Mark Ramseyer from Harvard Law School claiming—without substantial evidence—that the victim-survivors were prostitutes. This view initiated huge and heated scholarly debates around the world and was critically challenged by a transnational network of scholars and reported widely in the media. As outlined above, the living legacy of violence and trauma had multiple directions and effects. These include debates about terminologies, survivor-activists regaining their voices and agency, the advancement of transnational feminist collaboration and networks facilitating global forums, state and civic responses to war compensation and the development of educational resources, and academic discussions on the implication of this system of sexual slavery. The continuing ripples from the experiences and testimony of victim-survivors demonstrate the significance of this living legacy, which further generated struggles over the memorialisation of that legacy.

Politics of memorialisation: towards new redress movements

'Comfort women' redress movements today centre around two main activities. As victim-survivors of this system of sexual slavery were already in their sixties and seventies when they came forward, many survivors have passed away since they first testified to their painful experiences. Transnational feminist redress movements have, therefore, lately begun to organise around means by which to remember these women and inscribe representations of the injustice and harm that they suffered clearly onto history in order that younger and future generations can remember and acknowledge this legacy of violence and injustice. Building memorials to these women and establishing memorial centres and museums in Japan and other countries such as South Korea, China, the Philippines and Taiwan, as well as in Europe, North America and Australia, has become a crucial site of the politics of memorialisation over the past ten years. As the number of remaining survivors rapidly drops, resolving this issue while they are alive has become a matter of urgency. Furthermore, in response to the Japanese government's repeated failure to deal with this issue (including the ineffective or even harmful 2015 Japan–Korea Agreement which asserted that the issue would be resolved 'finally and irreversibly' by this bilateral deal),[3] feminist groups have more recently advocated the importance of taking a victim-centred approach to solving and remembering the issue.

Grandma Lee Yong-soo from Daegu in South Korea is one of the few remaining survivor-activists of the 'comfort women' system. She came forward as a victim in 1992, soon after Kim Hak-sun testified on her ordeal in public in 1991, after being inspired by Kim-Hak-sun's courage. Since then, Lee has tirelessly contributed to the campaign in South Korea and transnationally, demanding the Japanese government take full legal responsibility to achieve justice for victims of this history of sexual slavery. Most recently, she has become known through her campaign to take this issue to the International Court of Justice to gain international legal recognition that the system of 'comfort women' was a crime against humanity. Her struggle to accomplish her goal was captured in a documentary, *Unreported World: Justice for Japan's wartime sex slaves* produced and broadcasted by Channel 4, a British public-service television network in November 2021.

The documentary shows how in one of Lee's attempts to gain support from the South Korean government, she travelled to Seoul in November 2021 to lobby and meet with candidates for the presidential election scheduled in March 2022. She demanded that every candidate should seriously engage with this issue making every effort to resolve it (Roberts, 2021). Before she headed back home after these meetings, we see her taking the documentary presenter Krishnan Guru-Murthy to somewhere she claimed as 'her special place'. It turned out to be Namsan Park in Seoul, where a memorial to 'comfort women' was erected in 2019. It was built by British-American artist Steve Whyte, who gained an international reputation after he won a competition and installed his first memorial to 'comfort women' in San Francisco, the previous year in 2018. The memorial in Namsan Park is similar to the one in San Francisco. The San Francisco sculpture shows Kim Hak-sun gazing at three girls from Korea, China and the Philippines who stand in a circle turning their backs to each other but holding each other's hands. The difference between the two statues is that the circle formed by three girls in the Namsan Park statue is not closed as it is in the one in San Francisco. Instead, in the Namsan Park sculpture there is a space between the Korean and Filipina girls which enables visitors to the memorial to join in the circle and hold the hands of these girls an image of the 'Comfort Women' memorial at Namsan Park, Seoul, can be accessed at www.facebook.com/photo/?fbid=2534212683267659& set=pcb.2534215729934021).

Lee witnessed the installation project in Namsan Park unfold and attended the launch event on August 14, 2019—the International Memorial Day for 'Comfort Women'. When she visited the memorial this time with Guru-Murthy, she affectionately greeted three (statue) girls asking them how they have been, gently touching their cheeks as if they were her living granddaughters or someone very close to her. Then she turned to the statue of Kim Hak-sun and solemnly renewed her pledge to continue to fight until the day justice for women is achieved while also pouring out her anguished worry that her time is running out. The documentary eloquently illustrates two central sites of resistance for survivors and other feminist activists—testimonies and memorials—in their challenge to ongoing delays in justice for the victims of Japan's military sexual slavery.

Memorials to 'comfort women' victims

The first memorial to victim-survivors of the comfort women's system on public land was erected in Palisades Park, New Jersey near New York, USA in 2010, initiated by a Korean American civil organisation, Korean American Civic Empowerment (McCarthy & Hasunuma, 2018, p. 417). This was followed by installation of the Statue of a Girl of Peace in Seoul in December 2011. Various initiatives to build memorials have since unfolded not only in South Korea, but also in countries such as Australia, the United States, Canada,

182 Maki Kimura

China, the Philippines, and Germany. Unfortunately, however, these developments have led to disputes between right-wing groups and feminists over the politics of memorialisation and intensified right-wing attacks with regard to the latter.

The Statue of Peace—or the Statue of a Girl of Peace—in Seoul, built in front of the Japanese Embassy, is a statue of a young barefoot woman sitting on a chair with an empty chair next to her an image of the Statue of Peace, at Seoul, can be accessed at www.tripadvisor.com/LocationPhotoDirectLink-g294197-d13151759-i306116782-Statue_of_Peace-Seoul.html.

This statue was designed by sculptor couple Kim Seo-kyung and Kim Eun-sung and was erected to mark the 1000th Wednesday Demonstration. Rallies by the 'comfort women' have taken place here in Seoul every Wednesday since January 1992. The statue portrays a girl, wearing a traditional Korean dress to represent the loss of girlhood through being sexually abused by the Japanese military. Her hair is cropped to illuminate that women were taken away forcibly from their families; the bare feet and raised heels suggest the hardship and the difficult, unstable life that they had to endure during and after their experience of sexual abuse. Her clenched fists express the determination of the survivors to obtain the apology from the Japanese government and resolve the issue of their violation. The shadow behind the girl is an old woman representing the Wednesday demonstrators. The young girl sits on a chair to represent chairs that many survivors have brought to sit on during the demonstrations. The empty chair beside the young girl symbolises the spirits of those women who have already died to be part of the demonstration. The bird perched on the girl's shoulder is a symbol of peace and freedom, but also connects survivors with those women who have passed away. The inscription on 'the Statue for Peace' is based on the calligraphy of one of the survivors, Kim Bok-dong and states:

> December 14, 2011 marks the 1000th Wednesday demonstration for the solution of Japanese Military Sexual Slavery issue after its first rally on January 8, 1992 in front of the Japanese Embassy. This peace monument stands to commemorate the spirit and the deep history of the Wednesday Demonstration.
>
> (Okamoto & Kim, 2016, p. 26)

Kim Seo-kyung, one of the artists who made the statue, has stated that the memorial is designed to enhance communication with the audience through the presence of a life-sized girl and an empty chair which invites them to sit. It generates compassion towards both those who survived and those who did not, as well as encouraging the audience to recognise the campaign for justice for the 'comfort women while looking at the Japanese Embassy (Okamoto & Kim, 2016, pp. 21–34). A range of emotions is evident in the visitors who interact with the memorial. They sit on the empty chair next to the girl and/

or dress her with hats, scarves, gloves and shoes. The statue commemorates victim/survivors of the 'comfort women' system as the empty chair visibly symbolises and also commemorates the 20 years of activism of survivors at the Wednesday Demonstrations, where protesting women sat side by side on portable chairs facing the Japanese Embassy (Okamoto & Kim, 2016; Yang, 2016; Mackie & Crozier-De Rosa, 2019). Thus the experiences of violence and trauma that these women suffered and their ongoing struggles are a living legacy, a living testimony, to the continuing interplay of power dynamics which frame our understanding of social injustice of the past, present and future.

The dynamic impact of such memorials is revealed in responses to them. Since the erection of the Statue of a Girl of Peace in front of the Japanese Embassy, the Japanese government has repeatedly intervened to block projects to build memorials in South Korea and in other countries and also expressed their support for Japanese (expatriate) communities that oppose the construction of memorials. Most recently, in October 2020, Berlin Mitte District withdrew official approval for a memorial statue after the Japanese government raised concern. However, feminists from Germany, South Korea, Japan and beyond worked together and filed a complaint to the Japanese government. They also sent a petition to Berlin Mitte District Mayor, which resulted successfully in the Mitte District Council deciding to support the permanent display of the statue in December 2020.

If memorialisation may be said to have powerful effects and political effects, what is the impact of other memorials with the same (or similar) design and form in different places with different local narratives (of war)? Different memorial designs for victims/survivors of the 'comfort women' system can be identified, but many memorials have been developed and created by Kim Seo-kyung and Kim Eun-sung, based on four different designs. These artists have mostly finalised the design through consultation with the local people who would erect the memorial (Okamoto & Kim, 2016). The comparable successes of campaigns for erecting memorials for victim/survivors across the globe can partly be attributed to transnational feminist networks, as well as the coalition-building of diaspora politics and their efforts towards transnational commemoration (Hasunuma & McCarthy, 2019; Kwon, 2019; McCarthy & Hasunuma, 2018; Yoon, 2018). Yet, these memorials of similar design have been built in different places with distinctive (local) narratives of trauma and war, and thus may create differing experiences of memorialisation. These questions can further be explored by looking at the above-mentioned San Francisco and Namsan Park memorials. These memorials for victims of the 'comfort women' system provide one instance of the materialisation of the politics surrounding the legacy of injustice that these women suffered. They not only represent what is remembered and erased in the history, but also both transnational and localised struggles to achieve justice for those who have been long marginalised and silenced.

A Victim-centred approach

The request of victim-survivors for justice has been largely based on the claim that the Japanese government should take full responsibility for their involvement in the 'comfort women' system. This has been denied for many years and was further severely undermined by the 2015 Japan–Korea Agreement. The Agreement which asserted that the issue would be resolved 'finally and irreversibly' was initially widely publicised as a 'landmark' and 'breakthrough'. It was considered to represent the final achievement of a long-awaited settlement on this issue between Japan and South Korea (and possibly other Asian countries concerned). However, the Agreement gave rise to similar reactions to those associated with the Asian Women's Fund. Survivor-activists, and groups that support them, criticised the Japanese government and the Korean government on the grounds that they both had completely ignored the voices and wishes of victim-survivors. The activists expressed their frustration and anger that, despite government assertions that 'the issue is resolved finally and irreversibly', they were never consulted to develop this deal, thus ignoring women's efforts to seek justice extending over almost twenty-five years. The Agreement was condemned as mere diplomatic complicity in the face of pressure from the United States which was more concerned with ensuring the political stability of East Asia (given the rise of China and North Korea) than securing justice for victim-survivors.

The recommendations made to the Japanese government in the 12th Asian Solidarity Conference on Japan's Military Sexual Slavery held in 2014 clearly emphasised the significance of a victim-centred approach in solving this grave violation of human rights against women. Their demands include reflecting voices of victim-survivors, recognising the crucial role the Japanese government played in the organisation of the 'comfort women' system, acknowledging the continuing suffering of those women who fell victim to the system, and admitting that the system was a serious violation of human rights. Furthermore, they proposed that a variety of reparation measures should be undertaken with an offer of compensation to individual victims as demonstrable evidence of the sincerity of their apology, accounting for past actions and implementing preventative measures against future reoccurrence. These remedial measures had already been recommended to the Japanese government to fulfil their responsibilities in the final judgement of the Women's International War Crimes Tribunal for the Trial of Japanese Military Sexual Slavery held in December 2000. In addition, in various United Nations human rights mechanisms, recommendations have been repeatedly made to urge the Japanese government to commit to a lasting solution with a victim-centred approach, supporting survivor-activists' demands such as those outlined above. Some of these recommendations include concluding observations of the Committee on the Elimination of Racial Discrimination in 2018 (CERD/C/JPN/CO/10–11) and the Committee on the Elimination of Discrimination against Women in 2016 (CEDAW/C/JPN/CO/7–8).

The importance of listening to women's voices has been the centre of debates surrounding women's testimonies since they emerged in the 1990s but has resurfaced in the controversy surrounding the publication of *Comfort Women of the Empire* in 2013, by Park Yu-ha, Professor of Japanese Literature from South Korea. In response to the publication, victim survivors, including nine of them living in the House of Sharing (a communal residence for victim-survivors near Seoul) filed a lawsuit on the basis of defaming them. Feminists in South Korea and Japan condemned the Park's book as undermining survivor's testimonies, and this has encouraged feminists in Japan to develop a new methodology to engage with testimonies of victim-survivors (learning from their Korean counterparts) (Onozawa, 2017).

Since the victim-survivors came forward in the 1990s, right-wing politicians and critics in Japan have been arguing over the historical authenticity of their testimonies with feminists and left-wing historians, such as Yoshimi Yoshiaki and Suzuki Yuko (Kimura, 2016a, pp. 134–5). Right-wing politicians and critics have argued that these women were prostitutes in keeping with the system of state regulated prostitution within Japan and its colonies, which was legal during the time of the war and operated as a privatised system of 'comfort women' along with Japanese military expansion and the progress of war. Moreover, while the government of Japan has indicated that is sorry for what it deems the unfortunate and inadvertent brutality suffered by these women, it also insists that the women, in principle, gave their consent to become prostitutes and were paid accordingly. These perspectives ignore the suffering of these women on the basis of the assertion that they were prostitutes. However, they also highlight the inconsistency and incoherence of women's testimonies. Such perspectives and claim that the testimonies of the victim-survivors are not reliable and should not be considered as historical documentation of any systematic organisation of 'comfort women'.

By contrast, while the women's backgrounds and experience and the accounts of them are diverse, common narratives have emerged from their testimonies. Their narratives may be summarised as the women were taken by deception or force by Japanese soldiers or Japanese and colonial officials and coerced into having sex daily with a number of officers and soldiers without monetary recompense. Feminists and left-wing historians in Japan counter-argue that these testimonies are important as historical records which can uncover historical truths official documents have conveniently failed to reveal—that is, the Japanese government's involvement in and responsibility for sexually exploiting these women through coercion and violence. The stance of feminist and left-wing critics is in keeping with the position taken by feminist standpoint theorists, who claim that the dominant group's perception of reality, is 'partial and perverse', whereas the perspective of the oppressed is 'true' and 'liberatory' and can uncover 'real but concealed' social relations

(Hartsock, 1987, p. 9; Hekman, 1997, p. 343). In this context, feminists and critics on the left have claimed that the testimonies of 'comfort women' are a true representation of history. However, a problem with such claims is that supporters of the 'comfort women' are unable to offer a reasonable explanation as to why there are inconsistencies and incoherence in the women's testimonies (Kimura, 2008).

Only a few left-wing historians openly admit that women's testimonies contain some contradictions. However, while these commentators also argued that it is easy to identify 'errors' in some testimonies and discern which are the more accurate testimonies if reference is made to other historical documentation (Yoshimi & Kawada, 1997, pp. 73–6, Ishide, Kim & Kobayashi, 1997, pp. 92–3). Here the link between women's testimonies and historical truth is maintained. Some feminists have also asserted that these women suffer from post-traumatic stress disorder (PTSD) (Yang, 1997; Kuwayama, 1998) leaving memories fragmented, such that the women cannot provide coherent narratives regarding what happened to them. In this approach, the women's testimonies are seen as historical data, though possibly providing supplementary information, that can help to uncover and establish historical 'facts' and truth. More recently, however, feminists (in Japan) have started to embrace a more narrator-centred approach to testimonies, reflecting on a long-established feminist (oral history) practice of listening to women's voices (Gluck & Patai, 1997; Kim & Onozawa, 2020; Korean Council for the Women Drafted for Military Sexual Slavery by Japan 2000, 2020). This new approach to testimonies has further inspired feminist supporters to connect the legacy of Japan's military sexual slavery with contemporary cases of sexual violence in Japan and beyond, in order to create emotionally engaged 'affective' transnational feminist politics to advance social justice (Onozawa, 2017).

Conclusion

The transnational redress movements of/for victims of Japan's military sexual slavery have recently been organising themselves around the struggle to build memorials for women who fell victim to this systematic violence and sexual exploitation and renewed engagements with victim-survivors' voices. This shift has successfully illuminated power relations that connect past, present and future, but also highlights power relations that have erased, denied and undermined legacies of injustice.

This example of redress movement clearly illustrates, as Beasley and Papadelos emphasise in Chapter 1 of this volume, how legacies of injustice are not simply about the past impacting the present. It rather uncovers continuities as well as changes in the operation of power that can deny but also recognise these legacies of injustice. Contemporary feminist politics of remembering these victims of sexual slavery and their injuries is the very act of reconstituting power relations. Acknowledging the temporality of these power dynamics creates the possibility and capacity for resistance to build a more socially just future.

In this setting, Grandma Lee Yong-soo speaks of the continuing impact of the legacy of this injustice while also drawing attention to how it can contribute to the re-shaping the present and the future:

> If there are other conflicts, although there should be no more wars, but if there must be, I think things like "comfort women" should never happen again. This is a grave lesson for the international community. I hope the world engraves this lesson in their hearts.
>
> (Lee, 2021)

Notes

1 The Japanese right wing consists of a range of individuals—politicians, scholars, cultural critics, and other citizens—and groups that generally share nationalist and historical revisionist views and the Emperor centred history that deny the atrocity that the Japanese military committed during World War II and the Emperor's war responsibility.
2 However, in 2021 several textbooks which contain a brief commentary to 'comfort women' were approved for the first time since 2010.
3 In this agreement, then Prime Minister of Japan, Abe Shinzo, acknowledged the physical and psychological damage that victims of 'comfort women' system suffered and expressed 'his most sincere apologies and remorse to all the women who underwent immeasurable and painful experiences'. The governments of Japan and the Republic of Korea (ROK) decided (without consulting the survivors) to establish a foundation to be run by the government of the ROK and Japan to make a one-off contribution to its budge. It also hinted that the Republic of Korea would work towards removing the girls of peace statue built in front of the Embassy of Japan in Seoul (Kimura, 2016b).

References

Fight for Justice. (2022a). Who were the Japanese military "comfort women"?https://fightforjustice.info/?page_id=2760&lang=en.

Fight for Justice. (2022b). Hon, eizō gaido (Recommended books and recordings). http://fightforjustice.info/?page_id=17.

Gluck, S. B. & Patai, D. (Eds). (1991). *Women's Words: The Feminist Practice of Oral History*. New York & London: Routledge.

Hartsock, N. C. M. (1987). The Feminist Standpoint: Developing the Ground for a Specifically Feminist Historical Materialism. In S. Harding (Ed.), *Feminism and Methodology: social science issues* (pp. 157–180). Milton Keynes: The Open University.

Hasunuma, L. & McCarthy, M. M. (2019). Creating a Collective Memory of the Comfort Women in the US. *International Journal of Politics, Culture, and Society*, 32(2), 145–162.

Hekman, S. (1997). Truth and Method: Feminist Standpoint Theory Revisited. *Signs*, 22(2), 341–365.

House of Councillors of Japan. (2014). The 186th Session of the Diet, House of Councillors of Japan, Budget Committee Minutes, no. 13, March 14, 2014. https://kokkai.ndl.go.jp/minutes/api/v1/detailPDF/img/118615261X01320140314.

Ishide, N., P. Kim & Kobayashi, Y. (Eds). (1997). *"Nihongun ianfu" o dō oshieruka: kyōkasho ni kakare nakatta sensō* [*How to Teach the System of "Japan's Military Comfort Women": war erased from history textbooks*]. Tokyo: Nashinoki Sha.

The Japan Nationwide Action (The Japan Nationwide Action for Resolution of the Japan's Military 'Comfort Women' Issue. (2020). Dai hakkai sekai nihongun 'ianfu' memoriaru dē sekaishūkai, dai 1452 kai nihongun seidoreisei mondaikaiketsu no tame no teiki suiyōshūkai kishakaiken, keika hōkoku [The Eighth International Memorial Day for Japanese Military 'Comfort Women', International Solidarity Actions, 1452th regular Wednesday meeting to solve the issue of Japan's Military Sexual Slavery, press release and update. www.restoringhonor1000.info/2020/08/81452_13.html.

Kim, P. & Onozawa, A. (Eds). (2020). *Seibōryoku higai o kiku: 'Ianfu' kara gendai no seisakushu e* [*Listening to the victimisation of sexual violence: from 'comfort women' to contemporary forms of sexual exploitation*]. Tokyo: Iwanami Shoten.

Kimura, M. (2008). Narrative as a site of subject construction: through the "Comfort Women" Debate. *Feminist Theory*, 9(1), 5–24.

Kimura, M. (2016a). *Unfolding the 'Comfort Women' Debates: Modernity, Violence and Women's Voices*. Basingstoke: Palgrave Macmillan.

Kimura, M. (2016b, January 20). Japan's military sexual slavery: whose agreement? *openDemocracy, 50.50.* www.opendemocracy.net/en/5050/japans-military-sexual-sla very-whose-agreement.

Kimura, M. (2021). War Memorials: Embodying Traumatic Pasts and Constructing Memories of the Asia-Pacific War. In M. S. Micale and H. Pols (Eds), *Trauma in History: Asian Perspectives* (pp. 289–314). Oxford & New York: Berghahn.

Korean Council for the Women Drafted for Military Sexual Slavery by Japan 2000 (Josei Kokusai Senpan Hōtei Shōgen Chīmu 2000nen. (2020). *Kioku de kakinaosu rekishi: 'ianfu' sabaibā no katari o kiku* [*Rewriting history through memory: listening to 'comfort women' survivors' narratives*], Kim, P. & Furuhashi, A. (Eds and Transl.). Tokyo: Iwanami Shoten.

2000nen is part of the name of the author meaning the year 2000.

The Korean Council. (2021). *History*. https://womenandwar.net/kr/history-of-the-m ovement.

Kuwayama, N. (1998). Chigokujin "Ianfu" no Shintekigaishō to PTSD [Trauma and PTSD of Chinese "Comfort Women"]. *Kikan Senso Skinin Kenkyu*, 19, 10–19.

Kwon, V. S. (2019). The Sonyŏsang Phenomenon: Nationalism and Feminism Surrounding the "Comfort Women" Statue. *Korean Studies*, 43, 6–39.

Lee, Y. S. (2021). Interview with Lee Yong-soo: Unreported World documentary "Justice for Japan's wartime sex slaves" [video file], December 6. www.youtube.com/watch?v=IOVhJ6PS1BU.

Mackie, V. & Crozier-De Rosa, S. (2019). Remembering the Grandmothers: The International Movement to Commemorate the Survivors of Militarized Sexual Abuse in the Asia-Pacific War. The Asia-Pacific Journal Japan Focus, 17(4), 1–29. http s://apjjf.org/2019/04/MackieCrozierDeRosa.html.

McCarthy, M. M. & Hasunuma, L. C. (2018). Coalition building and mobilization: case studies of the comfort women memorials in the United States. *Politics, Groups and Identities* 6(3), 411–434.

Nagai, K., 2017. Hatan shitsutsu mo nao ikinobiru 'Nihongun mujitsuron' [The collapsing, but surviving contention of 'the Japanese military's innocence']. In Nakano, K., Itagaki, R., Kim, C., Okamoto, Y. & Kim, P. (Eds). *'Ianfu' mondai to mirai e no sekinin* [*The 'comfort women' issue and responsibility for the future*] (pp. 112–131). Tokyo: Ōtsuki Shuppan.

Nakano, T., Itagaki, R., Kim, C., Okamoto, Y. & Kim, P. (2017). Shōgenshū, terebi/rajio bangumi, eizō kiroku ichiran [List of collections of testimonies, TV/radio programmes and video recordings]. In Nakano, K., Itagaki, R., Kim, C., Okamoto, Y. & Kim, P.(Eds), *'Ianfu' mondai to mirai e no sekinin* [*The 'comfort women' issue and responsibility for the future*], (pp. 13–19). Tokyo: Ōtsuki Shuppan.

Okamoto, Y. & Kim, P. (Eds) (2016). *Naze Heiwano Shōjyo wa Suwari Tsuzukeru no ka* [*Why does 'the Statue for a Girl of Peace' Remain Seated? Engaging the Memory of Harming*]. Yokohama: Seori Shobo.

Onozawa, A. (2013). 'Ianfu' mondai to kōshōseido [The issue of 'comfort women' and state regulated prostitution]. In Nishino, R., Kim, P. & Onozawa, A. (Eds). *'Ianfu' basshingu o koete* [*Overcoming the 'comfort women' bashing*], (pp. 47–62). Tokyo: Ōtsuki Shuppan.

Onozawa, A. (2017). Feminizumu ga reikishishugi ni katan shinai tame ni: 'ianfu' higai shōgen to dō mukiau ka' [Avoiding feminism's becoming complicit with revisionism: how to engage with 'comfort women' survivors' testimonies]. In Nakano, K., Itagaki, R., Kim, C., Okamoto, Y. & Kim, P. (Eds). *'Ianfu' mondai to mirai e no sekinin* (The 'comfort women' issue and responsibility for the future), (pp. 152–171). Tokyo: Ōtsuki Shuppan.

Roberts, N. (Producer/Director). (2021). *Unreported World: Japan's Wartime Sex Slaves.* [Television broadcast], November 26. London: Channel 4 News.

Tawara, Y. (2013). Kyōkasho mondai to uyoku no dōkō [School textbook debates and right-wing activities]. In: Nishino R., Kim P. and Onozawa A. (Eds). *'Ianfu' basshingu o koete* [*Overcoming the 'comfort women' bashing*], (pp. 162–178). Tokyo: Ōtsuki Shuppan.

VAWW-NET Japan (2002). *Josei Kokusai Senpan Hōtei no zenkiroku I* [*The full record of the Women's International War Crimes Tribunal, part one*]. Tokyo: Ryokufū Shuppan.

Women Active Museum. (Akutibu Myūjiamu 'Joseitachi no Sensō to Heiwa Shiryōkan') (2006). *Josei Kokusai Senpan Hōtei no subete* [*Everything about the Women's International War Crimes Tribunal*]. Tokyo: Women Active Museum.

Women Active Museum. (2013). *Nihongun 'ianfu' mondai: subete no gimon ni kotaemasu* [*Answering all questions concerning the issue of Japan's Military Sexual Slavery*]. Tokyo: Gōdō Shuppan.

The Women's International War Crimes Tribunal for the Trial of Japan's Military Sexual Slavery. (2001). Judgement. https://archives.wam-peace.org/wt/wp-content/uploads/2020/03/Judgement.pdf.

Yang, C. J. (1997). 'Moto "Ianfu" ni miru "fukuzatsusei PTSD" ["Complex PTSD" suffered by former "comfort women"]'. *Kikan Senso Skinin Kenkyu*, 17, 26–31.

Yang, C. (2016). Heiwa no hi' ga tatsubasho 'Heiwaji [Peace Street,' where 'The Statue for Peace' stands]. In Okamoto, Y. & Kim, P. (Eds). (2016). *Naze Heiwano Shōjyo wa*

Suwari Tsuzukeru no ka [*Why does 'the Statue for a Girl of Peace' Remain Seated? Engaging the Memory of Harming*] (pp. 14–19). Yokohama: Seori Shobo.

Yang, C. (2020). Kibotane renzoku kōza: Nihongun 'ianfu' mondai kaiketsu undōshi I [Kibotane lecture series: the history of the movement for redress for Japan's military sexual slavery, part one] [Lecture handout for online lecture, delivered August 21, 2020].

Yoon, R. (2018) 'Erecting the "Comfort Women" Memorials: From Seoul to San Francisco, *de arte*, 53(2–3), 70–85.

Yoshimi, Y. & Kawada F. (Eds) (1997). *"Jyūgun Ianfu" o Meguru 30 no Uso to Shinjitsu* [*30 Truth and Lies about the Issue of 'Military Comfort Women'*]. Tokyo: Otsuki Shoten.

Chapter 11

Haunted by the Heteronorm: Contemporary Hollywood Romance

Chris Beasley

Introduction[1]

The central concern of this chapter is with the notion of living legacies of social injustice, referencing past social inequality in terms of its ongoing transmission in the present and the future. Such living legacies are typically identified with striking unusual moments/events or specific contained periods of time and very often articulated in relation to museums, monuments, days of remembrance, 'serious' non-fictional literature and documentary film. However, in this chapter the intention is to put forward a conception of legacy which considers the impact of social injustice in terms which do not confine it to the exceptional but instead locate it in the unquestioned everyday and find expression in the much more pervasive continuing shaping of memory to be found in popular culture. The focus of the chapter is upon fictional film and, in particular, on mass market Hollywood film. In order to grasp how past injustice continues to infuse the present and how the ongoing legacy of inequality shapes contemporary understandings of social justice, the global reach and impact of Hollywood film cannot be ignored. Legacies of social injustice are not only to be found in specific moments or bounded times nor in objects/institutions/events which publicly acknowledge these moments or times. Perhaps the most troubling and intransigent of these legacies arise from what is seemingly relatively unchanging and normalised such that they are rendered natural, eternal and thereby invisible.

This forms the basis of making use of the notion of 'living' legacies. Such a terminology entails an intensified emphasis upon understandings of power relations and social justice which go further than a simple sense of the past influencing the present. Living legacies is a language which insists that power is actively and thoroughly engaged in the constituting of present and future in ways that are so taken for granted that its encompassing fashioning of selves, practices, spaces and environments may be perceived as just being so. Ongoing normalisation of power works against recognition of the stickiness of social injustice and instead upholds linear expectations of increasingly progressive change over time. It is in this light that I consider what stories cultural forms

DOI: 10.4324/9781003311928-14

192 Chris Beasley

like Hollywood film continue to *tell* us about heteronormativity, thereby insistently instructing us in proper normality. The aim of such an analysis is to explore a possible means of responding to this normalising force.

Legacy: power as non-linear time and the "sticky" normal

Usage of the term 'legacy' enables power to be viewed as necessarily marked by temporality and as non-linear. Past social injustice is by no means simply of the past, but very often is a living continuity which may shape future social options. In this context, the notion of living legacy provides a means to re-imagine the relationship between power and time in ways that have implications for contemporary feminist/gender thinking. In keeping with the preoccupations of this volume, such an employment of legacy not only re-considers the relationship between power and time but offers an approach which suggests an alternative emphasis to recent feminist and new materialist accounts of power that stress ceaseless motion (Beasley, 2011, pp. 31–32), including influential Deleuzian-inflected frameworks that are inclined to emphasise power's fluidity (Braidotti, 2008, 2006; Colebrook & UK Research and Innovation, 2008). While I have considerable affinities and sympathies with the rejection of fixity in these various theoretical directions, the concern here is to bring to the foreground the "stickiness" of aggregations of power over time which fold the past into the present and may infect the future (Ahmed, 2007, pp. 11, 60, 89–95; Ahmed, 2004; Beasley & Holmes, 2021, pp. 15–33;). The folding non-linear temporalities of power relations highlight their slow or even long-standing sedentary character (Athanasiou et al., 2008; Beasley, 2011; Beasley & Bacchi, 2007). These temporalities limit potential for resistant "lines of flight" (Deleuze & Parnet, 2007) by endlessly proclaiming unequal power relations to be normal, everyday, eternal and unceasing. Thus, legacy is employed as a political concept which draws attention to the pleated persistence of the sticky normal.

Power and the sticky normal of social injustice in Popular Culture

While longstanding understandings of 'art' as distinct from and certainly not reducible to politics and social issues continue to be matters for debate, nevertheless cultural outputs like literature, art, music, television and social media as well as consumer experiences associated with them have increasingly been viewed as of significance in terms of the political zeitgeist (Berezin, 1997; Schiller, 1997). As can be seen in Chapters 3 and 10, monuments and other memorialising art works are usually explicitly not intended to be viewed as 'art for art's sake' but as openly conveying messages of social significance. By comparison, popular cultural forms (Storey, 2001) are often not recognised as central or significant in relation to the ongoing impact of social injustice and remain under-researched in this regard. Although recognition of culture as entwined with power is now at least not unusual with regard to representation-production, consumption and access to popular cultural forms (O'Brien & Oakley, 2015, pp. 2–4; Watts & Hodgson, 2019, pp. 1–22), it remains far less common to consider the effects of fictional films, and especially Hollywood films, in terms of the generation and legitimation of hegemonic power relations and specifically of social injustice. Surely Hollywood movies are just light-weight recreation, confections for entertainment? Why spend time on them in relation to the ongoing production of inequalities? In this context, it is not surprising that many analyses of the 'politics' of Hollywood film limit their examination to the government, the military or even more narrowly to American presidencies and, on the basis of this narrowed conception of 'the political', assert that Hollywood film is almost entirely simply 'entertainment' (Beasley & Brook, 2019, pp. 6–7). However, if politics is understood more broadly as operations of power, then all films, including fictional films, may be regarded as political (see Beasley & Brook, 2019, p. 3, pp. 15–16 note 2) and as enmeshed in power relations including social inequalities.

In 2019 Heather Brook and I completed a book, titled *The Cultural Politics of Hollywood Film: Power, Culture and Society* (Manchester University Press), which reflected on film and its implication in legacies of social injustice. In short, we drew attention in that work to three main points. Firstly, the impact of film on mass audiences is particularly significant when we are talking about Hollywood, a film industry which has unsurpassed global reach.[2] Secondly, film (including Hollywood film) can be shown to have an impact on people's thinking and behaviour—in direct and practical, as well as generalised and attitudinal ways (Hunter, 2003, p. 71). Lastly, this means that popular films are not simply instantly forgettable escapist popcorn but rather can be situated as a enabling the transmission of culture and its power relations, and relatedly as a repository and producer of cultural memory (Romanowski, 1993, p. 63).

Hollywood films would hardly be of great concern if the Hollywood film industry did not attract mass audiences, or if its output was small and its inter-national distribution limited. The cultural politics of Hollywood is a matter of considerable importance because the Hollywood film industry is synonymous with global dominance (in terms of audience reach, box-office appeal, pro-duction and distribution). In 2015 the Motion Picture Association of America stated that box office for US films was 71 per cent of the world market (Motion Picture Association of America, 2016). By 2019 this percentage had increased to 73 per cent (Loria, 2020; see also Screen Australia, 2020). More-over, the US share of many domestic national markets remains on a mono-polistic scale. For example, the US share of Australian box office market amounted to 84 per cent in 2016 (Motion Picture Distributors Association of Australia, 2017) and 80.5 per cent in the period 2018–20 (Screen Australia, 2021). This is not exceptional (Crane, 2014, p. 370; Durmaz et al., 2008, p. 5). In this setting, filmmakers, politicians, government bodies and business organisations are entirely convinced that films do have a significant social impact upon their mass audiences. For instance, members of Congress (from both major parties) asked the US Government Accountability Office in 2016 whether Chinese influence should result in greater attention to American "national security (…) concerns about propaganda and control of the media and 'soft power' institutions" (Beech, 2017, pp. 33–34). In much the same vein, the Chinese government has instituted a strict quota on imported big-budget feature films, a quota specifically introduced to counter the presumed problematic social effects on the Chinese people arising from imported (usually Hollywood) films (Beech, 2017, pp. 33–4; Wei & Shaw, 2016).

Such sensitivities within the US and Chinese governments indicate concerns regarding the influence of film and regarding their influence being linked to national agendas. Such concerns are by no means unfounded. A 2002 interview with Jack Valenti, the long-time President and CEO of the Motion Picture Association of America—Hollywood's peak body (Valenti, 2002; see also Alterman & Green, 2004)—revealed close co-operation between Hollywood and government security agendas in the wake of 9/11. Valenti vowed that Hollywood would "go to war" to actively support the US government. However, collusion between filmmakers and government is not limited to events like 9/11. Hozić (2001) describes this co-operation between filmmakers and government as now forming a kind of military-entertainment conglomerate dominating the global media space (see also Der Derian, 2001; Lin, 2002; Ryan & Kellner, 1988, pp. 210–16).[3]

Making use of a specifically 'cultural politics' approach to popular film means locating popular films (that is, mass market, mass audience films) as a form of "political technology"—a technology that generates and manipulates ideas, individual and collective identities and memories, inter-relational bodies and fictionalised flows by giving cinematic flesh to certain myths, narratives and characters (Beasley & Brook, 2019, pp. 2, 12). In brief, most Hollywood films—using Joseph Nye's terminology (2004)—can be shown to advance American "soft power" and—using Antonio Gramsci's account of consent to hegemony (1948[1991])—to advance a legitimating positive American self-image to Americans and around the world.

However, if Hollywood films are understood to have powerful socio-political effects, including those inflected by specifically US national agendas, it becomes crucial to reflect upon Hollywood's impact upon all of us around the globe, in terms of attending to legacies regarding social injustice. In this setting, heteronormativity casts a long shadow of past discrimination, marginalisation and violence into the present. The term broadly refers to the assumption that all people are naturally and normally, exclusively and exhaustively, either men or women and heterosexual (Butler, 1990).

Heteronormativity amounts to an all-encompassing insistence on the natural eternal normality of gendered heterosexuality such that it is presented as the only means to pleasure, acceptance, full personhood and love (Blakemore,

2016). As Martin and Kazyak (2009, p. 333) point out, its "pervasiveness lends it power" with the effect that "[i]t becomes difficult to imagine anything other than this form of social relationship or anyone outside of these bonds". Heteronormativity involves the specific construction of those who fail to occupy acceptable/normative gender or heterosexual social positionings and practices as 'other' and almost invariably as deficit (Jackson, 2006; Rubin, 1984). However, heteronormativity is also linked to a range of other social/institutional requirements which are not strictly limited to gender and sexuality subjectivities. These requirements include reproductive sexuality, gender-specified domestic living arrangements, intra-racial intimate relationships and modes of consumerism/consumption (Beasley et al., 2012, pp. 86–87; Martin & Kazyak, 2009, pp. 316–317), which continuously constitute hierarchical insider/outsider distinctions delimiting the former and resulting in an array of harms to the latter. The heteronorm thus legitimates the unrelenting policing of all genders and sexualities as it propounds a coherence, an "inner charmed circle" (Rubin, 1984, p. 282), against which not only pariah outsiders but also seeming insiders are judged (Beasley et al., 2012, p. 87; Warner, 1999, p. 27). Heteronormativity imposes an exacting price upon those deemed to be homosexual. Nevertheless, it is not simply a synonym for heterosexual but also suppresses diversity within heterosexuality and in relation to gender. Its variable impacts have fuelled and justified past social injustices, continuing to generate everything from social disapproval to rape and murder (see for example, Adelson, 2012; Human Rights Campaign, 2020; Lu et al., 2019; Yep, 2003). In this setting, how does Hollywood deal with heteronormativity? What does Hollywood say that has effects upon our views of intimate relationships today? Such questions are relevant because of substantial evidence that *what Hollywood says, matters*.

Power and sticky normality in contemporary Hollywood Romance

This chapter considers the more specific question of whether, and to what extent, Hollywood *romance* films reiterate, enforce or challenge inequality in intimate life by noting the reiteration of themes to global mass audiences. Hollywood romance movies diligently mobilise audience expectations of what is desirable, normal and enjoyable about intimate relationships. What do these reiterated formulations say about heteronormativity?

In Hollywood movies, 'normal' romance and desire is thoroughly heteronormative and validates both heterosexuality and gender distinction in a number of ways. In keeping with Joseph Nye's conception of "soft power" (2004), the attractions of the legitimate heteronormative community are 'sold' to audiences over and over again as preeminent and appealing. We are shown a community with which we should identify and wish to join and relatedly the abnormality and punitive consequences that will follow if we fail to do so—in keeping with Gramsci's conception of producing consent to the existing hegemonic status quo (1948[1991]). In this context, Hollywood romance relentlessly presents an interconnected set of heteronormative political myths. I will now briefly explore these mythological tropes in the particular context of contemporary Hollywood romantic comedies.[4]

All you need is [hetero] love—*particularly if you are a 'real' woman*

Women on screen in romantic comedies are often represented as committed to meaningful careers. Consider, for example, Kate Hudson's corporate lawyer "Liv" in *Bride Wars* (2009); and Sandra Bullock in almost all her romantic roles—FBI agent, lawyer, doctor, publishing executive and so on.[5] More than any other genre, romantic comedies feature career-conscious women. Yet, there is a less than subtle hint here that women who have succeeded are special women and thus appropriate objects of romantic desire. They are 'special' in other ways, too. Female leads in Hollywood romances are almost inevitably also young, white, slim, heterosexual, able-bodied, middleclass and conventionally beautiful. They provide what Barthes (1972, p. 49) described in terms of a celebrity 'alibi', an obfuscating substitution diverting attention from recognition of social inequality (see also Mane, 2012, pp. 2, 24). In short, the 'everyone' of romance movies is decidedly not an everywoman. Rather, these films offer the aspirational ideal of traditionally successful femininity re-cast as empowerment.[6] The limited and ambiguous shift in hierarchical gender politics within Hollywood rom-coms continues to depend heavily on sexuality, racial and other social privileges. Though egalitarianism and egalitarian intimacy is seemingly promoted, heteronormativity with its presumptions regarding gender and sexuality, continues to be insistently presented as for everyone and as virtually universal or at least as a universal aspiration to the point of its appearing inevitable and natural (Anderson, 2016; Dowd et al., 2021, Lauzen, 2021). Unsurprisingly, alongside these visions of empowered, beautiful women, the reiterated myth is that while (young, white, able-bodied) women today have the world at their feet, satisfaction and respect cannot be found in work alone. Indeed, in rom-coms, (hetero) love is represented as always and inevitably more worthy than anything else.

Hypermonogamy—*love's highest and normative form is exclusive and eternal heterosexual coupledom*

Elizabeth Emens coined the term "supermonogamy" to describe the idea that there is one (and only one) uniquely perfect soul-mate for every human being (Emens, 2004, p. 12). Here an alternative term is adopted, *hypermonogamy* (see Beasley & Brook, 2019, pp. 147–148). While Emens's "supermonogamy" stresses the overarching social approval attached to the "one and only one" idea, the 'hyper' in hypermonogamy suggests an emphasis that is simultaneously endorsed and elevated, yet anxious. This anxiety is evident in the strongly instructional elements of many rom-coms, such as *Hitch* (2005), *The 40 Year old Virgin* (2005) and *He's just not that into You* (2009) (see Behrendt & Tuccillo, 2004). Anxiety and instruction go hand in hand in the hypermono-gamous world of Hollywood romance since those who remain outside this community of coupledom are failures, as will shortly become evident.

Hypermonogamy is patently not available to or even suitable for everyone. Yet Hollywood romances insist on the preeminence of heterosexual couple-dom. The premise of *Something Borrowed* (2011) is that "Dex" (Colin Eggles-field) cannot resist revisiting his enduring attraction to his fiancé's best friend, "Rachel" (Ginnifer Goodwin). We are invited to imagine that in a world of more than seven billion people (and counting), Rachel's one true love, her only soul mate, is none other than the man her best friend is about to marry. Predictably, 'true' heterosexual love trumps years of loyal, same-sex friendship.

Gender polarity and complementarity

Romantic comedies almost inevitably see 'different' individuals pairing up. The focal difference, however, is almost always presented as gendered polarisation: if the female lead is neat, the male lead is messy; if the male lead is strait-laced and conventional, the female is non-conformist; and so on. Thus, in *Letters to Juliet* (2010), "Sophie" (Amanda Seyfried) is sentimental and romantic, while "Charlie" (Christopher Egan) is a hardnosed pragmatist. Katherine Heigl's "Jane" in *27 Dresses* (2008) is a kind and helpful friend, but her destined partner "Kevin" is cynical and shrewd. In romantic comedy, it does not matter whe-ther a woman is this or that; what matters is that she is one thing and the appropriately masculine man she meets is another. In this way, romantic comedies appear merely to reflect gender polarisation, but in fact also produce it—indeed insist upon it.

In addition, as noted earlier, despite some tweaking rom-coms maintain certain traditional gendered features. For instance, love and relationships are at the centre of successful femininity and male rom-com leads are presented as having certain traditionally masculine characteristics even if they are cast in less prestigious positions than female leads. For example, in *Fever Pitch* (2005) Drew Barrymore is a high-performing executive who finds her Prince Charming in the guise of a humble Boston Red Sox (American baseball team) fan. He might 'only' be a teacher, but he is identified with sports. Moreover, as might be expected, while female leads are invariably conventionally attractive, the aes-thetic margins of what constitutes a plausibly attractive person seem to be sig-nificantly more elastic for men. Consider Gerard Depardieu in *Green Card* (1990), Jack Black in *Shallow Hal* (2001), or Seth Rogen in *Knocked Up* (2007)—none of whom is obviously or conventionally handsome.[7]

However, male rom-com stars do often present a markedly 'softer' mascu-linity than their action hero counterparts. In *The Holiday* (2006) "Graham"

(Jude Law) admits to being easily moved to tears. In *Moonstruck* (1987) and *Serendipity* (2001) there are pivotal speeches by men regarding the necessity to relinquish rationality, to embrace emotionality in order to truly experience love—a far cry from the controlled authoritativeness of action heroes. Rowe labels this softer, more sensitive version of masculinity the "melodramatised man", arguing that his softening actually serves to supplement rather than undermine masculine authority (1995, pp. 196–197).[8]

In sum, even if gender identities are somewhat expanded in some contemporary Hollywood rom-coms, allowable variations on the gendered heteronorm are decidedly limited. Women can have more job possibilities and men can have a greater emotional/communicative range, but women and men are cast as necessarily different. Hence, gender difference, and distinct gender subjectivities, remain firmly in place.

Compulsory [gendered] hetero-destiny

Rom-coms endorse the message that the heterosexual couple is a necessary, natural unit, an endorsement that is repeated in rom-com treatments of single people as pitiful and unhappy. Adrienne Rich's (1980) account of "compulsory heterosexuality" remains relevant here. Rich argues that if heterosexuality were really as naturally and normally widespread as is claimed, there would be no need to systematise punishments directed at women who fail or refuse to comply. In rom-coms, protractedly single female characters are represented as almost inevitably desperate. A good example here is "Annie" (Kirsten Wiig) in *Bridesmaids* (2011). In the opening scene, Annie is engaged in comically gymnastic sex with her "fuck buddy". That she is his "number three girl" marks her as exploited or a little desperate—she is not valued or respected, not truly loved.

The same logic may be found in the portrayal of a range of single people as fat, ugly, hypersexual, or otherwise unlovable (think of Melissa McCarthy's character "Megan" in *Bridesmaids,* 2011; Rebel Wilson's "Fat Amy" in *Pitch Perfect,* 2012; Zach Galifianakis as "Alan" in *The Hangover,* 2009). And just in case we didn't get the message, in Hollywood rom-coms those who are 'happily' single are represented as the victims of false consciousness—playboys/playgirls who are shallow, irresponsible, immature or emotionally wounded.[9] Even when the notion of the hetero-couple appears to be the subject of critique and those who do not embrace coupledom seem at first not to be dismissed, hetero love returns recuperated and hence coupledom is reinstated as inevitable destiny. Thus, critics of the heteronormative couple in *Friends with Benefits* (2011) and *Friends with Kids* (2011) are revealed as damaged and ill-informed but come to 'see the light' (Cadwallader, 2012)

However, Hollywood's compulsory hetero-sexuality goes beyond sociality or psychology. Hollywood romantic comedies generally present love as a powerful human need whose shape is (to some extent, at least) figured as beyond human control. If a couple is 'meant' to be together, fate will bring

Haunted by the Heteronorm 199

them together. For example, in the first of a series of fateful coincidences in *Serendipity* (2001), the couple-to-be meets in a department store when both reach for the same pair of gloves. In *The Wedding Planner* (2001) "Mary" (Jennifer Lopez) causes a traffic accident and subsequently faints. Like Sleeping Beauty, she awakens to her rescuer, "Steve" (Matthew McConaughey). In romantic comedies, lovers are *destined* to meet and fall in love.

Though fate may engineer love, missing out on romance is not attributed to destiny. Rather, this terrible possibility is ascribed to personal inadequacy. The American independent movie *Kissing Jessica Stein* (2002) provides an exemplary account. "Jessica" (Jennifer Westfeldt) discusses her recent dating experience over a dinner with friends and rues the lack of decent single men. Her former boyfriend responds by launching an excoriating attack on Jessica, pronouncing that it is she who is the problem rather than the men she meets. This scene illustrates perfectly the sting in the tail that inevitably inheres in privileging of hypermonogamy and compulsory hetero-destiny. The reiterated political myths in rom-coms relentlessly police the normative 'us' and remind us of the problematic marginalised 'other'.

The romantic "coital imperative"

For the most part Hollywood romantic comedies are not very explicitly sexual (see for example, *My Big Fat Greek Wedding*, 2002; *Dirty Dancing*, 1987) and tend to represent sex through the lens of marriage, pregnancy and other synecdoches. Nonetheless, Hollywood rom-coms are built upon notions of sexual attraction and continue to provide relentless pedagogical lessons about 'proper' sex (Pearce, 2006), As Cadwallader (2012) among many others notes, heterosex is remarkably consistent and persistent in Hollywood romance. Heterosex is sex (no other forms are presented) and, when it does (relatively) explicitly appear, is equated with penis-vagina intercourse (Sandberg, 2013, p. 264). Men and women are necessarily and naturally driven by "the coital imperative" (Jackson, 1984, p. 44), the sexual dimension of Rich's "compulsory heterosexuality" (1980). Penises, without any other assistance (other than perhaps a preliminary bout of extended kissing), are the invisible means by which women gasp and moan and become orgasmic. Barring when sex is clearly constituted as comic,[10] clothes drop away, and women are then immediately able and keen to engage in intercourse and orgasm, wherever they are, no matter how uncomfortable or challenging the setting (showers, outdoors, in public, etc.), or the impediments they face, even if the women have never had sexual intercourse before (see *Love and Other Drugs*, 2010; *Nick and Norah's Infinite Playlist*, 2008; *My Big Fat Greek Wedding*, 2002; *Pretty Woman*, 1990) (Hayes & Ro, 2018; Lawless, 2019; Vaynshteyn, 2014). Erections apparently never fail to appear and no matter how urgent their desire, men remain silent, apart possibly from some heavy breathing.[11] Through this process, men's penises are insistently re-erected as *the* active essential. And significantly even penis-vagina intercourse takes a particular form: 'normal' hetero-sex appears as 'missionary-position'. Other options suggest something problematic or possibly ridiculous—see *Forgetting Sarah Marshall* (2010) (Brillson & Nesita, 2014).

Heterogendered transformation: the romance rite of passage and the evolved self

Romantic comedy's reliance on fate is matched by a paradoxical insistence that the protagonists acknowledge and act on their attraction. Love, like most other matters of value in Hollywood films, demands 'can-do' individualist will power and action. In rom-coms, love almost always requires mettle and some attendant risk of humiliation or rejection. Often, one or both romantic protagonists must find the courage to reveal some truth about their lives or feelings. In *Maid in Manhattan* (2002), for example, "Marisa" (Jennifer Lopez) eventually confesses that she is not the wealthy socialite would-be-Senator "Chris Marshall" (Ralph Fiennes) supposes her to be but is in fact a humble maid. And, in this movie, like countless others, the lead female character undertakes a makeover (Ferris, 2008), a transformation, on her romance journey.

Although both women and men lose self-control in rom-coms and are transformed emotionality, the rite of passage towards romantic adulthood takes decidedly different gendered forms. With few exceptions, only women are required to undergo physical transformation.[12] The 'magic makeover' for women very often involves a focus on improving her appearance such that they become appropriate objects of (men's) desire (see for example *The House Bunny,* 2008; *Miss Congeniality,* 2000; *She's All That,* 1999; *Moonstruck,* 1987). Moreover, women's emotional development through love is not strongly highlighted and is more frequently bound up in 'letting go' of control. By contrast, men's transformation is usually one limited to emotional maturation. Although men also lose self-control, their romance rite of passage is typically cast as a journey towards self-knowledge and care for others. It involves moving beyond adolescence/under-developed adulthood and becoming more responsive to women (Mortimer, 2010, pp. 62–65). Gender polarity is once again produced (and naturalised).

Similarly, while single women are routinely depicted as pathetically uncoupled (Kirsten Wiig in *Bridesmaids,* 2011) or obsessed with finding a man (Ginnifer Goodwin in *He's just not that into You,* 2009), men are rarely portrayed as actively or naturally interested in love. Rather, love finds them and invites them to reconsider what they have. Single men are represented as subject to a different kind of loneliness than women. In *Wedding Crashers* (2009), "Jeremy" (Vince Vaughan) and "John" (Owen Wilson) are first presented as joyously single, consuming 'easy' women at weddings like food from a buffet. As the narrative progresses, they become aware of how much more meaningful and rewarding their lives might become if they were to find—and keep—true love. As "Connor" (Matthew McConaughey) in *Ghosts of Girlfriends Past* (2009) comes to realise, even spectacularly successful womanising and unending opportunities for sexual pleasure is as nothing next to this.[13] Single men may be presented as 'happy bachelors', but their happiness is shallow or illusory. In Hollywood romance, women find what they obviously desperately need to be complete, while men find what they come to appreciate is unexpectedly good for them. As Michele Schreiber asserts, romance "mythologizes the redemptive qualities of love and heterosexual coupling" (2014, p. 27).

The unlovable limits of love

While love and heterosexual coupling are routinely mythologised as necessary, redemptive and available to everyone, those who remain unmatched are characterised as sad, lonely failures. This seeming paradox rests upon constructing the 'everyone' of Hollywood romance in certain ways. For example, while illness and disability are enduring themes in Hollywood, representations of sick or disabled people in romance films are anything but inclusive. Older people (those over 50) or relationships which cross social categories remain rare subjects. Hollywood has barely recognised black-white intimate relationships, let alone sexual scenes.

Moreover, reaching the 'promised land' of hypermonogamy is obviously not available to those who 'fail' its intrinsic hetero requirements. Even though homosexuality and other queer orientations are (in the United States and many other places) no longer so strongly proscribed, LGBTIQ characters almost never appear as romantic leads in Hollywood romance. Instead—like a number of other 'marked' categories—they are either excluded altogether or relegated to 'sidekick' roles—such as in the bro-mance *I Love You, Man* (2009), as well as in more traditional rom-coms like *As Good as it Gets* (1997) and *Friends with Benefits* (2011).

Countering Hollywood Heteronormativity

Hetero-love in Hollywood is not only preeminent, irresistible, obligatory, sexually restrictive and written in the stars; it completes you as a woman or man, as well as a human being. Missing out on hetero-love marks you as an outcast, nonentity, failure, runner-up or peripheral side-kick and, whatever one's relegation on this dreary score-card, as unhappy. The ongoing oppressive and damaging orthodoxy of heteronormativity continues apace. Hollywood romance films consistently reiterate—reflect, generate and demand—discriminatory heteronormative stories of intimate life. Yet, there is presently no register for the global promulgation of the insistent policing of this continuing legacy of social injustice, this selective memorialising of hegemonic normativity and suppression of alternatives.

The Bechdel-Wallace Test: implications for challenging heteronormativity in popular culture

By contrast, there has been in recent years some attempt to identify cinematic codes which reinforce gendered power relations and the subordination of women. The limitations of Hollywood's representations—that is, its ongoing privileging of men and subordination of women—have been rendered more visible to many through the application of the Bechdel Test or, more accurately, the Bechdel-Wallace Test.[14] In Alison Bechdel's 1985 comic strip one character explains her criteria for movie-going to another. These criteria include the presence of at least two women, who talk to each other and talk about something other than men. The Bechdel-Wallace test is a relatively blunt analytical instrument but is salient. In a study of more than 800 popular movies produced from 1950 to 2006, Amy Bleakley and her colleagues showed not only that male main characters outnumber female main characters by "more than two to one" but also that this pattern of women's under-representation has remained consistent over time (Bleakley et al., 2012, p. 75). The use of the Bechdel-Wallace Test reveals in broad terms that Hollywood film really does present an axiomatic masculinism. Moreover, in a practical sense, it has had a significant progressive impact on the gender content of films when employed to rank films.[15]

Cultural memories of discrimination and violence are very frequently erased, denied or declared redundant. However, as is evident in Chapters 10 and 12, the impact of these memories does not necessarily override possibilities for resistance and innovation. It is timely and important in this context to register heteronormativity, to make it visible, as well as providing opportunities for recognition of resistant, counter-hegemonic alternatives. In this setting, a new 'test' is suggested which—drawing the progressive impact of the Bechdel-Wallace Test—may be employed in assessing and hopefully influencing popular fictional films in future. The Beasley-Brook test has, like its originating predecessor, three elements, as well as bonus features.[16] These elements and bonus points are intended to highlight the ongoing pervasiveness of heteronormativity through rewarding challenges to it. Any fictional romance film which has all three elements should receive an A approval rating, two elements receive a B, one element generates a C ranking, and none produces a Fail (F). These elements are:

- at least one positive example of a character who is not cis-gendered and/or not heterosexual;
- at least one positive instance of a hetero singleton who does not become coupled, or other explicit indicators that hetero coupledom is not the only option for a satisfactory life; and
- no overtly negative comments concerning being single which are taken as self-evident (that is, no 'single-shaming')

A bonus star should be added (for example, A★) if there is at least one positive example of sexual practices beyond the heteronorm of legitimated sexual expression. In other words, a star is added if there is at least one instance which goes beyond heterosexual kissing/hugging or heterosexual intercourse.

Conclusion

As noted earlier in this chapter, the notion of living legacies of social injustice enables attention to the sticky 'normality' of power relations, a normality which for the most part renders inequality/discrimination as natural and therefore largely invisible. This suggests inertia as past injustice folds into the present and shapes the future. Yet, past and continuing injustice do not determine future directions. The frameworks concerning culture outlined previously indicate the ongoing weight of cultural legacies but not their inevitability. While Joseph Nye focusses upon the cultural production of notions of America as attractive nation—which he terms American "soft power", Gramsci attends to cultural production of consent to the status quo and thus to the significance of cultural forms like film in giving legitimacy to hegemonic American society and values. However, both note in different ways that legitimation and hegemony are not given and are produced through an ongoing cultural battle of ideas (Strinati, 2004, pp. 156–157; see also Murphy, 2003). In this setting, since what Hollywood says, matters, do Hollywood movies offer any glimpses of alternative *counter-hegemonic* perspectives?

The Hollywood film industry for the most part legitimates American state power and American individualist values (Beasley & Brook, 2019) and thus is deeply implicated in sustaining and validating the American 'political imaginary'—that is, hegemonic notions of national community and selfhood. It is likely that many Hollywood romances would be awarded a Beasley-Brook test ranking of F for Fail. In such a context, any alternative perspectives in Hollywood romance films are comparatively welcome. The question is whether it is possible to think of *any* Hollywood romance which, following the Beasley-Brook test, could be granted an A rating, (let alone an A★ one)? One example comes to mind. When my colleague Heather Brook and I pondered Hollywood romances which might offer counter-hegemonic glimpses—in that they provide some glimpses of critical response to heteronormativity—we thought that one story which deserved at least an A rating was *My Best Friend's Wedding*—if only for its ending. Here is a brief precis.

"Julianne" (played by Julia Roberts) receives a call from her lifelong friend "Michael". He is about to marry "Kimmy". Julianne realises then that she loves Michael and becomes intent on sabotaging the wedding, but in the end the wedding goes ahead. A gay male friend, "George" (Rupert Everett) who has throughout tried to offer her advice and support, calls her at the wedding reception. Unknown to Julianne, George is also at the reception and, to the

204 Chris Beasley

tune of a romantic song ("I say a little prayer"), they move toward each other. As the crowd parts and they meet, George speaks the immortal lines of a most unusual 'happy ending': "What the hell. Life goes on. Maybe there won't be marriage. Maybe there won't be sex (grimaces). But, my god, there'll be dancing!". He twirls her onto the dance floor as they fondly smile at each other.[17]

Dispiritingly, Hollywood's dominance as a producer and distributor of cinematic stories about sex, desire, love and intimacy have most often resulted in F for Fail narratives. However, this chapter is intended to give voice to hope that the ongoing legacy of the heteronorm in popular culture, as elsewhere, is at least sometimes challenged by alternative perspectives. Such perspectives may be further assisted by their recognition in forms of public ranking such as through the proposed Beasley-Brook test.

Notes

1 This chapter is a revised version of two papers I presented in June 2018 at the second OLIRN conference held at Karlstad University, Sweden, and at York University, United Kingdom. The co-authored papers arose from a co-authored book, Chris Beasley and Heather Brook (2019), *The cultural politics of contemporary Hollywood film: Power, culture and society*. The papers and book were written in consultation or in conjunction with my dear friend, Heather. She died as a result of breast cancer just before the age of 55 in 2019. She was my birthday twin, my intellectual companion, my much-loved mate. It seemed too peculiar to name her in the context of this chapter as my co-author, but I wish to acknowledge her here as my previous co-author and as joint source of most of the arguments and ideas that are in this work.

2 Hollywood films are popular films produced by major Hollywood studios for mass global audiences rather than independent, art-house or avant-garde productions. While the distinction between mass and art-house is reasonably straightforward, the distinction between majors and independents is becoming more difficult to establish. (Beasley & Brook, 2019, pp. 12, 16).

3 There are further compelling grounds for acknowledging that movies have an impact on audiences. This can be demonstrated in quite specific and practical sense when we look at the phenomenon of 'product placement' in films, which has a direct effect on sales (Segrave, 2004, p. 181).

4 As this chapter is concerned with considering past social injustice in the form of heteronormativity in relation to its ongoing transmission in the present and the future, the focus is upon relatively recent Hollywood films, mostly from 2000 onwards. The selection of films was also based upon their impact registered by commercial success—that is, those chosen had a mass and indeed international audience, as well as numerous popular assessments of 'best' or 'top' romantic comedies (see for example *Box Office Mojo* on Romantic Comedy and Rotten Tomatoes editorial guide).

5 The corresponding movies are *Miss Congeniality* (2000), *Two Weeks Notice* (2002), *The Lake House* (2006) and *The Proposal* (2009), to name just a selection.

6 If "raunch culture" passes off traditional sexualised objectification of women as the new empowerment in contemporary cultural mediums (Levy, 2005), romantic comedy provides its more respectable doppelganger. Both re-jig traditional

valuation of women in terms of their attractiveness as a marker of women's supposed new freedom and gender equality.

7 The disparity is one of a number of gendered double standards. One of the most obvious of these is that male rom-com protagonists (and indeed male stars in general) are thought to have much more enduring romantic appeal than women, whose 'shelf-life' is markedly shorter (Guo, 2016; Wilson, 2015). This restricted space for women is associated with markedly lower numbers of women working in the film industry (Lauzen, 2021).

8 Rowe, in keeping with Janice Radway's (1991) analysis of romance novels, stresses the softening of masculinity through romance, though of course the hero must not become 'too' soft (see also Mortimer, 2010, p. 49).

9 Male leads (and increasingly, female leads too) often start off as irresponsible, hypersexual playboy types (see for instance, *Crazy Stupid Love* (2011) and *Wedding Crashers* (2009).

10 For example, *The 40-Year-Old Virgin* (2005).

11 Gender distinction is even maintained in terms of noise-making in sexual activity.

12 Men are very rarely the subject of physical make-overs in order to attract women but see *Crazy Stupid Love* (2011).

13 As Connor succinctly puts it, following his realisation of the limits of bachelorhood, "Look at me. I'm empty, lonely, ghost of a man".

14 Bechdel credits the idea of the test to her friend Liz Wallace (Beasley & Brook, 2019, p. 129).

15 The introduction of use of the Bechdel A rating in Sweden resulted in marked changes in Swedish feature films with 80 per cent achieving an A rating in 2015 (up from 30 per cent at the initiation of the rating's usage) (Kang, 2016; Selisker, 2015).

16 This test offers a rather different ranking approach than the 'Vito Russo' test, The Vito Russo test has a wider scope in that it does not specify the kind of films or their production but is more limited in only dealing with the presence of LGBTIQ characters. It is thus more limited with regard to heteronormativity in only checking for issues included under the first element of the Beasley-Brook test. (Anderson, 2016).

17 See *My Best Friend's Wedding* (1997): There will be dancing. www.youtube.com/watch?v=Zsi7-dbKxP8—3.42minutes. Accessed March 2022.

References

Adelson, S. (2012). Practice parameter on gay, lesbian, or bisexual sexual orientation, gender nonconformity, and gender discordance in children and adolescents. *Journal of the American Academy of Child and Adolescent Psychiatry*, 51(9), September, 957–974.

Ahmed. S. (2004). Affective economies. *Social Text*, 22(2), 117–139.

Ahmed, S. (2007). *The cultural politics of emotion*. New York: Routledge.

Alterman, E. & Green, M. J. (2004). *The book on Bush: How George W. (mis)leads America*. London: Penguin.

Anderson, T. (2016). Here is why Hollywood also has an LGBT diversity issue. *Los Angeles Times*, May 2. www.latimes.com/entertainment/movies/la-et-mn-glaad-studio-lgbt-20160502-snap-htmlstory.html. Accessed October 2022.

Athanasiou, A., Hantzaroula, P. & Yannakopoulos, K. (2008). Towards a new epistemology:the "affective turn". *Historein*, 8, 5–16.

Barthes, R. (1972). *Mythologies*. New York: Hill & Wang.

Beasley, C. (2011). Libidinous politics: Heterosex, "transgression" and social change. *Australian Feminist Studies*, 26(67), 25–40.

Beasley, C. & Bacchi, C. (2007, December). Envisaging a new politics for an ethical future: Beyond trust, care and generosity towards an ethic of social flesh. *Feminist Theory*, 8(3), 279–298.

Beasley, C. & Brook, H. (2019). *The cultural politics of Hollywood film: Power, culture and society*. Manchester: Manchester University Press.

Beasley, C., Brook, H. & Holmes, M. (2012). *Heterosexuality in theory and practice*. New York: Routledge.

Beasley, C. & Holmes, M. (2021). *Internet dating: Intimacy and social change*. London & New York: Routledge.

Beech, H. (2017, February 6). Hollywood east: A movie-crazy China is making the global film industry in its image. *Time*, 30–36.

Behrendt, G. & Tuccillo, L. (2004). *He's just not that into you: The no-excuses truth to understanding guys*. New York: Simon Spotlight Entertainment.

Berezin, M. (1997). Politics and Culture: A Less Fissured Terrain. *Annual Review of Sociology*, 23, 361–383.

Blakemore, E. (2016, October 7). How Disney movies teach straightness. *Daily*. https://daily.jstor.org/how-disney-movies-teach-straightness. Accessed September 2021.

Bleakley, A, Jamieson, P. & Romer, D. (2012). Trends of sexual and violent content by gender in top-grossing US films, 1950–2006. *Journal of Adolescent Health*, 51(1), 73–79.

Box Office Mojo. (n.d.). Genre Keyword: Romantic Comedy. www.boxofficemojo.com/genre/sg2111762689. Accessed October 2022.

Braidotti, R. (2006). *Transpositions: On nomadic ethics*. Cambridge: Polity Press.

Braidotti, R. (2008). In spite of the times: The postsecular turn in feminism. *Theory, Culture & Society*, 25(6), 1–24.

Brillson, L. & Nesita, L. (2014), 10 ways the movies get sex wrong. *Refinery* 29. www.refinery29.com/en-us/2014/11/71957/movie-sex-tropes. Accessed September 2021.

Butler, J. (1990). *Gender trouble: Feminism and the subversion of identity*. London: Routledge.

Cadwallader, J. R. (2012). Like a horse and carriage: (Non)normativity in Hollywood romance. *M/C Journal*, 15(6). https://journal.media-culture.org.au/index.php/mcjournal/article/view/583. Accessed September 2021.

Colebrook, C. & UK Research and Innovation. (2008). Vitalism and the meaning of life in the philosophy and criticism of Gilles Deleuze. (https://gtr.ukri.org/projects?ref=AH%2FE003206%2F1). Accessed September 2021.

Crane, D. (2014). Cultural globalization and the dominance of the American film industry: cultural policies, national film industries, and transnational film. *International Journal of Cultural Policy*, 20(4), 365–382.

Dowd, J., Crabtree, A. & Cannon, B. (2021). Movies, gender, and social change: the Hollywood romance film. *Journal of Gender Studies*, September. doi:10.1080/09589236.2021.1979479.

Emens, E. (2004). Monogamy's law: compulsory monogamy and polyamorous existence. *New York Review of Law and Social Change*, 29(2), 277–376.

Deleuze, G. & Parnet, C. (2007). *Dialogues* II. New York: Columbia University Press.

Der Derian, J. (2001). *Virtuous war*. Boulder, CO: Westview Press.

Durmaz, B., Tan, Yigitcanlar, T. & Velibeyoglu, K. (2008). Creative Cities and the film industry: Antalya's transition to a Eurasion film centre. *The Open Urban Studies Journal*, 1, 1–10.

Ferris, S. (2008). Fashioning femininity in the makeover flick. In S. Ferris & M. Young (Eds), *Chick Flicks: Contemporary Women at the Movies* (pp. 41–57). New York & London: Routledge.

Gramsci, A. (1948[1991]). *Prison notebooks*: Volume 1. Translated by J. A. Buttigieg & A. Callari. New York: Columbia University Press.

Guo, J. (2016, September 19). Why the age of 40 is so important in Hollywood. *The Washington Post*. www.washingtonpost.com/news/wonk/wp/2016/09/19/these-charts-reveal-how-bad-the-film-industrys-sexism-is. Accessed September 2021.

Hayes, A. & Ro, C. (2018, April 2). 18 things women do in movies during sex that are totally unrealistic. *Buzzfeed*. www.buzzfeed.com/alliehayes/women-sex-in-movies-cliches. Accessed September 2021.

Hozić, A. (2001). *Hollywood: Space, power and fantasy in the American economy*. Ithaca, NY: Cornell University Press.

Human Rights Campaign. (2020). *Fatal violence against the transgender and gender non-conforming community in 2020*. www.hrc.org/resources/violence-against-the-trans-and-gender-non-conforming-community-in-2020. Accessed September 2021.

Hunter, L. (2003). The celluloid cubicle: regressive constructions of masculinity in 1990s office movies. *Journal of American Culture*, 26(1), 71–76.

Jackson, M. (1984). Sex research and the construction of sexuality: A tool of male supremacy? *Women's Studies International Forum*, 7, 43–51.

Jackson, S. (2006). Gender, sexuality and heterosexuality: The complexity (and limits) of heteronormativity. *Feminist Theory*, 7, 105–121.

Kang, I. (2016, February 17). What happened after Swedish theaters introduced a Bechdel rating for its movies? *IndieWire*. www.indiewire.com/2016/02/whathappened-after-swedish-theaters-introduced-a-bechdel-rating-for-its-movies-204746. Accessed 13 February 2017.

Lauzen, M. (2021). The celluloid ceiling: Behind-the-scenes employment of women on the top U.S. films of 2020. https://womenintvfilm.sdsu.edu/wp-content/uploads/2021/01/2020_Celluloid_Ceiling_Report.pdf. Accessed September 2021.

Lawless, S. (2019). Sex on screen is such an anticlimax for women. Where did it all go wrong? *Refinery* 29, October 30. www.refinery29.com/en-us/movie-sex-scenes-unrealistic-fake. Accessed September 2021.

Levy, A. (2005). *Female chauvinist pigs: Women and the rise of raunch culture*. New York: Free Press.

Lin, J. (2002). Review of *Hollywood*, by Aida Hosić. *The American Journal of Sociology*, 108(2), 477–478.

Loria, D. (2020, March 11). MPA: 2019 global box office and home entertainment surpasses $100 Billion. *BoxOffice Pro*. www.boxofficepro.com/mpa-2019-global-box-office-and-home-entertainment-surpasses-100-billion. Accessed September 2021.

Lu, A., LeBlanc, A. J. & Frost, D. M. (2019, July 1). Masculinity and minority stress among men in same-sex relationships. *Society of Mental Health*, 9(2), 259–275.

Mane, R. L. C. (2012) Using female empowerment as a cover story for whiteness and racial hierarchy in pop culture. PhD Dissertation, Department of Communication, University of Washington.

Martin, K. A. & Kazyak, E. (2009, June). Hetero-romantic love and heterosexiness in children's G-rated films. *Gender & Society*, 23(3), 315–336.

Mortimer, C. (2010). *Romantic comedy*. Routledge Film Guidebooks. London: Routledge.

Motion Picture Association of America. (2016). *2015 Theatrical Market Statistics Report*. www.motionpictures.org/research-docs/2015-theatrical-market-statistics-report. Accessed May 2018.

Motion Picture Association & China Film Co-Production Corporation. (2014). *China international film production handbook 2014*. www.mpa-i.org/wp-content/uploads/2014/Co-Production_Handbook_English.pdf. Accessed May 2018.

Motion Picture Distributors Association of Australia. (2017). Personal communication with Osman Kabbara, film data administrator.

Murphy, P. (2003). Without ideology? Rethinking hegemony in the age of transnational media. In L. Artz & Y. R. Kamalipour (Eds), *The globalization of corporate media hegemony* (pp. 55–75). Albany, NY: SUNY Press.

Nye, J. (2004). *Soft power: the means to success in world politics*. New York: PublicAffairs Books.

O'Brien, D. & Oakley, K. (2015). *Cultural value and inequality: A critical literature review*. A report commissioned by the Arts and Humanities Research Council's cultural value project. Arts and Humanities Research Council, Swindon, Wiltshire, United Kingdom. www.buzzfeed.com/alliehayes/women-sex-in-movies-cliches. Accessed September 2021.

Pearce, S. (2006). Sex and the cinema: what *American Pie* teaches the young. *Sex Education*, 6(4), 367–376.

Radway, J. (1991). *Reading the romance: Women, patriarchy and popular literature*, 2nd Edition. Chapel Hill, NC: University of Carolina Press.

Rich, A. (1980). Compulsory heterosexuality and lesbian existence. *Signs*, 5(4), 631–660.

Romanowski, W. D. (1993 Summer). Oliver Stone's *JFK*: Commercial filmmaking, cultural history, and conflict. *Journal of Popular Film and Television*, 21(2), 63–71.

Rotten Tomatoes editorial guide. (n.d.). The 200 best romantic comedies of all time. https://editorial.rottentomatoes.com/guide/best-romantic-comedies-of-all-time. Accessed October 2022.

Rowe, K. (1995). *The unruly woman: Gender and the genres of laughter*. Austin, TX: University of Texas Press.

Rubin, G. (1984). Thinking sex: Notes for a radical theory of the politics of sexuality. In Vance, C. (Ed.), *Pleasure and danger* (pp. 267–319). Boston, MA: Routledge.

Ryan, M. & Kellner, D. (1988). *Camera politica: the politics and ideology of contemporary Hollywood film*. Bloomington, IN: Indiana University Press.

Sandberg, L. (2013). Just feeling a naked body close to you: Men, sexuality and intimacy in later life. *Sexualities*, 16(3/4), 261–282.

Schiller, N. G. (1997). Cultural politics and the politics of culture. *Identities: Global Studies in Culture and Power*, 4(1), 1–7.

Schreiber, M. (2014). *American postfeminist cinema: Women, romance, and contemporary culture*. Edinburgh: Edinburgh University Press.

Screen Australia. (2021). Cinema industry trends: box office in Australia, 1977–2020. www.screenaustralia.gov.au/fact-finders/cinema/australian-films/feature-film-releases/box-office-share. Accessed September 2021.

Screen Australia. (2020). World rankings: Number of feature films produced and key cinema data, 2008–2019. www.screenaustralia.gov.au/fact-finders/international-context/world-rankings/feature-films-and-cinemas. Accessed September 2021.

Segrave, K. (2004). *Product placement in Hollywood films: a history*. Jefferson, NC: McFarland.

Selisker, S. (2015, Summer). The Bechdel test and the social form of character networks. *New Literary History*, 46(3), 505–523.

Storey, J. (2001). *Cultural theory and popular culture*. London: Pearson/Prentice Hall.

Strinati, D. (2004). *An introduction to theories of popular culture*, 2nd Edition. London: Routledge.

Valenti, J. (2002). Cinema and war: Hollywood's response to September 11 (Interview with Jack Valenti). *Harvard International Review*, 24(2). http://hir.harvard.edu/article/?a+1028.

Vaynshteyn, G. (2014). Why is sex so unrealistic in TV and Movies? *HelloGiggles*, September 12. https://hellogiggles.com/lifestyle/sex-unrealistic-tv-movies. Accessed September 2011.

Warner, M. (1999). *The trouble with normal: Sex, politics and the ethics of a queer life*. Cambridge, MA: Harvard University Press.

Watts, L. & Hodgson, D. (2019). *Social justice theory and practice for social work*. Singapore: Springer.

Wei, J. & Shaw, N. (2016, December 14). Now playing: new film law impacts the Chinese silver screen. *Lexology*.

Wilson, C. (2015, October 6). This chart shows Hollywood's glaring gender gap. *Time*. https://time.com/4062700/hollywood-gender-gap. Accessed September 2021.

Yep, G. A. (2003). The violence of heteronormativity in Communication Studies: Notes on injury, healing and queer world making. *Journal of Homosexuality*, 45(2–4),11–59.

Chapter 12

Challenging Criminalisation in the Commonwealth

Theorising Legacies and Colonialities in LGBTIQ Movement Strategies

Matthew Waites

Introduction

The British Empire's criminalisation of sexual acts between men, and sometimes between women, has left an enduring legal residue in many states; and this continuing regulation has inspired new forms of transnational lesbian, gay, bisexual, trans and intersex (LGBTI) movement activity oriented to the Commonwealth as the international organisation that persisted after formal decolonisation (Lennox & Waites, 2013). In international political and sociological analyses, it has thus become necessary to examine this transnational LGBTI activism—not presumed analytically synonymous with queer politics (Waites, 2019a)—in relation to colonialism, through critical engagement with postcolonial and decolonial perspectives (Said, 1978; Mignolo, 2007; Kollman & Waites, 2009; Waites, 2015; Waites, 2017; Waites, 2019b; Gomes da Costa Santos & Waites, 2019; Lennox, Tabengwa & Waites, 2021). The present chapter contributes to this task, especially by considering the analytical frameworks that can be deployed in such social analysis. In particular, it is suggested that the concepts of "coloniality" (Quijano, 1999, p. 41) and "living legacy" (Beasley & Papadelos, 2024) both speak in different ways to the urgent task of theorising how the history of colonialism influences present social relations, power and conflicts. Hence the chapter provides an opportunity to compare the relative value of these concepts, especially to consider how the critically influential concept coloniality might usefully be supplemented by living legacy, when considered in relation to specific observed contexts. This examination will use data from activity surrounding the most recent Commonwealth Heads of Government Meeting, held in London during 2018. The comparative consideration of coloniality and living legacy enables discussion of how these concepts relate to social and political theories and how they may be used differently to interpret various issues and settings.

The analysis here, however, is motivated by the need to address contemporary burning questions and strategic dilemmas in international LGBTI and queer politics, in relation to sexualities and genders globally. The question of how to take account of colonial histories in light of decolonising politics has

DOI: 10.4324/9781003311928-15

emerged as one of the most pivotal and contentious issues in the transnational politics of gender and sexuality. On the one hand, we find a symbolic politics of regret or apology used increasingly in societies that have been colonising, suggesting a politics of recognition used more than a politics of redistribution in relation to colonial histories—with reference to Nancy Fraser's (1995) well-known distinction between recognition and redistribution. This was somewhat illustrated when British Prime Minister Theresa May expressed "regret" for British colonial regulation of same-sex sexual acts at the London Common-wealth Heads of Government Meeting (May, 2018), while not engaging claims for economic reparations for colonialism (Rao, 2020, p. 8)—although her words were accompanied by some funding for United Kingdom (UK)-based non-governmental organisations (NGO) to work with partners in formerly colonised states (discussed below). On the other hand, some decolonial analysts and activists are using an escalating vocabulary emphasising "delinking" from Eurocentrism (Mignolo, 2007, p. 449), with a challenge to "neo-colonial epistemic categories" (Bakshi et al., 2016, p. 1). While contributing to critical analysis, this kind of decolonising approach has sometimes tended to ignore, unfairly critique or dismiss the politics and practices of human rights (Waites, 2020, pp. 41–42), or sustainable development goals, painting an excessively negative and homogenous picture of Western government actions that include contradictions. Movement strategies need to be underpinned by clear con-ceptualisation and nuanced analyses of relevant contexts, to recognise structural power relations simultaneously with scope for creative transnational alliances and agency.

In social theory, postmodern analyses (Lyotard, 1984) and reflexive mod-ernisation analyses (Giddens, 1991) have characterised certain privileged societies as independently advanced in problematic ways that tended to forget colonialism, as postcolonial sociology now argues (Bhambra & Holmwood, 2021). However, such flawed postmodern and late modern analyses did somewhat identify how certain privileged societies experienced emerging socio-cultural diversity and globalisation with increased scope for learning about different cultures through information technology, in "computerized" societies (Lyotard, 1984, p. 3). Beck's reflexive modernisation analysis gener-ated a misconceived social theory of cosmopolitanisation as a dynamic of European societies, yet was somewhat useful for empirically noticing cosmo-politan culture, though lacking colonial contextualisation (Beck, 2006). New social movement theories such as from Melucci also offered some insights, emphasising how technological and cultural changes created new scope for creative movements—including sexuality movements (Melucci, 1996; Waites, 2017). In this light, while the Commonwealth clearly is problematically formed in relation to colonialism both historically and in the present (Murphy, 2018), future decolonial analyses might risk overemphasising the coloniality of the Commonwealth by over-stating historical associations. There is a need for careful empirically-informed investigation of whether such organisations are opening up dialogical spaces—including for new kinds of LGBTI and queer movements.

To contribute such analysis, this chapter proceeds in several sections. The first section introduces concepts of colonialities and legacies from existing critical literatures, considering these in relation to social and sociological theories in order to open a dialogue between literatures, developed through the chapter. The second section reviews the British Empire's consequences for ongoing criminalisation and inequalities facing people outside heterosexual sexuality and gender norms defined by European colonialisms; this section provides an updated summary of such criminalisation in Commonwealth states and begins discussion of Commonwealth responses. A third section then turns to the specific context of the London Commonwealth Heads of Government Meeting to explore contestations of LGBTI political claims; the section summarises methodology, then analyses data collected from civil society settings including the Commonwealth People's Forum—by engaging the conceptual frameworks of coloniality and living legacy. The chapter's conclusion offers an evaluation of how the concepts of colonialities and living legacies should be applied, thus delivering a distinctive analysis conceptualising power and change in relation to the Commonwealth context.

Colonialities and Living Legacies: Rethinking Conceptual Frameworks

Important conceptual frameworks for thinking about enduring effects of imperialism and colonialism have been generated in post-colonial and decolonial studies, especially through concepts of the post-colonial and coloniality, and it is in this context that the potential contribution of the proposed concept "living legacies" needs to be considered and evaluated (Beasley & Papadelos, 2024). The idea of "legacy issues" is a concept that has crept into the policy discourse of certain governments, notably in Ireland regarding historical abuse of women and children, where Enright (2019, p. 46) has suggested that governmental use of legacy involves management of temporality—such that state legal strategies abruptly curtail the past's relevance in the present. However, the concept of "living legacies" suggested for critical analysis and social theory by Beasley and Papadelos (2024) is differently conceived, with an emphasis on ongoing legacies to stress the continuing relevance and effects of the past in the present. To consider the potential scope and benefits of such usage for understanding power, it is first important to consider existing uses of the concept post-colonial as well as of coloniality. It will also be beneficial to consider how each of these concepts with implied conceptual frameworks relate to social theory—especially to sociological theory, which may be absent or limited in use within some history or interdisciplinary scholarship, and in some post-colonial and decolonial analyses.

Challenging Criminalisation in the Commonwealth 213

Edward Said's *Orientalism* commenced the emergence of a new critical analysis of discourses that were shaped by European imperial power, yet persisted beyond formal decolonisation (Said, 1978). The new field became known as post-colonial studies, with works by Gayatri Chakravorty Spivak (1988) and Homi Bhabha (1994) among defining contributions. The concept of the post-colonial awkwardly emerged in the context of wider debates over post-structuralism and post-Marxism disturbing academia and the Left, especially as the ill-informed and late translating Anglo-American reception of Foucault's work from the 1980s conflated those studies with postmodernism. In subsequent discussions, post-colonial theorists sought to disentangle the post-colonial from the postmodern, to emphasise post-colonial contexts as experiencing many continuities with colonialism rather than simply detachment. For example, Ashcroft et al. (1995), as editors of *The Post-Colonial Studies Reader*, commented:

> 'Post-colonial' as we define it does not mean 'post-independence', or 'after colonialism', for this would be to falsely ascribe an end to the colonial process. Post-colonialism, rather, begins from the very first moment of colonial contact. It is the discourse of oppositionality which colonialism brings into being.
>
> (Ashcroft et al., 1995, p. 117)

Yet the concept of the post-colonial has proved vulnerable to recent critical disillusionment with post-isms, as analysts have stepped back from postmodern emphases on transformation to instead emphasise persistent power relations. It is in this context that the concept coloniality has found new favour. In this chapter, therefore, there will not be another attempt to re-mobilise the concept of the post-colonial—even while it is recognised that many post-colonial intellectuals have applied that concept in ways highlighting persistent colonial aspects. It seems that the concept post-colonial might be irrevocably associated with academic forms of analysis from a specific period of critical theorising that lack enduring resonance in public debates. In the present chapter the focus will be on examining the concept coloniality's applicability for interpreting persistent power associated with the colonial in the present, while noting that many post-colonial analytical frameworks seem consistent with this idea.

The origin of the concept coloniality is in the work of Anibal Quijano, who became associated with the grouping of decolonial theorists from Latin America. Quijano (2000, p. 533) proposed the conceptualisation of the "coloniality of power," to comprehend how understandings associated with a Eurocentric paradigm of knowledge associated with rationality, modernity and racial classification persist beyond formal decolonisation and the independence of states (Quijano, 1999, 2000). The coloniality of power thus emerged as a central critical concept in in global social theory, conceptualising knowledge frameworks as inter-related with sociality and subject-formation: "the

European paradigm of rational knowledge, was not only elaborated in the context of, but as a part of, a power structure that involved the European cultural domination" (Quijano, 1999, p. 47). From this work the concept of coloniality has been taken up by other decolonial theorists including Walter Mignolo (2007) and has circulated increasingly in critical analyses. Indicatively, in gender and sexuality studies coloniality is a prominent concept in Mignolo's Foreword for the collection *Decolonizing Sexualities* (Mignolo, 2016, p. vii), with an Introduction which advocates "queering coloniality" (Bakshi et al., 2016, p. 1).

In a special issue of *Feminist Review* on Coloniality in 2021, editors Purewal and Ung Loh comment that "Feminist studies remains mired in coloniality," referring to a "modern episteme of coloniality"; they cite Quijano in arguing for an "ongoing hegemony of the coloniality of power" and Mignolo's conjoining formulation "modernity/coloniality" (Purewal and Ung Loh, 2021, pp. 1, 3). They describe "coloniality as a violent, subjugating and exclusionary system" and advocate "delinking" (pp. 5, 6). Yet while Quijano (1999) rightly identified how Enlightenment thinkers used "rationality" as a pivotal signifier to represent Eurocentric modern thought as superior, Quijano's wider approach risks taking such modern Eurocentrism at its own word (or at least mirroring its discourse), by conceiving the discourses of reason, science and the modern in an integrated paradigm together with individual human subjectivities—while under-stating contradictions.

What are the limits of emphasising coloniality? Unmistakably, the concept extends the colonial into present social life. Whereas the post-colonial was posited as a distinct cultural form in which the colonial constituted only one part, articulated with a differentiation from colonialism, coloniality seems to place emphasis solely on the continuity of colonial influences. Hence the specific meaning of colonialism, which relative to imperialism is more associated with settlement, is a relevant context (Tuck & Yang, 2012). The conceptual shift from colonialism to coloniality tends to suggest a shift from systematic processes to more diffuse social processes, cultural tendencies and affects, with more uncertain outcomes. Yet as many post-colonial and decolonial theorists now converge in use of the concept coloniality, it seems that some analytical nuances gained in debates over post-colonialism may be being lost. Quijano's (2000) characterisation of Eurocentrism as an integrated paradigm combining emphases on the human, rationality and science offers a somewhat reductive account of epistemology—given how rationalism and empiricism were in tension in Enlightenment philosophy, for example (Cottingham, 1984)—and is echoed in Boaventura da Sousa Santos's (2014) account of *Epistemologies of the South*. Many problems with current critical usage of coloniality are connected to this reductive conceptualisation of Eurocentrism's epistemological paradigm. Critical theorists of coloniality seem unable or unwilling to see positive aspects in discourses and practices of human rights, for example (Bakshi et al, 2016); the decolonial framework seems to assume human rights are static in their association with coloniality, precluding consideration of whether definition shifts through re-articulation, as discussed elsewhere (Waites, 2020, p. 41). Engaging further with specific examples of contexts where these concepts are contested may better reveal the complexity and difficult dilemmas that exist. A new conceptualisation of living legacies in social theory may help to analyse such contexts, and perhaps supplement the concept coloniality, by offering a different way to recognise effects of the past.

To be clear, this specific chapter assumes the concept of coloniality (and coloniality of power) as valuable and established in critical theory and social theory by Quijano and subsequent decolonial theorists. The concept coloniality can contribute much to social analysis. However, in a context where coloniality is already established as a concept in critical and social theories, the distinctive purpose of this chapter is to consider whether and how an additional concept such as living legacy might be of value. Living legacy might be a concept that could fill an analytical space to conceptualise aspects of European or Western culture (sometimes presented as global) that involve effects of Eurocentric colonialism and its epistemological paradigm, yet can no longer be described as colonial (given that concept's associations with settlement and occupation). This chapter does not imply that living legacy has greater merit; rather it suggests that living legacy might work alongside coloniality, each with a specific analytical contribution. To investigate these issues in a specific context first requires outlining the Commonwealth's relationship to criminalisation of people outside heterosexual norms.

Criminalisation of Sexual and Gender Minorities in the Commonwealth

The British Empire criminalised sexual acts between male persons in law across its territories, sometimes in ways that also potentially encompassed sexual acts between females (Human Rights Watch, 2008). Since 2000, especially since a legal case in India against Section 377 of the Indian Penal Code, there has been extensive global activism by sexual and gender minority movements pressing for decriminalisation in various states. National struggles for decriminalisation and human rights have been analysed in various Commonwealth countries (Lennox & Waites, 2013).

The Commonwealth is an international organisation comprising 54 member states, and the Commonwealth Secretariat remains based at Marlborough House in London (Commonwealth Secretariat, 2021). As at October 2021 a total of 35 Member States in the Commonwealth have laws that criminalise some or all private consensual adult same-sex sexual acts (Human Dignity Trust, 2021; for an overview of recent decriminalisations, see: Lennox, Tabengwa and Waites, 2021). Most of these laws were directly created by the British Empire; sometimes statutes have been reformulated. Recent decriminalisations have occurred in Mozambique (2015), Nauru (2016), the Seychelles

(2016), Belize (2016), India (2018) and Botswana (2019, upheld by the Court of Appeal in 2021), with Trinidad and Tobago's ruling (2018) subject to Privy Council appeal (Lennox, Tabengwa and Waites, 2021, p. 34). Many changes have occurred through the courts, as in Belize, Trinidad and Tobago, India and Botswana for example (Waites, 2019a; Waites, 2019b). Only rarely has change occurred through parliaments, as in Mozambique's penal code reform (Gomes da Costa Santos & Waites, 2021). Meanwhile in a distinctive case of gender regulation in Guyana, cross-dressing was illegal under a British Empire law until a decriminalisation in 2021—whereas sexual acts between males remain illegal (DeRoy & Baynes Henry, 2018; Newsroom, 2021).

Debates and controversy over the role of the Commonwealth in relation to decriminalisation and human rights for sexual and gender minorities have pushed colonial histories onto the organisation's agenda for discussion. Questions of whether the Commonwealth can provide a forum for relevant discussions of sexuality and gender, or offer an institutional lead, are situated in wider debates over the relevance of the Commonwealth in the contemporary world. Indian politician Srinivasan (2006) characterised the organisation as "Nobody's Commonwealth" in the new millennium, and Murphy (2018) has offered a critique of *The Empire's New Clothes* which castigates pervasive elitism. This makes the Commonwealth a highly suitable setting in which to investigate the relative analytical value of coloniality and living legacy.

Researching the London Commonwealth Heads of Government Meeting

Research drawn on in this discussion occurred through fieldwork in London concerning the London Commonwealth Heads of Government Meeting held on April 19–20, 2018, with the main focus of data-collection on preceding civil society forums (April 16–18) and other civil society activity. The Commonwealth Heads of Government Meeting itself is a bi-annual meeting, hosted by the current Chair country, with deliberations of state leaders not accessible to the public or researchers. The focus here is on Commonwealth civil society as it manifested in relation to the London event, and especially where this involved interventions by LGBTI or other sexual and gender minority actors or opposing actors. Civil society is not understood here as only existing in the four official civil society forums organised by the Commonwealth Foundation— the People's Forum, the Women's Forum, the Business Forum and the Youth Forum; rather, it also includes informal and disorganised interactions, including in physical spaces, conventional media and online social media. Four main research methods of data-collection were used: observation of the People's Forum as the largest official civil society forum, organised by the Commonwealth Foundation; social media analysis; collection of newspaper coverage from the UK, Jamaica, India and Kenya; and observation of civil society events including protests outside official forums. In this contribution, the data used is mainly from observation of the People's Forum and from wider observation of civil society events and institutional arrangements in London. Ethical approval was received from the University of Glasgow's College of Social Sciences.

To research the formal civil society forums, the People's Forum was selected as the most important. Owing to registration for approximately 350 places filling up almost immediately, the method of observation online was used, as much of the People's Forum was transmitted live on camera via the Commonwealth Heads of Government Meeting website—replicating experiences of the excluded majority. To research informal Commonwealth civil society involved attending a range of events, from queer street protests to a panel discussion at the British Library—using participant observation as a present but silent observer for a somewhat ethnographic approach. Initial data was supplemented with further documentary and online sources related to emerging themes, especially pages and documents from Commonwealth organisations' websites.

To draw out relevant issues and consider the relevance of colonialities and legacies as analytical concepts, the data-analysis here involves selecting key examples that can serve as a useful basis for examination and speak to relevant concerns. The analysis offered is an exploratory contribution to ongoing debates. The approach adopted is to consider the potential relevance of the two concepts coloniality and living legacy in relation to a series of themes: language; British government regret; and institutional agenda-setting.

Language

One of the most significant effects of British colonialism, though easy to miss for some Anglophone researchers when examining interactions within British settings, is the establishment of English as the most privileged international language. Yet in critical analysis, post-structuralism and studies of translation politics have taught us to attend to the forms of discourse (Foucault, 1979; Picq & Cottet, 2019). The exclusive use of English was apparent throughout research at the London Commonwealth Heads of Government Meeting and in associated civil society.

All the official civil society forums were conducted in English, without translation. In this respect the entire event continued certain forms of cultural erasure. Moreover, the pervasiveness of English also extended well beyond the official forums. The more elite newspapers which reported the event in many Commonwealth countries are also delivered in English; for example, the *Times of India* and the *Jamaica Observer*, for which coverage was surveyed. Social media discussion on the Commonwealth Heads of Government Meeting hashtags was also entirely in English. This was particularly interesting since the Commonwealth Foundation promoted the hashtags by advertising an inclusive "global conversation." Yet the limits of a conversation in English can be seen in relation to discussion of sexuality and gender. Lesbian, gay, bisexual, trans and intersex and the associated acronym LGBTI are all English language concepts that initially emerged in Western contexts; they have major limitations for a potential global conversation that would ideally engage with indigenous and non-western cultural conceptions of sexuality and gender.

However, can the pervasiveness of the English language be simply described as continuing coloniality? To interpret the emergence of English as the predominant global language only in terms of coloniality would be to miss the ways that shared language is a facilitator of communication and conversations and can be a medium for generating new meanings. This is the case even despite the clear histories where indigenous languages have been destroyed and displaced by the imposition of English. The English language has not only been a vehicle for colonial beliefs, it has also been a medium for some anti-colonial resistances. Hence the privileged status of English at the London Commonwealth Heads of Government Meeting provides an example where the concept living legacy may be more helpful for an overall characterisation of the language than coloniality, even while coloniality would be evident in specific instances. This might imply the legitimacy of continuing to use English as the central language for conversations in Commonwealth contexts, while also critically implying that those using English should deploy it with a historical awareness of how the language became established—and hence an ongoing critical attention to issues of translation and cultural differences in contexts of power.

British Government Regret

Theresa May made a speech to the combined civil society forums that included a statement of deep "regret" for the British Empire's criminalisation of same-sex sexual acts, marking a significant new intervention:

> Across the Commonwealth, discriminatory laws made many years ago, continue to affect the lives of many people, criminalizing same-sex relations, and failing to protect women and girls. I am all too aware that these laws were often put in place by my own country. They were wrong then, and they are wrong now. As the United Kingdom's Prime Minister, I deeply regret both the fact that such laws were introduced, and the legacy of discrimination, violence and even death that persists today. As a family of nations we must respect one another's cultures and traditions, but we must do so in a manner consistent with our common value of equality, a value that is clearly stated in the Commonwealth Charter. (...) Nobody should face persecution or discrimination because of who they are or who they love. The UK stands ready to support any Commonwealth member that wants to reform such outdated legislation.
>
> (May, 2018)

The following day, the Home Secretary announced that the UK would provide £5.6 million pounds for a new Equality and Justice Alliance, comprising the Kaleidoscope Trust, Human Dignity Trust, the Royal Commonwealth Society and Sisters for Change, working on rights for women and girls (Butterworth, 2018). This funding was to support legal work with governments considering reforms, and while the funding was given to British-based NGOs working internationally, it was underpinned by commitments of these NGOs to work with partners in formerly colonised states. Hence some of the benefits did accrue to organisations in the Global South, and some such funding has continued beyond the initial two year projects (Human Dignity Trust, 2020).

Theresa May's government also funded the UK's first LGBT international development project *Strong in Diversity Bold on Inclusion* from 2019, initially assigning £12 million for work on inclusion in five African countries, as part of the (then) Department for International Development's UK AID Connect programme (HIVOS, 2019). This had ambiguous prospects in light of long-standing critiques of international development. That said, UK AID Connect innovated with 'co-creation' phases of nine months to enable partner organisations—including from the Global South—to co-design projects. However, after the co-creation phase (in which the present author represented University of Glasgow as a partner), funding for the main second phase was withdrawn by Boris Johnson's government during 2020 in the context of Covid-19 and wider cuts to international aid.

Rahul Rao in *Out of Time: The Queer Politics of Postcoloniality* has provided a critical discussion of British political discourses of "atonement" in relation to the history of criminalisation of sexual acts between men (and sometimes between women), focusing mainly on parliamentary discourse but also referring to Theresa May's 2018 speech (Rao, 2020, pp. 8–9):

> This discourse of atonement is remarkable in emanating from sections of the British political establishment not known for their eagerness to acknowledge the ravages of empire, and it sits uncomfortably with their continuing unwillingness to reckon with monumental imperial crimes such as slavery.
>
> (Rao, 2020, p. 9)

Rao's analysis emphasises how British politicians' interest in addressing history regarding sexual orientation contrasts with such politicians' lack of interest in claims for reparations addressing slavery—raised, for example, by leaders from Jamaica (Rao, 2020, pp. 107–135).

While Rao's emphasis is on how discourses are used by British political actors in ways that avoid material obligations, they do not mention the financial commitment of £5.6 million that was made by the UK government in 2018. This is despite Rao's critical approach generally emphasising the need for attention to material dimensions of international politics, including in the introduction of the concept "homocapitalism" to conceptualise how business advocates for LGBT rights (Rao, 2020, pp. 136–173). Much of Rao's discussion focuses on times before 2018 (Rao, 2020, pp. 107–135), yet the effect is to imply that the British government approach to atonement is only discursive, whereas there has also been a financial element. The British government is not only engaging in a symbolic or discursive politics but also in certain limited kinds of material politics that imply an element of taking responsibility, even while on a minor scale. In short, Rao's central argument brings attention to the British government's failure to adequately address reparations. Funding reparations for slavery is a very different approach from funding NGOs working on LGBT human rights or development. However, it is still worth noting that the British government approach to addressing colonialism's effects regarding criminalisation of same-sex sexual relations is not only discursive, and that the material element focused on funding for North/South partnership work (albeit accompanied by the problematic power relations that I have discussed elsewhere) (Waites, 2019b).

In this light, May's speech does not seem appropriate to characterise in terms of coloniality overall, even if there remain traces of coloniality in aspects of the British government's approach, especially the selection of this issue (unlike slavery reparations). Rather, the speech itself expresses and seeks to address certain complexities of a post-colonial context, though awkwardly focusing on only one dimension. The concept of living legacy is some help here, since it gives expression to the present relevance of the past, which is apparent in the speech. However, while the concept living legacy is broadly political as it is used in this volume (see Beasley & Papadelos, 2024, Chapter 1), it does not necessarily assign visible responsibility. The concept is therefore assisted by articulation with a suitable critical analysis of colonialism. Potentially a shift from emphasis on coloniality to living legacy may be problematic if living legacy is taken up in a form that appears politically neutral and benign. Both these concepts need contextualising within a wider radical conceptualisation of power as existing even where there is not awareness of its functioning (Lukes, 2005); this enables understanding of how power structures that emerged through colonialism persist in certain respects. Even where there is no longer a colonising process or coloniality, there may still be an ongoing occupation of a historically established position of power through new social processes, understood as living legacy. Analytically it seems not appropriate to assume that any identifiable power relations necessarily imply ongoing coloniality, although this is sometimes the case.

Institutional Agenda-Setting in The Commonwealth People's Forum

The People's Forum appeared as an official gathering of over 350 civil society representatives, held over three days with the theme of 'Inclusive Governance'; yet the limited numbers participating made it less sizeable than many conferences, constraining representation from the 53 Commonwealth countries. The Forum was held in the Queen Elizabeth II Conference Centre, opposite the UK Parliament. Applications to register, largely to represent NGOs, are decided by the Commonwealth Foundation. I confirmed in person on the first day that entry was refused, with security guards standing by—as if undertaking a little Gramscian ethnomethodological breaching experiment (Garfinkel, 1967), revealing the coercion underpinning civil society (Thomas, 2009). Live transmissions were therefore watched online, while partially transcribing and taking notes. The Meeting website broadcast only one forum—predominantly the People's Forum—without recordings, thus limiting external engagement (HM Government and The Commonwealth, 2018).

Central findings concern the importance of agenda-setting, particularly by the Commonwealth Foundation. Here we may think of political communications literature on agenda-setting (Scheufele, 2000); but also Erving Goffman's dramaturgical sociology, emphasising what happens "backstage", behind the scenes (Goffman, 1959, p. 114). The Commonwealth Foundation is an organisation that has run forums for Meetings since 1991 (Onslow and Kandiah, 2018, p. 66); it is formally distinct from the host government yet must work closely with that government's representatives to plan the events. The Foundation describes itself first as "the Commonwealth agency for civil society," yet it is also an international organisation "established" and "funded" by and "reporting to, governments" (Commonwealth Foundation, 2018a).

The Foundation was established as a charity from 1965 but was reformed to become an intergovernmental organisation in 1982 and is funded by contributions from member governments (Commonwealth Foundation, 2012, pp. 6, 34). Moreover, the Foundation has its address at Marlborough House, Pall Mall, interestingly sharing residence with the Commonwealth Secretariat. This location highlights the British organisational base and associated colonial influences. It also demonstrates the considerable likelihood of informal as well as formal communications and influence between the Secretariat and the Foundation, as well as the British government and civil service. These spatial arrangements seem likely to give rise to circulations of power that are sometimes unconscious and unintentional for individual actors (for example, chance meetings within buildings or through social networks), some of which could be usefully characterised via living legacies, as well as organised power structures where coloniality is more relevant. This seems crucial to understanding the institutional, structural context that shaped the agenda of what is called the People's Forum.

According to the Foundation, it "formulates and validates the themes, focus areas and aims of the event in active consultation with civic voices from around the Commonwealth" (Das, 2018). The Forum was to focus on Sustainable Development Goal 16 "Promote, just, peaceful and inclusive societies," particularly inclusion (Das, 2018). The Foundation involved a seven-member external Content Design Committee, made up of civil society actors from Bangladesh, Ghana, Jamaica, Malaysia, Malta, Samoa and the United Kingdom. However, the agenda was tightly controlled; though it was possible to apply to run a delegate-led session, there were only three 30 minute sessions during lunchtimes, for no more than 30 people, and topics were not advertised in the programme (Commonwealth Foundation, 2018b).

Significant research findings concerned the People's Forum's rigid format, lacking participation. There was a fixed agenda with a series of selected speakers addressing a seated audience from a platform. From the published agenda and observation, the only opportunities allowed for delegate discussion in small groups were over lunch or coffee. There was thus very little scheduled time for questions or substantial dialogue in the manner that Fraser (2014), for example, might look for in a transnational public sphere.

The intriguing role of backstage agenda–setting was particularly apparent in the selection of speakers. This certainly worked in the favour of The Commonwealth Equality Network, since its Chair Rosanna Flamer-Caldera from Sri Lanka was very prominently scheduled after the first keynote, to start the first panel titled *Inside the Margins*. It seems likely that Commonwealth Foundation agenda-setters may have been informally influenced by London-based actors including The Commonwealth Equality Network—for which Kaleidoscope Trust in London provides the Secretariat—the UK government or the Commonwealth Secretariat. The UK LGBT organisation Kaleidoscope Trust has played a central formative role in the creation, agenda-setting and resourcing of The Commonwealth Equality Network (Waites, 2017). Hence the representation of international sexuality and gender politics at the Commonwealth Meeting through The Commonwealth Equality Network implied a certain framing, in which a collective of activists sympathetically oriented to engaging the Commonwealth were foregrounded.

The powers that be at the Commonwealth Foundation had scheduled the novelist Ben Okri as the opening keynote speaker, to set the tone with a talk titled *Ending Exclusion: A Path to Renewal*—to be directly followed by Flamer-Caldera. Okri (1991) was the winner of the Booker Prize for his novel *The Famished Road*, that draws from his youthful experiences of life in Nigeria, and he is often labelled as an example of postcolonial or African literature. However, while born in Nigeria in 1959, as a child he lived in Peckham, inner-city London, until moving to Nigeria in 1968, then moved to the UK again in 1978 (*Penman Times*, 2016; British Council, 2018). From 1988 he lived in Notting Hill. Thus, Okri has lived for considerable periods in the UK, though often labelled only a "Nigerian writer" (Encyclopedia Britannica, 2018).

Okri's speech was carefully designed to open the People's Forum by advancing a narrative of progressive inclusion. However, this was proposed in rather abstract and simplistic terms, including such literary wisdoms as "there are some people in life who don't like stories, they are the full stops" whereas "we should aim to instead be a semi-colon, or a dash," "discoverers not concluders"—signalling continuity and forward movement. Here it can be seen

Challenging Criminalisation in the Commonwealth 223

that Commonwealth governance had selected a figure from the London literary establishment as a performer to represent Africans; and that the arts were summoned into the service of a form of progressivism. Okri was positioned to narrate a renewal of the Commonwealth that implicitly led into the LGBTI rights agenda, alongside other valuable agendas for indigenous people and refugees. This was used to set the stage for Flamer-Caldera, a Sri Lankan LGBTI activist. An African voice was crucial for those in power, yet this voice from Africa had also taken shape in the UK.

The staging thus represented an African voice calling forth a discourse about inclusion from LGBTI people, entering a conversation, without any African outside cosmopolitan circles being involved in that discussion. Markedly absent from this and a related later afternoon session on *Legislative Reform in the Commonwealth* were homophobic voices, not only (for example) from the Pentecostal churches that fuelled bigotry in Uganda, but also from more moderate heterosexist positions. The positioning of Flamer-Caldera and the later session were certainly no coincidence. The afternoon session *Legislative Reform in the Commonwealth* was co-curated by The Commonwealth Equality Network, with all speakers supporting LGBTI rights. A different agonistic politics, emphasising democracy's need for expressed conflict and debate (Mouffe, 2005), would not have constituted the event like this selective liberal cosmopolitanism.

The staging by the Commonwealth Foundation thus brought in only certain kinds of different voices, though occasionally radical decolonising voices. An astonishing moment came when the poet Karlo Mila—of Tongan, Samoan and European heritage and from New Zealand (Poetry Foundation, 2022)—was invited to speak immediately after Theresa May and Bill Gates; the audience suddenly intent:

> Indeed, we've entered this
> strange garden
> in this city,
> epicentre of epitaph,
> epitome of empire.
> The stones in the squares
> remind us
> that we all died for this.
> The war memorials murmur
> numbers not names.
> We bring our dead with us
> and they are already here.
> Not just the ones marked by marble.
> But our ancestors,
> the original inhabitants
> of the lands 'discovered'.

Who lie in the unmarked graves
and unmentioned massacres,
in battles unspoken of
in untaught wars
We carry them like stones
in our bodies.
They too contribute
towards this commonwealth.
  (for full poem, see: Mila, 2018. See
    also: Mila, 2020, pp. 185-188)

Yet what becomes clear is how the arts were used in this space. Both Okri and Mila were introduced to gesture towards radical possibilities. Together with comments from many Global South speakers, these contributions made characterisation of the event overall only in terms of coloniality unrealistic. Yet on central issues including economics there was a lack of connection between these aspirations and the lack of substantive policy debate, necessary to be effectively political in the sense of actualising change.

Conclusion

This chapter has provided an original critical analysis of civil society contexts associated with the London Commonwealth Heads of Government Meeting in 2018, and the analysis has provided a basis on which to reflect on the value of concepts of coloniality and living legacy. The analysis focused on three themes. Regarding language, the predominance of English was noted, but it has been argued that coloniality is an insufficient way to describe the use of English in itself and that critical analysis should turn greater attention to whether and how English is used with an awareness of cultural differences and power relations. Regarding British Prime Minister Theresa May's expression of regret for historical criminalisation of same-sex sexual acts, it has been argued that this needs to be interpreted not only as a discourse of atonement, but with acknowledgement of some emergent material practices of funding to address historical responsibility, even while these have been limited. Regarding institutional agenda-setting, it has been argued that the Commonwealth Foundation based in London played a key role in agenda-setting for the Commonwealth People's Forum, and that the orchestration of discussion clearly worked in favour of The Commonwealth Equality Network as an organisation constituting a particular representation of international LGBTI movement politics, through scheduling of sympathetic speakers. This does tend to show how the sedimentation of Commonwealth institutions in London leads to networking in the British capital between Commonwealth organisations and London-based NGOs, with effects in structuring power.

The analysis has provided an opportunity to reflect on the extension of coloniality as a concept in social analysis and suggests that the contribution that the concept living legacy can make in relation to this. Coloniality has certainly emerged as an indispensable concept in contemporary social theory. However, the original use of the concept by Quijano (2000) created scope for all Eurocentric culture to be negatively associated with coloniality, whereas currently not all of European or Western culture is Eurocentric. Therefore, there is a need to modify Quijano's decolonial analysis by drawing insights from aspects of postmodern, reflexive modernisation and new social movement theory characterisations of post-industrial societies, partially helpful to the extent that these enable recognition of some changing socio-cultural forms involving certain kinds of cross-cultural learning about cultural differences and types of cosmopolitan sensibility (Beck, 2006), albeit mainly liberal pluralist rather than critical. Rather differently and more helpfully, Gilroy's work on racism and culture in *After Empire* suggests analysing British social and cultural contexts as sites of ongoing contestations structured by racialisation, neither entirely stuck in coloniality nor necessarily progressing via cosmopolitanisation. Gilroy has drawn attention to "post-colonial conviviality" in cities like London, involving living with difference rather than a blurring or erasure of all differences (Gilroy, 2004).

Interpreted in this light, the Commonwealth Heads of Government Meeting and Commonwealth civil society appear as more complex settings than a decolonial analysis focused only on coloniality would suggest. It is highly significant that even in London, the British Government and allies were not able to achieve a Heads of Government statement that explicitly challenged criminalisation or addressed sexual orientation, gender identity or sex characteristics (Commonwealth Heads of Government, 2018); and hence the Commonwealth appears far from a simple vehicle of British sexual nationalism or coloniality. Rather than all powerful, the Commonwealth risks irrelevance. Rather than Prime Minister Theresa May speaking a Conservative party line, her comments appear to have been highly influenced by the NGO Kaleidoscope Trust with its discourse of challenging colonial laws "sensitively, (...) particularly given our colonial past" (Crerar, 2018).

Meanwhile regarding Commonwealth civil society: rather than the research here revealing an entirely exclusionary elitist context, it has suggested subtle agenda-setting by civil society elites like the Commonwealth Foundation to enable selected Southern voices, LGBTI voices and Southern LGBTI voices such as Rosanna Flamer-Caldera—a lesbian person of colour from Sri Lanka—to find representation in Commonwealth forums. The Commonwealth Equality Network should not be reductively characterised, as suggested by the published account of activist Ibtisam Ahmed from Bangladesh who participated at the London Meeting: "Having been fortunate enough to be in the room myself, I can attest to the group championing context-specific solutions towards decriminalisation and decolonisation, rejecting the cookie-cutter neoliberal approach" (Ahmed, 2019, p. 108). However—drawing from Gilroy—it can be suggested that the Commonwealth Foundation's staging of civil society forums seems to have been imbued with a particular selective and managed cosmopolitan post-colonial conviviality that could only represent certain differences, rather than a broader, agonistic conception of the political.

The present analysis nevertheless points to the value of continuing engagement with the Commonwealth by LGBTI activists from formerly colonised states as one part of a multi-sited and strategic politics across many contexts. In particular, it is important to appreciate the role of cultural politics which has always been central in LGBTI and queer politics—as in Pride. Hence the contributions of activists making political claims at the London Meeting itself had significant effects.

The analysis thus does not support a decolonial politics of 'delinking' (Mignolo, 2007) as a political strategy across all sites, or in relation to the Commonwealth generally. Such an approach would not grasp the leading roles of actors like Flamer-Caldera from formerly colonised contexts in producing new kinds of Commonwealth discourse that challenge colonial practices including criminalisation. Owing to its colonial associations, there is a risk of the Commonwealth being performatively dismissed in decolonial queer discourse; but despite their limitations the Commonwealth civil society forums remain internationally rare as spaces where sexual and gender minority movements can represent themselves safely in relation to intergovernmental institutions, in some contrast to the limited availability of such regional spaces—in Africa or Asia, for example.

Therefore, while there remain areas where analysis of coloniality in Eurocentric culture needs to be further extended, there also appears a risk that the current popularity of coloniality in critical theory risks leading to over-extension. The concept of living legacies may play a useful role in social theory here, capturing a need to highlight the ongoing relevance of histories even where there is not a colonial process. Yet living legacies will need to be carefully articulated with wider conceptions of power and colonialism in critical analyses, in order to fulfil this role.

Acknowledgement

Matthew Waites and Taylor & Francis gratefully acknowledge permission to reproduce an extract from *Poem for the Commonwealth 2018* from: Karlo Mila 2020. *Goddess Muscle*. Wellington: Huia Publishers. Reproduced by permission of Huia publishers. Matthew Waites also says a big thank you to Karlo Mila for supporting and enabling this reprint.

References

Ahmed, I. (2019). Decolonising queer Bangladesh: Neoliberalism against LGBTQ+ emancipation. In M. L. Picy & C. Cottet (Eds), *Sexuality and translation in world politics* (pp. 101–111). Bristol: E-International Relations.

Ashcroft, B., Griffiths, G. & Tiffin, H. (1995). Introduction. In B. Ashcroft, G. Griffiths & H. Tiffin (Eds), *The post-colonial studies reader* (pp. 117–118). London: Routledge.

Bakshi, S., Jivraj, S. & Posocco, S. (2016). Introduction. In S. Bakshi, S. Jivraj & S. Posocco (Eds), *Decolonizing sexualities: Transnational perspectives, critical interventions* (pp. 1–15). Oxford: Counterpress.

Beasley, C. & Papadelos, P. (2022). *Ongoing legacies – introduction*. In C. Beasley & P. Papadelos (Eds), *Living legacies of social injustice: Power and social change* (pp. x). Abingdon: Routledge.

Beck, U. (2006). *The cosmopolitan vision*. Cambridge: Polity Press.

Bhabha, H. (1994). *The location of culture*. London: Routledge.

Bhambra, G. K. & Holmwood, J. (2021). *Colonialism and modern social theory*. Cambridge: Polity Press.

British Council. (2018). *Ben Okri: Biography*. https://literature.britishcouncil.org/writer/ben-okri. Accessed 2021.

Butterworth, B. (2018, April 19). Amber Rudd announces major fund to help end anti-gay laws in Commonwealth countries. *Pink News*. www.pinknews.co.uk/2018/04/19/amber-rudd-announces-major-fund-to-help-end-anti-gay-laws-in-commonwealth-countries.

Commonwealth Heads of Government. (2018). Commonwealth Heads of Government Meeting communiqué: "Towards a Common Future". www.chogm2018.org.uk/sites/default/files/CHOGM%202018%20Communique.pdf.

Commonwealth Foundation. (2012). Strategic plan 2012–16. https://commonwealthfoundation.com/wp-content/uploads/2012/10/Commonwealth_Foundation_Strategic_Plan.pdf.

Commonwealth Foundation. (2018a). About us. https://commonwealthfoundation.com/about-us.

Commonwealth Foundation. (2018b). Delegate-led sessions at CPF 2018: submission form. https://commonwealthfoundation.com/cpf2018-delegate-led-sessions.

Commonwealth Secretariat. (2021). The Commonwealth. https://thecommonwealth.org.

Cottingham, J. (1984). *Rationalism*. London: Paladin.

Crerarr, P. (2018, April 16) Theresa May urged to apologise for Britain's anti-gay colonial past. *The Guardian*. www.theguardian.com/world/2018/apr/16/theresa-may-urged-to-apologise-for-britains-anti-gay-colonial-past.

Das, S. (2018). Just, peaceful and inclusive societies: CPF 2018 programme takes shape. https://commonwealthfoundation.com/blog/just-peaceful-inclusive-societies-cpf-2018-programme-takes-shape.

DeRoy, P. & Baynes Henry, N. (2018). Violence and LGBT human rights in Guyana. In N. Nicol, A. Jjuuko, R. Lusimbo, N. Mulé, S. Ursel, A. Wahab & P. Waugh (Eds), *Envisioning global LGBT human rights: (Neo)colonialism, neoliberalism, resistance and hope* (pp. 157–176). London: University of London Press.

Encyclopedia Britannica. (2018). Ben Okri: Nigerian writer. www.britannica.com/biography/Ben-Okri.

Enright, M. (2019). 'No. I won't go back': National time, trauma and legacies of symphysiotomy in Ireland. In S. Benyon-Jones & E. Grabham (Eds), *Law and time* (pp.46–74). Abingdon: Routledge.

Foucault, M. (1979). *The history of sexuality. Volume 1: An introduction*. London: Allen Lane.

Fraser, N. (1995). From redistribution to recognition? Dilemmas of justice in a 'post-socialist' age. *New Left Review* 212, 68–93.

Fraser, N. (2014). Transnationalizing the public sphere: On the legitimacy and efficacy of public opinion in a post-Westphalian world. In K. Nash (Ed.), *Transnationalizing the public sphere* (pp. 8–42). Cambridge: Polity Press.

Garfinkel, H. (1967). *Studies in ethnomethodology*. Englewood Cliffs, NJ: Prentice-Hall.

Giddens, A. (1991). *Modernity and self-identity*. Cambridge: Polity Press.

Gilroy, P. (2004). *After empire: Melancholia or convivial culture?*Abingdon: Routledge.

Goffman, E. (1959). *The presentation of self in everyday life*. London: Penguin.

Gomes da Costa Santos, G. & Waites, M. (2019). Comparative colonialisms for queer analysis: Comparing British and Portuguese colonial legacies for same-sex sexualities and gender diversity in Africa—setting a transnational research agenda. *International Review of Sociology*, 29(2), 297–326.

Gomes da Costa Santos, G. & Waites, M. (2021). Analysing African Advances Against Homophobia in Mozambique: how decriminalisation and anti-discrimination reforms proceed without LGBT identities. *Sexuality & Culture*, doi:10.1007/s12119-021-09908-8.

HIVOS. (2019). *UK Government commits £12 million to promote LGBT+ inclusion.* March 26.https://hivos.org/news/uk-government-commits-12-million-to-prom ote-lgbt-inclusion.

HM Government & The Commonwealth. (2018). Commonwealth Heads of Government Meeting London 2018. www.chogm2018.org.uk.

Human Dignity Trust. (2020). Changing laws, changing lives—HDT secures renewed UK funding for acclaimed work helping governments eradicate archaic laws. October 9. www.humandignitytrust.org/news/changing-laws-changing-lives-hdt-secures-renewed-uk-funding-for-acclaimed-work-helping-governments-eradicate-archaic-laws.

Human Dignity Trust. (2021). Changing laws, changing lives: Good practice indicators. Indicator 15 consensual same-sex sexual activity is not a crime. www.humandignity trust.org/reform/indicators/15.

Human Rights Watch. (2008). *This alien legacy: The origins of 'sodomy' laws in British colonialism*. New York: Human Rights Watch.

Kollman, K. & Waites, M. (2009). The global politics of lesbian, gay, bisexual and transgender human rights: an introduction. *Contemporary Politics*, 15(1), 1–17.

Lennox, C. & Waites, M. (Eds) (2013). *Human rights, sexual orientation and gender identity in the Commonwealth: Struggles for decriminalisation and change*. London: School of Advanced Study.

Lennox, C, Tabengwa, M. & Waites, M. (2021) Contesting lesbian, gay and bisexual human rights in the Commonwealth. In P. Gerber (Ed.), *Worldwide perspectives on lesbians, gays and bisexuals. Volume 3: The global picture* (pp. 31–54). Santa Barbara, CA: Praeger Press.

Lukes, S. (2005) *Power: A radical view*, 2nd Edition. Basingstoke: Palgrave Macmillan.

Lyotard, J. F. (1984). *The postmodern condition: A Report on Knowledge*. Manchester: Manchester University Press.

May, T. (2018). PM speaks at the Commonwealth Joint Forum plenary, April 17. www.gov.uk/government/speeches/pm-speaks-at-the-commonwealth-joint-forum-plenary-17-april-2018.

Melucci, A. (1996). *Challenging codes: Collective action in the information age*. Cambridge: Cambridge University Press.

Mignolo, W. (2007). Delinking: the rhetoric of modernity, the logic of coloniality and the grammar of de-coloniality. *Cultural Studies*, 21(2–3), 449–514.

Mignolo, W. (2016). Foreword: decolonial body-geo-politics at large. In S. Bakshi, S. Jivraj and S. Posocco (Eds), *Decolonizing sexualities: Transnational perspectives, critical interventions* (pp. vii–xviii). Oxford: Counterpress.

Mila, K. (2018). Poem for the Commonwealth 2018. www.addastories.org/poem-commonwealth-2018.

Mila, K. (2020) *Goddess muscle*. Wellington: Huia Publishers.

Mouffe, C. (2005) *On the political*. London: Routledge.

Murphy, P. (2018). *The empire's new clothes: The myth of the Commonwealth*. London: Hurst.

Newsroom. (2021, August 10) Cross-dressing formally removed as criminal offence from Guyana's law. *Newsroom*. https://newsroom.gy/2021/08/10/cross-dressing-formally-removed-as-criminal-offence-from-guyanas-law.

Okri, B. (1991). *The famished road*. London: Vintage.

Onslow, S. & Kandiah, M. (2018). Britain in the Commonwealth: the 1997 Edinburgh summit witness seminar. School of Advanced Study. https://sas-space.sas.ac.uk/9215.

Penman Times. (2016). Biography of a great African poet: Ben Okri. https://medium.com/@kennedyanthony95/biography-of-a-great-african-poet-ben-okri-ae4c577174d4.

Picq, M. L. & Cottet, C. (2019) Introduction. In M. L. Picy & C. Cottet (Eds), *Sexuality and translation in world politics* (pp. 1–12). Bristol: E-International Relations.

Poetry Foundation. (2022). Karlo Mila. www.poetryfoundation.org/poets/karlo-mila.

Purewal, N. & Ung Loh, J. (2021). Coloniality and feminist collusion: Breaking free, thinking anew, *Feminist Review* 128(1), 1–12.

Quijano, A. (1999). Coloniality and modernity/rationality. In G. Therborn & L. L. Wallenius (Eds), *Globalizations and modernities: Experiences and perspectives of Europe and Latin America* (pp. 41–51). Stockholm: FRN.

Quijano, A. (2000). Coloniality of power, Eurocentrism and Latin America, *Nepantla: Views from the South*, 1(3), 533–580.

Rao, R. (2020). *Out of time: The queer politics of postcoloniality*. Oxford: Oxford University Press.

Said, E. (1978). *Orientalism*. London: Routledge & Kegan Paul.

Scheufele, D. A. (2000). Agenda-setting, priming and framing revisited: another look at cognitive effects of political communication, *Mass Communication & Society*, 3(2-3), 297–316.

de Sousa Santos, B. (2014). *Epistemologies of the south: Justice against epistemicide*. Abingdon: Routledge.

Spivak, G. C. (1988). Can the subaltern speak? In C. Nelson & L. Grossberg (Eds), *Marxism and the interpretation of culture* (pp. 66–111). Chicago, IL: University of Illinois.

Srinivasan, K. (2006). Nobody's Commonwealth? The Commonwealth in Britain's post-imperial adjustment, *Commonwealth and Comparative Politics* 44(2), 257–269.

Thomas, P. (2009). *The Gramscian moment: Philosophy, hegemony and Marxism*. Leiden: Brill.

Tuck, E. & Yang, E.W. (2012). Decolonization is not a metaphor. *Decolonization: Indigeneity, education and society* 1(1), 1–40.

Waites, M. (2015). The new trans-national politics of LGBT human rights in the Commonwealth: What can UK NGOs learn from the global South? In F. Stella, Y. Taylor, T. Reynolds & A. Rogers (Eds), *Sexuality, citizenship and belonging: Transnational and intersectional perspectives* (pp. 73–94). London: Routledge.

Waites, M. (2017). LGBTI organizations navigating imperial contexts: the Kaleidoscope Trust, the Commonwealth and the need for a decolonizing, intersectional politics. *Sociological Review*, 65(4), 644–662.

Waites, M. (2019a). LGBT and queer politics in the Commonwealth. In D. Haider-Markel (Ed.), *Oxford encyclopedia of LGBT politics and policy*. Oxford: Oxford University Press. doi:10.1093/acrefore/9780190228637.013.1257.

Waites, M. (2019b). Decolonizing the boomerang effect in global queer politics: A new critical framework for sociological analysis of human rights contestation. *International Sociology*, 34(4), 382–401.

Waites, M. (2020). Global sexualities: Towards a reconciliation between decolonial analysis and human rights. In Z. Davy, A. C. Santos, C. Bertone, R. Thoreson & S. E. Wieringa (Eds), *The SAGE Handbook of Global Sexualities* (pp. 33–56). London: Sage Publications.

Chapter 13

Re-imagining Legacy (Power-Time) and Social Change

Chris Beasley and Pam Papadelos

This book has as its task re-considering power in its entanglements with time through the key notion of legacy, and more specifically living legacy, as a means to interrupting social injustice and advancing social justice. As noted in the opening chapter (Beasley & Papadelos, 2024), attention to power's temporal location involves recognition of injustice and by this means invites possibilities for social change. The theme of legacy in this setting requires awareness of the ways injustice can be rendered invisible, silent, in the context of time. Discounting the legacies of past injustices compounds the vulnerability of those most in need and increases the probability of their needs being ignored as "the past is not a simple object of knowledge but the milieu within which we think" (Colebrook, 2009, p. 12). Thus, the framework of legacy, and in particular, 'living legacies', allows us to interrogate the past while simultaneously enabling attention to its continuing ramifications. And since power relations may be through time erased, denied or declared redundant, including through normalising them, the concept 'living legacies' focusses upon bringing to light spectres of past injustices which haunt the present and potentially inhibit alternative directions to come. Legacy—though weighted by its connections to the past—is thus ironically intimately linked with the present and amounts to an invitation to the future.

Thus, it is fitting that this final chapter begins with some thoughts on key ideas around the notion of legacy which are featured in this book, namely its relationship with power and justice and, importantly, possibilities for re-imagining the future. To do this we draw broadly upon interplays between the works of Jacques Derrida (1986) and Sarah Ahmed (2004a, 2004b) as they may be employed to inform discussion of power relations and justice. In the case of Derrida, his terms 'aporia' and 'promise' potentially open up ways of thinking about social justice as a political project (see also for a related discussion, Beasley & Bacchi, 2007).[1] The chapters in this book call for political change. The terms 'aporia' and 'promise' locate both the responsibility and promise of a future that attends to social change. Literally, aporia, derived from the Greek (ἀπορία), means "an absence of path (...) the immobilisation of thinking, the impossibility of advancing" (Derrida, 1986, p. 132). While we are inclined to

DOI: 10.4324/9781003311928-16

232 Pam Beasley and Pam Papadelos

employ this terminology through the less apparently impermeable lens of Ahmed's concept of 'stickiness' (2004a), we note that the seeming impossibility of enacting change, while simultaneously demanding it, haunts many of the chapters in this book. Derrida's account of aporia also "gives or promises the thinking of the path, provokes the thinking of the very possibility of what still remains unthinkable or unthought, indeed, impossible" (Derrida, 1986, p. 132) and thus registers the materiality of responsibility, of an 'optimism of the will' (Gramsci, 1977; Antonini, 2019), which is evoked at the point of seemingly impossible or seemingly unthinkable scenarios (Derrida, 1999). The promise is for a future, not a future that we can predict, but a 'to come', a future that we cannot anticipate. Thus, Derrida introduces the 'not yet/to come' to image this future (*l'à-venir*), rather than be confined to the word 'future', as the word future as it currently stands becomes reducible to the present (Derrida, 1986). The not yet/to come is entirely unknown, contingent, and unexpected where (im)possible possibilities can be realised. It refers to an altogether different future based on what has been precluded in the past and present. In other words, aporia does not signal a *telos* or end, rather, it signals the impossibility of knowing (in advance) what, if anything, will result. The potential for change is captured in the uncertainty of what will come. The future that allows for the unknown can potentially be transformative; it offers an open engagement and the hope of otherwise, of justice-to-come.[2] However, both Derrida (1986) and Ahmed (2004b) do not perceive this hope for the future or the future itself as forged out of any singular vision or struggle. The uncertainty of the future and of justice-to-come is precisely co-terminus with the uncertainty of political imaginaries that require some form of collectivity and some mutuality in relationship with the Other.[3] As Ahmed (2004b, p. 189) notes, even if "we do live on common ground",

> [s]olidarity does not assume that our struggles are the same struggles, or that our pain is the same pain, or that our hope is for the same future.
>
> (2004b, p. 189)

> The impossibility of 'fellow feeling' is itself (…) a call for action, and a demand for collective politics, as a politics based not on the possibility that we might be reconciled, but on learning to live with the impossibility of reconciliation, or learning that we live with and beside each other, and yet we are not as one.
>
> (2004b, p. 39)

In light of the unpredictable challenges of this diversity, Derrida's justice-to-come and Ahmed's 'stickiness' provide useful concepts for highlighting the way that social justice as expressed in the chapters in this book, is not a linear process and therefore cannot be secured or absolutely acquired; it is an

Re-imagining Legacy (Power-Time) and Social Change   233

ongoing project. The past haunts the present and compels us to right wrongs entailing an ethical responsibility to futures/others.

The notion of living legacies provides a useful framework for understanding how events relegated to the past, or more precisely their effects, impact on current policies, ideologies and ultimately people's lives. The effects of these legacies are dynamic as they respond to and are shaped by the present. However, "each text, word, fragment and image of past (…) acts as an always present resistance (or insistence) to a simple moving forward or living on" (Colebrook, 2009, p. 13). Identifying "the stickiness from the past" and seizing opportunities opens up new futures or a justice-to-come. Thus, living legacies provides a framework that is not linear, constant or static, but one that allows for an exploration or reconstruction of the past that is meaningful in the present. It suggests that what 'sticks' in the present is of concern and it pays special attention to how that 'stickiness' causes harm, such that new futures are possible—that is, justice-to-come. The spectres of past injustice suffuse the chapters of this book. For instance, Alison Dundon's chapter (Chapter 2) discusses the stickiness of legacies of violence and injustice against women in Papua New Guinea, which adhere despite various laws that criminalise domestic and family violence. She argues that the normalisation of violence against women is imbedded in everyday practices and, although it is instituted in the past, also shapes the present and potentially the future. Therefore, Dundon calls for these legacies to be interrupted by challenging the unequal power relations in communities and the violence women encounter when engaged with legal structures and institutions. Justice-to-come will not be available to women in Papua New Guinea through changes to law and policies if these legacies are not addressed.

Another instance, where the framework of living legacies is useful is in understanding ancestral loss and cultural harm bought about by assimilationist policies of previous Australian governments. Wanganeen and Szorenyi's chapter discuss this framework in relation to the 'stolen generations' of Aboriginal children in Australia. Such a framework allows for an understanding of the present which stem from legacies of past assimilation policies, but also look towards the future, a justice-to-come where the 'stolen generation' find an avenue to deal with their grief and to heal. Through this framing the authors not only give voice to the impact of the injustice of 'stolen generation' policies but also validate these stories, which is a step towards reconceptualising power and redressing injustice.

How might these exemplars assist us to reconfigure power understood in terms of time? Davina Cooper (2021, 2013), Paisley Currah (2022a, 2022b) and Nick Gill (2010, 2020) alert us to conceptualising power relations not only through recognition and acknowledgement but additionally through imagining otherwise. In this spirit, we wish to elaborate what this book might offer to analysis of power relations and their futures. As noted in the opening chapter of this volume (Beasley & Papadelos), the focus on legacy enables a novel approach to power, time and change. This approach highlights that power relations do not invoke time understood as linear, let alone as progressive, but rather makes manifest that they are not inevitably directional, deliberative, exceptional, fast paced or solid. The lack of fixity outlined does not however necessarily denote movement but rather continuous permeability. The opening chapter and, many if not most of the chapters which follow, indicate that power's forms may indeed be sticky, largely unchanging for lengthy periods of time and seemingly impervious to change.

In keeping with porous framings of power offered by Cooper (2021), Currah (2022a) and Gill (2020), we wish to balance this sense of the substance, the weight of legacies of injustice, without displacing these scholars' intention to 'denaturalise' and re-imagine power. In this volume our stress is upon power's temporality and thus its implication in past, present and future. The expansive permeability described encompasses individual, communal, national and international contexts, draws attention to a range of small-scale and larger frames of reference, and refers to what is striking, shocking, distinctive and exceptional as well as that which is normalised, ordinary and everyday. Moreover, such inclusivity is not one-way. It is not all production-action.

Cooper (2013, 2019, 2021), Currah (2022a) and Gill (2020) are particularly attentive to deconstructing massed forms of power from the perspective of the state and governance—even if this perspective is tempered by a concern with intimacy and with alternative spaces (see also Canaday et al., 2021). Their works tend in consequence to be especially helpful when considering power's productions or actions. In this volume we are notably attentive to a somewhat different imagining which includes the impact or effects of power. As Currah (2022a; 2022c) points out, power relations undertaken by the state are myriad, inconsistent and significantly at times inadvertent. We would add to this that the inclusion of power's effects inevitably brings to the fore possibilities of resistance and hence alternative re-imaginings including those of the future.

We suggest that what is at stake here may be considered as not only a matter of re-imagining terms/concepts and their relation to actualities (see Cooper, 2021; see also Odogwu 2015). We also aim here to *re-image* power-time and change. How might power-time *look* in light of legacies of social injustice and with an eye to what Cooper (2021, p. 893) calls "a progressive transformative politics" that might enable reconstructive and prefigurative directions around which to organise and re-shape the future. In this setting, Chapter 10 (Kimura) and Chapter 11 (Beasley) offer examples of a means to configure a progressive transformative politics. Kimura's chapter engages with efforts to acknowledge and memorialise the treatment of 'comfort women' during World War II. The act of memorialisation in the form of statues has the potential to transform the future; first, the statues invite solidarity and recognition and, second, they encourage the Japanese government to be accountable for past injustices. Beasley stresses the need to make heteronormativity visible in Hollywood films. However, while visibility is important it is equally important to configure aspirational methods to challenge heteronormativity. To this end Beasley offers a 'test' to identify counter-hegemonic examples as a political intervention that can transform and re-organise representations in popular culture.

This edited collection involves attention to *social* injustice and *social* change. No doubt another book is needed to develop additional political imaginaries of change beyond the socio-political relations of human beings. All the same, the term legacy also depends upon and is entwined with the land and physical world upon which social injustices arise. Such an entanglement is for example a necessary background in chapters by Wanganeen and Szorenyi, Papadelos, Kaur, and Waites, among others. To *re-image* power-time and change in this setting is to engage with a notion of power-time as multiple forces, continuously both productive and responsive. Instead of power being conceived as a property that is owned, as something vertical, top-down, event/site-oriented, describable as a regime or period and as only capable of reconstitution through the interventions of the young, it seems more unruly. Though not chaotic, formless or disordered, power entwined with time is capable of visualisation as rather more like a lumpy folding over, as potentially circular, spiralling, or rippling, as multiple forces which may flow, fan or otherwise spread out, remain still on the surface yet perhaps show signs of seething undercurrents, or even as capable of becoming solid and unmoveable, freezing over. Swallows on mass in flight and roosting provide one possible image (see Vance, 2012) for this notion of power-time as multiple forces.

There are pitfalls and limits in all such attempts to reimagine and re-image power-time and hence change. No doubt one concern in relation to the term, legacy, is that it may be taken up as a solidification that inhibits rather than opens up forces. As Diana Seuss' poem, 'Weeds' (2022), reminds us, memory, for example, may be delimiting. Indeed, she insists that memory is not a place for respite. It can be a guide but not a place to dwell.

Waites, in this volume, similarly insists that legacy must always be paired with the political to enable negentropy, the re-making of new forms and practices such as social justice. Legacy risks what might amount to an unhelpful repetitive reiteration of harms, which is one possible interpretation of Liddle's analysis of the impact of violence inflicted upon the Pontian Greeks or, in the language employed by Wanganeen and Szorenyi in their chapter, of unresolved grief that generates a corralling of imagination, innovation and resistance. It is possible to read this volume from the perspective of sadness, pity, of hierarchical altruism, requiring a response that restates *noblesse oblige* and thus retains the power of those who care in relation to those who are deemed vulnerable and requiring care (Beasley & Bacchi, 2007; Bacchi & Beasley, 2002; see also Bacchi, 2022). Reconfiguring power-time as the swirling swallows of multiple forces instead casts legacy as a political imaginary which works against the danger of political condescension or, in Braidotti's terms, political melancholia (Braidotti, 2010, p. 45).

What are the implications of this for a reconfiguring of change? We suggest that Cooper's focus upon the reconstructive and prefigurative provides a means to take up the lens of power-time as multiple forces and, rather than this imagery appearing as simply a multifaceted panoply that might encourage exhausted compliance, entrenchment in trauma or despair, attends to particular formations which encourage counter-strategies with regard to social injustice. In this vein, we propose attention to terminologies of heterodoxy[4] like 'transgression' and 'subversion' which provide bridging vocabularies linked to progressive political imaginaries situated between localised/private/intimate innovations/oppositional conduct (micropolitics) and more public organised movements/struggles/institutional developments connected with so-called big P politics and more public languages like 'dissent', 'protest' and 'utopias' (see Beasley, 2011, p. 27; Beasley, 2015; Beasley et al., 2012, p. 88; Beasley et al., 2015; Papadelos et al., 2021). This focus upon progressive social change—which may be characterised as alteration in social patterns through time to advance social justice—involves challenging and highly contested concerns (Harper & Leicht, 2015, p. 5, see also Bridges, 2019, p. 30). Hence, we refer here to a framework originally developed to chart and trace shifts towards progressive social change in relation to heterosexuality and masculinity (Beasley, 2015). The most recent version of this framework—contextualised in terms of masculinity (Papadelos et al., 2021)—outlines non-normative scenarios along a continuum of practices.

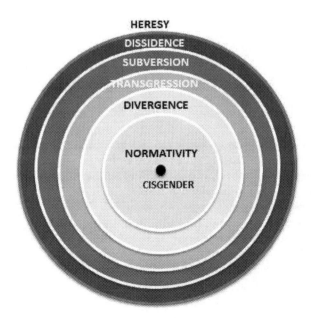

Figure 13.1 Masculinity – from normative to heretical
Sources: Beasley, 2015; Papadelos et al., 2021

These practices depart from a normative core to encompass a potentially non-normative terrain stretching from heterodoxical possibilities to the entirely heretical. In order to make use of the reconfigured account of power-time as multiple forces, which might provide potential for social change, we propose placing particular emphasis upon the scenarios of *transgression* and *subversion*. Transgression, in this configuration, describes instances where the normative core is relatively temporarily disrupted or diverted, and hence where possibilities for social change and social justice are experienced, even if only fleetingly. An example of transgression can be seen in Chapter 5 where Andrada maps the mythologising of the 'traditional' American family in an effort to understand and address the stigma experienced by single mothers, particularly black single mothers. A sign of transgression in her argument arises in relation to the uptake and partial if growing acceptance of single mothering, even if only in relation to white women and only relatively conceivable in recent times.

Subversion in this account of heterodoxical practices moves beyond the transgressive, displacing power relations that serve to maintain social injustice. Marcus, in Chapter 6, may be seen as outlining moves beyond the relatively contingent character of transgression to more decided and deliberate practices of resistance to mainstream marginalisation in her account of Gypsy/Travellers in Scotland. Whereas transgression involves temporary and not usually deliberate departures from the conventional hegemonic, subversion involves more conscious and continuing undermining of privileged norms. Subversion may not always be radical, but nevertheless upsets assumed norms, sometimes in quiet ways (Papadelos et al., 2021, p. 7). These two heterodoxical scenarios allow attention to practices that can involve intimate and not only public and collective heterodoxies.[5] They may take many forms, arising from the arts such as in films and statues, as well as from written memoirs and memorialising events, media connectivities online, collaborative activism and everyday communal or otherwise unconventional life (Beasley, 2015). Importantly, as the term heterodoxy connotes, these departures from normative conventions may involve mundane activities and are not always clearly or inevitably in opposition to the normative.

Nevertheless, while unconventional conduct offers a beginning, this must be paired with progressive directions. In previous work we have made use of some vocabularies which describe a variety of effects of power-time, of legacies of social injustice. This use involved drawing upon and developing work by several writers to build a more nuanced and expansive account of the character of social change, in particular with regard to gender (Ahmed, 2006; Andersson et al., 2009; Beasley, 2015; Thompson, 2014). The vocabularies we employed indicate modes of experience associated with progressive change. Our intention has been to flesh out a model of social change that allows for an array of individual and collective practices/experiences reflecting degrees of change, which include, becoming aware of injustice, coming up against rejection and policing of alternative options, equivocating between mainstream and resistant directions, strategically turning back and forth between conformity and innovation depending upon contexts, synthesising elements of normative and alternative practices/responses into other configurations of power-time and actively risking non-conformity. These modes of experience regarding change may be described in shorthand form as *disorientation, straightening, vacillation, swivelling, hybridisation and breaching respectively* (Papadelos et al., 2021, p. 8; Beasley, 2015).

Such terms suggest *qualitative markers* for identifying practices that open up possibilities for social change. The chapters in the book offer a range of instances which refer to these modes of experience. Andrada's piece on single mothers may be said to offer exemplars of *straightening* and *hybridisation* arising in relation to mythologies of the 'good mother' (married, white) and the 'bad' or othered mother (unmarried, non-white) stigmatising single black mothers. Both of these mythologised figures, as Andrada points out, take the form of authorising narratives within the USA with subsequent effects upon single mothers and indeed mothers *per se* in that setting. Papadelos's chapter on ageing migrants in Australia also aligns with *straightening* as Greek migrants respond to ongoing patterns of power and privilege in Australian society. Yet, their responses also involve *vacillating* and *swivelling* as they both comply with and resist their marginalisation. Dundon's contribution about domestic violence in Papua New Guinea suggests *disorientation* regarding advancing alternative views in relation to women's rights based on unfamiliar discourses of gender equality, yet there are some signs of *swivelling*, of a moving back and forth between the accepted view of women's rightful subordination and a less orthodox feminist stance that encourages social change. Additionally, Kimura's chapter on 'comfort women' and Liddle's chapter on Pontian Greeks could be seen in terms of *breaching* as they both consider practices that demand recognition and justice for past atrocities. Another instance of *breaching* may be found in Marcus's discussion of Scottish Gypsy/Travellers. Participants in the study outlined in her chapter use silence to empower their community by defying the dominant gaze, thus enabling the possibility of alternative futures. These examples illustrate the many moments in the book where the multiple forces of power entangled with time, and their accompanying legacies of injustice require us to re-consider concepts and actualising practices that enable progressive social change.

This book outlines legacies of injustice but does not simply describe or condemn them so much as indicating the differing productions/actions of power-time and its differing effects including heterodoxical modes of social resistance. In concluding this exploration, we reimagine and re-image power-time with the aim of considering how struggles to resist social injustice might in practical terms respond to the notion of power-time as multiple forces. From the instances raised in the book, we argue that such struggles are assisted by emphasising pathways that can respond to these swirling forces. Our suggestion is to develop counter-strategies which concentrate upon enhancing practices of transgression and subversion and which promote and support modes of experience that advance progressive change.

Living Legacies of Social Injustice: Power, Time and Social Change is a contribution towards the reimagining and re-imaging of power-time and hence the reconfiguring of alternative pathways, to the re-configuring of otherwise, of justice-to-come. As Maya Angelou (1986) says, no matter how oppressive and obdurate existing forms of sociality might seem, there will always be ways to defy them and, in her terms, to 'rise'.

Notes

1 See Papadelos (2010) for a more detailed discussion of these concepts.
2 This hope for social justice implies directions regarding democracy, which might connect with Derrida's discussions of the 'to come'. The promise of a democracy-to-come is an affirmation, and a yet to be thought, "always insufficient and future", yet like all promises, it has to be kept (Derrida, 1997, p. 306). The future as a 'to come' will not reproduce or invoke the present, but it will affect the present; it will have consequences. Thus, the 'to come' that is invoked by Derrida opens a democratic space for the Other (see Derrida, 1988).
3 Working through the past, the not yet or the 'to come', will necessarily reinvent the Other and consequently "'we' will become something other; our response to the other will reinvent 'us'" (Derrida 1992, p. 342).
4 Drawing on previous work attending to heterosexuality and masculinity (Beasley, 2015), 'heterodoxy' refers to a leaning toward the unorthodox, the non-normative. Heterodoxy is that which is at variance with, or that which differs or departs from the accepted, the standard, the status quo, the orthodox, without necessarily being its opposite. The term heterodoxy is employed in this context to re-conceptualise power-time outside of the mainstream with regard to raising the possibility of alternative futures.
5 In this context the term heterodoxy is used to indicate the fissures in normative representations rather than necessarily identifying revolutionary changes.

References

Ahmed, S. (2006). *Queer phenomenology: Orientations, objects, others*. Durham, NC: Duke University Press.
Ahmed, S. (2004a). Affective economies. *Social Text*, 22(2), 117–139.
Ahmed, S. (2004b). *The cultural politics of emotion*. Edinburgh: Edinburgh University Press.
Andersson, S., Amunsdotter, E., Svensson, M. & Däldehög, A. S. (2009). *Middle managers as change agents*. Stockholm: The Gender Network at Fiber Optic Valley.
Angelou, M. (1986). *And still I rise*. London: Hachette Digital.
Antonini, F. (2019). Pessimism of the intellect, optimism of the will: Gramsci's political thought in the last miscellaneous notebooks. *Rethinking Marxism*, 31(1), 42–57.
Bacchi, C. (2022). "Becoming more mortal": governing through "risk", "vulnerability" and "underlying" health conditions. Blog, February 27. https://carolbacchi.com/

2022/02/27/becoming-more-mortal-governing-through-risk-vulnerability-and-underl
ying-health-conditions. Accessed May 2022.

Bacchi, C. & Beasley, C. (2002). Citizen bodies: Is embodied citizenship a contradiction
in terms? *Critical Social Policy*, 22(2), Iss. 71, May, 324–352.

Beasley, C. (2011). Libidinous politics: Heterosex, "transgression" and social change.
Australian Feminist Studies, 26(67), 25–40.

Beasley, C. (2015). Libidinal heterodoxy: Heterosexuality, hetero-masculinity and
"transgression". *Men and Masculinities*, 18(2), June, 140–158.

Beasley, C. & Bacchi, C. (2007). Envisaging a new politics for an ethical future: Beyond
trust, care and generosity towards an ethic of social flesh. *Feminist Theory*, 8(3),
December, 279–298.

Beasley, C., Brook, H. & Holmes, M. (2012). Heterosexuality in theory and practice. In
Advances in Feminist Studies and Intersectionality Series. London & New York:
Routledge.

Beasley, C., Brook, H. & Holmes, M. (2015). Heterodoxy: Challenging orthodoxies
about heterosexuality. *Sexualities*, 18(5–6), September, 681–697.

Braidotti, R. (2010). On putting the active back into activism. *New Formations*, 68
(Spring), 42–57.

Bridges, T. (2019). The costs of exclusionary practices in masculinities studies'. *Men and
Masculinities*, 22(1), 16–33.

Canaday, M., Cott, N. & Self, R. (2021). *Intimate states: Gender, sexuality, and governance
in modern US history*. Chicago, IL: University of Chicago Press.

Colebrook, C. (2009). Stratigraphic time, women's time. *Australian Feminist Studies*, 24
(59), 11–16.

Cooper, D. (2013). *Everyday utopias: The conceptual life of promising spaces*. Durham, NC &
London: Duke University Press.

Cooper, D. (2019). *Feeling like a state: Desire, denial, and the recasting of authority*. Durham,
NC & London: Duke University Press.

Cooper, D. (2021). The urgent task of reimagining the state. *Critical Legal Thinking*, 8
April (criticallegalthinking.com). Accessed June 2022.

Currah, P. (2022a). The asymmetry of gender: Paisley Currah, interviewed by Lucy
Jakub and Max Nelson. *The New York Review of Books*, May 28 (nybooks.com).
Accessed June 2022.

Currah, P. (2022b). What sex does. *The New York Review of Books*, May 27 (nybooks.
com). Accessed June 2022.

Currah, P. (2022c). *Sex is as sex does: Governing transgender identity*. New York: New
York University Press.

Derrida, J. (1986). *Memoires: For Paul de Man*. Trans. C. Lindsay, J. Culler & E. Cadava.
New York: Columbia University Press.

Derrida, J. (1988). The politics of friendship. *The Journal of Philosophy*, 85(11), 632–644.

Derrida, J. (1992). *Acts of literature*. New York & London: Routledge.

Derrida, J. (1997). *The politics of friendship*. Trans. G. Collins. London & New York:
Verso.

Derrida, J. (1999). Themes from recent work, 13 August. Paper presented at Seymour
Theatre, Sydney: Sydney Seminars.

Gill, N. (2010). Tracing the imaginations of the state: The spatial consequences of different state concepts among asylum activist organisations. *Antipode*, 42(5), 1048–1070.

Gill, N. (2020). Border abolition and how to achieve it. In D. Cooper, N. Dhawan & J. Newman (Eds), *Reimagining the state: Theoretical challenges and transformative possibilities*, (pp. 231–250). Abingdon & New York: Routledge.

Gramsci, A. (1977). *Selections from political writings Vol 1 1910–1920*, trans. J. Matthews, London: Lawrence & Wishart.

Harper, C. L. & Leicht, K. T. (2015). *Exploring social change: America and the world*. New York: Routledge.

Odogwu, W. (2015). *Book review of Everyday utopias. Feminist Legal Studies*, 23, 215–219.

Papadelos, P. (2010). *From revolution to deconstruction: Exploring feminist theory and practice in Australia*. Bern: Peter Lang.

Papadelos, P., Beasley, C. & Treagus, M. (2021). Social change and masculinities: exploring favourable spaces? *Journal of Sociology*, published online November 11. doi:10.1177/14407833211048241. Accessed June 2022.

Seuss, D. (2022). Weeds. *The New York Review of Books*, June 23 (nybooks.com). Accessed June 2022.

Thompson, T. (2014) *Queer Lives in Fiji*. Unpublished PhD thesis, University of Auckland, New Zealand.

Vance, M. (2012). Amazing tree swallow roost, January 1. https://youtu.be/EiTzo S1OZD0. Accessed June 2022.

Index

affective economies 59, 61
Ahmed, S. 10, 43, 59, 61–62, 63, 65, 67, 78, 84, 98, 106, 136, 138, 141, 231–232
Angelou, M. 239
apology(ies) 7, 154, 178, 182, 184, 211
assimilation 97, 109, 136–138, 140, 142, 145, 146–147

Backs, L. 105
Brandhorst, R., Baldassar, L. and Wilding, R. 133
Barthes, R. 196
Bauman, Z. 60
bearing witness 34, 49
Beasley-Brook test 202, 203–204, 205n16
Beck, U. 211
Bechdel, A. 202, 205n14
Bechdel Test 202, 205n15; *see also* Bechdel-Wallace Test
Bechdel-Wallace Test 202
Belton, B. 93, 108
Benedict, R. 61
Bhabha, H. 68, 213
Bilge, S. 96
Bleakley, A. 202
Bourdieu, P. 136, 149n2
Brah, A. 140
Braidotti, R. 235

Calwell, A. 134–135, 137
Carbado, D. W., Crenshaw, K. W., Mays, V. M. and Tomlinson, B. 96
Clark, C. R. 97
collective memory 8, 39–40, 65, 146; *see also* social memory; cultural memory
collective nostalgia 74, 80, 84

colonial(ism) 9, 12, 26, 29, 57–69, 93, 95, 136–137, 149n3, 210–215, 225–226; 'colonial gaze' 166; colonialities 12, 210, 212, 217; decolonial 12, 210–215, 225, 226; neo-colonial 211; postcolonial 3, 4, 5, 10, 61, 65, 66, 68, 93, 95–96, 108, 210–213, 222, 225
'comfort stations' 175, 176
'comfort women' 173–174; 176–187
commemoration(s) 9, 39, 40, 42, 44–45, 47–49, 51, 52, 101, 183
compulsory heterosexuality 198, 199
Cooper, E. 234, 235
Connell, R. 83
cultural memory 6, 7, 8, 193
cultural politics 3, 12, 193, 194, 226
Currah, P. 233, 234

Damousi, J. 146,
Deleuze, G. 5, 14n3, 192
Derrida, J. 231–2, 239n2
displacement 10, 13, 63, 116–129, 135, 141

Enright, M. 140, 212
Emens, E. 196
emotional reflexivity 118–125, 128
Eurocentrism 211, 213–215, 225

Fanon, F. 63
Faulkner, W. 7
Ferguson, K. 100, 108
Foucault, M. 14n3, 100, 213
Fraser, N. 211
Freud, S. 67
friendship(s) 11, 117–118, 120, 122–128, 178, 197

genocide 8, 9, 49–51, 94, 154, 155, 156, 160, 166; cultural genocide 155
Gill, N. 233, 234
Gilroy, P. 65–66, 68, 225
Glenn, C. 100
Goffman, E. 221
Gramsci, A. 194, 196, 203, 221
grief (and loss) 11, 39, 47, 118, 128, 146–147, 153, 160–166, 233, 235; 'Griefology' 153, 162–163, 166–167, 168n14
Gupta, D. T., James, C. E., Maaka, R. C. A., Galabuzi, G. E. and Anderson, C. 97

Hall, S. 95, 108
heteronormativity 6, 12, 84–85, 192, 194–203, 204n4, 205n16, 234
Heuss, H. 94
holocaust 45, 47–50, 51, 52n14
hypermonogamy 196–197, 199, 201; see also supermonogamy

inequality 3, 12, 22, 24, 28, 30, 34, 191, 195, 196, 203
intersectionality 3, 4, 10, 83, 84, 95–96,

Jeffery, D. 58
Johnson, C. 7
Johnson, T. A. 100
Jolly, M. 22, 26, 28, 30
Jupp, J. 136

Kenrick, D. and Clark, C. 97
Kristeva, J. 69

Ladson-Billings, G. 105
legacy: living legacy and ongoing legacy 2–3, 133–134; ongoing legacy 8, 9, 10, 23, 73, 76, 94, 99–100, 125, 133, 146, 167n9, 191, 204, 212
Lopez, I. H. 95
Lorde, A. 96, 104
Loriggio, F. 134
Luhmann, S. 7–8

Marx, K. 63; post-Marxism 213
Martin, K. A. and Kazyak, E. 195
Mead, M. 61
Melucci, A. 211
memorialisation 6, 12, 39, 101, 173–4, 180, 182–183, 192, 234; memorial(s) 9,

12, 39, 44–45, 47, 51, 52n10, 173, 178, 180–183, 186; monument(s) 9, 47, 48, 49, 51, 52n10, 182, 191, 192, 219
Mignolo, W. 214
migration 9, 11, 63, 64, 94, 133–138, 140, 142, 146–148; immigration 136–137
multiculturalism 134, 136–138, 142,
Mila, K 223–224
Mirza, H. S. 95, 96, 100
moral economy 58–60, 62, 63, 66, 69
moral panic 58–59, 63–65, 70n4, 101

navigation 118, 128
Neat, T. 97
Nietzsche, F. 59–61,
normalisation 1, 6, 12, 22, 24, 32, 58, 100, 191–195, 200, 202, 231, 233, 236–237, 239n5
Nunga 155, 156, 159, 161
Nye, J. 194, 195, 203

Okri, B. 222–223
OLIRN 4, 14, 204n1
ongoing legacy see legacy
'other' (the) 10, 57–68, 95, 101, 232, 239n2, 239n3; othered and othering 10, 57, 73, 75, 76, 82, 83, 95, 101, 108, 109, 122, 238,

power 2; power relations 1–6, 8, 11, 12, 13n2, 14n3, 22–23, 30, 34, 51, 61–62, 69, 94, 95, 103, 105, 117, 120, 124–128, 133–134, 166, 174, 186, 191–193, 201–203, 211, 213, 220, 224, 231–234, 237; power-time 235–236, 237–239, 239n2; soft power 194–195, 203; weak power 108; see also cultural politics

Quijano, A. 213–215

racialisation(s) 58, 95, 117, 225,
racism 57, 62–63, 69, 94, 137–138, 141–142, 156, 157, 162, 166, 225; racist 65, 77, 78, 98, 101, 103, 106, 136, 145, 146, 154, 160, 167
Radway, J. 205n8
Rao, R. 219–220
Razack, S. 102
Reddy, W. M. 118

244 Index

refugee(s) 11, 41, 45, 117–129, 223,
resistance 7, 12, 39, 46, 48, 52n8,
  78, 93, 100, 105–106, 109, 142,
  136, 138, 173–174, 181, 187, 202,
  233–238
Rich, A. 198, 199
Richardson, J. 101
Rochat, P. 98
Rowe, K. 198, 205n8
Rushdie, S. 106

Said, E. 213
Schreiber, M. 201
Schröter, M. 99
silence 6, 10, 11, 25, 26, 29, 48, 57, 93,
  99–109, 166, 183, 231, 238
social change 1, 4, 10, 12, 13, 33, 102, 117,
  127, 231, 232, 235–239
social memory 39
social justice 1–4, 9, 26, 33–34, 99, 102,
  108–109, 134, 154, 174, 191, 193–195,
  203, 231–232, 235–238, 239n2
Spivak, G. C. 213
stigma 10, 13, 75–76, 78–84, 85n1,
  85n13, 85n14, 237
'stolen generations' 3, 11, 33, 153,
  154, 233
Suess, D. 235
supermonogamy 196
'survivor-activists' 176–177, 180–186

time 1–14, 22, 59, 61, 66, 69, 118, 125,
  133–134, 142, 191, 192, 231–239, 239n4
trauma 133, 135, 140, 147
trust (distrust) 11, 105, 118–120,
  122–123, 126, 128, 160–161

Valenti, J. 194
victim-survivors 174–176, 178–180,
  185–186
violence: 7, 8, 21–24, 41, 51, 117,
  126–127, 156–158, 160, 166, 174, 195,
  218; domestic violence 9–10, 21,
  24–30, 32, 33, 34n1, 34n2, 34n4, 35,
  41, 43, 57–59, 65–66, 68, 70, 158,
  233; gendered violence 9, 21, 23,
  25–26, 29–31, 33, 68, 96, 175, 233;
  honour-based violence 56–57, 68,
  70n2; sexual slavery 12, 173–180;
  sexual violence 12, 13, 24, 26, 28,
  30–33, 34n3, 34n4, 173–177,
  186–187; slow violence 22, 23, 30,
  32–34; structural violence 22, 23, 29,
  33–34, 100
Virdee, S. 94

Wallace, L. 205n14
war crimes 42, 50, 177, 184
whiteness 63, 70n6, 106, 108

Žižek, S. 68